Multiculturalism in Transit

INTERNATIONAL POLITICAL CURRENTS
A Friedrich-Ebert-Stiftung Series

General Editor: Dieter Dettke

Vol. 1: Toward a Global Civil Society
   Edited by Michael Walzer

Vol. 2: Universities in the Twenty-First Century
   Edited by Steven Muller

Vol. 3: Multiculturalism in Transit: A German-American Exchange
   Edited by Klaus J. Milich and Jeffrey M. Peck

Vol. 4: The Challenge of Globalization for Germany's Social
   Democracy: A Policy Agenda for the Twenty-First Century
   Edited by Dieter Dettke

Multiculturalism in Transit

A German-American Exchange

Edited by

Klaus J. Milich

and

Jeffrey M. Peck

Berghahn Books
NEW YORK • OXFORD

Published in 1998 by

Berghahn Books
Editorial offices:
55 John Street, 3rd Floor, New York, NY 10038 USA
3, NewTec Place, Magdalen Road, Oxford, OX4 1RE, UK

Library of Congress Cataloging-in-Publication Data
Multiculturalism in transit : a German-American exchange / edited by
    Klaus J. Milich and Jeffrey M. Peck.
        p.   cm. – (International political currents ; v. 3)
    Includes bibliographical references and index.
    ISBN 1-57181-163-X (acid-free paper)
    1. Pluralism (Social sciences)–United States. 2. Pluralism
(Social sciences)–Germany. 3. United States–Relations–Germany.
4. Germany–Relations–United States. 5. United States–Ethnic
relations. 6. Germany–Ethnic relations. I. Milich, Klaus J.
II. Peck, Jeffrey M., 1950–   . III. Series: International
political currents ; vol. 3.
E184.A1M86   1998
305.8'00973–dc21   98-26838
                                                                        CIP

British Library Cataloguing in Publication Data
A CIP catalogue record for this book is available from
the British Library.

Printed in the United States on acid-free paper

Contents

Foreword

Dieter Dettke

Multiculturalism is and will remain a controversial issue both in the United States and Germany for many years to come. Therefore, a German-American exchange on the key issues should prompt a healthy debate bound to yield substantial results.

More than anything else it is "otherness" which divides, left and right, determining who is an outcast and who belongs to the group.

How we deal and live with otherness also says a lot about the character of our own society. We now understand that there is no panacea. Under the conditions of globalization, assimilation alone is not the answer to immigration. More and more people live in an environment that transcends national borders—once a privilege experienced only by upper class business people and intellectuals. Today, workers, clerks, and technicians, for example, have bi-national and international experiences and the recent globalization of services has brought many ordinary people into contact with a growing international environment.

Modern communications—radio, television, telephone and the print media—are not only an assimilating force as once regarded, but also a medium with which to maintain one's own identity in a foreign environment. One has only to look at the numerous Spanish speaking television and radio shows filling the airwaves in California and Texas, or Turkish broadcasting and print media in Berlin as evidence.

Modern communications enable people to practice multiculturalism. However, what seems to be an opportunity for some is a threat for others. Those wishing to live in a homogeneous society would most likely not be willing to accept multiculturalism.

- Yet, the reality of German life today is that
- the country has a population of 8 percent non-citizens
- in cities like Frankfurt/Main the number of non-citizens approaches 25 percent
- in states like Hessen there is a population of more than 15 percent lacking German citizenship
- in a city like Hamburg there are many churches and temples of all religions, serving the Buddhist, Islamic, and Christian minorities, as well as others

A multicultural society, however, needs multicultural people and this, unfortunately, is not automatically the result of more international experience on an individual level. This needs to be nurtured.

It is true, there is no homogeneous society anywhere in Europe. The peoples of Europe are mixed in many different ways: race, religion, and beliefs, and there can be no peaceful return to homogeneity, nor should we desire it.

So the issue is to help create a political culture and the political and legal instruments to be different without fear. German citizenship laws need adjustment, too. Naturalization is still a rare exception occurring only after a lengthy and tedious process. The allowance of dual citizenship would also help to solve problems. Most importantly, the narrow concept of ethnicity as a basis for German citizenship needs to be enlarged.

This publication, the result of a conference co-hosted by the Center for German and European Studies at Georgetown University, the Institute for English and American Studies at Humboldt University in Berlin, and the Washington Office of the Friedrich Ebert Foundation, contributes not only to an enlightened debate, but also to actual progress in the long road to a more benign environment for otherness.

March 1998   Washington, D.C.

Introduction

Klaus J. Milich and Jeffrey M. Peck

In an international academic environment, where not only scholars but also theories, concepts, and terms travel and assume global and universal connotations, the local and the particular seem to have dropped out of sight. Hybridity and positioning, traveling theory and situated knowledge, indeterminacy and ambiguity have become productive issues in the discipline of Cultural Studies, but have obscured the appreciation of local contexts. Terms like modernity, postmodernity, feminism, gender, and, of course, multiculturalism are cases in point. More than any other notion, multiculturalism has provoked scholars in the humanities and the social sciences to transcend national boundaries and to interpret this term as part of an international network of cultural relations. However, as this term takes on both global and local connotations and unfolds different semantic fields in Germany and the United States, careful attention must be paid to the "national" historical, political, social, and institutional contexts in which it appears, circulates, and accrues meanings. Recognizing the particular conditions and different ideological concepts that shape this term and its meanings may indeed dispel common criticism that the term and the claims made in its name are vague and incoherent.

These problems became quite clear when the two editors of this volume met at a conference in Berlin six years ago where scholars in German-American Studies and American- German Studies were attempting to come to terms with the different meanings of multiculturalism in the two countries and the two disciplines. Although multiculturalism has obviously become a central issue in both North American and German public and academic discourses, these scholars were becoming quite aware of the different politics and policies of multiculturalism in Germany and the United States. It seemed that decisions made in the political sphere did not sufficiently take into account notions of culture and its potential definitions. In fact, ongoing political debates in Germany about immigration, asylum, and citizenship emphasize the differences between German and American cultural and political notions of multiculturalism. While one could always "become an American," German nationality could never really be adopted, because it is based on an ethno-racial concept of Germanness, incorporated in *ius sanguinis* (citizenship based on blood). While German culture has traditionally merely adopted foreign cultures to its own without questioning its own premises, American culture has, as an "immigrant society," always been faced with constantly transforming its culture and questioning the assumptions of "What is an American?"

In short, while multiculturalism in Germany is still being discussed along the line of an inside/outside or we/you matrix, "otherness" and alterity in the United States has moved from the margin to the center and spurred a discussion about the differences within. Furthermore, the reunification of Germany, as a unique example of multiculturalism, has made the discussion of a new culture concept more urgent than ever before. The traditional fusion of national and cultural identity based on the construction of ethnic homogeneity that has always been challenged by the imprint of "foreign" peoples in Germany has become an even more compelling issue in recent years. In other words, reunification and the question of "integrating foreigners" have provoked a discussion about Germany—which does not consider itself "ein Einwanderungsland" (an immigration country)—as a potential multicultural society.

In the United States, the discussion about American self-definition has reached a stage where it is played out in the status of minority cultures and their representation in the American canon. This debate culminated in the quarrel about "political correctness." Allen Bloom's term "the closing of the American mind" was one of the significant conservative versions at the basis of the call for a "new synthesis." While the notion of multiculturalism has moved into German political and cultural debate, in the United States one can perceive an opposite turn. Starting a number of years ago with the works of conservatives like E.D.Hirsch, William Bennett, and, of course, Bloom himself, who wanted to solidify a unified American culture, the United States is showing signs of closing itself off from the very concept of culture that has been so foundational. Recent polemics about immigration illustrate and reinforce this development. The diametrically opposed tendencies that developed simultaneously in both countries could simply put be described as the shift from an open to a closed concept of culture in the United States and the reverse in Germany. Although there are currently tendencies in American universities against multicultural curricula, cultural studies, and identity politics, these progressive notions are so widely institutionalized that it is hard to imagine that they will disappear. In fact, in a world where migration, telecommunication, and market economies represent global movements of human and financial resources, multiculturalism appropriates part of the cultural side of this political and economic process. If modernity is equated with nineteenth-century discrete nation-states and imperial ventures, and postmodernity is thought to represent the cultural logic of late twentieth-century international political economy, telecommunication, and global movements of human and financial resources, then multiculturalism appropriates parts of this postmodern culture.

In order to enlarge and deepen our discussion, we decided together with Günter H. Lenz to assemble colleagues from a variety of disciplines in our two fields from both sides of the Atlantic. We asked them how they would take into account both the universal and the particular without either contributing to new metanarratives, or falling prey to a provincial nationalism by discussing cultural differences in terms of national character. In other words, how can we accommodate the advances of poststructuralism with a postnational discourse that is neither indiscriminately international nor simplistically national?

Conflicts between African Americans and Jews in the United States and the status of Turks and Jews in Germany, for example, raise questions about whether comparisons can be made between these groups, both within the two countries and transnationally. A static comparative perspective does not take into account the constantly shifting topics, theories, disciplines, and national interests; a more dynamic comparison of multiculturalism is necessary for a comprehensive understanding of intercultural relations between disciplines and nations beyond the merely internal and domestic. In order to come to terms with comparative perspectives, the idealistic German *Begriffsgeschichte* (concept formation) took for granted the geopolitical and historical conditions under which categories such as multiculturalism came into being. It merely traced the transfer of terms from author to author in the Romantic sense. Our contextualized comparative method however makes explicit how a discursive field constitutes the meanings from which an individual author draws. Following this approach, the essays in this volume consider terms themselves, such as multiculturalism, feminism, gender, nationality, and discipline as discursive fields, and unpack their universal *and* particular, i.e., their global *and* local meanings, from both sides of the Atlantic.

Thus, our discussion of multiculturalism in the United States and Germany became an occasion to cross boundaries at every turn, be they national, academic, or disciplinary. Multiculturalism became more than a subject of study, an analysis of Turks in Germany or African Americans in the United States, but a critical perspective for analyzing not only the discourses of otherness and difference, but also the concepts of American and German cultural formation in general. For multiculturalism is more than just about race and ethnicity; it also stresses other cultural categories such as feminism and gender, as well as geopolitical divisions such as Eastern and Western Germany. In short, the analysis of a single cultural term becomes metonymic for revealing an entire cultural formation.

We found it particularly fruitful at this historical juncture to bring together German and American scholars working on multiculturalism in both countries. From their various disciplinary perspectives in a crosscultural context, they discussed their common concerns about the perception of the "other" in the variety of literary, political, historical, and cultural (re)presentations that permeate both the United States and Germany. As both the subject and object of study, the participating representatives of German and American Cultural Studies created a chiasmus that made clear that both disciplines themselves were sites of multiculturalism. Simultaneously connected through subject matter and the structures of national disciplines, and separated by national differences, this unusual intercultural situation became a rich field for discovering how multiculturalism was inflected or even constituted by German or American national identities. Germans talking about America and Americans talking about Germany became a very literal test case for determining how not only national interests, but also institutional conditions and disciplinary structures specific to one or the other country formed central notions, concepts, epistemologies, methodologies, and subjects.

As American Studies in the United States developed against the backdrop of an American multiculturalism, it therefore questioned any value system of a universal literary and historical tradition that did not take into account differences based on race, ethnicity, and gender. While American Studies programs were transferred in part from the United States to some German universities — not without controversy — German Studies as a new discipline had trouble differentiating itself from the traditional American *Germanistik* that was so influenced by Germany and its immigrant academics. American-German Studies was only able to develop interdisciplinary paradigms and apply them to multicultural questions in Germany, at least in part, because of a heterogeneous culture concept in the United States that formed the basis of American Cultural Studies.

While volumes produced from conferences never fulfill all the expectations of their origins, this collection makes a strong case for the necessity to take an interdisciplinary approach to multiculturalism in both the American and German environments. Literary criticism, cultural studies, history, anthropology, and political science are all represented, as is the unique situation of a divided Germany that produced alternative interpretations of American culture. The international (transatlantic) and interdisciplinary component produced new angles of vision for understanding the extent to which multiculturalism is manifold. The shifting perspectives have recalibrated how narrowly or how broadly, how high or how low, we see our subject and employ our methods of analysis. National "interests" (*Erkenntnisinteressen*) in the German sense have been seen to be always at play and always at stake, even when we least expect them or want to acknowledge their presence. Generational differences as well, in both America and Germany, inflect our investments as professors of literature or political science. Ultimately, understanding "the foreign" is a discovery of oneself and one's own prejudices as much as the discovery of the other. Multiculturalism becomes more than a political epithet encompassing liberal calls for openness, on the one hand, or, on the other, a label to be attacked by conservatives in the crossfire of debates on political correctness. It achieves a status as a kind of critical hermeneutic, which mediates an activity of self-reflection and knowledge. We think that more attention needs to be paid to this dimension of multiculturalism for its future as a catalyst for intellectual and political change.

Are concepts of nation still applicable in a multicultural world? What role do the intellectual and academic discourses on multiculturalism play in the public debate in Germany and the United States? In which ways can scholars contribute to the decisions made in the political sphere and does the urgency of the immediate and everyday concerns for civil and human rights leave space for the theorizing about difference, otherness, and the definition of culture?

We take the opportunity to express our gratitude for the financial support we received from various German and American sources. Our thanks go to the Friedrich Ebert Foundation, Washington, particularly to Dieter Dettke for his generous support and encouragement, to the Center for German and European Studies, as well as to Georgetown University and Humboldt University, Berlin.

A collaborative project such as *Multiculturalism in Transit* depends on the shared time and effort of those who gave their energy generously. The editors wish to thank in particular all participants and contributors to this volume. We especially want to acknowledge Robin Floyd and Richard Wiggers, who did so much of the organizational groundwork for the conference, Elise Brayton and Barbara Serfozo, who word-processed the manuscripts into their final form. Two people, however, deserve a special note: Günter H. Lenz for his support in organizing the conference and Heidrun Suhr for her advice and encouragement at the initial stage of this project. Apart from their professional expertise, we are particularly grateful for their solidarity and long-standing friendship.

Part I

THEORIZING COMPARISONS

1. The Uses of Comparison

Gisela Welz

When scholars who belong to *one* academic discipline but work in either one of *two* national academic frameworks meet in order to explore similarities and differences in their work, the basic tenets of comparative methodologies are fulfilled: what is being compared must share some fundamental traits—practitioners of Cultural Studies have topical interests and theoretical concerns in common—and the compared items must also be clearly separate and discontinuous. Cultural Studies are conducted in academic settings that differ because of the intellectual histories of their societies and because of variations in the social conditions and infrastructures of producing knowledge.

What do we stand to gain by comparing German and American styles of doing Cultural Studies? Or, to pose the question in a more general way, what are the uses of comparison? When engaging in comparison, we should be aware of what comparison as an epistemological tool entails. One reason that suggests the need for a critical exploration of comparison is that much comparative work in the social sciences has been implicated in the type of scientific inquiry labeled "positivist." Another reason is that there is something to learn from the critiques of comparativism that have been emerging in anthropology since the 1960s. When developing a comparative perspective on our own work, it is useful to consider how the operation of comparing cultures works, what its problems, but also its potentials are. Certainly, there is no clear analogy between cross-cultural comparison in anthropology and a comparison of national styles in Cultural Studies. However, recent discussions in cultural anthropology could contribute to an understanding of the differences and disjunctures within the emergent (trans)national discipline(s) of Cultural Studies. This essay will tap into current debates about the intellectual place of comparison in cultural anthropology, outlining major shortcomings of cross-cultural comparison, but also recapturing some of the inherently critical potential of comparison.

The history of comparative methodology is closely connected with the disciplinary development of anthropology. Before anthropology even became a scholarly discipline, anthropological concerns had already taken shape in the systematic gathering of data about the ways of life, languages, beliefs, and artifacts of primitive peoples. These collections were carried out by overseas travelers who had devised questionnaires as guidelines for the observation and description of whatever contemporary indigenous societies they might encounter. In the disciplinary historiography of anthropology, however, the invention of cross-cultural comparison is closely aligned with the emergence of the evolutionist paradigm. Indeed, as Johannes Fabian's acidly ironic description conveys, the comparative method, "this omnivorous intellectual machine permitting the 'equal' treatment of human culture at all times and in all places"[1] was hailed as the most celebrated scientific achievement of that period. Fabian emphasizes that comparative methodology set the "epistemological conditions under which ethnography and ethnology took shape; and they were also the conditions under which an emerging anthropological praxis (research, writing, teaching) came to be linked to colonialism and imperialism."[2] Succeeding evolutionism, diffusionist theory focused on retracing the spread of cultural ideas and artifacts from one culture to the next. Cross-cultural comparison became an indispensable tool for the historical reconstruction of cultural diffusion. With the advent of functionalism in anthropology,[3] cross-cultural comparison emerged as the principal methodology for finding transculturally valid laws that govern all of human social life: "By comparing a sufficient number of diverse types we discover uniformities that are more general, and thus may

1. Johannes Fabian, *Time and the Other: How Anthropology Makes Its Object* (New York, 1983), 17.

2. Ibid., 17.

3. For a periodization of comparative approaches in anthropology, see Sharon Siddique, "Anthropologie, Soziologie und Cultural Analysis," in *Zwischen den Kulturen. Die Sozialwissenschaften vor dem Problem des Kulturvergleichs*, ed. Joachim Matthes, Sonderband Soziale Welt 8 (Göttingen, 1992), 37–47. See also Laura Nader, "Comparative Consciousness," in *Assessing Cultural Anthropology*, ed. Robert Borofsky (New York, 1994), 84–94.

reach to the discovery of principles or laws that are universal in human society," as British social anthropologist Radcliffe-Brown put it succinctly in 1921.[4] Relinquishing some, but not much of the generalizing thrust of earlier social anthropology, more recent approaches in European structural functionalism and postwar American cultural anthropology generally agree that cross-cultural comparison no longer serves to determine the underlying transcultural laws. Instead, comparison serves to inquire into the interplay of so-called variable and invariable factors that shape social relations in a given culture by contrasting them with others like them, often in a controlled sample of regionally equivalent cultural groupings. This approach entails systematically collecting and analyzing transcultural data in categories such as descent and kinship terminology, marriage rules and avoidance taboos, household composition and residential patterns, techniques of subsistence, or social responses to ecological crises.

Predictably, when functionalism came under attack within anthropology, the assumption that one could arrive at generalizations about human nature by way of cross-cultural comparison was challenged and discarded. Also, a strongly relativist school emerging in postwar American cultural anthropology seemed to have made way for particularist approaches to the study of other cultures. Finally, new developments in the cultural anthropology of the sixties, such as the interpretive approach of Symbolic Anthropology, predicated a significant shift away from comparative work in anthropology. Most notably, Clifford Geertz's championing of "thick description" cleared the way for an approach that he himself has characterized as "not to generalize across cases but to generalize within them."[5] It became legitimate to acquire anthropological knowledge by immersing oneself in-depth in one culture and in the ethnographic representation of one individual case-study, thus avoiding the pitfalls of comparativism by doing away with explicitly cross-cultural perspectives altogether. Following Geertz's example, many of the critical and reflexive approaches in anthropology since the 1960s have rejected cross-cultural comparison. In anthropological praxis and in academic institutions, a schism emerged, dividing non-comparatists from comparatists, and particularists from generalists. As is often the case with dichotomies that allow a wide range of approaches to either

4. A. R. Radcliffe-Brown, *Method in Social Anthropology* (Chicago and London, 1976), 80.
5. Clifford Geertz, "Thick Description: Toward an Interpretive Theory of Culture," in *Interpretation of Cultures: Selected Essays* (New York, 1973), 26.

side of an epistemological divide, this schism seems to have prevented discussions on comparison in anthropology for some time. Currently, however, a re-evaluation of comparison among critical anthropologists can be observed that explicitly engages anthropology's predicament of "being in culture while looking at culture"[6]—a predicament shared with Cultural Studies—while arguing for the achievement of what Laura Nader calls "comparative consciousness," a critical sense of how comparison operates and to what ends it has been used and could be used in the future.

Obviously, so far, it is only with difficulty that the account of the role of comparative approaches in the disciplinary history of anthropology, can be productively applied to the issue of how to compare national styles of conducting scholarly work within one transnational disciplinary framework. However, it is precisely the current reassessment of cross-cultural comparison in anthropology that, in its move to critique past practices within the discipline, sheds light on some of the more problematical implications of comparativism. To my mind, there seem to be four common traps comparatists can fall into: (1) *Fragmenting cultural wholes.* Comparative methodologies in anthropology have tended to and often continue to delimit their objects to fit taxonomic classifications, thereby fragmenting cultural wholes into transculturally comparable bits and pieces. In order to make comparisons, one has to sort through a vast amount of information on cultures and make it fit into categories that one counts on being transculturally valid. It is almost inevitable that contextual meanings and culturally specific relations are lost in the process. (2) *Denying linkages between cultures.* By treating the cultures under comparison as discrete and separate units, cross-cultural comparison constructs social groups or societies as neatly bounded, which they generally are not (and never have been). Cross-cultural comparison often denies linkages and influences between cultures. (3) *Freezing cultures in time.* Cross-cultural comparison "presupposes a freezing of the time frame," writes Johannes Fabian in his critique of functionalist comparison: "Practically, concentration on cultural configurations and patterns resulted in . . . an overwhelming concern with the description of states."[7] Synchronizing cultures for the purposes of comparison de-emphasizes historical change and historicity in general. (4) *Hiding the comparatist from view.* The anthropologist conducting the

6. James Clifford, *The Predicament of Culture: Twentieth-Century Ethnography, Literature, and Art* (Cambridge and London, 1988), 9.

7. Fabian, *Time and the Other*, 20.

comparison of two or more usually non-Western indigenous cultures writes himself out of the process.[8] His or her subject position is made out to be that of the objective observer who is purportedly above or beyond culture. Cross-cultural comparison as an operation tends to cloak power and privilege shaping the hierarchical relations between observer and observed or between comparer and compared. Also, by pretending that its goal is to deal with other cultures, cross-cultural comparison obviates the fact that it is strongly implicated with Western cultures, and that the most important divide emphasized by the comparison is not between those other cultures but between the anthropologist's own culture and those he or she represents and images as the Other.

Recent original approaches to comparison that have emerged in anthropology in the past decade take up the challenge posed by these deeply problematic operations. American cultural anthropologists George E. Marcus and Michael Fischer elaborate on the critical potential of an operation they do not call comparison, but instead label as the "juxtaposition" of cultural representations. British social anthropologist Marilyn Strathern claims that the very basis for cross-cultural comparison has disappeared in what she describes as a postplural world, and her American colleague Laura Nader reflects on a new comparative consciousness in anthropology.

In their widely acclaimed 1986 book *Anthropology as Cultural Critique*, George E. Marcus and Michael Fischer[9] define a new role for anthropology as one of the key disciplines in the humanities. To some extent, they attribute the discipline's newly prominent position to the discovery or recovery of its comparative potential. Anthropological comparison, so they claim, can offer critiques on Western societies. This critical impetus is predicated on a comparatist move that, if we believe Marcus and Fischer, has disposed of many of the problems of cross-cultural comparison along with its name. What they call "juxtaposition . . . is a matching of ethnography abroad with ethnography at home. The idea is to use the substantive facts about another culture as a probe into the specific facts about a subject of criticism at home."[10] Rather than arranging comparison ostensibly around perceived differences between a variety

8. For a forceful critique of this stance, see Joachim Matthes, "'Zwischen' den Kulturen?" in *Zwischen den Kulturen. Die Sozialwissenschaften vor dem Problem des Kulturvergleichs*, ed. idem, Sonderband Soziale Welt 8 (Göttingen, 1992), 3–9.

9. George E. Marcus and Michael M. J. Fischer, *Anthropology as Cultural Critique: An Experimental Moment in the Human Sciences* (Chicago and London, 1986).

10. Ibid., 138.

of non-Western cultures "out there" and leaving the underlying us-them dualism between "the West and the rest" unmarked, juxtaposition as an operation in cultural anthropology explicitly pairs the anthropologist's own society with a contrasting non-Western example. Rather than remaining dualistic and opposing, however, such comparisons are always informed by the entire body of knowledge that anthropology has produced, thus introducing as a third perspective "multiple other-cultural references."[11] Another major difference to prior comparative approaches lies in the fact that Marcus and Fischer speak of juxtaposing representations of cultures rather than of comparing actual cultures. In a number of contemporary works in anthropology, they see a kind of "playing off other cultural realities against our own" that adequately realizes the potential of anthropology for cultural critique—a critique aimed at our own culture and at "the normally unexamined assumptions by which we operate and through which we encounter members of other cultures."[12]

Marilyn Strathern in her 1992 essay, "Parts and Wholes: Refiguring Relationships in a Post-Plural World," in turn addresses some of the unexamined assumptions that guide her American colleagues Marcus and Fischer in their championing of cross-cultural juxtaposition. To regard cultures as "wholes," as bounded units and entities meaningful unto themselves, according to Marilyn Strathern is an activity that belongs to a "recent, pluralist past," when anthropology could still perceive the world as a "replication of like units (a multitude of distinctive but analogous societies)."[13] Clearly, Marcus and Fischer's suggestions for a new mode of comparison are predicated on this now obsolete assumption, as Strathern claims: "The pluralist vision of a world of distinctive, total societies has dissolved into a post-plural one."[14] Postplurality means a sustained cultural interchange and borrowing whereby "elements cut from diverse times and places can be recombined, though they cannot fit together as a whole."[15] If we subscribe to Strathern's view, to criticize a comparatist perspective for not understanding "each society as a whole," but "as an object dismantled by our own categories"[16] becomes

11. Ibid., 139.
12. Ibid., ix–x.
13. Marilyn Strathern, "Parts and Wholes: Refiguring Relationships in a Post-Plural World," in *Conceptualizing Society*, ed. Adam Kuper (London, 1992), 77.
14. Ibid.,77.
15. Ibid.,75.
16. Ibid.

meaningless. She rejects the idea that a comparative perspective should acknowledge cultures as wholes rather than as assemblages of parts. In a recursively comparative move that uses indigenous notions of kinship and belonging to question some of anthropology's core precepts, Marilyn Strathern instead suggests that native epistemologies are much more comfortable with the idea of cultural fragmentation (and with social relations that need to be invented over and over again) than the ethnographers who strain to make non-Western cultures fit a so-called holistic model of culture as a closed, seamless, and internally consistent system.

American cultural anthropologist Laura Nader also demands that non-Western perspectives should be included in the comparatist enterprise. In her 1994 essay, "Comparative Consciousness," she urges anthropology to rethink what she calls its wholesale debunking of comparison. She claims that "without comparison, we literally lose consciousness and become victims of the bounds of thinkable thought."[17] However, what she has in mind when she uses the term comparison has little in common with the controlled methodology of cross-cultural comparison employed by the functionalists. Indeed, she opts for developing a type of comparative perspective that overcomes all of the problems listed before, instead thinking about "the possibility of a comparative consciousness that illuminates connections—between local and global, between past and present, between anthropologists and those they study. . . . Comparative methodologies that are useful in examining the current world situation must include the interactive aspects of the global movement of people, goods, and ideas."[18] Also, she rejects the notion that cross-cultural comparison can only be done from the privileged position of the Western anthropologist. Rather, as she points out, non-Western authors and indigenous peoples have always engaged in cross-cultural comparisons of their own, and any comparative venture anthropology is embarking on today should not only acknowledge the insights of non-Western observers, but scrutinize and utilize their categories of comparison as well.

In these three author's attempts at inventing new types of comparative approaches, anthropology has sought to free itself of a legacy that rejected intra- and intercultural influences as "impurities," placed indigenous cultures in an ahistorical "ethnographic present," and claimed the position of an objective observer for

17. Nader, "Comparative Consciousness," 86.
18. Ibid., 86f.

practitioners of a discipline deeply implicated in a politics of "us and them." But does the formation of a new comparative consciousness in cultural anthropology also speak to the endeavor of bringing a comparative perspective to scholarly practices in the academy? As observed before, there is no clear analogy between comparing cultures and comparing national subdivisions of a transnational scholarly discipline. However, if we seek to compare the types of academic institutions in which the field of Cultural Studies is established in different societies, if we intend to compare the ways in which it is taught, debated, and written about at universities in various national contexts, or to inquire into the influences of the specific developments of intellectual history on national incarnations of Cultural Studies, some suggestions on how to best proceed can be gleaned from anthropology's struggle with comparativism:

1. *"A capacity for thinking about fluid situations."*[19] The critiques developed by Laura Nader and Marilyn Strathern speak forcefully to the necessity for cross-cultural comparison to address linkages and connections between cultures, rather than constructing them as neatly bounded, separate entities. This challenges us to reflect on how we construct the entities we set out to compare when we talk about a comparative perspective on the transnational discipline of Cultural Studies.

2. *Contextual meanings.* Comparison to some extent applies categories cross-culturally that tend to homogenize local meanings and contextual variation. That is why it is so important to engage in "the challenge of rethinking the culturally specific meanings of some of the key-terms of the field," and to remind ourselves of the fact that these "cannot be treated in isolation from questions of power and politics."[20] To give an example, the German word *multikulturell* carries a meaning that is not covered by the semantics of American multicultural terminology.[21]

3. *Historicity.* Because cross-cultural comparison to some degree has to synchronize processes in different societies, there is

19. Ibid., 86.

20. Prospectus, Symposium "Cultural Studies in Comparative Perspective," Institut für Anglistik und Amerikanistik, Humboldt Universität zu Berlin, 27–28 June 1996.

21. See Gisela Welz, "Multikulturelle Diskurse: Differenzerfahrung als ethnologischer und gesellschaftlicher Topos in Deutschland und den USA," in *Amerikastudien/American Studies* 38, no. 2 (1993); 265–272; Günter H. Lenz, "Transnational American Studies: Conceptualizing Multicultural Identities and Communities—Some Notes," in *Fremde Texte verstehen. Festschrift für Lothar Bredella,* ed. Herbert Christ and Michael K. Legutke (Tübingen, 1996), 191.

always the danger of concealing discontinuities and disjunctures. How can we compare the disciplinary trajectories of Cultural Studies in different societies without freezing on-going processes in easy-to-compare developmental stages? Can the histories of Cultural Studies actually be represented as evolutionary narratives?

4. *Reflexivity and the positional predicament.* Cultural Studies is pervaded by an awareness of "looking at culture while being in culture." While speaking poignantly to the positional predicament of Cultural Studies, this statement also allows for a curious "black-boxing" of which culture we are "in" and which culture we are "looking at." How do we position ourselves and our disciplinary subject(s) culturally? Does it suffice to identify a scholar doing Cultural Studies in or on Germany or the United States as a German or an American? Or does a simple dualism that employs nationality as a categorical marker mask other, more complex divisions?

The conventional historiography of science constructs evolutionary narratives of prominent scholars who act as founding fathers for so-called schools. While these are, more often than not, nationally defined in origin and scope and associated with national developments in intellectual history, this approach rarely engages comparison. Beyond a few studies comparing national academic "cultures"—mostly limited to the natural sciences—the sociology of science has not developed a comparative methodology—or theory—devoted to the question of nationally or culturally specific styles within transnationally established disciplines. However, some of the sociological and epistemological approaches emerging in science theory that address the constitution of scholarly disciplines might be productively applied to an inquiry into national styles within a transnational discipline. For instance, Pierre Bourdieu's reflexive analysis of the sociological discipline scrutinizes what he calls the "scientific subconscious" and brings to light the unspoken *doxa* that limit and guide the surface struggles between orthodox and heterodox disciplinary approaches.[22] Ian Hacking, in turn, coins the term "style of reasoning" to denote the conventionalized modes of knowledge production, of argument and debate that remain largely tacit within a discipline. These guard what is considered to be within or without

22. Pierre Bourdieu, "Narzißtische Reflexivität und wissenschaftliche Reflexivität," in *Kultur, soziale Praxis, Text. Die Krise der ethnographischen Repräsentation,* eds. Eberhard Berg and Martin Fuchs (Frankfurt/Main, 1993), 365–374.

the borders of the disciplinary subject,[23] and what kind of statement could be regarded as being what Michel Foucault calls "dans le vrai"[24] of a given discipline. By conceptualizing scholarly endeavors as a cultural practice, these approaches could help position the discipline within different societal frameworks and comparatively relate those to each other.

However, it may not be useful or even correct to construct the entities to be compared as nationally identified subdivisions or subdisciplines of a transnational discipline called Cultural Studies. We need to ask whether the term discipline is adequately descriptive of Cultural Studies. Certainly, if one were to apply the criteria that sociologists of science have evolved to define and measure disciplinarity,[25] the status of Cultural Studies as a discipline is somewhat questionable: disciplinarity does seem to require a degree of institutional consolidation and standardization of knowledge that Cultural Studies appears to have not, or not yet, achieved. On the other hand, do we even strive for disciplinarity in this more conventional sense? The *Wissenschaftslandschaften* (sciencescapes) of late modern societies are becoming decidedly postplural in much the same sense as Marilyn Strathern uses the term. It is not at all certain whether disciplinarity will remain the dominant model for the social organization of knowledge. Also, national sciencescapes are becoming effectively globalized, with a definite increase in transnational communication and with the emergence of a global academic labor market. On both counts, because of its nondisciplinary or transdisciplinary status, and because of its strongly transnational impetus, Cultural Studies may well be a forerunner of future developments.

23. Ian Hacking, "Language, Truth and Reason," in *Rationality and Relativism*, eds. Martin Hollis and Steven Lukes (Cambridge, 1982), 48–66.

24. Michel Foucault, *Die Ordnung des Diskurses. Inauguralvorlesung am Collège de France—2. Dezember 1970* (Munich, 1974), 24.

25. Wolfgang Kroh and Günter Küppers, *Die Selbstorganisation der Wissenschaft* (Frankfurt/Main, 1989).

2. Race, Color ... and Creed

Timothy Brennan

It is widely assumed that the U.S. Constitution protects citizens against discrimination on the basis of "race, color, or creed." In fact, there are no explicit protections for freedom of conscience in the Constitution apart from Article I, which protects against "prohibiting the free exercise" of religion.

Stony Brook, where I taught, is heralded for its medical staff and at least one Nobel Prize-winning physicist. Like most non-Ivy League or would-be Ivy League schools elsewhere in the country—especially in state schools dependent on state funding—its center of gravity is the hard sciences. Anyone positioned in the humanities at a major research institution will likely be familiar with a situation in which corporate grants and national science awards create, as in a laboratory, administrative favors and faculty clout. An entire wing of the university supposedly open to all students and faculty (in Stony Brook's case, the Office of International Studies, for example) is actually not as open as its name implies. Like certain Italian bars on the fringes of black neighborhoods—which pretend to be closed for business when the wrong clientele comes around—it is an office with an explicit constituency. Like other departments at Stony Brook, International Studies is actually a private resource center for the university's scientists, and it is the scientists alone who, as a bloc, can expect regular perquisites in the form of lower teaching loads, teaching assistants' support, travel monies, regular merit pay increases, and even most-favored parking status. It is no surprise then that the science professors tend to converse in hushed tones about the importance of what they do as distinct from the humanities.[1] Although whatever the claim to privilege might be, it certainly cannot be comparative public recognition, since the English Department (to take only that wing of the humanities I happen to occupy) boasts a Pulitzer Prize-winning poet, a Pulitzer Prize-winning feature journalist, a best-selling novelist, commissioning editors for Verso and Cambridge University Presses, a film critic whose work has been translated into five languages, and so on and so forth.

In the university senate this familiar academic judgment on disciplinary hierarchy—whose power derives from reflecting a well-known public common sense on the usefulness of science—is not always even hidden. Although no special benches are assigned to them, the chairs where the scientists sit are typically set apart from those of the professors in the so-called "soft" disciplines as if in some restaging of urban "redlining." Indeed, the campus itself is divided elsewhere by a similar politics of space, with the scientists in the newer and taller buildings by the president's office; the humanities huddled in the older, sparer buildings housing the cafeterias; and the social sciences somewhere vaguely in between. The university, then, has its barrios, its good and bad side of the tracks both literally and figuratively, and the rules-making system is definitely not based on the principle of one-person-one-vote.

With that sort of atmosphere on his mind, my provost recently admitted that this division I've been describing—between disciplinary mentalities or methodological communities—was a difference, basically, of "culture." While trying to cheer some of us up at Stony Brook's Humanities Institute during a very favorable outside review, he said that the sciences needed us to show them that they were not above criticism, and that their methods were not the only ones. Speaking as a biologist himself, he affirmed that the scientists existed in a culture that was different from ours. If the funding and preference patterns were going to change, or if he was to be given any leverage in his arguments before the university president during

1. Cf. the classic debate about Charles Percy Snow's 1959 Rede Lecture at Cambridge University on the difference between the humanities and social sciences, published as *The Two Cultures and a Second Look: An Expanded Version of The Two Cultures and the Scientific Revolution* (New York, 1963); the responses by Frank Raymond Leavis, "Two Cultures? The Significance of C.P.Snow," *Richmond Lectures* (London, 1962) and Lionel Trilling, "The Leavis-Snow Controversy," *Beyond Culture: Essays on Literature and Learning* (New York, 1968); and the previous debate between Matthew Arnold and T.H. Huxley about Arnold's 1882 Rede Lecture "Literature and Science," *Philistinism in England and America: The Complete Prose Works of Matthew Arnold*, ed. Robert Henry Super (Ann Arbor, 1974) vol. 10.

the next round of Albany budget cuts, we humanities professors had to find a way to articulate our culture to a public that now widely assumed its inferiority. This manner of identifying communities of belief is key to the debate over multiculturalism today, and it takes us into a very different territory than the one to which we are accustomed.

Far much more customary are the rash of attempts by journalists and literary critics lately to complain that the word "cultural" in multiculturalism is a euphemism. It has been concocted, they aver, by those who simply do not want to own up to the fact that culture almost *always* means "race."[2] Therefore, because most people draw the battle lines in this country over race, what had to be devised was a tangential, somewhat technical term that reminds one of good things like inclusion and tolerance, and this was "multiculturalism." What I've tried to suggest right here at the beginning is that culture as a term is not always about race, or at least does not have to be. What, in other words, is a culture of science, and how is it different from a culture of the humanities? In the willful way I've described my campus above, I've suggested that *this* understanding of culture recalls many of the same biases, acts of exclusion, and arrogance that the understanding of race and ethnicity does. Cultural difference based on conflicting mentalities, positions, or doctrines can and does lead to ghettoization, violence, and even censorship. In that way, belief or a belief-system has a direct and unacknowledged impact on multiculturalism. What are cultures of belief, and what role do they play in discrimination? What roles should they play?

The United States

There is no need to replace race, ethnicity, gender, national origin, or sexual orientation with a new term; and in spite of my opening, I am not interested only in academic disciplines as "belief cultures." Often considered to be tendentious slogans, for example, the categories of race/class/gender are as unavoidable as the abstraction "Renaissance" in a history of European painting, and necessarily follow from rendering inequality more visibly an issue. The point here rather would be to extend, not delimit, freedom. To do so appropriately, one has to look in the direction of that particularly dense and (paradoxically) invisible set of discriminations against

2. Walter Benn Michaels, "Race into Culture: A Critical Genealogy of Cultural Identity," *Critical Inquiry* 18, vol. 4 (Summer 1992): 655–85.

conscience, which are dangerous not because all conscience is equal, but because it is not. While a modest "free speech" is protected as a legal abstraction, there are no safeguards for conscience in the workplace that "discriminate"—openly and judiciously and with a full sense of what it means to do so—on the basis of the *content* of conscience.

Few of us want to address directly the tangled problems of belief, for reasons I will be occupied with below. My focus on beliefs or opinions here stems, obviously, from an opinion of my own, which has to do with the conviction that in matters of knowledge, policy making, and social amelioration, affiliation matters at least as much as filiation. We write and speak about what we know or care about; or rather—what we care about, we learn about and therefore know. It is a bitter sort of injustice when a person becomes a second-class employee on the basis of what he or she created for themselves. The most decisive question ultimately is not what one has been born into or how one comes off in a social setting that attributes character to phenotype or accent. The most decisive question is what one is drawn to or makes.

One might initially see this claim as too meritorious to be refutable, and yet it is precisely what often escapes notice. One has only to ask how it has affected recent efforts at academic reform to realize the reversible stakes in a politics of position-as-belief. Apparently antagonistic to affirmative action, for example, the claim actually supports it, since affirmative action attempts to allow *doing* to take place freely, to not be foreclosed by a certain perception of being. On the other hand, at least one of the absent theoretical moves in the attempt to reach affirmative action's goals is precisely a shift from identity to position or location—and by this I mean not locale as in place of birth or native habitation, but social location, one's circle of friends, one's range of reading, one's contacts and habits, or conditions of travel.

We have an enormous problem with the stubbornness that assumes, for example, that American-based scholars whose family background or nominal lineage is Lebanese, Nigerian, or Mexican will write books or give speeches of greater depth or poignancy on Lebanon, Nigeria, or Mexico. Entire careers, not only the speakers-lists of conferences or magazine round tables, operate with a brittle confidence in this questionable homology between knowledge and being, analytical depth and skin color, judgment and surname. A "cellular epistemology" covers the thinking and (more importantly) the policy-making of academic reformers and liberal politicians *as well as* public commentators and mainstream news organizations. In spite of the crucial points of dissonance between the media and academic progressives on matters ranging from the value of Cultural Studies to the role of research in undergraduate humanities education, there is no disagreement about the equation between black scholars and "black" thinking, if one can use such a term. I use it here, at any rate, with intentional irony to refer to views about the questionable centrality of the English language in a world where a small minority actually speak it, about the vibrancy and longevity of foreign popular cultures not already subsumed into the U.S. media, or about the competitive aesthetic brilliance of, say, Caribbean music when placed alongside European literature. In both venues, the defense of culturally dissonant thinking is given permission to *be* only in the imaginary form of the black scholar, and in this sense one could say that a more general political environment tolerates cultures of belief only when bled through a racial or ethnic mask as though, in some horrible reenactment of a Jim Carrey film, the mask becomes the person, and belief as such becomes invisible as an issue of prejudice.

And here one understands the force of the word "prejudice" to be distinct from discrimination in its positive connotations (the "discriminating mind"), in which the rejection of specific views would be well-justified for being based on a reasoned assessment or a careful weighing of positions rather than an atmospheric disgust or frustration with outlooks or orientations that, very much like the California tourist in Mali, cannot wait to return home to a securer and more inviting set of conventions. Beliefs breed ways of being, and the intolerance toward some has less to do with scholarly refutations than with a palpable unease in the presence of lifestyles that demand of the stranger a painful cultural conversion.

Outside the relative social fairness and moral conscience of the university, sites of opinion-forming and decision making—Congress, the Washington talk shows, and somewhat less so, influential news feature and interview programs such as *Nightline* and *60 Minutes*—are so overwhelmingly white (or so predictably tokenized) that equations between affirmative action and alternative values seem almost automatic. However, here various media-watch organizations have succeeded in popularizing the matter of creed in the race/class/gender nexus. Nonetheless, a set of arguments against gender and racial oppression are firmly in place, even though those arguments have not achieved anything like racial or gender equality. There is a good deal of evidence, in fact, that the unofficial is becoming the official—that trends in business and government are actually moving from de facto segregation to an open declaration that minority exclusion is justified—a shift in policy that mirrors the rise in anti-immigrant violence, growing numbers of police brutality cases, sharp increases in governmental recourse to the death penalty, and extraordinary campaigns by white supremacist organizations best exemplified, perhaps, by the recent wave of arson against black churches in the South.[3] Such campaigns and policy changes are not being enacted, however, without resistance. A firm rhetoric of racial and gender inclusion still remains a part of the common culture.

What seems more and more to be missing is a language combating discrimination against belief and the cultures it generates. Even in the relatively pallid disputes between white senators from South Carolina and white senators from Massachusetts, in which a culture of postindustrial welfare liberalism vies with Dixie recidivism, issues of belief bear on the above developments with painful clarity even as they are swept from conversation in a flurry of clichéd codes for *race*: the "bell curve," "teenage pregnancy," the "drug problem," the "decline of the cities." Again, constitutionally creed has a much less clear legal status in discrimination suits than gender and race do, and when raised at all creed is almost always considered to be a matter of *religious* freedom. Creed in that sense is either not an issue at all, or it is an issue largely equated in the United States with church or religion. Thus, the discourse of freedom of conscience—with the exception of recent protests against the attack on arts funding or the banning of books in public schools—is mostly limited to issues like school prayer, Catholics or Jews denied membership in country clubs, the tax-free status of radio preachers, and similar cases.

One might argue that there are at least two exceptions to this claim about the unacceptable limits of our nation's religious focus: the Federal Communications Commission's (FCC) "Fairness Doctrine," which requires television and radio stations to provide contrasting points of view; and asylum law, which stipulates the right to asylum of those with a "well-founded fear of persecution because of their race, religion, nationality, political opinions, or membership

3. See two recent rulings, one by the Federal Appeals Court against the University of Texas, the other by the Federal Communications Commission: Peter Appelbome, "National Desk," *New York Times*, 22 March 1996, B8; Edmund L. Andrews, "FCC is Said to Seek an End to Preference on Sex and Race," *New York Times*, 22 June 1995, D1.

in a social group."[4] And yet it seems significant that the first of these regulations was overturned by the Circuit Court of Appeals in 1987 and was never applied vigorously or with wide range; and the second relates not to domestic rights but to international ones, thereby displacing the concept of discrimination based on opinions from the presumably central democratic polity to other parts of the world, which are then judged from this center as though they were the only places where ill-treatment against those with unapproved political opinions actually occurred.[5]

From the legal standpoint, creed cannot simply be equated with religion. To do so is not to recognize what it is. While legal protections against discrimination based on creed are deliberately excluded from the statutes, there is a persistent rhetorical undertone in discussions of public policy that such biases do not occur. In other words, what is done on purpose is not being justified purposively. The ensuing false consciousness monopolizes for race, gender, and religion (much less sexual orientation) the issue of prejudice itself, and one suspects that there is a certain comfort in this bad faith with broader ideological resonances—views borrowed perhaps from nineteenth-century European social theory having to do with the strong explanatory force of *nature*, on the one hand, and an older sense of Christian guilt, on the other, such that inequality of access or opportunity is heinous to those who cannot help being what they are, but allowable for those who choose what they are. Theoretically, of course, the distinction is never argued or even faced. Why should what one chooses freely—why should what we *make* of ourselves—be any less protected than the ineradicable conditions of birth? Even with the rather questionable criterion suggesting that active choice places one with justice in the play of power's whims, is it really true that choosing one's membership in a belief culture is always free? The Amish child, the Hasidic youth, the teenage Klan member, the red diaper baby, inherit as much as choose, their ideologies.

As a particularly diligent form of legal protection against gender and racial bias, affirmative action (before its late demise) was nevertheless weak and decentralized. Neither federal law nor executive order, it was rather a loose collection of local or institutional policies carried out in the spirit of a sense of right that had been chiseled out

---

4. R. Terry Ellmore, *Broadcasting Law and Regulations* (Blue Ridge Summit, 1982), 209; Celia W. Dugger, "Woman's Plea for Asylum Puts Tribal Ritual on Trial," *New York Times*, 15 April 1996, A1 and B4.

5. William B. Ray, *The Ups and Downs of Radio-TV Regulations* (Ames, 1990), 89.

of the commons through an arduous process of political mobilizations in the 1960s and early 1970s. Conjuring here the principle of a generalized mood or perception of what constitutes fairness—and implying thereby the importance of such moods for the more concrete decisions made in their aura—brings us again to the term multiculturalism, which has come into its own at precisely the time that affirmative action has suffered a series of defeats. One has to wonder whether the success of the one is not linked to the failure of the other. Put another way: how can a person defend the dignity of unapproved *identities* (the "bitch," the "fag," the "wetback," the alien) while prying them away from those *ideologies* that historically accompanied their modest ascent to a kind of recognition— ideologies that were not always socialist (many of them were anything but) although they were usually characterized as "red" by mainstream commentators?

Creed is all but nonexistent as a topic within multiculturalism and—as the list of possible belief cultures above implies—it is avoided for compelling reasons. To begin with, there is the matter of priorities. As I said, launching an attack on discriminations based on political or disciplinary points of view—which are *chosen*—seems less compelling to many than attacks on discriminations which are not chosen, and which cannot be hidden the way views can, at least theoretically. U.S. military gay policy—"don't ask, don't tell"—replicates the assumption (again primarily Christian) that like the market, will is free, and inasmuch as freedom bequeaths absolute responsibility, credit or blame must go to whatever nature does not endow. In this case, perhaps, we see where the dispute over the etiology of homosexuality is most obvious and most legally crucial. It exists as fallout in the never adequately resolved discourse of those moral guardians who see gayness as a "lifestyle choice," and (by contrast) those gay men and women who speak of having been born into their sexuality.

Although usually conceived as a question of identity, gay rights clearly spills over here into the vexed issue of belief by highlighting one of discrimination's central principles: that one can be punished for what one actively does but not passively is. If that principle is principally unstated, inconsistency is the reason. For not only are the varieties of religious faith choices treated as the inevitabilities of birthright—although they are no more inevitable than other views inherited from family—but the rationale of radical responsibility is haphazard in the law. One, for example, is held guilty for violating laws of which one is ignorant. And one born a Swiss citizen has no right to enter English territory, for example. Having simply to accept one's fate in regard to ideas or convictions but not in regard to identity is an issue carried out as though it were independent of the content of the views themselves, in the sense that Amnesty International, for example, has often defended victims of torture and imprisonment only so long as they were unaffiliated recipients of violence rather than organized members of groups fighting the very atrocities Amnesty International abhors: the young father caught by mistake in a police sweep rather than the guerrilla fighter whose ideological discipline arms him to prevent these tragedies from occurring.

A more intractable and equally reasonable sort of barrier to introducing creed into a properly multicultural problematic is the difficulty of distinguishing real patterns of bias based on beliefs, on the one hand, from simple idiosyncracies or occasional clashes of personality, on the other. In other words, since it is in the nature of institutional life for individuals to feel unappreciated, not listened to, or secretly outmaneuvered by enemies or rivals who skirt democratic processes, how can one ever hope to eradicate the strong suspicion of being discriminated against on the basis of one's views? How can one in practice distinguish between ruffled feathers or the zero sum game of perquisite disbursements in underfunded colleges, say, and ideological repressions that warrant a civil rights claim? They are not the same thing, and yet it is very difficult in practice to distinguish the one from the other. The apparent difficulty in enforcing the right to conscience in practice becomes, therefore, an argument against attempting it.

But finally, there is another—and I think the most powerful—reason for avoidance. And this is simply that anyone who seriously thinks about the issue soon discovers that they *want* discrimination based on creed—that they want to preserve the right to accept or reject candidates, coworkers, or colleagues on the basis of what they think.[6] The framers of the U.S. Constitution certainly understood this need. And this need is recognized again at a number of micro levels throughout the system. On university hiring committees, for example, one's support *might* be entirely on the basis of stronger vitae, easier eloquence, sparkle of intelligence, and other supposedly neutral criteria. Chances are, though, that the committee prefers one candidate's reading of Bakhtin to others, is delighted

6. For an interesting recent treatment of this issue, see Stanley Fish, *There's No Such Thing as Free Speech, and It's a Good Thing, Too* (New York and Oxford, 1994), 110 and 113.

by her anecdotes about baseball, is impressed by her involvement in the Palestine Defense Committee, and in other ways "gets along" with her because, in a manner they are not likely to think about consciously, she is someone they recognize as living in their culture of belief. Few would want to give up their prerogative to reject a scholar who believed (as many do) that no literature other than English literature is worth reading, that African cultures are inferior or tangential to the development of America, that college students should be seen and not heard, and that poor people are beasts who ought better be taught a useful skill like typing than the *Duino Elegies.* In betraying my own set of convictions, I also realize, of course, that there are other positions of equal validity to those who hold them. This, I imagine, is what commentators mean when they talk about "tolerance." And yet, even though it is always espoused piously, tolerance is never meant to be sweeping. It always has inherent limits. In spite of the fact that almost no enlightened middle-class professor *only* accepts his own point of view, there is no reason to slip into thinking of oneself—or to identify in others—the benignness usually accorded pluralism. The point after all is not whether we accept views different from our own but whether we can admit all of them—even those fatal to our own. Almost no one rejects censorship when pressed long enough on individual examples. We need to have a public reckoning over the convenient piety, heard almost everywhere, that one opposes censorship in toto. For to admit that all of us have limits, removes the issue from a pseudo-religious principle and places it in the realm of program and policy in which a more honest discussion can take place.

Naturally there are dangers in this effort. As embarrassing as it might be to have an open debate over the limits, and even the acceptability, of censorship, there is no other way to combat the unofficial *Berufsverbot* of the American university and media than to keep tabs, in open court, on exactly who gets fired, non-promoted, or put down—and for what reason.[7] Under public scrutiny, I would argue, the assumed equality or balance of discrimination on the basis of belief (or at least its haphazard, merely local, character) would no longer be tenable. We would be able to give a general name to the creed or creeds that are most targeted and could begin to come to grips with the political and social meanings of the kind of discrimination that is massively going on today—especially in

7. In the Federal Republic of Germany, the term *Berufsverbot* referred to the job ban in the public service for members of the Communist Party, as well as for those perceived to be sympathetic to it.

those fields where ideas are the raw materials of work: film production, writing for newspapers and magazines, and teaching and writing at the university. A number of people might rush to point out the obscenity of comparing contemporary U.S. censorship with Saudi crackdowns on pornography, the jailing of dissidents in the former Eastern Bloc, or the public execution of witches in seventeenth-century Salem—to mention some of the more familiar examples of censorship when the matter is discussed in the media. But if the virulence of its actions, and the principle of its execution, are different from these cases, what are they? Is it ingenuous to argue that the documented cases of people fired from their jobs, refused publication, hounded out of town, and even on occasion jailed or lynched, are all aberrations and all unlinked by the semblance of a common principle? If most of us recognize the fact of a "color line," for example—a phrase that stands for the general international embarrassment of American racism—is there not also a cultural dominant whose censorship predilections can be given a name? I would like now to do that.

To begin to tackle this problem, we could begin by observing that at least until the Christian Coalition achieves more power, the U.S. principle of censorship is not religious per se. Only a little provocation is needed to see that the principle is rather a "religion of state"—a solidly liberal dogma about the importance of taking the middle road against the extremism of two sides. Forged in the fundamental ambiguity of the postwar period, when the U.S. government was riven by the untenable paradox of distrusting the ally that won the war (the Soviet Union) while relying for expertise and information on the well-trained castoffs and survivors among the Germans who immigrated here amidst quiet fanfare, religion of state became a dogma from which it has been simply intolerable to vary. With convenient echoes of the golden mean of the *Reader's Digest* classics, the unstated principle of evading the tyrannies of Hitler/Stalin metamorphosed in a number of useful ways. The moral lesson that the United States created in the postwar period was that America, by definition, occupied a terrain suspended between the unrelieved mayhem of left and right fanatics outside its borders. It was only a matter of time before these "fanatics" became interchangeable.

Ever since the remarkable pronouncements of Jean Kirkpatrick regarding the difference between (good) "authoritarian" regimes in the Third World and properly (bad) socialist ones, the attempts of a type of right wing extremism to enter the mainstream have

begun to change this calculus. While the pieties of balance still govern the pluralist discourse of the media, an insurgent wing of the
Republican party, along with certain policy analysts, antigovernment
militia groups, and traditional white supremacist organizations, are
trying hard to defend verbally—not only to enact quietly—the principles of intolerance and compulsory belief in *their* cultures, with
gun (or appropriations bill) in hand. It would be fair to say that the
religion of the "middle way" has never been in more danger. It is an
interesting moment.

The secular religion of balance paradoxically helped cripple progressive opposition movements and paved the way for the very right
wing assault that now threatens balance itself. The specious golden
mean, by staking out a middle that was nothing of the sort, and sti-
fling the opposition to America's unhealthy postwar affair with right
wing generals and domestic strongmen—sanctified by the increasingly meaningless term "communist"—nurtured the extremism that
now rises up from the darkness to demand payment. This history
would have been different if we had accepted guilt for our acts of
censorship. What sort of weight, then, could the sanctimonious con-
trasts between the land of the "free press" and the lands of unfree-
dom in the Eastern Bloc have had? We would have been forced to
have a discussion about *which* views we favored and why.

Whatever the systemic disparities between East and West were,
they were not censorship. There were different styles of execution,
perhaps, even different levels of intensity, but not fundamentally
different motives or effects. Once one comes clean on this matter,
there is nothing left to do but fight over which views are acceptable
and which are not. If this sounds uncomfortably close to the procedural outlooks of the Christian Coalition, one has to accept the
comparison procedurally. But overestimating the significance of a
purely formal similarity is the staple of the religion of the middle
way. In that view, if two states jail dissidents, pass laws limiting the
rights of movement, wage wars against foreign powers, and insist on
a role in determining the curriculum of the public schools, these
two states are equivalent. The problem with this untenable equiva-
lence is that it falls apart once one explores individual cases; it suppresses the questions "for whom?" "on whose behalf?" "how many?"
"to what end?." In the United States, therefore, it is perfectly coherent to argue against the prohibition of flag-burning while arguing
for the prohibition of displaying the Confederate flag. The apparent formal inconsistency is a ruse that hides the more important
fact that the one flag stands for the free expression that permits its

own burning, while the other champions slavery. Less important than agreeing with this position is agreeing to argue it politically (that is, more honestly) rather than abstractly. One can defend democracy without holding to the ridiculous claim that no censorship exists here, and to do so with the idea that otherwise, America would simply make no difference.

In spite of the history I have laid out, there is a sense in which creed has not really been so overlooked in discussions of multiculturalism as I have been suggesting. For the claim fails to take account of the "political correctness" debate itself, which was exactly an appeal from the right to defend those discriminated against for unpopular views. The point seems decisive, and yet it is deceptive. Accusations are often only confessions of practice. It takes no specially equipped Washington insider to discover that when a congressman complains of "big government" he is really arguing for corporate mergers and a vastly strengthened federal system of criminal penalties and re-armed police departments; that when he protests the capital's "business as usual" he is posing as a rebel and outsider while opposing any mild reforms of business as usual in Washington; and that when he cries about right wing students and "traditional" professors suffering on "p.c." campuses, he is really talking about his own campaign to purge the universities of progressive teachers and innovative graduate students, or to create the climate in which others can do it for him.

Liberal piety is precisely the weapon of those whose illiberal designs are a matter of public record and a matter of conspicuous public bragging. This is the contradiction that escapes notice in the absence of debate over cultures of belief. Thus, the only response by the academy to charges that some conservative students or professors were suffering because of their views was to say: no they are not, we are open to everyone, these events never happened. And it is true, in fact, that the right has not suffered in the university. But it is not true that we are open to everyone, nor should we be. What was *not* said in response to the p.c.-opponents was that the left rather than the right is the victim of discrimination in the university. Younger professors identified with, say, postcolonial theory or Cultural Studies, radical economists, labor historians, scientists involved in critiques of scientific rationality are typically the ones denied promotion or told to change their interests or be expelled. The acceptable middle road in journalism and the media has become so belligerently conservative that no author in or near the politics of the New Deal can easily earn a living, at least not without finding a manner of expressing those beliefs as entertainment, or in a way that is rife with qualifications, in a ghastly act of cowering. Film and even television still have openings, by contrast, although purges within alternative radio (one thinks of KPFA in Los Angeles) are a sign that anyone with links to a past of unions, of parties, much less of socialism is in constant threat of being fired. Although following a predictable postwar set of antagonisms, these acts of systematic censorship are, in terms of the university at least, closely related to movements of race, gender, and class, although not along the expected lines of identity.

The term "minority discourse," for example, refers not only to new canons and new professors. As an emerging bid for mainstream status, minority discourse is rather an atmosphere—a sort of background noise—within which progressive institutional changes have begun to take place. The right understands this very well, which is why its budget cuts on the Hill have consistently been prepared by an avant-garde on the cultural front. What is happening in the attacks on public education cannot be seen in a burrowing sort of way at the level of the department or even the "profession" as it is often called. If we look at these attacks historically, we can begin to see that the normality of a thing in the universities called English studies, art appreciation, philosophy and so on—the humanities—represented an interim moment between types of industrial training in the mid-nineteenth century and the current service-oriented university. The service university has for a long time been the reality, of course, at community colleges, but is now becoming more pronounced in public or state research institutions and extends even, in a weaker and more tentative way, to well-endowed private universities. At the level of state schools, this service means nonintellectual, practical skills like math, writing, and so on; at Yale or Harvard, service takes the form of a utilitarian use of the canon as secular religious instruction.

The point, then, is that the liberal arts as a site of open-ended questioning, of vaguer and more satisfying means of cultural development, spiritual refinement, and theoretical inquiry central to the "quality of life"— a process we have all grown up believing was a more or less standard feature of higher education—is now largely seen as an obsolete privilege, or as a frill that was never intended for those upon whom it is now bestowed. And the reason for this is that the constituencies have changed. Liberal arts has the function of polishing the veneer of class-arrival, in much the way that the Southern plantocracy in Thomas Jefferson's time taught their daughters how to play piano and to recite poetry. This type of training, mutatis mutandis, is being withdrawn today in part because a dissonance exists between its logic and its constituency. The logic is high-cultural finishing; the constituency is, more and more, white working-class and black and Latino youth. Those kinds of students do not need *that* kind of training, at least if it costs money.[8]

How do cultures of belief affect these policies? I would like to revive here the idea I raised above about the U.S. secular religion of the middle way, which so forcefully exerts its influence at every level of public and professional life, and which has produced more than one scapegoat and act of ostracism. To weight the case—that is, to take an example from the least likely source, and therefore to make the case even stronger—let us look at a typical document from university Cultural Studies—that is, precisely from that wing of university life attacked for its p.c. excesses, its racial fixations, and its creeping socialism. The following comes from a document written by a well-known humanities institute defending its role in, as it puts it, "the organization of knowledge in the university." Identifying as its foils those Allan Bloom-like theories that culture decays when there is a lack of training in the Western canon, the document has its response ready to hand. Humanities centers, it says, must be about "questioning" and "contesting," not simply providing fixed answers in gruff tones like Bloom. The principle espoused is what it describes as a welcome loss of faith in the philosophical traditions of Darwin, Marx, and Freud. For that loss leads to a "plethora of competing voices all claiming access and inclusion in the cultural sphere" and has, most welcomely, "produced a situation of undecidability, a jostling for claims to have the 'truth' that reveals there is none."

What this document shows, I would argue, is that the creation of new academic fields often leads to a double-consciousness. In its attempt to assuage the religion of the middle way, it paints a utopian portrait that the right wing has no trouble exposing as rank idealism. It opts for a strategy of meandering rather than of confrontation, and therefore allows the confrontations that cannot be avoided to take place in quiet under a veil of "undecidability" and

---

8. I, of course, am not emphasizing here those other factors in the defunding of higher education that have to do with declining tax bases as a result of homeowner or stock-jobber revolts, corporate shock treatment as a result of executive fears that schools are not producing the *kind* of skilled workers and managers they need, and the (not unimportant) factor of inertia, in that education has always been an easy target in budget cuts by virtue of the anti-intellectual perception of it as a debit cost rather than an investment.

choral "voices." It is especially the disenfranchised, of course, who hate hearing there is no truth; and again the issue of creed joins the issues of discrimination based on race, class, and gender. In the field of postcolonialism, too, that double-consciousness is shot through with a self-defeating gesture: how to resist the assumptions that surround us in a center of empire—how to resist them even while being hired to promote them in understanding, giving, and tolerant ways. It is the immense *subtlety* of imperial attitudes at this level that needs more analysis, and yet discrimination on the basis of creed (as I have outlined it here) prevents that analysis. That may be said even to be its goal.

Germany

For many of the reasons above, the issue of multiculturalism in Germany has a potent set of lessons about cultures of belief mistaken for race. In a country whose extensive American Studies and Cultural Studies programs have developed the discourse of ethnic fissure and national unity as they exist in the United States, and whose initial forays into multiculturalism repeat the gesture of looking at important social upheavals among immigrant populations of Turks, Kurds, Africans, and Vietnamese; very little has been said *in this context* about the clashes between the belief cultures of East and West. Judging from the table talk in fashionable Berlin restaurants after unification about the East German "prolies" (proletariat), a nagging ethnocentrism exists there too—based not on race or nationality but on the cultural training that creed creates.

I simply do not know the German situation as well as that of the United States, so what I say is based on the role German unification has had *here*, or with obvious reference to here—about the kinds of evaluations it has fostered in the United States. What strikes one initially is the sheer extent of recognition of belief as *culture* in the German context, and yet the eager flight from that recognition's consequences. In a rather too appealingly enigmatic way, for example, Christa Wolf has spoken of the West's "catalog of values different from those in the East ... implanted in its people."[9] Andreas Huyssen took a similar position: "before 1990 there were two German states, but presumably one nation. There is now again one German

9. Christa Wolf, "Parting from Phantoms: The Business of Germany," *PMLA* 111, no. 2: 404.

nation-state, but two national identities."[10] Michael Weck deliberately grasped the parallels between the brands of ideology and multicultural notions of "difference" when he spoke of the West's "orientalizing" of the East Germans. They had been, he observed, constructed as "the *wild* and *ungezahmt* (wild and undomesticated)" in the very breath that they were labeled "authoritarian and autocratic"—as overly Prussian with *urdeutsch* (archetypical German) habits that needed to give way to the enlightenment principles of the free market.[11] Hans Joachim Maaz—an East German psychologist adapting to the times—went so far as to call the East Germans "psychologically defective, infected by a 'virus' of a pathological social deformation."[12]

This transformation of socialist would-be countrymen into quasi-racial aliens is here overlaid on a traditional repugnance that Westerners in Europe have felt for those further East. That is, in order not to be misled by the virulence of objectifying belief as culture, one had to point to historical patterns that resemble it along traditional "racial" lines. As Wolf points out, "the look of contempt aimed from West to East has a long tradition,"[13] a feeling of civilizational superiority dating back to centuries of ridicule of the Slavs, and only intensified by the blunt politics of the Russian occupation (which took place even, as Wolf observes, among the "liberated" East Germans, who would tell racist jokes about Russian hygiene in the glory year of 1945). All that being said, the *Wessi* (West German) distaste for the *Ossi* (East German) at present seems clearly to be an incomprehension in the face of rhythms of life and ethical disparities arising from two to three generations of politically divergent training. The cultures are distinct for all to see, even while existing among peoples who share contiguous territory, language, common history, and the physical characteristics typically given the name "race": in other words, everything that the specialists tell us constitutes a nation. There is no better place, perhaps, than Germany to witness the vitality and cogency of what we are calling here "cultures of belief."

And these differences? John Borneman finds them in the very experience of space and time itself: "[In the G.D.R.] one could possess (*besitzen*) buildings but not land. The ability to occupy space

10. Andreas Huyssen, *Twilight Memories: Marking Time in a Culture of Amnesia* (New York and London, 1995), 74.

11. Quoted in John Borneman, "Time-Space Compression and the Continental Divide in German Subjectivity," *New Formations* 21 (Winter 1993): 112.

12. Ibid., 113.

13. Wolf, "Parting from Phantoms," 402.

(*besetzen*) was extremely restricted. This limitation in the possibilities for private valuation, through occupying or making one's own of public space in the G.D.R., created a peculiar relationship to what Freud called *Besetzung* and in English is translated as 'cathexis'. The libidinal attachment and investment in an object, specifically property, was truncated."[14] Borneman's essay goes much further, in fact, inferring instincts of great psychological depth from the surface phenomena of political principle. He is persuasive in doing so, although the inferences themselves are made with Wessi eyes, so that we are told, for example, that "with the building of the Wall in August 1961, space in the East was shaped by a sense of confinement and closure" even though it is widely known by now that the East Germans conceived it (with some justice as the 1990–95 period would show) as *protection* from the West's hungry incursions into their fledgling ways of life—what Borneman later refers to as the West's "imperial attitude towards space."[15] Thus, as an Ossi, Wolf focuses instead on the cleaning up by the West of what it considered the East's ideological extremists in an egregiously one-sided act of arrogant conquest and invasion. Agents of the new power poured over the files left behind by the G.D.R. state—documents that "reduce people's personal histories to simple patterns of yes or no, black or white, guilty or innocent": "I thought then and still think that this credulous faith in files is possible only in Germany. I shall not forget, nor do I want to forget, the physical sensation of being replaced, piece by piece and limb by limb, by another person who was built to suit the media and seeing an empty place arise at the spot where I 'really' was."[16] As Wolf implies, but nowhere states as directly as I will now, this cleansing of those with the wrong attitudes toward property and the wrong attitudes toward space—attitudes, after all, that extended to immensely admirable child care, education, anti–sex discrimination, and maternity leave policies—was a process fertilized by a phalanx of cultural barbs.[17] These barbs are familiar enough as forms of racial demonizing, directed (in Wolf's words) against "brothers and sisters from a family we don't know: ill-bred, plebeian, proletarian, and yet demanding."[18]

14. Borneman, "Time-Space Compression," 105.
15. Ibid., 104 and 106.
16. Wolf, "Parting from Phantoms," 402.
17. For a treatment of East Germany's exceptional legislation in regard to women, and its collapse after unification, see Lynn Duggan and Nancy Folbre, "Women and Children Last: East Germany Did It Better," *New York Times*, 8 January 1994, A23.
18. Wolf, "Parting from Phantoms," 402.

As a well-known author of novels classified feminist or dissident in the West, Wolf is given a great deal of play in the media here. But there has been no serious effort to present the extensive work by East German scholars or West Germans sympathetic to the East German plight following the coercions of unification. Daniela Dahn's ironically titled *Westwärts und nicht vergessen,* for example—a take-off on the socialist labor song of the 1930s, "Vorwärts und nicht vergessen"—analyses the reasons for her discomfort at being (before unification) a compulsory antifascist and (after) a compulsory member of the New Germany. An Easterner "in spite of herself," she mercilessly deals with the contradictions of socialist culture in a wonderful inversion of the familiar comment about the Nazis. In the G.D.R., she explains the problem was not the banality of evil but "The Banality of Good." She dissects this before moving on to explore the "mentality of the colonized" that the East now wrestles with in its new role as a conquered people.[19] A much more patiently sociological work can be found in *Die produktive Kraft der Unfreiheit,* which is, for all that, a less concertedly rallying and opinionated work than is often found here.[20] And best of all, perhaps, the work of the "Alternative Commission of Inquiry," *Unfrieden in Deutschland,* which criticizes the purging of the schools of G.D.R. influence after the Fall, and attempts tentatively to spell out the matter from the Easterner's point of view.[21] Work like this, to my knowledge, either does not exist at all or is very difficult to come by in the United States.

What we do have is writing like that of Andreas Huyssen, who as a professor with intimate knowledge both of Germany and the United States, and with personal knowledge of the forms of multiculturalism on American campuses, is important to look at here. A brilliantly influential scholar of postmodernism with a reputation as a leftist a decade ago, he surprised some readers with his recent chapter from *Twilight Memories* entitled, "After the Wall: The Failure of German Intellectuals." For one thing, his mood of impatient tutelage there seemed particularly inappropriate in an era that he himself characterized as one of mutuality and unity. The idea that one speaking from the territory of triumph could actually learn

19. Daniela Dahn, *Westwärts und nicht vergessen* (Berlin, 1996), 7, 33, and 148.

20. Ralf-Dietmar Hegel, Martin Müller, and Michael Wolf, *Die produktive Kraft der Unfreiheit: Eine empirische Studie zu ostdeutschen Biographien in der "Wendezeit,"* (Milow, 1994).

21. Gerd Buddin, Hans Dahlke, and Adolf Kossakowski, eds., *Unfrieden in Deutschland* (Berlin, 1994).

something from the vanquished is quickly dispelled in an emphatic demand that all sides concede not so much the defeat as the internal spiritual collapse of G.D.R. culture: "One of the more depressing aspects of the year of unification, however, is the unwillingness and inability of many left and liberal intellectuals to admit error, to analyze the nature of their delusions and political projections, and to admit that a thorough reorientation is the order of the day."[22] It is certainly understandable that one would hold Huyssen's views here—many do. What surprises me, though, is the peevishness—the fussy implication that anyone who did not was intellectually hollow or dishonest. As a fairly typical example of Huyssen's tone, the passage immediately strikes one as extremism carried out in the name of moderation. Precisely the banner of "criticism" that the intellectuals of his title ought to uphold, it seems to me, is folded up and tucked away in an ill-tempered scolding, as though he had completely lost sight of the fact that the defeat of the Soviet Bloc did not spell its impossibility, only its military and economic inadequacy at *this* time, against *these* enemies. With opinions that sound frighteningly close at times to the U.S. State Department, he confuses the proofs of history with the history the conquerors allow to be true. Corrupt or unworkable systems are not the only ones razed by more powerful opponents, after all. If one had indeed to consider the possibility that socialism was a "delusion," was it not also true that one had to ponder whether the Fall was better seen as part of the well-known historical pattern of superior civilizations overrun by barbarians—China by the Mongols, Mohenjo Daro by the Aryans, Teotihuacan by the *barbados* of retarded Catholic Spain?

His insistence on the assertively "obvious" analysis that the Fall of the Berlin Wall demonstrates the irredeemable unpopularity of socialist culture and the final confirmation of consumerist attractions is delivered only months before the Russian elections made this a doubtful conclusion indeed. The analysis does read, in fact, a little disturbingly like the words of the Spanish clerics who willingly counseled malleable Aztecs to repent following the death of Moctecuzohma. So, in the clerical workshops of the Mexican sixteenth century, Christianized *indios* busily wrote a version of the past commissioned by the Spanish crown! It is not, however, that Huyssen is wrong to point out the offensive practices of the East German state—the Stasi's files on an estimated *third of the population*, the restrictions on travel, the deeply conservative educational policies,

22. Huyssen, *"Twilight Memories,"* 39.

the oppressive ultramoralism of public discourse, and so on—nor to needle the West German left for its own inability to accommodate or even explain the rush of East Germans "for the discount bins in Western department stores." It is only the alarming insensitivity toward the correspondences between the East-West conflict and a supposedly messier and more shamefaced racial and civilizational bias toward the non-European—what traditionally lies, in other words, at the core of multiculturalism. Apparently outside his scope, Huyssen deals with these correspondences only tangentially and dismissively: "East and West German intellectuals, who, after the collapse of the benefit of mutual exoticism, had found it immensely difficult to talk to each other, discovered common ground in a ritualistic, Third World theology and an anti-imperialism that mixes blatant and subtle anti-Americanism and plain disregard for the Iraqi threats to Israel with touches of latent and not so latent anti-semitism."[23] Are we to suppose that a camaraderie based on saying "no" to the everyday atrocities against the Third World is as unfounded and fanatical as the sly word "theology" implies? The stand-by allusion to "threats to Israel" in the wake of the Iraqi massacre known as the Gulf War is, if one may say so, obscene in this context, as medical supplies, electricity, basic foodstuffs, and logistical support continue to be denied to that country, and as Iraqi children continue to die in droves through the policies of an America that Huyssen is concerned we might be too harsh toward while condemning its (fictional?) "imperialism."

These views, it seems to me, have very much to do with the secular religion of the middle way, which must repudiate the notion that belief cultures even exist. Thus Huyssen laments that the brutal pressures in the process of unification will only create the *myth* of a "nostalgic G.D.R. identity" allowing some to indulge in the tired refrain that "'Westerners will never understand [it] since they have not lived it.'"[24] Even as he shows at each turn the cultural dissonance that makes indecipherable for him the value system he consigns to an untimely death, he confidently pushes on as though such claims to a meaningful otherness were merely presumptuous. He speaks instead, as most victors do, of discovering "our common ground." And of course, as a matter of doctrine, that ground must lie in an imaginary middle space, just as his heroes in the Fall narrative are those East European revolutions that preceded the Fall itself, which according

23. Ibid., 41.
24. Ibid., 43.

to Huyssen, "foregrounded civil rights, thus attempting to shed the murderous left-right scheme of earlier bourgeois revolutions."[25]

How intemperate, though, to lay the transparency of "civil rights" over the discolored map of post-1990 Eastern Europe! The heroes of his "revolutions" hardly deserve such praise—from Václav Havel's outlawing of the Communist Party, to Lech Walesa's frightening policies toward women's choice, to Yeltsin's unspeakable shelling of the Russian Parliament, to the well-known horrors of Bosnia with Croatia emergent. It does not do to cast these crimes as initial stumblings or unforeseen snags in a generally positive process when these are the intentional consequences of the very forces held up as clarions of democracy. Even if one conceded Huyssen's point that "it is not only that Westerners do not understand the complexities of life in the GDR The reverse is also true,"[26] we would have to say that the realities of media penetration and now forceful repatriation have made the incomprehension deeply incommensurate.The Ossis obviously know the West much better than the Wessis were ever allowed to know the East. The leap of imagination, therefore, must go in the direction of the culture of the prolies, who with justice see themselves like Picts kneeling at the feet of the Saxon lords, told to learn a new language and religion. It is something of an understatement to observe that the following sentiments are not likely to breed mutual understanding: "The discourse of colonization and of a new Manchester capitalism overtaking the former GDR runs rampant among intellectuals when in fact the problem is that industrial capital does not colonize enough, does not build up or take over production facilities that would provide jobs and income to the beleaguered communities in the East."[27] The unmentionable truth in the process Huyssen describes as industrial capital not "colonizing enough," of course, is this: the tempting financial arrangements that permit investment to pay off for speculators in this globalized "out-shipping" of services depend on depressed wages, the absence of safety or pollution standards, and a heavily policed workforce. These little inhumanities tend to be more easily forced on people who are perceived (in Kipling's words) as the "lesser folk and wild." Hence, "prolies."

Multiculturalism, then, is intimately about cultures of belief, just as the so-called Third World is about the East-West conflict. No

25. Ibid., 45.
26. Ibid., 48.
27. Ibid.

social conjuncture shows this more forcefully than "unified" Germany, where a multiculturalism imported from the United States is enriched by the inescapable reality of one people that is really two, and whose culture diverges over issues of property, community, social accessibility, and the character of their respective utopias, rather than skin color, accent, or religion. The point now is to face such a notion of culture, and to give it the seriousness it deserves.

3. The Politics of Difference: Theories and Practice in a Comparative U.S.-German Perspective

Berndt Ostendorf

> "Daddy, what are we?"
> "What do you mean?"
> "You know, where are we from? Are we Italian, Irish,
> Jewish; you know like that?"
> "Well, we're from here; we're Americans."
> "Daddy!!! What am I going to say in school?"
>
> — *John Garvey*[1]

This paper will focus on the cognitive differences between the multiculturalism debates in Germany and the United States and on the dichotomy between the (academic) theory and the (political) practice of multiculturalism in the United States. These multiculturalism debates are primarily due to the historically specific organization of cultural and national identity, but also to the fact that each political culture has its actual strengths and weaknesses for which multicultural agendas serve as a therapeutic, countervailing balance. In other words, both countries' debates are tied to specific historical wounds of collective memory and the deficits of the existing political systems. This fact may help explain why the discourse of difference and the nurture of ethnic *Gemeinschaft* (community) is popular on the left in America and on the right in Germany.

1. John Garvey, "My Problem with Multi-Cultural Education," *Race Traitor* 1, no. 2 (Winter 1993): 18–25.

Secondly, in both countries a politics of difference reacts to a current global realignment of capitalism: to the change from a national to a global division of labor and hence to the emergence of new patterns of labor migration or dislocation (refugees) that have affected first the American and then the German society and polity. Add to this the disappearance of "work" at the end of the social democratic century and the "Thirdworldization" of the First World (split labor market). With the decline of classical labor we witness a turn away from "class" and toward "culture" or "identity" as the new key words of political mobilization. Concurrently there is talk of a decline of the nation-state (in Western Europe) and a waning of the belief in a universalist consensus (in the United States) and, as a compensatory reaction, the emergence of a new microdemocratic mood for ever more sensitive recognition of ever smaller difference and/or Gemeinschaft. What kind of politics (domestic or global) does this pedagogical and anthropological (vaguely Herderian and noticeably Nietzschean) archaeology of wrongs translate into? What happens when a well-intended and enlightened politics of difference is translated under the given global and national economic conditions into political practice? Is cultural fragmentation the best way to react to economic globalization? What are their costs and benefits for a civil society?

Frank-Olaf Radtke, a staunch defender of the Enlightenment Project, listed five ways of dealing with the ethnic "other," options which extend from rigid separation to complete inclusion:[2]

1. Radical separation, which may take several historical forms: repatriation, expulsion, ethnic cleansing and genocide, all based on differences of race, national origin, and religion.
2. Ghettoization or, more precisely, asymmetrical apartheid—the subordinate group in the "host" society is without civil rights and has a special subordinate or "alien" status such as that of guest workers.
3. Corporate or hard multiculturalism with a political and juridical recognition of group rights effecting the political equality of groups not of individuals.
4. Hyphenate pluralism (or soft multiculturalism) with a (negotiable) division à la Hannah Arendt between a private and a public sphere. The former sphere is particularistic and subordinate, the latter

2. Frank-Olaf Radtke, "Multikulturell - Das Gesellschaftsdesign der 90er Jahre," *Informationsdienst zur Ausländerarbeit*, no. 4 (1990): 27–34. See also his contribution "Multikulturalismus: Ein Postmoderner Nachfahre des Nationalismus," in *Multikulturelle Gesellschaft. Modell Amerika?*, ed. B. Ostendorf (Munich, 1994), 229–236. Unless otherwise noted, all translations are my own.

universalistic and dominant. In other words, particularistic group rights are recognized so long as these do not interfere with universal individualistic rights. A graded distinction is made between the private ethnic *l'homme* and the public *citoyen*.

5. Radical inclusion—the integration of the other regardless of race, national origin and religion.

These options are quite familiar from history, and they are currently operative in political practice all over the world. They range from legal inequality (1) to legal equality (5). In terms of a politics of difference, we move from a *negative recognition of difference* (1) to *indifference towards difference* (5).[3]

However, both of these radical options discriminate against the men and women who are and want to be different, and particularly against those who have no choice. The first discriminates in principle, the second tends to discriminate in practice. This dilemma of difference lurks at the core of the current conflict over multiculturalism. In her book *Making "All" the Difference*, Martha Minow, former assistant to Supreme Court Justice Thurgood Marshall, captures the dilemma well: "When does treating people differently emphasize their differences and stigmatize or hinder them on that basis? and when does treating people the same become insensitive to their difference and likely to stigmatize or hinder them on *that* basis?… The stigma of difference may be recreated both by ignoring and by focusing on it."[4] Regrettably the Manichean disposition in the American moral imagination tends to draw the players in this debate into mutually exclusive camps which reinforce and stabilize each other. We might want to divide them into the ignorers and the focusers, fully armed with a rhetoric of invective: "You nasty focuser, you blind ignorer." Alan Wolfe argues that both the defense and the abolition of difference or of boundaries is an essential part of an unending sociogenesis, which unfolds as a negotiation between inevitably particularistic communities within an inevitably universalistic liberal state.[5] This sounds "balanced" in theory, but how does it work in practice and how do tacit assumptions in the American and German public cultures control or affect the meaning of difference and of boundaries?

3. The morphology of *gleichgültig* highlights the fact that indifference towards difference presupposes equal rights.

4. Martha Minow, *Making "All" the Difference: Inclusion, Exclusion, and American Law* (Ithaca, 1990), 20.

5. Alan Wolfe, "Democracy versus Sociology: Boundaries and Their Political Consequences," in *Cultivating Differences: Symbolic Boundaries and the Making of Inequality*, eds. Michèle Lamong and Marcel Fournier (Chicago, 1992), 309–325.

At this juncture a first cognitive dissonance between Germany and the United States appears in the semantics of difference. Not only does the "ethnic other" have a specific historical ring in Germany, but the two radical options, separatism vs. integration, are grounded in different pragmatic political force fields. In short, the two debates, though apparently similar in their rhetoric and utopias, react to and filter through different historical wounds. In Germany the hidden choreography of the debate is defined by the fall of liberalism after 1848 and by the Holocaust; in the United States by the coexistence of the success of liberalism (for white males) and its failure (for blacks and women, Native Americans and Hispanics). In Germany "to make a difference" stands in the shadow of *Sonderbehandlung* (special treatment), *Endlösung* (final solution) or, more recently, of *Fremdenfeindlichkeit* (xenophobia), all of which are compounded by unification woes. Hence politically conscious Germans such as Frank-Olaf Radtke are loath to consider a politics of ethnic or cultural difference as a "countervailing balance" to the excesses of liberalism: integration and assimilation. With an eye on the failure of liberalism after 1848 and on the Holocaust, they argue for the fifth option, complete legal equality.

In the United States the quest of ethnic groups for a politics of difference and cultural autonomy had a positive and a negative motive. After the liberal principle of individual civil rights was achieved in the courts (1954–1965), the economic and social chances of African Americans, Native Americans, and Hispanics did not improve as expected. Full political citizenship, blacks were first to find out, did not protect them against social or economic discrimination. Such victims of discrimination needed help not as individual American citizens but as members of these groups. The affirmative step was to transfer the principle of equal rights from the individual to ethnic groups. This positive push for recognition of group rights was reinforced by a negative, "republican or communitarian" reaction towards the corrosive effects of a possessive individualism on the one hand and the "stultifying" process of Americanization and mass cultural homogenization on the other. Conservative communitarians worried that core republican values were in decline as an inevitable consequence of "too much" liberalism. Countercultural communitarians attacked patterns of hegemony (Gramsci) and power (Foucault) of an all too repressive state and blamed the current crisis of civil society on "too little" liberalism. Both groups, however, reinforced the positive connotation of difference and of small communities within a liberal American frame.

The squaring of the circle, as it were, was found in a binary switch. Divisive, negative ascription was changed by an act of consciousness raising into a positive identity, expressed in the slogan "Black is beautiful," a transformation that worked remarkably well, albeit more effectively in the culture industry than in social relations. The formerly negative recognition of difference was transvalued into the recognition of "positive" difference. Behind this reversal, I recognize a specifically American spin, the power of positive thinking that derives from the victorious Armenian heritage in the management of religious difference. When the belief in the equality of individuals was applied to groups, this led inevitably to the problematical assumption that all cultures must be accepted as equally good. To Europeans this is an instance of American exceptionalist optimism.

With one eye on Quebec, Charles Taylor argues in his essay *Multiculturalism: The Politics of Recognition,* for such a positive revaluation of cultural difference and for the possibility of a "liberal Quebec nationalism." One of Taylor's approving respondents, Michael Walzer, with one eye on the United States, formulates the two types of liberal goods that need to be protected in a post-Civil Rights state: individual freedom and group or ethnic loyalty. "The first kind of liberalism ("Liberalism One") is committed in the strongest possible way to individual rights and, almost as a deduction from this, to a rigorously neutral state, that is, a state without cultural or religious projects or, indeed any sort of collective goals beyond the personal freedom and the physical security, welfare, and safety of its citizens. The second kind of liberalism ("Liberalism Two") allows for a state committed to the survival and flourishing of a particular nation, culture, or religion, or of a (limited) set of nations, cultures, and religions...." In other words, Liberalism One is, in terms of culture or religion, "contentless" and merely guarantees the pursuit of happiness to a plurality of individual citizen. Liberalism Two on the other hand protects a normative idea of belonging, of the "good society" and the "right values," which would guarantee group survival. Liberalism One represents the classic American position; Liberalism Two, the classic German position. This fact is not lost on Walzer. For he feels constrained to add a caveat—after a long dash, which the German language appropriately calls *Gedankenstrich* (the American equivalent would be "on second thought"): "—so long as the basic rights of citizens who have different commitments or no such commitments at all are protected."[6] In other words, according to Walzer, Liberalism Two, which Taylor considers at this time the more urgent policy, keeps its innocence only under the stern vigilance of Liberalism One.

Here we run into the communitarian dilemma that not only mirrors a key problem of multiculturalism, but also brings out the "American" or "exceptionalist" character of the debate: how to prevent the cultural loyalties of Liberalism Two from becoming "normative" or "essential" and how to prevent boundaries, designed to protect one minority, from being exclusive to other minorities. Though ethnic cultures and boundaries based on endowment are by any classic anthropological definition normative, how can they be made voluntary? According to some communitarians their ideal of community should be "uncoerced." Here we have, in Goethe's words, *des Pudels Kern*, the core of the multicultural and communitarian dilemma: the balance (or imbalance) between the freedom and necessity of belonging. And here the European and American stories diverge.

Classic American Liberalism One abolished the necessity of belonging, yet the United States cherished the notion of a national Gemeinschaft, represented by a repository of republican, communitarian values beyond the constitution that Gunnar Myrdal called the "American Creed" and others in the wake of Rousseau a "Civil Religion." This extra-constitutional sense of belonging to a *Wertegemeinschaft* (community of shared values), conservative communitarians claim, is now endangered by a rampant Liberalism One on the one hand and by a new particularistic congeries of all sorts of prenational Gemeinschaften such as blacks, Native Americans, women, gays. Both of these notions of Gemeinschaft are in tension with Liberalism One.

Apart from this communitarian quandary (whose genesis will be explored below) we run into a profound cognitive dissonance

---

6. The title of the second edition adds one word, "Examining" to Taylor's title and therewith a note of caution: Michael Walzer, *Multiculturalism: Examining the Politics of Recognition* (Princeton, 1994), 99; with additional essays by Jürgen Habermas and Anthony Appiah. See also Walzer's "Multiculturalism and Individualism," *Dissent* (Spring 1994): 185–191 and Andrew Stark, "Vive le Québec anglophone!" *TLS*, 22 September 1995, 16. Louis Menand unravels some of the contradictions in "Blind Date: Liberalism and the Allure of Culture," *Transition* (Fall 1995): 70–81. Needless to say the term "liberal" is frought with transatlantic ambiguity. American and German usage vary considerably: see Dietmar Herz, *Republik und Verfassung. Die theoretischen Grundlagen einer liberalen Staatsordnung*, Ph.D. diss., Sozialwissenschaftliche Fakultät, Munich, 1995.

between the United States and Germany, or indeed between the New World and Europe. There is a marked difference in the organization of cultural identity, particularly as concerns the historically sedimented traditions of "individualism" and "community," which constitute the pillars of Liberalism One and Liberalism Two respectively. In the language of jazz, let me run these key concepts, individualism and community, through German and American changes.

For Americans, individualism rests on a belief in the freedom and integrity or inviolability of the individual. The rigorous protection of the individual manifests itself best in crises like war. In World War II it was the U.S. government's policy to minimize the loss of American citizens, and consequently the United States "sacrificed" a mere 350,000 individuals—much to Stalin's chagrin—whereas Soviet Russia lost forty times as many. Wherever an American citizen is in danger, as Tom Lehrer has it, America "sends the Marines." The second pillar of the national faith is voluntarism (as opposed to coercion) and its corollary, freedom of choice rather than unfree fate or deterministic descent. Americans insist that politics be implemented according to the "consent of the governed" rather than the descent of the group. Hence, there is the demand, often observed in the breach, but renewed and reclaimed in the course of American history, of one man [*sic*], one vote and of no taxation without representation.[7] All of this boils down to one important difference: *Amerikaner kann man werden durch freie Wahl* (One can become an American of his/her own free will). Hence the United States has had an *Einbürgerungsgesetz* (naturalization law) since 1800 and Germany has had a *Staatsangehörigkeitsgesetz* (national membership law) since 1913. *Man wird Amerikaner. Aber man ist Deutscher.* (One becomes an American. But one is German.) When in doubt, Americans favor inclusion on the basis of freedom and

7. In other words, America's liberal *Bürgerrechte* (citizens' rights), like its Coke, have become so "classic" to the postmodern imagination as to be boring, thus inviting ill-advised attempts to improve them. Moreover, the virtuous *citoyen* living in a moral city upon an exceptional hill is called upon to be a model for the world—much to the chagrin of that world. This missionary habit of the American heart has already affected the international multicultural debate. Benjamin Barber suggests in a recent article that the United States should export its brand of multiculturalism worldwide. The article's title, "Global Multiculturalism and the American Experiment," is properly exceptionalist, published fittingly in the *World Policy Journal* 10, no.1 (Spring 1993): 47–55. Barber thinks that the American model of multiculturalism (he means soft pluralism) and a federalism along the lines of the Articles of Confederation could be a viable model for multiethnic countries. I detect a note of exceptionalist condescension in wanting to export the constitutional lemon that did not work in America.

voluntaristic choice regardless of culture, religion, or national origin, in short, Liberalism One; when in doubt, Germans favor exclusion on the basis of cultural or religious incompatibility for the protection of normative Gemeinschaft and essential descent groups, in short, Liberalism Two. And some Germans would gladly do without Walzer's caveat as some of the recent attacks on the *Bundesverfassungsgericht* after its crucifix decision, all allegedly based on *"gesundes Volksempfinden"*(what the common man thinks[8]), amply demonstrate.[9]

Despite frequent jeremiads by communitarian Cassandras who bemoan the effects of a corrosive individualism and the decline of republican virtues, Americans in their role as political agents will come up with the following spontaneous free associations when the word individualism pops up. On a plane from Frankfurt/Main to Washington, D.C. in March 1995, after watching *Forrest Gump* with my two neighbors, I tried it out on them: to my left a Jewish New York liberal, to my right a Polish-American follower of Pat Robertson, both who despite their ideological differences got along famously on a first name basis. (Germans find this social civility across political divides mildly disturbing.) Although from diametrically opposed ideological camps, the two agreed that the state should not interfere with or curtail the freedom of choice of individuals. But they also defined the role of the individual in society by stewardship, by duties and obligations. Both stressed the moral framework of a civil religion, both insisted that ethics are a matter of individual responsibility, not of the state. Yet their notion of voluntarism was embedded in a sense of duty toward the public good, the common wealth. How did Jonathan Edwards put it? "Where much is given, much is demanded." Both gave me Gunnar Myrdal's *American Creed*. (I should add that they did disagree on causes and remedies of poverty and the role of government.)

Americans may now fear that I begin to sound like William Buckley, the mouthpiece of American jingoism. Not at all. I am articulating the *klammheimliche* (secret) envy of a German looking at bipartisan approval of certain principles of enlightened liberalism buttressed by a republican civil religion, principles that *verspätete*

---

8. *"Gesundes Volksempfinden"* is a term found in jurisprudence, albeit of questionable legitimacy after the Nazis instrumentalized it for their purposes. It refers to populist passions: what the common man thinks.

9. Hans Ulrich Wehler, "Der Kampf gegen Karlsruhe. Wie die Advokaten des gekränkten Volksempfindens die Axt an unsere Verfassungsordnung legen," *Die Zeit*, no. 49 (1 December 1995): 73.

Nationen (delayed nations)[10] or democracies without a successful revolution so often lack. And this difference in tacit assumptions is borne out by recent comparative polls on values in Western democracies, which *The Economist* reported with understandable envy under the Eurocentric headline, "An Odd Place: America."[11] The question "which good do you value higher, 'freedom' or 'equality'" received quite different responses from Germans and Americans. Indeed the difference would question the allegedly successful Americanization of (West) Germans.

In the United States, 72 percent of the respondents opted for freedom, only 20 percent for equality. In (West) Germany, 37 percent chose freedom, but 39 percent would have equality. Raising the ante, the pollsters asked if government should equalize income disparities that are due to the free market system. And a whopping 80 percent of the Americans said no, but 59 percent of the Germans approved. Of Italians and Austrians, a solid 80 percent called for the state to right the wrongs of poverty.[12] Americanization of Germany? Perhaps, but only relatively speaking. American freedom, on the other hand, is, in Isaiah Berlin's classic definition, a "freedom from interference of the state" and "freedom to do your own thing." In America the state should be weak and inactive, the individual strong and active; in Germany, where the state has a history of being strong and active, the individual tends to be weak and inactive. This continues to be a habit of the heart across political divides.[13]

What are the spontaneous associations when a concerned student of German history and a reader of the German press such as myself considers Gemeinschaft, that is Walzer's Liberalism Two? Gemeinschaft, as the majority of Germans would define it, is constituted by culture, religion, or linguistic or regional ethnicity. You are a German, a Catholic, a Bavarian, a Volga-, or *Sudetendeutscher.* There is a strong undertow of determinism buttressed by "collective

10. Helmut Plessner, *Die verspätete Nation. Über die politische Verführbarkeit bürgerlichen Geistes* (Stuttgart, 1959).

11. "American Values," *The Economist,* 5 September 1992.

12. *The Economist,* with raised eyebrows, marvels: "in Germany 'solidarity' is an obsession. The constitution itself calls for 'unity of living standards in the federal territory.' In four decades the pursuit of solidarity has not eliminated economic differences among regions, but it has smoothed them out, and it has also given Germany relatively even distribution of income among classes." 30 September 1995, 21.

13. Thomas Nipperdey subtitled his *Deutsche Geschichte 1800–1866: Bürgerwelt und starker Staat* (Munich, 1983). According to a recent poll by the *Süddeutsche Zeitung,* East German approval of the German liberal constitutional republic is low and 44 percent favor a return to a "starker Staat" (stronger state), 5 January 1996.

memories" (M. Halbwachs) in the *Begriffsgeschichte* (concept formation) and the current popular use of Gemeinschaft.[14] The *Feststellung* (observation) "Herr Bubis, Sie sind doch Jude" (But you are a Jew, Mr. Bubis), recently heard in Rostock, harbors a tacit political agenda quite different from such a query in New York. From the tacit privileging of Gemeinschaft in German political culture, it follows that the autonomy and self-determination of the collective takes precedent over the rights of dissenting individuals: you are one crab in a crab basket full of mutually entangled crabs. What about the freedom to differ? If one crab tries to crawl out, the others will pull him back. Within such Gemeinschaften, in crises such as war, the individual serves as cannon fodder for the national, ethnic, and religious cause. *Für das Vaterland gestorben. Dulce est pro patria mori.* You find yourself as a member of a *Schicksalsgemeinschaft* (fated community) (Carl Schmitt), or as a member of a *Volks-* or *Abstammungsgemeinschaft* (peoples' or descendants' community) (Minister of the Interior Kanther) complete with genealogical myths. On the constructivist end, you are a member of a *Solidargemeinschaft* (community of solidarity) or of what Habermas refers to as a *Sozialisationsgemeinschaft* (socialization community), yet all of them are defined by an inevitable *Angehörigkeit* (belonging).

What about one man, one vote? Surely, Germans believe in it, thanks to a "Westernization" of our Basic Law (due to American pressure), but historical or collective memories and ideological configurations persist. Indeed, in keeping with Liberalism Two the protection of a *deutsches Volk* (German people) is part of our Basic Law. There is even a trickle-down effect. When a member of a Bavarian *Trachtenverein* (traditional costume club) was asked on the radio why he dressed up each weekend and wore a funny hat, he did not answer "Because I like it," but "Der Schutz der Tradition ist Paragraph eins unserer Statuten." ("The protection of tradition is one of our group by-laws.") How better could one capture the normative bond of Gemeinschaft or the protection of its cultural content. Inevitably then *"Mir san Mir"* (we are we) as the Bavarians will

14. Manfred Riedel, "Gesellschaft, Gemeinschaft," *Geschichtliche Grundbegriffe*, vol. 2 (Stuttgart, 1979), 859, comments on the reactionary turn in the understanding of Gemeinschaft as an oppositional term to *Gesellschaft.* It needs to be remembered that the Holocaust sensitized post-Second World War Germany to questions of racialism or "racial" difference, yet because of the ethnic cleansing, postwar Germany is a more homogeneous Gemeinschaft than Weimar. On basic differences between German and American notions of community, see Hans Vorländer, "Ein vorläufiges Nachwort zur deutschen Kommunitarismusdebatte," *Forschungsjournal NSB* 8, no. 3 (1955): 39–43.

doggedly insist,[15] though the 1828 Brockhaus, albeit from a hostile Prussian point of view, identified them as "ein *vermischtes,* räuberisches Bergvolk" (a mixed, rapacious mountain people). Hence it follows that Gemeinschafts-oriented people would have a *Staatsangehörigkeitsgesetz* (citizenship law) and that candidates for the German civil service have to present a *Staatsangehörigkeitsnachweis* (proof of "membership in the nation") that reaches back six generations into the miasmic mist of miscegenation.

Let me turn to the spontaneous fantasies of a modal, i.e., statistically average, German when s/he hears of individualism within the given ideology of Gemeinschaft. Again I exaggerate for the sake of dragging tacit *Selbstverständlichkeiten* (taken-for-granted terms) out of their ideological closets. For "gemeinschafty" Germans, individualism evokes anomie or egotism, narcissism, and libertinism. Lack of solidarity and a penchant for hedonism or self-indulgence are traits that Germans over the years have recognized "instantly" as a "fault" in the American system. From Heinrich Heine, over Sigmund Freud, to Heiner Müller this has been the *Vorbehalt gegen Amerika* (reservation about America), the land where according to leading Germans, liberty quickly degenerated into libertinism. Liberty, according to this German view, has by itself no moral or cultural content; it is merely "procedure." Along with Henry James, Germans would recognize the lack of proper institutions and traditions: *Kulturlose Amerikaner* (culture-less Americans). Robert Bellah and Amitai Etzioni continue in this rhetorical vein, albeit from a republican American perspective, and call for a new sense of community as a countervailing balance to Liberalism One. Not surprisingly then, in the poll of the *Economist,* the German vote for freedom ranked below the vote for solidarity and 59 percent of the people wanted the government to equalize income disparity.

Not that solidarity is in itself an illiberal force or that a consensus on values does not sit well with a liberal polity. Far from it, as Montesquieu, Rousseau, and I would argue. Indeed some of the best traditions of German political culture are grounded in communitarian habits. One such virtue, solidarity, is expressed in the higher vote for equality, and it bears directly upon the German multicultural debate. One reason why the debate on individual and civil rights is underdeveloped in Germany today—even among the ethnic groups themselves—has to do with the consequence of a

15. "*Mir san Mir*" is the Bavarian identity marker. The best translation I can find in the U.S. is in black southern culture where there is a saying "nothing like being us," which has the same ironic signifying twist.

strong working class solidarity and with a "systemic or structural ethics" of a paternalistic "strong state" from the Fuggers over the Krupps to Norbert Blüm. Indeed the worry about income disparity is a basic element in the concept of *soziale Marktwirtschaft* (social market economy), which all parties including the conservatives embrace. The fact that workers in Germany, including foreign-born workers, enjoy a degree of job security and fringe benefits unheard of in America has in the past reduced their need to claim "civil rights" that would enable them to fight in a competitive, "free" market system over diminishing resources with other citizens under conditions of "equal opportunity." Add to this an open and inexpensive educational system and you knock two of the most powerful motives for the rise of multiculturalism in the United States clean out of the German picture. Indeed, it is the lack of job security in the United States and the high cost of education that make "individual rights," "equal opportunity," and "access to resources" such important political instruments in American free market competition under conditions of a zero-sum game. Is it an accident that the debate gained momentum in the period of a moral and economic slump from the late 1960s onward and fully emerged when Ronald Reagan began to deconstruct the welfare state and the New Deal? For a Greek or Turkish worker whose safe job at the BMW or Siemens plants is protected by German labor law, the questions of civil rights and empowerment within the German political culture are of a decidedly secondary order. You would, in fact, be hard put to find a Turkish BMW worker willing to emigrate to America and exchange a safe job without civil rights for the sake of civil rights without a job.

Therefore, it is not surprising that the German "crisis of multiculturalism" was first felt when the second generation *Gastarbeiterkinder* (guest workers' children), came of age. This second generation did not enjoy the job safety of their parents and had no rights as citizens although, in marked contrast to their parents, they were born and raised in Germany. Whereas their mothers and fathers rested comfortably in a non-assimilationist attitude of "*abwarten und Tee trinken*" (wait and see, literally—wait and drink tea), the second generation began to experience an identity crisis, that is, the dual pull of being de facto German, but de jure *Ausländer* (foreigner). Worse yet, they faced the double jeopardy of being unemployed and of having no rights. As the German labor market over the past ten years has become more deregulated and privatized, the need for an American-type multiculturalism may indeed increase. American-type multiculturalism, then, wants to equip individuals with the juridical-liberal instruments to weather the hazards of an economic liberalism. As Sir Ralph Dahrendorf puts it, "[economic] liberalism can live with a great deal of inequality ... as long as the equality of chances is secured."[16]

Marked differences between the United States and Germany also become apparent when comparing the notion of community. Let me chart the semantic range of American meanings of community by quoting from dissertations defending the American creed, such as Huntington's *American Politics:The Promise of Disharmony*, or from current communitarian jeremiads, such as Robert Bellah's *Habits of the Heart* and *The Good Society*. We could even start at the beginning and quote the Mayflower Compact, which was "voluntarily agreed upon." Voluntarism was a key concept in the early Republic, when individuals flexed their muscles and exercised their new freedoms guaranteed in the constitution and the amendments. German observers on the Right have always marveled at American *Selbsthilfeorganisationen* (self-help organizations) and the more encompassing definition of the private sector, and our Left successfully imported civil disobedience and *Bürgerinitiativen* (citizens' initiatives) in the late 1960s.[17] Many "voluntary" associations of the "private" sector, let me hasten to add, are too often stabilized by social Darwinistic advantages such as money, family status, chauvinism, and racism. No wonder that social Darwinism as a social philosophy for the selection of the fittest was so successful in America. Therefore gemeinschafty Germans will tend to characterize the American principle of freedom as *heuchlerisch* (hypocritical), at least in its social Darwinist practice.[18] But the point I want to make is that the cultural principle of voluntarism is so deeply embedded in the

16. *Die Zeit*, 2 December 1994, 13. See also *Die angewandte Aufklärung. Gesellschaft und Soziologie in Amerika* (Munich, 1963).

17. Robert Bach in his essay "Recrafting the Common Good: Immigration and Community," *The Annals of the American Academy of Political and Social Sciences*, no. 530 (November 1993): 164, emphasizes the role of voluntarism as a way of negotiating cultural difference. "Voluntary associations, organized formally or informally, provide the energy, resources, and direction for community building. They mobilize private and group standards, obligations, and responsibilities and are especially important in shaping culture and discourse." See also Robert Wuthnow, "The Voluntary Sector: Legacy of the Past, Hope for the Future?" in *Between States and Markets: The Voluntary Sector in Comparative Perspective*, ed. Robert Wuthnow (Princeton, 1991), 3–29.

18. They are joined by American communitarians: Ann Swidler, "Inequality and American Culture: The Persistence of Voluntarism," *American Behavioral Scientist* 35, no. 4/5 (March/June 1992): 606–629, and of course by Marxists: C.B. MacPherson,

American unconscious and in political practice that it is simply taken for granted *as being natural*, even by the American Left. It is telling that even conservative communitarians, who desire a return to normative values, insist that the change in the habits of the heart should be voluntary.

Not only income disparity (Reagan's voluntary poor), but even "ethnicity," the ultimate determinant of identity by descent, has come under the sway of voluntarism. Mary C. Water's *Ethnic Option: Choosing Identities in America* (1990) concludes that "ethnicity is increasingly a personal choice of whether to be ethnic at all ... it matters only in voluntary ways.... First, I believe it stems from two contradictory desires in the American character: a quest for community on the one hand and a desire for individuality on the other." She quotes the official instructions for the census takers for the 1990 census: "List the ethnic group with which the person *identifies*." How did that get into the instructions for a census which is supposed to form the solid statistical rock for policy making? Through voluntary associations, in this case through the active lobbying on the part of *white* ethnic leaders in Washington.[19] There is an interesting process at work here. The essentialist or primordial quality of descent *(Abstammung)* acquires, in the American political process (that is in the free exercise of white individual rights), an exceptional or voluntaristic quality, a privilege, I repeat, which extends primarily to white ethnics. You cannot choose not to be black though this has been tried close to the color line in the tradition of "passing."[20]

Translated back into the political process, however, ethnicity becomes essential again (in both meanings) when the division of

Die politische Philosophie des Besitzindividualismus, 2nd edition (Frankfurt/Main, 1987). See also Hans Joas, "Gemeinschaft und Demokratie in den USA. Die vergessene Vorgeschichte der Kommunitarismus-Diskussion," in *Gemeinschaft und Gerechtigkeit,* eds. Micha Brumlik and Hauke Brunkhorst (Frankfurt/Main, 1993), 49–62. For a comparative view: Helmut K. Anheier, Lester M. Salamon, and Edith Archambault, "Participating Citizens: U.S.-European Comparisons in Volunteer Action," *Public Perspective* 5 (March-April 1994): 16–18, 34. I owe the coinage "gemeinschafty" to Werner Sollors.

19. And thereby hangs a tale. Mary Waters writes "symbolic ethnicity persists because of its ideological 'fit' with racist beliefs." *Ethnic Options. Choosing Identities in America* (Berkeley, 1990), 147. On the balance between consent and descent cf. Werner Sollors, *Beyond Ethnicity* (New York, 1986).

20. Shirlee Taylor Haizlip recounts how she restored missing branches of her family tree in "Passing," *American Heritage* (February/March 1995): 46–54. This problem is heatedly debated in *Lure and Loathing: Essays on Race, Identity, and the Ambivalence of Assimilation,* ed. Gerald Early (New York, 1993).

political spoils along an ethnic or a color line, as in affirmative ger-
rymandering or quotas, has to be administered and defended as
public policy. Voluntary or de-essentialized ethnicity recoups its
normative losses in democratic proceduralism under the given patterns of inequality of the market. This curious process of voluntary
de-essentialization and procedural or juridical re-essentialization
is, I believe, the cause of much of the current resentment among
white ethnic males and explains the crisis of affirmative action.
Quite clearly African and Native Americans have not enjoyed the
privilege of voluntarizing community. They had no choice or wanted
no choice. Continued racism was the dividing line between voluntary white and involuntary nonwhite ethnicity. Indeed, racism kept
African and Native American communities and community bond-
ing alive (cf. the black church, secret lodges, Social Aid and Plea-
sure Clubs, etc.). Hence the sense of community among African
and Native Americans has an "Un-American," almost Bavarian ring
to it, one reason, perhaps, why there seems to be an elective affinity
between community-oriented Germans and African or Native Americans.[21] This compensatory role of community as antidote to
structural racism within American liberalism explains why the "white
ethnic" American Michael Walzer, who enjoys the privilege of an
ethnic option, has no choice but to consider the protection of
minority-community a "liberal" cause.[22] This idea, I submit, is not
exportable to Europe without loosing its liberal innocence.

The process of de-essentialization may best be explained by looking at another tacit *Selbstverständlichkeit* or taken-for-granted term of
the American political creed: the role of religion in the public
sphere. For I suspect that the voluntarization of ethnicity is modeled on the manner in which "primordial" religious loyalties (as in
the absolute dictum "una sancta catholica" or "once a Jew always a
Jew") were denominationalized in the young Republic. Denominationalism, which has by this time become a deep seated political
faith, is the American way of pulling the political teeth of religious
passions (cf. Federalist 10). The two parts of this crucial compromise on religious difference are set down in the First Amendment.

21. In Bavaria and Baden-Württemberg there are a number of *Indianervereine*.
These are clubs with a lower middle-class membership (often drawn from the crafts)
that cultivate and recreate Native American tribal traditions complete with tepees,
war paint, and corn dances.

22. Anna Whiting-Sorrell, a member of the Salish-Kootenai tribe, writes that the
salient feature of Indianness is "a strong sense of community," "a strong sense of
belonging," and a "strong sense of rituals." "Life Is Belonging." *Treatment Today* 7, no.
1 (Spring 1995).

First, the two freedoms "from and to": (1) the free exercise clause, which gives each individual the freedom to exercise his/her religious faith without interference from the state and from other individuals and, as a consequence, (2) the anti-establishment clause, which aims to prevent the rise of any sort of unique ecclesiastic, dogmatic, or institutional religious power. Hence America has no ecclesia, no state church, no institutional religious power. And the power sharing between church and state—typical of the Concordat (of June 1933) between the German government and the Vatican—is to the average American decidedly "the work of the devil." Not surprisingly, American denominations are notoriously weak on dogma (no teeth), but high on general morality or on principles of a civil religion (lots of saliva). The latter is best characterized by the buzzword of the canon debate, the "Judeo-Christian tradition."[23] In the course of American history, the organization of ethnic difference has fallen in line: the free exercise of ethnic difference is widely accepted, but most Americans, including members of ethnic groups, are hesitant, if not wary, of the establishment of ethnic difference as political or consociational power. Interestingly, ethnic elites want it more than the rank and file. The quasi-religious nature of the battle over this core value may be explained by its roots in the First Amendment heritage. As Germans would say, "Hier geht's ans Eingemachte" (This is where the going gets rough).

Since our focus is difference, we can now make a difference between "denominational" ethnicity, which enjoys general support, and "established" or "dogmatic" ethnicity, which has so far failed to convince a clear majority of Americans, even of African Americans. A preference for a denominational ethnicity is borne out by a poll, entitled "What Ordinary Americans Think about Multiculturalism,"

23. B. Ostendorf, "Identitätsstiftende Geschichte: Religion und Öffentlichkeit in den USA," *Merkur* (May 1995) and Jürgen Gebhardt, "Amerikanismus - Politische Kultur und Zivilreligion in den USA," *Aus Politik und Zeitgeschichte* B49, 30 November 1990, 3–18. The old civil religion based on a denominational consensus is in a deep crisis. One consequence has been the rise of the new evangelicalism or televangelism, that is the new fundamentalism, which represents not a regression to the Middle Ages, but a voluntaristic realignment of denominationalism. The old denominations are breaking apart at the liberal/conservative fault line and realign as pluralist para-churches or megachurches or as electronic communities drawing their members from those established denominations now in decline. This process is driven by voluntarism, which continues unabated into a virtual and New Age phase, cf. Charles S. Clark, "Religion in America," *CQ Researcher*, 25 November 1994, 1035–1041, who says that people, more than ever, "shop around" for a custom-made religion that fits their particular lifestyle and moral universe. Robert Wuthnow, *The Restructuring of American Religion* (Princeton, 1988).

conducted among the most postmodern and, in my view, least ordinary Americans, namely Southern Californians. The preliminary results were presented at the annual meeting of the American Political Science Association, 1 September 1994, by four of our academic colleagues: David Sears, Jack Citrin, Sharmaine Vidanage, and Nicholas Valentino, a research team that represents a properly balanced ethnic ticket like the bomber crews in Hollywood's Second World War movies. This is their—to me quite unsurprising—conclusion: "We have found that the mass public—*more or less irrespective of ethnicity*—is sympathetic to culturally diverse groups. There is a respectful recognition of diverse heritages. But there is little mass support, at this time, for official recognition of these ethnic differences or for special entitlements attached to them. And this lack of mass support for particularistic multiculturalism holds despite much *more supportive elite rhetoric* and official policy both in California generally and in the Los Angeles area" (my emphasis). If Southern Californians think so, what about the folks in Peoria? And the authors end somewhat enigmatically: "This gulf between elite and mass creates a dynamic that might have a number of long-term outcomes." I will speculate on that gulf and its outcomes a bit later.[24]

Germany has no First Amendment tradition for the domestication of religious difference. But while Germans have accepted the institutional empowerment of religion in the Concordat, they take revenge by freely exercising their right of not going to church and of not confusing personal morality and political talent. Nobody cares whether Kohl or Waigel have affairs or believe in God. And neither of the two would be caught dead quoting the Bible. Yet, without a First Amendment history, no liberal constitutional tradition exists for de-essentializing difference, whence difference in Germany remains inescapably *essential*. Indeed the discourse on the "politics of difference" along the boundary lines of Gemeinschaft has an almost exclusive right wing tradition. This fact was brought home to me when I presented current American theories of multiculturalism (Charles Taylor, Martha Minow, Iris Marion Young,

24. Daniel Yankelovich attributes the birth of the new politics of "Ressentiment" (Nietzsche) to this widening gulf. "Three Destructive Trends: Can They Be Reversed," Lecture presented at the National Civic League's one hundredth National Conference on Governance, 11 November 1994. Seymour Martin Lipset in turn argues that "clearly, the American political system—though distrusted and ineffective in dealing with major social problems—is in no real danger." "Malaise and Resiliency in America," *Journal of Democracy* 6, no. 3 (July 1995): 17. Lipset observes not a decline, but a realignment of voluntaristic energy under postmodern, post-Fordist conditions. See also his *American Exceptionalism: A Double-Edged Sword* (New York, 1996).

Michael Walzer) to the Council members of the City of Munich. The person most interested in Walzer's Liberalism Two (including its afterthought) turned out to be the press secretary of the Republikaner, who welcomed this unexpected support for his party's platform from the American left. Therefore Frank-Olaf Radtke is correct when he argues within the given German multicultural debate: "Multikulturalismus bleibt auf halbem Wege stehen." (Multiculturalism is stuck in first gear.) He means "auf halbem Wege" (halfway) to an enlightened citizenship law and to a political culture honoring consent, not descent, a position that we have yet to reach. Hard multiculturalism is entirely compatible with our right wing's efforts to keep the difference between Germans and Turks intact. When liberal Germans such as Daniel Cohn-Bendit and Thomas Schmid speak of *multikulturelle Gesellschaft* (multicultural society), they mean hyphenated pluralism (option four) with a strong tendency toward integration (option five), in short what the United States practiced until 1965.[25] The press secretary of the Republikaner would gladly import the more radical politics of difference (option three) of Taylor, Young, and Minow to Germany as a compromise, which would allow him to exercise a modicum of *Fremdenfeindlichkeit* (unfriendliness toward strangers) without running the risk of being *verfassungsfeindlich* (unfriendliness toward the constitution). Indeed the model of a politics of difference or of an "ecological protection of diversity" has by now been adopted by members of the ruling Christian Democratic Party.[26]

Let me now address a second theme: the dichotomy between the theory and practice of multiculturalism. The core attitudes of and discourses on individual identity and community have to be seen in the larger context of structural changes and of global and post-Fordist realignments. The most encompassing frame is the increasingly global economic order which, though global, has an American face. Secondly, there have been marked changes in the political orders of Germany and the United States—both changes were accompanied by national debates. Thirdly, the order of words. Here not only the *national* organization and management of theoretical and academic

25. "Die kulturelle Identität hat in der multikulturellen Gesellschaft eine Grenze ... Religions- und Kulturimperialismus stoßen in einer freiheitlichen Gesellschaft an die immanenten Schranken der modernen Verfassung." Daniel Cohn-Bendit and Thomas Schmid, *Heimat Babylon. Das Wagnis der multikulturellen Demokratie* (Hamburg, 1992), 21.

26. Sabine von Dirke presents a cogent analysis of various ideological positions of the Right and Left in "Multikulti: The German Debate on Multiculturalism," *German Studies Review* 17, no. 3 (October 1994): 513–536.

debates is of interest, but also the *international* marketing of American multicultural agendas as new academic commodity. This factor receives little attention from the American agenda setters of multiculturalism. To wit, in America the studied gaze focused upon the "other" is accompanied by relatively little historical self-reflection or by any interest in comparative experiences in other parts of the world. The parochialism of the current debate is nowhere more evident than in its ignorance of the vigorous debates between 1945–1955 in the United States on intercultural education and interethnic tolerance, or of similar debates around the turn of the century in the Austro-Hungarian Empire.[27]

Economy

There has been a realignment of global capitalism from centralized Fordism to deregulated post-Fordism and from a national to a new international division of labor.[28] The deindustrialization of the First World and the relocation of manufactures to threshold countries has as a consequence led to the loss of the blue-collar sector as a middle-class income ladder in the United States, particularly for African Americans and white ethnics.[29] Since they were and are at odds over multicultural agendas, this loss of middle-class income options must be seen as the economic engine of the multicultural debate. The relocation of manufactures has created new patterns of "transnational" labor migration, particularly from so-called threshold countries: from the Caribbean, Mexico, Korea, Philippines, and Taiwan, nations which supply the majority of the so-called new new immigration, groups which benefit from affirmative action initially set aside for blacks.

The increasing mobility of people and the global proliferation of products has led to what Benjamin Barber calls a "McWorld." In keeping with the metaphor, this new world has an American face.[30]

27. Otto Bauer, *Die Nationalitätenfrage und die Sozialdemokratie* (Vienna, 1907), 23; Werner Sollors, "DE PLURIBUS UNA/E PLURIBUS UNUS: Mathew Arnold, George Orwell, Holocaust und Assimilation. Bemerkungen zur amerikanischen Multikulturalismusdebatte," in *Multikulturelle Gesellschaft. Modell Amerika?* ed. Berndt Ostendorf (Munich, 1994).

28. For a succinct summary, cf. David Harvey, *The Condition of Postmodernity* (New York, 1989).

29. John Cassidy, "Who Killed the Middle Class? The Economy is Fine, but Most Americans Are Not ..." *New Yorker,* 16 October 1995, 83–90.

30. Benjamin Barber, "Jihad versus McWorld," *Atlantic,* March 1992.

A related factor is the increasing illegality or temporality of migrants' status ("birds of passage") and the decreasing willingness or need of incoming groups to assimilate.[31] Instead, diasporic networking keeps national bonds alive and has, in some instances, led to new forms of long-distance nationalism. Most troubling, however, is the aggressive growth of a split labor market that will inevitably lead to the Thirdworldization of the First World and to the perpetuation of a welfare-dependent class which in turn legitimates antiwelfare arguments. We are witnessing the return of working conditions in Los Angeles and New York that Friedrich Engels and Charles Dickens encountered in nineteenth-century Manchester and London. The ever-growing megacities are the recipients of 75 percent of the new illegal migration, which brings sweatshops back to New York and hastens the ungovernability of Los Angeles.[32] It also generates interethnic conflict, currently in California, along the lines of "legality" and "entitlements."

Polity—Politics—Policy

There have been changes in the definition of what constitutes national identity or unity. What are the new forms of belonging in the context of both *Gesellschaft* (society) and *Gemeinschaft* (community)? Looking primarily at the United States since 1965 we note certain changes. There has been a marked decline of a national consensus and a breakdown of centralism. Indeed all types of "centrisms" are currently encountering a bad press on the Left or on the Right. Using the example of Jewish assimilation in Germany, Malcolm X identified assimilation as a form of ethnic suicide. His stand was crucial in the articulation of a black politics of difference. There is a new microdemocratic mood favoring cultural nationalism;

31. Alejandro Portes and Min Zhou, "Should Immigrants Assimilate?" *The Public Interest* (Summer 1994): 18–33.

32. Simon Head, "The New, Ruthless Economy," *The New York Review of Books*, 29 February 1996. Cf. David Harvey, "Klassenbeziehungen. Soziale Gerechtigkeit und die Politik der Differenz," in *Multikulturelle Gesellschaft. Modell Amerika?* ed. Berndt Ostendorf (Munich, 1994) and Peter Drucker, "The Age of Social Transformation," *The Atlantic Monthly*, November 1994. On the effects of the new immigration on the split labor market cf. Thomas Muller, *Immigrants and the American City* (New York, 1993) and Nicolaus Mills, *Arguing Immigration: The Debate over the Changing Face of America* (New York, 1994). And Jeff Madrick writes: "Differences in income are greater now than at any other time since the 1930s, giving the US the most unequal distribution of income in the advanced world." "The End of Affluence," *New York Review of Books*, 21 September 1995, 14.

particularistic, local knowledge; and local power rather than trans-ethnic, national coalitions. In a way, localism and the distrust of central government (or powerful unions) used to be as conserva-tive and as American as apple pie. The new fragmentation of the left along the lines of "differences" cheered on by French master thinkers gives the American anti-egalitarian screw another, some claim unintended, right wing turn.

Taylor and Walzer discussed the general definition of belonging and loyalty: what is the role of individual rights (universalism and centralism) vs. group rights (particularism, empowerment of dif-ferential identities)? Is a balance politically feasible, or must group rights be controlled by individual rights? Is justice without some sort of metanarrative or a residual belief in the autonomous subject possible?[33] The emergence and political recognition of subunits and of subgroups within national politics (gays, lesbians, ethnic groups, women) was accompanied by a demand to make the previ-ously private (cultural) endowment public. But where to draw the line? What differences should remain private, what differences (such as sexual preferences) must be made public through a forced outing for the benefit of subcommunities? What differences must be depoliticized and what differences must be politicized, what dif-ferences must be ignored and what differences focused on? And, hardest of all, which cultural differences are "good" and which are "bad"? Again the Arminian solution was to declare all differences "good," thereby establishing in the United States—and this is a first in human history—congeries of no-fault cultures. As a skeptical, historically wizened European, I believe that some cultures can be, and have been, positively evil. Indeed, *Kulturpessimismus* (cultural pessimism) is, ever since Simmel and Freud, a German (if not Euro-pean) habit of the heart.

We have witnessed since 1960 the decline of class orientation, that is the decline of the old union-based working-class cultures as carriers of a political New Deal consensus. Loyalty shifted from class differences to differences of endowment, a development many old Leftists with one leg in the historical past regret. John Higham

33. American legal practice has of late recognized a "cultural" defense, i.e., judges take into account extenuating circumstances on the basis of cultural beliefs. Cf. Paul J. Magnarella, "Justice in a Culturally Pluralistic Society: The Cultural Defense on Trial," *Journal of Ethnic Studies* 19, no. 3 (1996): 65–84. Again how to "measure" a legally recognizable difference is the problem. Courts will be filled with anthropol-ogists, who must decide whether Vietnamese wife beaters may continue their prac-tice on multicultural grounds.

writes: "Multiculturalism fosters cultures of endowment while drawing a veil over the cultures of class."[34] Add to this the disappearance of work. Lean production, automation, and mediatization has made a large part of the classical working class obsolete, and we have seen, over the past twenty years, the rise of a permanently unemployable underclass, a reserve army only of consumption, not of production. Unemployment of one third of the population, some economists have suggested, is entirely compatible with a booming economy. The new icons of the age are (1) unemployed, useless, and homeless people, (2) illegal minimum wage laborers, Robert Reich's "in-person servers," and (3) the political refugees and asylum seekers. There are seventy million displaced persons on the move, ten times more than in 1970.

Traveling Culture Theory: The New World Order of Words and Its American Management

The following issues are so problematical, the attendant debate so cacophonous, and the mudslinging so blinding that I will only mark questions and problem areas without making value judgements for fear of being excommunicated from my interpretive community. When cultural boundaries become "political," there is a procedural need to define what constitutes cultural difference and who is to define it. The root problem is that the key term in this debate, culture, is a vague and essentially contested concept. In the United States, an egalitarian concept of culture stands in the tradition of leftist discourses (from Franz Boas onward), in Germany a hierarchical notion of *Kultur* has made it the buzzword of reactionaries. But what indeed, under close scrutiny, is culture or what are the dominant religious-ethnic cultures and counter-, sub-, regional cultures and what are they to whom? Are cultures closed aggregates with integrity, inviolability, and autonomy, hence with stable boundaries that will stand up in court—courts that now have to decide whose gambling casino is tax-exempt? What about the center and periphery of cultures? What about high and low culture? What about power and the power brokers in a culture? Is any "normative" culture desirable? What consequences does the displacement of the idea of the integrity, autonomy, and inviolability of the individual and its grafting onto "cultures" and to "groups" have? I fear that the

34. John Higham, in *Multikulturelle Gesellschaft*, ed. Ostendorf, 120.

term—when used as a political ersatz term—camouflages the newly emerging power relations quite effectively, while enhancing political fragmentation and economic clustering along the lines of cultural difference. What political forms does cultural diversity produce? Federalism, minority enclaves, separate but equal apartheid, or permanent Civil War?[35] The market, at any rate, welcomes the fragmentation of its target groups into culturally distinct lifestyle clusters, thus creating individualized customers for the products of a new and improved McWorld.

What is race (racism) and who defines it? Where is, demographically speaking, the color line and why is it wherever it is? Is the color line socially, culturally, or genetically constructed? Is that drop of black blood enough to "soil" the "great white race"? And what in turn is "whiteness"?[36] Though the anthropological legitimacy of "race" is questionable, must we accept the inevitability of racial division because racism is a social fact? If we do, we are effectively saying, "because there is social racism we should keep its pseudo-anthropological boundaries alive." Are not the strategies for a positive politics of difference as likely to stabilize racial paranoias and boundaries as were its negative antecedents? Claude Levi-Strauss thought so when he refused to sign an antiracism drive. The fact that racism, despite all efforts to reduce it, has increased since 1965 cannot be blamed on individual racists or majority racism alone. A more basic problem, it seems to me, lies elsewhere: race has been instrumentalized over the centuries to legitimate the unequal distribution of resources.

What is ethnic identity? Where is the line between ethnic voluntarism vs. ethnic determinism? Who decides who you are—yourself, the government, or anthropologists appointed by courts? What about the reemergence of "blood and soil" in multicultural discourses? Is it possible to choose your ethnic, racial, gender identity, or is this partly determined? Does option (the freedom to choose) become deterministic in the procedural democratic and juridical process?

Is the politicization of culture-talk, race-talk and ethnicity-talk a textual or representational ersatz for having given up the fight for

35. Philip Fisher interprets American culture as an unending Civil War, modifying Kenneth Burke's metaphor of culture as an "unending conversation." "American Literary and Cultural Studies since the Civil War," in *Redrawing the Boundaries: The Transformation of English and American Literary Studies*, eds. Stephen Greenblatt and Giles Gunn (New York, 1992).

36. Peter Erickson, "Seeing White," *Transition* 67, no. 5.3 (Fall 1995): 166–187.

structural change? A Corporate Executive Officer quipped: "Multi-cultural canons are cheaper than social change." Postmodernism and the new eclecticism celebrate the disappearance of norms or period styles against which to rebel. What does the simultaneity and spatialization of all cultural options, particularly in the cultural industry, signify? Who promotes it, who profits from the new post-modern, hedonistic McWorld, old left communitarians such as Christopher Lasch ask rightly.

Deconstruction and poststructuralism articulate the problem of the extent and limits of social constructivism. Should we decon-struct the idea of the autonomous subject, of civil rights, and free speech as Stanley Fish suggests? Is everything up for grabs and reducible to "unconscious" power games that people or "interpre-tive communities" play?[37]

I suspect this practice has a systemic dimension. Are we witness-ing a closing of ranks between a right wing destruction and a left wing "deconstruction" of the Enlightenment? This overlapping consensus of an anti-enlightenment bias, which has come into the American debate via a gallicized Nietzsche and a politically immu-nized Heidegger, and the curious reemergence of Carl Schmitt in leftist discourse need to be watched with some alarm. It all boils down to one question: can we do without a reconstructed enlight-enment? How can we maintain ethical guidelines or "regulative ideas" (Kant) without some sort of modified juridical universal-ism?[38] As enlightenment principles lose their support on the left, the right, now firmly ensconced in Washington, pushes successfully for a return to nineteenth century social Darwinism. Does the new left know what it is doing, or has it merely isolated clean theory ("us") from dirty political practice ("them") and taken refuge in

37. Stanley Fish who "argues that standards do not transcend the particular points of view of the communities that interpret them" is faulted by Alan Wolfe for his fail-ure to explain or "deconstruct" the notion of "community" satisfactorily. "Algorith-mic Justice," in *Deconstruction and the Possibility of Justice*, eds. Drucilla Cornell, Michel Rosenfeld, and David Gray Carlson (New York, 1992), 361–386. By essentializing community, the American Left connects with algorithmic or radical communitarian theories of justice.

38. Stephen Holmes, "The Community Trap," in *The Anatomy of Antiliberalism* (Cambridge, 1993). Also Alan Wolfe, "Algorithmic Justice," 382f; who argues that our "potential can only be realized, not by denying humanism, but by welcoming it, by recognizing that what makes us human is our ability to shape and interpret rules according to the contexts in which we find ourselves." Conversely, Alfred Rosenberg in his *Mythus des 20. Jahrhunderts* placed "nordische Gemeinschaft" (nordic commu-nity) against "rassenlosen Universalismus," (raceless universalism) as quoted in Reinhard Merker, *Die bildenden Kunst im Nationalsozialismus* (Cologne, 1983), 65.

the former; a withdrawal from national politics to local "communities" of discourse?

Postcolonialism, postnationalism, and transnationalism. The new international diasporas with their pockets of long-distance nationalisms—Irish Republican Army, Euskadi Ta Askatasuna, Islam, Hindus, Kurds represent new patterns of ethnic organization.[39] Diasporic networking is also at work in the establishment of academic agendas. After multiculturalism is passé, postcolonialism or transnationalism will be eminently marketable.

How do ecological concerns fit in with multiculturalism? Is it ecologically "reasonable" that Germany is adding one million people annually to its urban population and that the majority of new immigrants to the United States end up in five megacities? What about ecology and country-to-city migration worldwide? What is the geopolitical balance between massive intervention to save the spotted owl and obvious boredom with genocide-ecocide in Rwanda, Liberia, and Haiti? Does moral urgency depend on the mediated management of representation? Is it real only after CNN has been there or after symbolic analysts have adopted it as an agenda? In the age of cyborgs and virtual realities, what indeed is real?

The dichotomizing post-Fordist megatrends, running off in the direction of national cultural fragmentation and economic globalization, are everywhere in evidence. In a way, the changes in polity and culture are epiphenomena, sometimes helpless reactions to larger economic convulsions. And many people, particularly after the collapse of all socialist agendas, prefer to treat economic megatrends as God-given, and withdraw with a shrug into their respective universes of discourse.

In the tradition of German Kulturpessimismus, I would want to turn the focus on ourselves and consider the role of academic elites. What strikes me first of all is that scant attention is paid to the increasing class divisions within groups or "cultures of endowment," that is to the fact that there are *rich and poor* women, gays, blacks, Hispanics with very different needs. The role of the new elites within these groups needs to be looked at. What are their particular interests in this power game? If, as Barbara Herrnstein Smith argues, "we are always, so to speak, calculating how things 'figure' for us—always pricing them, so to speak in relation to the total economy of our personal universe"[40] what does this say for our

39. Zossi Shain, "Ethnic Diasporas and U.S. Foreign Policy," *Political Science Quarterly* 109, no. 5 (1994–1995), 811–841. There is a new journal called *Diaspora.*
40. Barbara Herrnstein Smith, *Contingencies of Value* (Cambridge, 1988), 42.

role in stabilizing the market? Are we part of the problem or part of the solution? Are we role models and Talented Tenths (DuBois) or are we perhaps not Orwellian, rather Huxleyan nomenclatures? The late Christopher Lasch fired off one last republican salvo before he left us for the *True and Only Heaven* (the title of one of his last books). In *The Revolt of the Elites*, he addresses the complicity of academic elites in stabilizing the split labor market.[41] The new icon of the split labor market is not hard to find: this is the baby-boomer political appointee with an illegal minimum-wage housekeeper. On the left Zoe Baird and on the right Michael Huffington were caught at it. We have here, in the words of Robert Reich, the well-paid "symbolic analysts" who hire a minimum wage "in-person server," or, in Aldous Huxley's old-fashioned words: overinsured and over-paid "alpha people" hiring underinsured and underpaid "gamma people." The Green reader of the *TAZ* in Berlin who takes pride in his economic good sense to have his apartment renovated by inex-pensive but excellent Polish craftsmen (instead of expensive Ger-man ones) makes use of the emerging German equivalent of the American split labor market.[42]

Let me address an example of a more complicated complicity which includes most of us, even rigorously well-intentioned liber-als. One obvious growth industry is the health food market. This market with its large demand for manual labor would collapse instantly without the constant flow of illegal workers across po-rous borders. Hence Clinton's resolve to "regain control over our borders" is—if not downright hypocritical—clearly counterpro-ductive healthwise. Moreover, there is a concerted and program-matic effort among health-conscious Americans to put ever more vegetables on our tables, and everyone would agree that this is good for all our arteries. But this is, very drastically put, what I mean by a growing contradiction between our heads and heart, between theory and practice, between open arteries and closed borders. Currently, Congress is getting ready to amend the new immigration bill to allow 240,000 visas for Mexican guest workers at minimum wages.

41. Christopher Lasch, *The Revolt of the Elites and the Betrayal of Democracy* (New York, 1995). Abstracted in *Harpers* (November 1994).

42. A liberal view: Robert B. Reich, *The Work of Nations* (New York, 1991); and a conservative assessment: Peter Drucker, *Post-Capitalist Society* (New York, 1993). Also Drucker, "The Age of Social Transformation," *The Atlantic Monthly*, November 1994. Dieter Dettke assesses the current climate, "Amerika nach den Zwischenwahlen: Revolution von Rechts?" Occasional Papers, *Friedrich Ebert Stiftung*, 1995.

Three years ago in an article entitled "The Costs of Multicultur-alism," I summarized my misgivings about the unintended and long-range consequences of a politics of difference.[43]

This widening dichotomy between the well-educated professional up-per middle-class [Reich's symbolic analysts] that can afford to have principles and an undereducated underclass that is not able to cope with material survival translates the soft multiculturalism of enlight-ened educational theory into a hard political multiculturalism of the streets. Could it be that the new and largely academic discourse of "gen-der-race-ethnicity" serves to repress a consideration of the more diffi-cult issues of income division and poverty, which to many postmodern, poststructuralist Americans, even to some liberals, seem so intractable and boring. Could it be that academic multiculturalism avoids a serious consideration of poverty by favoring a discourse of difference along the lines of race, ethnicity and gender; in short, that it represents an overde-termination of "cultural" discourses and a repression of new income divisions at the very moment when these begin to hurt [primarily those who are not part of the discourse]. The American liberal conscience is of course more allergic to injustice on the basis of race rather than on the basis of class. Compassion for the economically disadvantaged is held in check by a tacit belief in achievement oriented individualism and the attendant anarchism (of doing your own thing) of which even the hardiest leftist is not quite immune. Thence it is much easier to rally the bad consciences around the issues of racism, sexism, ablism, etc., rather than economic inequality. Yet, the hurts of town and the dis-course of gown are farther than ever apart within my own memory. It is indicative of the current fragmentation of a liberal agenda and of the academization of leftist political culture in the US that it took a conser-vative, Kevin Phillips, the herald of Nixon's Southern strategy, to point out the new class divisions in his *The Politics of Rich and Poor: Wealth and the American Electorate in the Reagan Aftermath, 1990.*[44]

And of all the opinion leaders it was the British *Economist* (a staunch defender of liberalism and its free market principles for 150 years running) that pointed out with some alarm the social contradictions

43. Berndt Ostendorf, *The Costs of Multiculturalism,* Working Paper no. 50, J. F. Kennedy Institut, Berlin, 1992, 50 pp. (May be ordered free of charge.) A shorter German version is also available, "Der Preis des Multikulturalismus. Entwicklungen in den USA," *Merkur* (September/October 1992): 846–862.

44. In a strange inversion of political platforms, the right wing Republican presi-dential candidate Pat Buchanan courts the embattled working class and sounds like a former union leader: "What is an economy for if not so that workers and their fam-ilies can enjoy the good life their parents knew, so that incomes rise with every year of hard work ..." *The Times Picayune,* 27 March 1995, B5. The column is entitled "Learn from Pat."

emerging from these economic disparities in the United States.[45] It is a Bakhtinian and carnevalesque world indeed where economic liberals ask the classic questions of the left.

With an eye on the growing gap between rich and poor, the German vote for *Gleichheit* (equality) and *Solidarität* (solidarity) takes on a different significance. For the time being, German working-class solidarity seems to hold, as the recent successful strike in the spring of 1995 indicates, and it holds all ethnic workers with jobs in its communitarian embrace. But there are clear signs that the "social democratic century" is over and that the global pressure of a new economic liberalism with its push for deregulation, privatization, and deunionization is winning the day. There is also a strong indication that widespread urban unemployment, particularly of second-generation ethnic youth, is compatible with a booming economy. All these trends are challenges to the *Solidargemeinschaft* (community of solidarity) that may well lead to a new aggressive competition between generations, sexes, and ethnic groups and that may threaten the relative solidarity of German and ethnic workers. With the ongoing liberalization of the market it may be necessary for Germany to adopt American liberal policies for the handling of competitive difference (Liberalism One). Better yet would be to maintain as much of the tradition of solidarity as is politically possible, supplement it with a countervailing sense of civil rights, and stabilize these goods in a system of checks and balances.[46]

What about the United States? As the centennial of a Supreme Court decision, *Plessy vs. Ferguson* (1896), approaches, a decision which marked the nadir of race relations and represented the pinnacle of a politics of negative difference, the United States seems to be drifting toward a politics of apartheid and into an economic social Darwinist fragmentation, albeit in a postmodern and post-Fordist guise, a fragmentation that target group researchers quite cheerfully refer to as "the clustering of America." Perhaps the time has come to follow three strategies: first to reaffirm (with Michael Walzer) the universalist principle of *Gleich-Gültigkeit* (indifference) established

45. "Slicing the Cake: The Rights and Wrongs of Inequality," *The Economist*, 5 November 1994; and "Rich North, Hungry South," *The Economist*, 1 October 1994.
46. Like Walzer, Ronald Dworkin identifies two liberalisms, one based on neutrality (Walzer's Liberalism One). But his second liberalism is not based on cultural Gemeinschaft, but "on a positive commitment to an egalitarian morality." *A Matter of Principle* (Cambridge, 1985), 205. Cf. Michael Walzer, ed., *Toward a Global Civil Society* (New York, 1995), particularly the contributions by Jean Elshtain, William Galston, Philip Selznick, Otto Kallscheuer, and Norman Birnbaum.

by *Brown vs. Board of Education, Topeka, Kansas* (1954) and, secondly, to combine this liberal view of citizenship with efforts to revitalize community networks not within but *across* ethnic, racial, and gender divides (cheered on by communitarians). (Admittedly, this sounds easier than it is.) And third, form transethnic and postnational coalitions across all differences of endowment in order try to deal more effectively with the major national and global problems of poverty and income rather than to refine, as Freud put it in his 1930 assessment of Balkan politics, the diverse "narcissisms of minor difference."[47]

Both American and German political cultures should, in the words of David Hollinger, "widen the circle of the 'we,'" denominationalize old and new differences, accept them without either *Angst* or undue *Fremdenfreundlichkeit* (xenophile), and get on with "reconstructing" a new balance between individual freedom and group solidarity toward a postethnic civil and economically just society to which there are a host of rotten alternatives.[48] James Madison, who as one of the founding fathers is clearly on the wrong side of the poststructuralist moral divide, identified the root cause of all divisive factions in Federalist 10: "But the most common and durable source of factions has been the various and unequal distribution of property." Gemeinschafty Germans would agree and, although the *Solidaritätsabgabe* (handling of solidarity) is under some flak, the belief in solidarity, as the *Economist* marvels, continues to be a German "obsession."[49] The majority of Americans, 80 percent according to the *Economist*, would disagree. And yet, the safeguarding and long range stability of Liberalism One or Two may well depend on this piece of pragmatic, Madisonian wisdom.

47. S. Freud, "Civilization and Its Discontent," in *Standard Edition of the Complete Psychological Works of Sigmund Freud*, vol. 11, ed. James Strachey (London, 1930).

48. D.A. Hollinger, "How Wide the Circle of the 'We'? American Intellectuals and the Problem of Ethnos since World War II," *The American Historical Review* 98, no. 2 (April 1993): 317–337. See also Manning Marable, "Beyond Racial Identity Politics: Towards a Liberation Theory for Multicultural Democracy," *Race & Class* 35, no. 1 (1993).

49. In a debate on the origins of national factionalism, Heinrich August Winkler echoes Madison: "Je befriedigender die Lösungen der Partizipations- und Redistributionsprobleme in den Augen der Mitglieder einer Gesellschaft sind, desto weniger anfällig ist diese Gesellschaft für Nationalismus." *Nationalismus* (Königstein, 1985), 32.

Part II

GENDER AND RACE— TWO CATEGORIES OF MULTICULTURALISM

4. Gender in a Transatlantic Perspective

Renate Hof

It is almost impossible to remember a time when people were not talking about differences. The question of how difference is constituted as a concept has become one of the central issues of feminist criticism and Cultural Studies. There are doubtless a number of historical, sociopolitical, and philosophical reasons for this development, and it is certainly true that, within this context, U.S.-American theories have played a leading role. "Given the international division of labor of the imperialist centuries," writes Gayatri Spivak in "French Feminism Revisited: Ethics and Politics," "it is quite appropriate that the best critique of the European ethico-politico-social universals, those regulative concepts, should come from the North Atlantic."[1] The slight irony of these words is enhanced by the fact that much of the critique of universalism seems to have been imported to the United States from European poststructuralist theories. In any case, however, U.S.-American theoretical approaches and methods have strongly affected the various European discourses on feminism. To reduce this situation to an *impact* of American culture seems to me an understatement. As far as feminist theories are concerned, I would rather agree with Rosi Braidotti who, in a recent interview with Judith Butler, has called Europe "a bit of a colony in the realm of women's studies." This, as she goes on to say, "makes us *dependent* upon the commercial, financial, and discursive power of American feminists."[2]

Talking about colonies, dependencies and one-sided power relations may be one way of describing or characterizing the notion of

1. Gayatri Spivak, "French Feminism Revisited: Ethics and Politics," in *Feminists Theorize the Political*, eds. Judith Butler and Joan Scott (New York, 1992), 57.
2. Rosi Braidotti, "Feminism By Any Other Name," *differences* 6, no. 2/3 (1994): 30.

impact as a particularly strong and influential force. As such—especially if one doesn't *welcome* this kind of impact—such a force can only be dismissed in order to develop one's own *original* thoughts. What is neglected within this line of argument, however, is not only the fact that we cannot control these influences. More important, or rather, more seriously flawed seems to me the underlying notion of impact itself, i.e., the implication of a one-directional movement, in which concepts, theories, and paradigms are imposed by one culture upon the other. In a world-wide web of what Edward Said has called "traveling theories," this premise is incompatible with the changes that theories necessarily undergo as they move from one intellectual location to another.

In what follows, I would like to consider some of the transformations that occur when certain theories are wrenched out of their American context and become recontextualized in the European academy. My focus will be on feminist theories of difference, in particular on the concept of gender as it is at present being discussed within the German academic and intellectual environment. While it is certainly true that there has been an increasing academic interest in feminist theories during the last few years—along with a certain shift of perspective as far as topics and subjects are concerned—there is still a lot of confusion about gender as a category of analysis. Discussions usually start with a kind of struggle over the meaning of this term which, for some scholars, signifies "gender identity," for others "gender difference," while still others simply use the term as a synonym for "gender roles." In other words: while the title of this paper—"Gender in a Transatlantic Perspective"—seems to imply that we *know* what to compare, it is unclear exactly what the term refers to, especially since the problem raised by gender difference and its relation to cultural difference is one about how processes of identification and recognition work.

As gender itself cannot be separated from the ways in which it is put into discourse, we can only look at how the term is actually being used in different contexts. In this respect, it is worth remembering what Raymond Williams wrote about the importance of language change. In his book *Culture and Society*, he claims that, "In the last decade of the eighteenth century, and in the first half of the nineteenth century, a number of words, which are now of capital importance, came for the first time into common English use, or, where they had already been generally used in the language, acquired new and important meanings.... Five words are the key points.... They are *industry, democracy, class, art, and culture*.... The changes in their use bear witness to a general change in our characteristic way of thinking about our common life: about our social, political, and economic institutions."[3] What Williams could not foresee in 1958 was how feminist scholars would change the meaning of the term gender to emphasize the extent to which our thinking about these social, political, and economic institutions is connected to our changing notions of "femininity" and "masculinity."[4]

While gender was originally used exclusively as a grammatical term, it has taken on new meanings in recent decades.[5] Although there were references to "equality of the sexes," "feminism," "freedom for women," "motherhood," "sex differences," etc., the term *gender* had no place at all in the numerous books about women that were published during the 1960s and in the first half of the 1970s. Since then the term has been used in contrast to terms like sex and sexual difference for the explicit purpose of creating a space in which socially mediated classifications between men and women could be explored apart from biological classifications. There has been an increasing interest in gender as a social category in order to gain new insights into the cultural organization of the relations between the sexes.

We now tend to recognize this critique of the naturalization of sexual difference as part of a general critique of universalizing theories, metanarratives, and totalizing typologies. Research on women, however, was not "invented" by the twentieth-century women's movement. While feminist politics have always been a response to women's actual—i.e., marginalized—position in society, the problem of sexual difference itself has a long history. It has always been a contested area, and, for centuries, there has been a "philosophy of the sexes." Virginia Woolf was one of the first to expose this longstanding tradition. In *A Room of One's Own* she explicitly, and ironically, revealed men's desire to solve the "riddle of femininity": "Have you any notion how many books are written about women in

3. Raymond Williams, *Culture and Society, 1780–1959* (London, 1987), xi.
4. This point is made strongly by the editors of a special issue on "Gender, Politics, and Power," *Daedalus* 116, no. 4 (Fall 1987).
5. The history of this concept, or rather, the fact that gender was not "invented" by feminist critics, but had a specific meaning not only in linguistics but also in biology and psychology, adds to the complexity of the term. For a more detailed historical account, see Donna Haraway, "Gender for a Marxist Dictionary: The Sexual Politics of a Word," in *Simians, Cyborgs, and Women: the Reinvention of Nature* (New York, 1991), 127–48; Teresa de Lauretis, "Eccentric Subjects: Feminist Theory and Historical Consciousness," *Feminist Studies* 1 (1990): 115–50.

the course of one year? Have you any notion how many are written by men? Are you aware that you are, perhaps, the most discussed animal in the universe?"[6] It was only with the advent of Women's Studies at American universities that the "woman question"—for the first time in history—was given a chance to be discussed by women scholars themselves. In Germany, however, the women's movement has had neither any noticeable influence on the curricula and canons of academic disciplines nor upon the notion and politics of culture in general.[7] And since women have been "the most discussed animals in the universe," it is certainly worth thinking about *why*, at least at German universities, research on women —*Frauenforschung*—became a "minor topic" as soon as women insisted on participating in that research.

Thus, the difficulties that German scholars obviously have with the concept of gender cannot merely be reduced to problems of translation or "terminology." On the contrary, they point to the inevitable discontinuities, leaps, and asymmetries that occur when discourses meet with those created in or having grown out of specific historical, social, and political circumstances. Within this context the following two statements seem to me of particular importance. The first one is a point made by Berndt Ostendorf in his essay "The Politics of Difference: Theories and Practice in a Comparative U.S.-German Perspective" arguing that "the discourse of difference and the nurture of ethnic *Gemeinschaft* is popular on the left in America and on the right in Germany."[8] The second statement comes from an interview with Derrida in which he claims that "one can never decide properly whether [a] particular term implies complicity with or a break from existent ideology."[9] Both statements are instructive because they necessitate a rethinking of the culturally specific history of apparently universal terms such as, for instance, "difference," "modernism," "postmodernism," "feminism," "gender," or "multiculturalism." The meanings of these terms not only take on different connotations in different places but force us to reconceptualize the notion of impact itself. What is implied is a self-critical evaluation of the history of one's own discourse and practice, thus providing a firmer basis for a methodology that is

6. Virginia Woolf, *A Room of One's Own* (New York, 1957), 28.

7. In the German humanities disciplines 4.6 percent of the professors are female, in the natural sciences the situation is not quite as good.

8. Berndt Ostendorf, "The Politics of Difference," this volume, chap. 3, p. 36.

9. Jacques Derrida, "Choréographies," Interview with Christie V. MacDonald, *Diacritics* 12 (1982): 74.

aware of itself as conditioned by "situated knowledges"—to use the title of a well-known essay by Donna Haraway.[10]

One of the reasons for the ongoing confusion about the concept of gender can be traced back to the more or less total nonexistence of Women's Studies at German universities. While in the United States the concept has developed as a consequence of Women's Studies and feminist theories, in Germany the most effective critique of social inequalities has been raised by women outside the university. There is, however, a paradox faced by any social change movement, including feminism: its critique is necessarily determined by the nature of the prevailing social system, and its meanings are embedded in that system. Thus, the recent interest in the concept of gender in the German academic and intellectual environment raises the question of which sociopolitical differences between the two locations are responsible for the different statuses of academic feminism in the two countries. What happens to this concept in a country where feminist criticism has never been taken very seriously? What kind of border has in fact been crossed?

Within U.S.-American feminist theories, gender was initially meant to demonstrate that "adding" women was not just a matter of making social or cultural analysis more comprehensive. It was a concept developed to contest the naturalization of sexual difference. Hence a great deal of research over the past few decades has been devoted to documenting and seeking to identify the sources of gender inequalities. In a way—apart from the civil rights movement—the focus on gender as a category of analysis can be seen as an attempt to come to terms with the notion of difference, before contemporary social and cultural theories exhibited an almost obsessive concern with issues of difference. And since deciding on differences is one way of delineating identities, feminist scholars have been struggling with the question of how or to what degree women might be the same or similar without being identical.

Early feminist analyses exemplified the tendency to treat gender (and woman) as a unitary category of analysis and to show how hierarchical power relations repeatedly rendered women invisible. By now, however, the assertion of the nonuniversal status of the category "woman" is almost a commonplace.[11] What was important was the attempt to provide socially, as opposed to biologically,

10. Donna Haraway, "Situated Knowledges: The Science Question in Feminism and the Privilege of Partial Perspective," *Feminist Studies* 14 (Fall 1988): 575–599.
11. As the following quotation shows, this fact has already been used to attack the whole feminist enterprise: "How can one assert the claims and needs of women, if

based accounts of women's position in society and of the origins of gender difference. Whatever role biology was playing, it was not determining gender. In short: the concept of gender selects and gives meaning to sexual difference. It is concerned with representations of social relations that construct our knowledge of men and women and inform social and scientific practices. Like race and class, gender—as a socially prescribed relationship—cannot be renounced voluntarily. Providing a framework of differential analysis, the concept has been developed to contest not sexual difference but the interpretation, or rather naturalization, of this difference. As "a primary way of signifying relationships of power,"[12] it was meant to account for the social and cultural *evaluation* of masculinity and femininity. As such, the concept can be seen as an attempt to reconceptualize the notion of difference itself. What is at stake, is a rethinking of methodology, or epistemology, and not just adding a feminist perspective to various other methods.

All this is certainly well-known. Equally well-known seem to be the rather stereotypical distinctions between Anglo-American feminism on the one hand and so-called continental feminism on the other. Depending on the "eye of the beholder," these descriptions, more often than not, tend to provide an almost ridiculous picture of the "other's" theoretical and epistemological standpoint. A theory of language as transparency on the one hand *versus* European poststructuralist notions of the materiality of the signifier on the other; a belief in a recoverable history, in the conscious over the unconscious *versus* poststructuralist emphases of structure over subject, of signification over meaning.[13]

Instead of classifying German academic feminism as *either* Anglo-American *or* continental, it seems to me more important that we first try to understand the reasons for this "uneven theoretical development." In this respect, the institutionalization of Women's Studies at American universities has been only one aspect. Equally important is the fact that the notion of difference seems to be differently ingrained and perceived in public discourses both in

---

the female is indeterminate?" cf. Eugene Goodheart, "Against Coercion," *New Literary History* 19, no. 1 (1987): 180.

12. Joan Scott, "Gender as a Useful Category of Analysis," *Gender and the Politics of History* (New York, 1988), 44.

13. It would be a valuable task to analyze the particular construction of U.S.-American and French feminism that has emerged in German feminist writings and compare these constructions with similar analyses in other countries.

Germany and the United States. In Germany, for instance, it is still impossible to forget about the specific use of the term—as rooted in fascism with its own hierarchical and exclusionary ways of thinking. In this history, difference has been predicated on relations of domination and exclusion. Hence, to be "different from" came to mean "less than," to be *worth* less than.[14] In addition—and here again I quote from the Butler/Braidotti-interview—"the historical problems related to difference in general and 'sexual difference' in particular are extremely relevant *politically* in the European community today.... 'Difference,' in the age of the disintegration of the Eastern Bloc, is a lethally relevant term.... Fragmentation and the reappraisal of difference in a post-structuralist mode can only be perceived at best ironically and at worst tragically, by somebody living in Zagreb, not to speak of Dubrovnik or Sarajevo."[15]

Most of the controversies about the concept of gender in Germany have to do with the contradictions surrounding the question of difference. And these contradictions, in turn, are closely connected with the strained relationship between universalism and particularism.[16] The reception of Judith Butler's book *Gender Trouble* is a case in point. The translation appeared in 1991, one year after its publication in the United States. It has "engendered" a controversial academic discussion about Gender Studies in Germany. However, as there has never been any widespread and detailed *theoretical* debate about why this concept was introduced in the first place, the book has confronted the German academic establishment with an almost impossible task—figuring out how to deal with gender and "gender trouble" *simultaneously*, i.e., determining how to come to terms with "the paradox that American

14. "Difference being tied to hierarchy and inequality is a fatal memory," writes Michael Geyer in his essay, "Multiculturalism and the Politics of General Education." "It is linked in the United States to slavery and in India to colonialism. In the German case, where this latter notion of difference is implicated in the Holocaust, it is still too painful to think for the offspring of both perpetrators and victims." And he even claims that the "strenuous efforts of Habermas to think a rational public sphere and his quick rejection of any alternative are among the most telling examples of this taboo." *Critical Inquiry* 19, no. 3 (1993): 522.

15. Braidotti, "Feminism By Any Other Name," 45.

16. It is certainly no coincidence that a heated debate is at present being carried on about the critique of universalism in the name of particulars. The journal *differences*, for instance, has recently devoted a special issue to this topic (7, no. 1, 1995). I elaborate on this question in a longer essay entitled "'To think is to forget differences': Rethinking the Ambiguous Notion of Universality."

feminist theory today is based on the very notion of gender that it problematizes, complicates, and, in some cases, undermines."[17]

One of the major issues which, mainly as a consequence of this translation, is being discussed today has to do with the division between sex and gender. While the underlying idea was a notion that gender was socially constructed, not determined by biology, this assumption has been unable to theorize the relationship between these two concepts. It was still based on a natural, sexual dichotomy. The problem was that the elaboration of the social determinations of gender seemed to deny the historical construction of sex and the body as a sociohistorical product, rather than a fixed, transhistorical category.

The discussion itself might be helpful, because both the sex/gender distinction as well as the critique of this distinction have reopened the question of the nature/culture relationship. What is lost in Germany, however, at least within the academic appropriation of gender as a category of analysis, is not only the *political* notion of gender as it has emerged out of feminism as a political movement, but also a more general debate about the relationship between sexuality and the production of knowledge, about the production of knowledge as a political enterprise, i.e., about the philosophical and institutional bases of social and cultural criticism.

The following quotation is an apt—and by no means unique—example of this lack of awareness that certain forms of generalizations are incompatible with the concepts of multiculturalism, gender, and difference:

> We are, after all, human beings before we are male or female, black or white, heterosexual or gay, young or old, European, African, American. Admittedly, this is a creed or a programme that will not go down well with the political activists among contemporary literary critics. But with a little patience and a great deal of scholarly thoroughness more might be achieved in the long run for the issues of multiculturalism, gender, race, or class than with all those fiery declarations of war against liberal humanism or logocentrism with which the followers of poststructuralism and postmodernism try to leave their mark on culture.[18]

These words cannot be easily dismissed because—in addition to explaining some features of the uneven theoretical development

---

17. Rosi Braidotti, "Theories of Gender," in *Transformations in Personhood and Culture after Theory*, eds. Christie McDonald and Gary Will (University Park, 1994), 145.
18. Jürgen Schlaeger, "Cultural Poetics or Literary Anthropology?" *Real* 10 (1994): 79.

in the two countries—they might even provide an answer to the question of why both the women's movement and feminist criticism in Germany have had neither any noticeable influence on academic research nor upon the notion and politics of academic life in general. The article stresses the "need to reclaim literature from the now rampant textual Darwinism" and it explicitly deplores the fact that theory, particularly contemporary literary theory, may have to give up its claim to universal relevancy. It gives us a number of explanations of why, in the United States, the radicalization of difference is the only game left worth playing, and why Europeans generally are less keen on playing it. One reason is said to be the impact of theory on literary criticism in the United States, where race, gender, and class are increasingly recognized as central constituents of the "melting pot" and where difference as an epistemological principle seemed to legitimize the new vision of a multicultural society. The second reason is that multiculturalism as a view embraces multiplicity instead of identity. And this, apparently, is part of a network of problems, issues, and needs that are characteristic of current American, but not of European, intellectual life.

Could it be that, against this backdrop, the recent *academic* interest in feminist theories, especially in the concept of gender with its emphasis on difference, serves as a means of displacement? That talking about American gender theories provides an opportunity to defer confrontation with our own historically specific notions of difference? The fact that at German universities, feminist theories have been integrated—if at all—mainly into American Studies departments raises some disturbing questions, not only with respect to the "uneven theoretical development" in the two countries, but also in terms of the role and function of German-American Studies themselves. For as German Americanists we seem to be confronted with a special dilemma insofar as the object or subject matter of our research is marked, or characterized by cultural diversity, difference, and multiplicity, while our critical writing is necessarily shaped by the nature of our own prevailing social and cultural system. This dilemma forces us to be particularly clear about our own interest in differences, especially in a cultural sphere that still conceives of itself as more or less homogeneous. It forces us to reconceptualize the process of differentiation itself, i.e., the fact that people are not discriminated against *because* they are already different, but that, on the contrary, difference and the salience of different identities are produced by discrimination, a process "that establishes the superiority or the typicality or the universality of some in terms of the inferiority or atypicality or particularity of others."[19] Without a reconceptualization of the still predominant view of a homogeneous German culture, there is at least a certain danger that academic feminism in Germany might take on a similar *rhetorical* function as the one that—in the United States—academic multiculturalism has arrogated to itself.

19. Joan Scott, "Multiculturalism and the Politics of Identity," *October* 61 (1992): 15.

5. Feminisms in Transit: American Feminist Germanists Construct a Multicultural Germany

Sara Lennox

In their afterword to the 1994 *Women in German Yearbook*, editors Jeanette Clausen and Sara Friedrichsmeyer call upon Women in German (WIG) members to commit themselves to the production of a feminist literary criticism "that is truly international and multicultural." "We are not the first to recommend that *Germanistik* become more international, more heterogeneous," Clausen and Friedrichsmeyer add, "but we are the first to suggest that WIG can and should play a leadership role in providing direction for that change...."[1] This essay explores how and why American feminist Germanists came to position themselves at the forefront of efforts to construct a multicultural German Studies by investigating the multiethnic, multinational origins of American feminism's syncretic methodologies. Imported into German Studies in the mid-1980s by influential American feminist Germanists, those methods provided WIG members with an optic that allowed them to emphasize the heterogeneity of German identities and conceive Germany to be a multicultural country. By the 1990s, as I will show, American feminist Germanists had helped to constitute American-German Studies as a field whose multicultural emphases made it a discipline distinctly different from German *Germanistik*.

A somewhat different version of this essay was published in the *Zeitschrift für Germanistik*, no. 3 (1996). All translations from the German in this chapter are the author's.

1. Jeanette Clausen and Sara Friedrichsmeyer, "WIG 2000: Feminism and the Future of *Germanistik*," in *Women in German Yearbook 10*, eds. Jeanette Clausen and Sara Friedrichsmeyer (Lincoln, 1994), 269.

Retrospective accounts of the origins of American feminism often invoke the title of Adrienne Rich's 1978 lyric volume *The Dream of a Common Language* to characterize the assumptions about the homogeneity of female interests on which much 1970s feminism was premised: all women would join together in universal sisterhood once they had freed themselves from their oppression by men.[2] But by the early 1980s, as many narratives of the history of American feminism recall, the vigorous interventions of American women of color at a series of explosive conferences and in a variety of influential anthologies had forced white feminists to confront the question of differences among women and their own implication in structures of oppression. As Teresa de Lauretis has detailed, feminists of the 1970s had mostly anchored their analyses to the single axis of gender as sexual difference and advanced two distinct, though intersecting, political strategies that could both be contained within the boundaries of hegemonic cultural discourses: some feminists argued for status and rights equal to men's with an "ideology of the same," while others, often defining themselves as feminist separatists, sought to construct a counterhegemonic discourse that, in its anglophone variant, would produce a "women's language" or "women's culture," or, as in the francophone *écriture féminine*, "would reclaim a symptomatic language of the body ... presumed to be subversive of the 'phallocentric' order of culture."[3] But the spirited objections of American women of color to such "quasi-metanarratives"[4] encouraged many American feminists of the 1980s to renounce the celebrations of *fémininité tout court* that had characterized both American radical feminism and the theoretical position they had termed "French feminism." In Donna Haraway's words, "White women ... discovered (that is, were forced kicking and screaming to notice) the non-innocence of the category 'woman.'"[5]

2. Sara Lennox, "Feministische Aufbrüche: Impulse aus den USA und Frankreich," in *Frauen Literatur Geschichte*, eds. Hiltrud Gnüg and Renate Möhrmann (Stuttgart, 1985), 392; Marianne Hirsch and Evelyn Fox Keller, "Conclusion: Practicing Conflict in Feminist Theory," in *Conflicts in Feminism*, eds. Marianne Hirsch and Evelyn Fox Keller (New York, 1990), 379; Nancy Kaiser, *Selbst bewußt: Frauen in den USA* (Leipzig, 1994), 11.

3. Teresa de Lauretis, "Eccentric Subjects: Feminist Theory and Historical Consciousness," *Feminist Studies* 16, no. 1 (Spring 1990): 132.

4. Nancy Fraser and Linda Nicholson, "Social Criticism without Philosophy," in *Feminism/Postmodernism*, ed. Linda Nicholson (New York, 1990), 27.

5. Donna J. Haraway, *Simians, Cyborgs, and Women: The Reinvention of Nature* (New York, 1991), 157.

American feminist scholars' far-reaching reconceptualization of their field in the 1980s can thus be read as their effort to repudiate their essentializing views of "woman" and elaborate a methodology that would allow them to understand and describe how women differ. If a certain appropriation of poststructuralism had allowed American and German feminists of the 1970s and early 1980s to view the stark binary opposition between men and women as the single difference founding a singular, monolithic "phallogocentric" system that had excluded women from discourse and power, American feminists of the mid-1980s, spurred on by the critique of racism, now used other elements of poststructuralist thought to challenge totalizing theories and unitary identities. That appropriation of French theory was often inflected or modulated by an attentiveness to historical specificity enabled by German Critical Theory, British neo-Marxism, and/or postcolonial theory. Robert Young has maintained in his provocative study *White Mythologies* that poststructuralism itself, evidently a multicultural product of French critical engagement with German theorists like Hegel, Marx, Nietzsche, Freud, and Heidegger, may also be read as a response to colonial struggles for liberation, especially the Algerian War of Independence, which forced a wide range of French and other thinkers to reassess their allegiance to "grand narratives of legitimation," to contest ethnocentrism, and to decolonize the forms of Western thought. As Young has put it, "Postmodernism can best be defined as European culture's awareness that it is no longer the unquestioned and dominant center of the world."[6] The origins of the new approach, which produced a transformation of American feminist scholarship without parallel in Germany, are thus multinational and a consequence of multiple theoretical displacements: as de Lauretis has put it, "feminist theory came into its own, or became possible as such ... in a postcolonial model."[7]

The new method of the 1980s now made it possible for American feminists to recognize that the female subject was not a product merely of categories of sexual difference, but was instead "shifting and multiply organized across variable axes of difference,"[8] including those of race, nationality, ethnicity, class, and sexuality. Though the term "gender," used to designate the social organization of sexual difference as distinct from the biological

6. Robert Young, *White Mythologies: Writing History and the West* (New York, 1990), 19.

7. de Lauretis, "Eccentric Subjects: Feminist Theory and Historical Consciousness," 131.

8. Ibid., 116.

raw material of sex, had already entered the American feminist vocabulary by the mid-1970s, attention to ethnic specificity in scholarship of the 1980s and 1990s made it possible for feminists to repudiate entirely what Linda Nicholson has termed "biological foundationalism," to recognize that "we cannot look to the body to ground cross-cultural claims about the male-female distinction,"[9] and to investigate the production of the sexed body across time and culture.

Expanding upon the structuralist/poststructuralist postulate that all meaning is relational, American feminists now advanced a concept of gender as a social construction that allows particular societies to define masculinity and femininity as opposite, if dialectically related terms. Like Foucault's notion of sexuality, de Lauretis argued, "gender is not a property of bodies or something originally existent in human beings, but 'the set of effects produced in bodies, behaviors, and social relations,' in Foucault's words, by the deployment of 'a complex political technology.'"[10] American feminists now regarded masculinity and femininity as unstable and constantly changing products of historically and culturally specific social practices, and they viewed various cultural products and arenas as sites of struggle where different, potentially contradictory gender definitions intersect and contend.

Acknowledging that the term "women" at best described a hybrid grouping linked only by tenuous and provisional coalitions, American feminists argued for new conceptions of feminist political practice that would free the category women from any stable referent and allow it to be reconfigured anew in each new instance,[11] while they simultaneously advanced a conception of feminist "positionality" to describe the specific location from which particular women can act and speak. Finally, as Jane Gallop argued at the 1994 Modern Language Association convention, American feminists' increasing emphasis on the multiple constituents of male and female identity made it possible for them even to decenter gender itself and instead emphasize its articulation with other social categories, particularly enabling investigations of how racial and ethnic ideologies

9. Linda Nicholson, "Interpreting *Gender*," *Signs* 20, no. 1 (Autumn 1994): 82–83.

10. Teresa de Lauretis, *Technologies of Gender: Essays on Theory, Film, and Fiction* (Bloomington, 1987), 3 citing Michel Foucault, *History of Sexuality*, trans. Robert Hurley, vol. 1 (New York, 1978), 127.

11. See Judith Butler, "Contingent Foundations," in *Feminist Contentions: A Philosophical Exchange*, eds. Seyla Benhabib, Judith Butler, Drucilla Cornell, and Nancy Fraser (New York, 1995).

and discourses—say, "whiteness" or "Germanness"—are critical to the production of particular varieties of masculinity and femininity. Though this feminist paradigm shift began outside of German Studies, in the course of the 1980s, American feminist Germanists (whom I will define here as feminist Germanists living and working in the United States, whatever their citizenship or country of origin) increasingly deployed interpretive models developed in other areas of American feminism for their investigation of gender issues in Germany. Those new analytical frameworks comprised an intervention into American-German Studies by American feminism that helped to constitute American-German Studies as a field that also increasingly conceived its German subject matter as variegated and heterogeneous. American feminist methodologies were introduced to American-German Studies in the mid-1980s by influential feminist Germanists like Biddy Martin and Leslie Adelson, who used the new theoretical approaches to address the intersection of race and gender. In "Feminist Politics: What's Home Got to Do with It?" published in 1986 in an important interdisciplinary anthology, *Feminist Studies/Critical Studies,* Martin and her colleague Chandra Talpade Mohanty showed how racial identifications underwrite gender identity through their reading of an autobiographical narrative by Minnie Bruce Pratt, a white Christian lesbian from the American South. A product of her confrontation with her race and class privilege, Pratt's narrative, Martin and Mohanty maintain, comprises "a complicated working out of the relationship between home, identity, and community that calls into question the notion of a coherent, historically continuous, stable identity" and works to expose "the exclusions and repressions which support the seeming homogeneity, stability, and self-evidence of 'white identity.'"[12] As Pratt comes to understand that the denial of positionality "is itself based on privilege, on a refusal to accept responsibility for one's implication in actual historical or social relations,"[13] she also rejects the easy opposition of victims and perpetrators, and advances a new concept of power as resulting from "multiple, overlapping, intersecting systems or relations that are historically constructed and recreated through everyday practices and interactions."[14] Placing their examination of Pratt's text explicitly in the context of challenges raised by

12. Biddy Martin and Chandra Talpade Mohanty, "Feminist Politics: What's Home Got to Do With It?" in *Feminist Studies/Critical Studies,* ed. Teresa de Lauretis (Bloomington, 1986), 193.
13. Ibid., 208.
14. Ibid., 209.

American women of color, Martin and Mohanty read it through a poststructuralist lens that allows them to assert that white women's confrontation with their racial positioning unsettles the terms of their self-definition and forces them to reconceive female identity as heterogeneous, shifting, and often self-contradictory.

Leslie Adelson's essay "Racism and Feminist Aesthetics: The Provocation of Anne Duden's *The Opening of the Mouth*," published in 1988 in *Signs*, the United States's most prestigious feminist journal, draws upon a wide range of current theoretical approaches borrowed from American feminism, poststructuralism, and German Critical Theory to undertake a related project. "Scrutinizing," as she puts it, "not only historicized and racialized constructions of gender, but also engendered and racialized constructions of German history and national identity,"[15] Adelson examines the potentially racist implications of a white German woman author's use of images of blackness, including a group of violent black GIs who attack the white female narrator. Adelson's premise in investigating Duden's book is the "very real possibility that specific manifestations of feminism may be implicated in systems of oppression not determined by gender alone."[16] Though Duden's text, Adelson argues, reveals an affinity to écriture féminine in its portrait of the female body as a site of opposition to the dominant order, Duden's inability to recognize the multiple constituents of gender, her failure to understand that "women are included and excluded from dominant orders in *different ways* depending on factors such as race, class, age, religion, sexual preference, and national context,"[17] undercuts the oppositional potential of her narrative. The racism of the text's central image, gives the lie to the alleged universality of woman-centered texts, and, Adelson concludes, "forces us to acknowledge that the experience of femaleness is historically, socially, and racially specific."[18]

For feminist German Studies, the transformations in feminist methodology accomplished by Martin/Mohanty's and Adelson's essays are threefold. First, unlike much earlier scholarship in *Germanistik*, which has mainly derived its analytical models from Germany, these essays are squarely located within the context of an ongoing *American* feminist discussion, whose debates they help to

15. Leslie Adelson, *Making Bodies, Making History: Feminism and German Identity* (Lincoln, 1993), 35.

16. Leslie Adelson, "Racism and Feminist Aesthetics: The Provocation of Anne Duden's *Opening of the Mouth*," *Signs* 13, no. 2 (Winter 1988): 235.

17. Ibid., 241–42.

18. Ibid., 236.

advance. (Particularly, the Martin/Mohanty article has been very influential within U.S. feminist scholarship.) Secondly, the methodology of these essays is very centrally indebted to their critical U.S. feminist appropriation of French poststructuralism, whose paradigms and terminology they thereby introduce to U.S.-German Studies (feminist and otherwise). And finally, their essays elaborate such sophisticated methodologies specifically in order to investigate the intersection of gender and race, emphasizing that within feminist studies it should henceforth be impossible to talk about gender without also showing how gender is always inflected by the heterogeneous categories of race, nationality, and ethnicity.

Though Martin and Adelson have always been at the forefront of American feminist theory, within American feminist German Studies (as within American academic feminism in general) the appropriation of the new American feminist models was a more contentious and discontinuous one that took various forms over the course of the 1980s: including a growing discomfort with monocausal models derived from German Germanistik (including those of German feminism), vigorous denunciations of poststructuralism in some camps and growing enthusiasm for it in others, and an increasing engagement with American feminist paradigms. The interventions of Jewish-American women at the Women in German conference in 1980 marked the first organizational break with homogeneous conceptions of female identity. But in part because of the adamant resistance to poststructuralism in Germany and in American-German departments (many American feminist Germanists associated poststructuralism only with German feminism's infatuation with an écriture féminine already discredited in the United States), that practical rupture could only slowly translate itself into an adequate method.

Martin's "Zwischenbilanz der feministischen Germanistik," published in Frank Trommler's *Germanistik in den USA* in 1989, captured a particular moment in that process. Basing her analysis on a reading of issues of the *Women in German Newsletter* published in 1986–87, Martin noted (correctly, in my recollection) a tendency on the part of some members of Women in German to construct a polemical "opposition between political engagement, democratic process, and empirical reality on the one hand [their own American position] and [German/French] theory, textuality, and trendiness on the other."[19] Perhaps Martin was correct to attribute some

19. Biddy Martin, "Zwischenbilanz der feministischen Debatten," in *Germanistik in den USA: Neue Entwicklungen und Methoden,* ed. Frank Trommler (Opladen, 1989), 172.

portion of American feminist Germanists' hostility to poststructuralism to their isolation within American-German departments, notorious in the 1980s for their "resistance to Lacanian psychoanalysis, Derridean deconstruction, Althusserian Marxism, and Foucauldian discourse theory."[20] But it is also possible to read that antipathy to French theory (also evident in other areas of American feminist scholarship) as an oblique response to the debates about gender and race within American feminism: feminist Germanists recognized at least dimly that, in its inability to conceptualize women's difference from each other, the 1970s variant of poststructuralism (like Duden's novel) actively perpetuated the hegemonic white feminist concepts that women of color had challenged. Yet, except for insisting that historical specificity was crucial, they otherwise remained at a loss to propose an alternative model.

But Martin also emphasized that the response of Women in German members to poststructuralism was nonsynchronous; by the mid-1980s, "a series of scholars within and outside of WIG, especially in film theory" had already begun to address the "overlaps of feminism and poststructuralism."[21] As Martin's own work had already shown, that polarization of the two positions was a false one, as she now argued: "These polemics ... conceal what many feminist scholars within and outside of *Germanistik* recognize as the positive potential of the poststructuralist dissolution of identity, unity, and truth."[22] Moreover, Martin maintained that feminist engagement with poststructuralism played a decisive role in transforming all of German Studies; it was via "the feminist interest in 'modern French theory'" that the "'theory discussion' was introduced into the field of *Germanistik*."[23]

By the beginning of the 1990s, as essays in the leading publication of American feminist German Studies, the *Women in German Yearbook*, show, the new American feminist paradigm whose central tenet was the challenge to feminist essentialism enabled by the intersection of French theory and American antiracism, had, despite ongoing debates about specifics, assumed virtual control of the field of American feminist German Studies. Quite different, even contradictory in their formulation of feminist responses to other issues, three position papers published in the 1992 *Yearbook* reveal their common indebtedness to American feminist debates in

20. Ibid., 171.
21. Ibid., 172.
22. Ibid., 173.
23. Ibid., 171.

the formulation of key arguments of feminist theory that each attempts to outline. Barbara Becker-Cantarino focuses on gender. Addressing "Feministische Germanistik in Deutschland" and the most German of the three, Becker-Cantarino's paper nonetheless discloses her American feminist roots (as well as her grounding in German sociohistorical methods). She does this in her vehement critique of "the obfuscation inherent in the ontological pursuit of 'Weiblichkeit' [femininity]"[24] and her charge to feminists instead to adopt "the open category 'Geschlecht'" (a term that she uses, as her footnotes to American sources reveal, to translate "gender"), a "historical, social, cultural construct which is open for individual, social, temporal, and spatial variation and historical change."[25] Becker-Cantarino does not address French theory's role in helping American feminism reconceptualize gender and acknowledges a French influence on her own formulations only in her encouragement to feminist scholars to explore the relationship of gender relations to "*Signifikationspraxis*" and "*Repräsentation.*"[26] Her essay does not acknowledge the instability of gender and displays a confidence in empirical investigations of real women that feminists less sanguine about the unproblematic relationship of representation and reality might find troubling. But her rejection of feminist essentialism and her insistence on gender as a relational concept embedded in a historical context would not have been possible without the debates about women and difference that rent American feminism in the 1980s.

Gisela Brinker-Gabler's subtle essay, "Alterity-Marginality-Difference: On Inventing Places for Women," focuses directly on those debates by rehearsing the genealogy of American feminist theory. She locates the origins of both French and American feminist readings of poststructuralism in theories of subject-decentering which allowed Hélène Cixous, Cathérine Clément, and Luce Irigaray to construct notions of "the feminine" as an "empty space beyond the symbolic male order," écriture féminine as "a potential language reflective of the female (or maternal) body" and "'speaking (as) woman' beyond logocentric discourse." But, Brinker-Gabler emphasizes, "numerous more recent studies" by Anglo-American theorists have rejected feminist concepts of "alterity" that fail to question

---

24. Barbara Becker-Cantarino, "Feministische Germanistik in Deutschland. Rückblick und sechs Thesen," in *Women in German Yearbook 8*, eds. Jeanette Clausen and Sara Friedrichsmeyer (Lincoln, 1992), 219.
25. Ibid., 228.
26. Ibid.

the coherence of the category "woman": "by emphasizing cultural modalities (Hull/Scott/Smith, Anzaldua/Moraga, Mohanty/Russo/Torres); by pointing out the multiplicity of social and political intersections in which 'gender' is produced (Scott, Riley); and also by criticizing the concept of one original and true sex, which is claimed to be one of the effects of a specific power structure and its language of presumptive heterosexuality (Haraway 1989, Butler 1990)."[27] Examining two essays by me, Adelson's "Racism and Feminist Aesthetics," and Martin's "Zwischenbilanz der feministischen Germanistik," Brinker-Gabler identifies thorny problems that feminist theory has not yet resolved: if the female subject is entirely socially constructed, how is female resistance possible? Does some residue of the female body escape social construction, or is even anatomy a social product? If feminists can no longer rely on women's solidarity but only their partial and provisional affiliations, how can they challenge existing power structures? Despite their different emphases on gender, the body, and the text, these essays and Brinker-Gabler's display a common American feminist lineage deriving from feminist debates arising from "the poststructuralist attack on the subject, the reexamination of the category 'woman,' the theorizing of differences, not only of class, but of race, ethnicity, and sexual orientation."[28]

Joeres's "'Language Is Also a Place of Struggle': The Language of Feminism and the Language of American *Germanistik*," the final paper of the volume, stresses the alliance of American feminist German Studies with other areas of American feminist scholarship.

27. Gisela Brinker-Gabler, "Alterity-Marginality-Difference: On Inventing Places for Women," in *Women in German Yearbook 8*, eds. Jeanette Clausen and Sara Friedrichsmeyer (Lincoln, 1992), 238. Gloria T. Hull, Patricia Bell Scott, and Barbara Smith's *All the Women Are White, All the Blacks Are Men, but Some of Us Are Brave: Black Women's Studies* (Old Westbury, NY, 1982); Cherrie Moraga and Gloria Anzaldua's *This Bridge Called My Back: Writings by Radical Women of Color* (New York, 1982); and Chandra Talpade Mohanty, Ann Russo, and Lourdes Torres's *Third World Women and the Politics of Feminism* (Bloomington, 1991) are path-breaking edited collections in which women of color pose far-reaching questions about the models of women's oppression and liberation that white feminists had elaborated. In Joan Scott's *Gender and the Politics of History* (New York, 1988) and Denise Riley's *Am I That Name? Feminism and the Category of "Women" in History* (New York, 1988), these two feminist historians urge feminist scholars to attend more carefully to historical specificity when theorizing women's experience. Donna Haraway's *Primate Visions: Gender, Race, and Nature in the World of Modern Science* (New York, 1989) and Judith Butler's *Gender Trouble: Feminism and the Subversion of Identity* (New York, 1990) propose provocative new concepts and categories for understanding gender and femininity.

28. Ibid., 240.

The author laments what she portrays as the absolute lack of connection between Germanistik and feminism, not merely "apples and oranges," but more like "elephants and parsley."[29] Joeres issues an ultimatum to her field: should male Germanists continue to dismiss feminism, feminists will simply withdraw. "They will certainly align themselves with Women's Studies departments, I suspect, but as members of German departments they will also be likely to pay less attention to those of their Germanist colleagues who ignore them and the methods they employ."[30] Meanwhile male Germanists' refusal to engage with feminism works condemns the field to irrelevance: "If *Germanistik* continues in large part to ignore what it is that feminism does and continues to do, it will find itself in an increasingly isolated position of its own making."[31] Consigning her unreconstructed male colleagues to the backwaters of literary scholarship, Joeres's manifesto declares that American feminist German Studies are now the mainstream.

The majority of the essays in the five volumes of the *Yearbook* published in the 1990s mostly bear out Joeres's contention that American feminist Germanists are mainly indifferent to Germanistik, now drawing their inspiration, as Ricarda Schmidt had proposed in the 1991 *Yearbook*, from the "contemporary debates of Anglo-American feminists from the fields of psychology, sociology, film, literary theory as well as American Studies, English Studies, and French Studies."[32] Attesting to the heterogeneity of feminism in the wide and contradictory range of interdisciplinary approaches on which they draw, those essays mainly turn to approaches developed by U.S. or British feminist scholars to provide the perspective from which they read German texts.

The use of an American lens through which to view German texts and culture had several consequences for feminist German Studies. First, a close study of feminist scholarship written in the past decade by American and German feminists could demonstrate that American feminists have elaborated quite different notions of German masculinity and femininity than prevail in Germany itself. Because "gender," rather than "Weiblichkeit," is the central term of

29. Ruth-Ellen Boetcher Joeres, "'Language Is Also a Place of Struggle': The Language of Feminism and the Language of American *Germanistik*," in *Women in German Yearbook 8*, eds. Jeanette Clausen and Sara Friedrichsmeyer (Lincoln, 1992), 248.

30. Ibid., 255.

31. Ibid.

32. Ricarda Schmidt, "Theoretische Orientierungen in feministischer Literaturwissenschaft und Sozialphilosophie," in *Women in German Yearbook 7* (Lincoln, 1991), 89.

analysis, American feminist scholars emphasize women's implication in and contributions to general history: how, for instance, representations of femininity affect portraits of masculinity (Marjorie Gelus on Kleist) and how the emergence and transformation of the public sphere is affected by women's participation and exclusion (Ute Brandes on baroque women writers, Ruth-Ellen Joeres on the women romantics, Rick McCormick on gender anxieties in Weimar cinema, Liz Mittman on G.D.R. women writers). They showed how, beyond the *Opfer/Täter* (victim/perpetrator) dichotomy that has characterized much German feminism, women participate in and reinforce oppressive social and discursive structures (M.R. Sperberg-McQueen on Hrotswitha, Gertrud Bauer Pickar on *Die Judenbuche*); they explored how gender and ethnic, nation, and/or cultural identities are negotiated (Karen Remmler on gender and the remembrance of the Holocaust, Karin Eysel on *Kassandra*, Konstanze Streese and Kerry Shea on *Bagdad Cafe*); they revealed how gender definitions themselves are unstable and contest discursive productions (Susan Signe Morrison on texts by fifteenth-century noblewomen, Christl Griesshaber-Weninger on Harsdörffer's *Frauenzimmer Gesprächsspiele*, Kirsten Belgum on *Die Gartenlaube*, Katrin Sieg on East German women dramatists).

But secondly and more importantly for my argument here, the American feminist perspective that allowed feminist Germanists to perceive multiplicity rather than homogeneity also allowed them to construct a multicultural Germany. As racism and xenophobia intensified in Germany after unification, many American feminists, already sensitized to issues of race by the American women's movement, now conceived it to be a matter of moral urgency to draw attention to Germany's diverse populations. Consequently they took the lead in moving multicultural issues to the forefront of German Studies in special issues of journals, conferences, and scholarly studies of the literature and culture of immigrants, Jews, and Germans of color. Though their attention to minority cultures in Germany was not motivated by feminism alone, members of Women in German like Arlene Aikiko Teraoka, Azade Seyhan, and Heidrun Suhr have been in the forefront of efforts to interrogate German constructions of otherness, to challenge Germans' conception of themselves as inhabitants of a monocultural country, and to make the literary and cultural productions of ethnic minorities in Germany a visible presence within German Studies. With the publication of the 1989 special issue of *New German Critique*, they contributed a milestone in American-German Studies.

WIG members were a moving force behind conferences focusing on multiculturalism in Germany and elsewhere: Gisela Brinker-Gabler's "The Question of the Other" at SUNY Binghamton (1991), Angelika Bammer's "Displacements: Cultural Identities in Question" at Emory University (1991), Arlene Teraoka and Rick McCormick's "Xenophobia in Germany: National and Cultural Identities Since Unification" in Minneapolis (1994), and Heidrun Suhr's "Minority Discourses in Contemporary Germany and the United States" at NYU (1995). As an organization, Women in German also focused its annual conferences on questions of multiculturalism in Germany and on women who represented and could speak about the varieties of German women. At WIG's 1991 conference, documentary filmmaker Deborah Lefkowitz presented her film *Intervals of Silence: Being Jewish in Germany;* Afro-German writer Ika Hügel and antiracist scholar and activist Dagmar Schultz were WIG's guests in 1992; in 1993 Ruth Klüger, long a WIG member, read from her autobiography *weiter leben;* in 1995, an interdisciplinary panel discussed the film *Beruf: Neo-Nazi;* and in 1996 WIG invited the Romanian writer Herta Müller and Czech writer Libusa Monikova, both of whom live in Germany and publish in German.

Perhaps American feminist Germanists' continued interest in East German women, frequent guests at WIG conferences, also derives from their commitment to German multiplicity or even from the American feminist engagement with women of color. In a provocative forthcoming book, sociologist Myra Marx Ferree argues that the distinctive analysis of East German feminism resembles black feminist thought in the United States in its emphasis on the complementarity of employment and motherhood and in its refusal to define men as the enemy. Throughout the 1990s, increasing numbers of established feminist scholars and many graduate students also focused their research and teaching on questions of race, ethnicity, and national identity in Germany, and a number of volumes addressing various aspects of multiculturalism in the German past and present written or edited by WIG members are currently in preparation. Berndt Ostendorf remarked at the Georgetown University conference, where the papers in this collection originated, that a discourse of difference is the province of the left in the United States but the right in Germany. If this is true, then U.S. feminist Germanists revealed the Americanness of the perspective that informed their inquiries into racial and ethnic constructions (and also guided the relatively small number of usually American, frequently Jewish, male Germanists engaged in similar projects) in their conviction that only an emphasis on ethnic heterogeneity and particularity rather than universalist inclusionism comprised an adequate response to what they conceived to be threats to democracy in Germany.

In their attempts to reconfigure Germanness, I want finally to argue here, American feminists have also captured some key terrain in the current generationally based battle over the contours of American Germanistik. If, as Frank Trommler has argued, German émigrés who oriented their intellectual production toward the Federal Republic played a leading role in defining the field of German Studies from the fifties to the early 1970s, then since the 1970s most younger faculty hired by U.S.-German departments have been American-trained, whatever their citizenship or country of origin. That younger generation is now poised to assume leadership of the field, proclaiming, in the words of Marc Weiner, the former editor of *German Quarterly*, that "German Studies in the United States has begun to develop an identity increasingly different from that of its counterpart (German) Germanistik, as manifested in a variety of intellectual paradigms that differ from those abroad."[33] In that as-yet undecided contest and within a field that many observers acknowledge to be increasingly "Americanized" and "feminized" (e.g., Nollendorfs), feminists have placed themselves decisively on the side of new methods and new contents and have aggressively promoted their position in areas over which they wield influence. At the 1994 MLA convention, for instance, the winner of the MLA's first-ever Aldo and Jeanne Scaglione Prize for the best book in Germanic languages and literatures was Leslie Adelson's *Making Bodies, Making History* (one chapter of which is her essay "Racism and Feminist Aesthetics"). That book, "commingling social theory and semiotics while confronting recent discussions about race, gender, and ethnicity,"[34] as the Prize Committee declared, can now be represented as setting the standards of excellence against which subsequent scholarly works of American-German Studies must henceforth be measured.

As well, for several years male and female feminist Germanists have held a majority of seats on most of the five-member Divisional Committees of the Modern Language Associations, established for each major period of German literature and responsible for determining

---

33. Marc Weiner, "Letter from the New Editor of The *German Quarterly*," *AATG Newsletter* 30, no. 1 (Fall 1994).

34. Prize Selection Committee, "Prize Citation," Presidential Address. San Diego Convention Center. 28 December 1994.

the topics of the MLA convention's major forums. As a consequence, at recent MLA conventions those forums have focused overwhelmingly on aspects of race, gender, ethnicity, or sexuality in the various epochs of German literature (a development to which more conservative members of the profession responded by not attending the sessions).

Feminist Germanists' American emphasis on multiculturalism has been particularly evident in forums dealing with questions of colonial and minority discourse: at the 1994 convention, the three sessions of the division on the nineteenth and early twentieth centuries addressed colonialism, while the three sessions of the twentieth-century division examined minority literature; in 1995 the three nineteenth- and early twentieth-century forums dealt with colonial fantasies, while one twentieth-century forum and a special session considered postcolonial perspectives. If, as Frank Trommler maintained at the 1994 German Studies Association convention, multiculturalism now marks American-German Studies' moral frontier, American feminist Germanists are prepared to traverse it, leading their discipline in the direction of a new conception of their discipline and of the entire field of German culture.

Marc Weiner, among others, has remarked upon the methodological distinctions that separate German Germanistik from American-German Studies: "At least in the more rarified sphere of the C-4 German *Lehrstuhl*, Germanistik in general has continued to favor philological research, the descriptive impartment of documentary material, and new-critical readings over the newer kinds of research developed in America within, say, the past ten to fifteen years. 'Culture studies' and poststructuralist theory, and the disparate issues, interests, and approaches that generally fall under those terms, are but some examples of the paradigms that distinguish American German Studies from its European counterpart."[35] As I hope I have shown here, those methods entered American-German Studies in some good part because American feminist Germanists, like their sister scholars in other fields, were attempting to develop methodological tools to describe women's differences from one another. And with this new method came also a commitment to perceiving heterogeneity in their German object of investigation. As the study of colonial discourse and postcoloniality now moves center stage in North American Cultural Studies, the subject of recent special issues of *Critical Inquiry, Social Text, Diacritics, Ariel, Yale French Studies, PMLA,* and *Signs* ("Postcolonial studies is everywhere," Russell Jacoby

35. Ibid.

observed in the September/October 1995 issue of *Lingua franca*),[36] American feminist Germanists have again played a major role in making colonialism/postcolonialism a focus of German Studies. As a consequence of their initiatives, many U.S. Germanists now view their subject matter through a distinctly American lens that allows them to perceive a multicultural Germany located within the larger context of a multicultural world. That, the editors of the *Women in German Yearbook* maintain, is indeed the appropriate aim of a feminist German Studies seeking to overcome its "Eurocentric" or even "Germanocentric" biases: "The shared concerns of feminism and multiculturalism create an opportunity as well as a kind of moral imperative for change that can lead us beyond the borders based in 'national' literatures to a truly international and intercultural understanding of issues vital to us all."[37]

36. Russell Jacoby, "Marginal Returns: The Trouble with Post-Colonial Theory," *Lingua franca* 5, no. 6 (September/October 1995): 30.

37. Jeanette Clausen and Sara Friedrichmeyer, "WIG 2000," 271.

6. The Germanification of Black Women's Literature

Anne Koenen

The literatures of women of color have provided some of the most exciting contributions to multiculturalism accounts that map the intersections and contradictory locations of gender, ethnicity/race, class, and sexual orientation. These formerly marginalized fictions, dedicated to the utopian project of "creating a new reality rooted in diversity and equality,"[1] have moved to the center of contemporary American literature. That literature can no longer be conceptualized as a canonized mainstream tradition (represented by the writing of white men) with marginal ethnic literatures and a marginal women's literature; instead, these women's voices, now central, have redefined the mainstream as well. Over the last decades, American literature has become a truly multicultural literature, not in the sense of adding other perspectives, but of radically challenging established notions of reality and questioning tacit assumptions about gender and race. The result is not a mere expansion of the canon, not a matter of mere addition or subtraction of material—but a revision, reinterpretation, and transformation of canonized work.

In contrast, German literature still represents itself as homogeneous, as a tradition founded and perpetuated by great (predominantly male) writers firmly embedded in German culture. The political debates about multiculturalism in German society do not find an equivalent in the form of fictions of immigrants—there is

---

1. Joanne M. Braxton and Andrée Nicola McLaughlin, eds., *Wild Women in the Whirlwind* (New Brunswick, 1990), xlvi.

no Italian-German or Turkish-German literature that would correspond to Chinese-American or African-American literature. How then does the German public, how do the German media react when confronted with a multicultural literature?[2] In the following, I want to sketch and analyze some typical reactions.

A first observation concerns a blatant limitation of range: while I have spoken of the literatures of women of color, the German media—with very few exceptions—only discusses black women's literature, and here only the two most prominent figures, Toni Morrison and, to a lesser extent, Alice Walker.[3] Although other writers like Leslie Marmon Silko and Amy Tan have been translated, their presence is not acknowledged.[4] Thus, multiculturalism is narrowed to biculturalism, and the complexity and diversity of contemporary American reality and literature is reduced to a polarized duality of white versus black. Morrison and Walker are virtually never discussed in a multicultural context, that dimension of their work—its relevance for American literature and its dialogue with other literatures by women and ethnic minorities— is ignored.

Even taking African-American women's literature seriously is a recent development: Rowohlt, the publisher of Morrison's novels, reports that in 1986 the chief editor of the arts and humanities section of an influential newspaper stated that such literature was nonexistent for his newspaper (he had never read a single line

2. Except for two examples, I'll deal with print media, including the Swiss *Neue Zürcher Zeitung*. I have analyzed a total of fifty-one reviews and review-essays; twenty-seven of these were published between 1979 and 1989 (only nine before 1986, when Spielberg's movie *The Color Purple* was released; after 1986, another nine reviews were published), twenty-four between 1990 and 1993. Of the "early" reviews, six deal with Morrison's novels; most deal with Spielberg's movie and more or less explicitly with Walker's novel on which the movie is based. Prior to the release of the movie, there had been only three reviews of *The Color Purple*.

3. Among the publications of black women's novels in German are: Toni Morrison, *The Bluest Eye/Sehr blaue Augen*, 1969/1979; *Song of Solomon/Solomons Lied*, 1977/1979; *Sula*, 1973/1980; Gloria Naylor, *The Women of Brewster Place/Die Frauen von Brewster Place*, 1982/1984; Ann Petry, *The Street/Die Straße*, 1946/1948; Toni Morrison, *Tar Baby/Teerbaby*, 1981/1983; Alice Walker, *Meridian*, 1984; *The Color Purple/ Die Farbe Lila*, 1986; *The Temple of My Familiar/Im Tempel meines Herzens*, 1990; Maya Angelou, *I Know Why the Caged Bird Sings*, 1969; Sandra Young, *Ein Rattenloch ist kein Vogelnest* (not published in the United States); Gayl Jones, *The Birdcatcher/Die Vogelfängerin*, 1985/1986; Margaret Walker, *Jubilee*, 1966/1988; Toni Morrison, *Beloved/ Menschenkind*, 1987/1989; *Jazz*, 1993.

4. Gert Raeithel, "Die zweite Zeit der Büffel" (on Leslie Marmon Silko's *Hüter der Weisheit*), *Spiegel* 17 (1993): 252–55.

written by Morrison).[5] There are nearly no reviews of *Sula* and *The Bluest Eye*, published in 1979 and 1980 respectively, a few more about *Song of Solomon* (1979) and *Tar Baby* (published in 1983); only with the publication of *Beloved* in 1989 is there a widening of critical interest in the media.

Two events—one the release of Spielberg's film version of Walker's *The Color Purple*, the other the Nobel Prize for Morrison—attracted more attention than the publication of novels and led to a peak in critical interest in 1986 and 1993 respectively.

Two particularly telling incidents (both broadcast on German television in 1993) may serve to give a general impression of reactions to multicultural literatures. The first incidence was in the *Literarische Quartett*, a show in which literary critics discuss the latest publications, in this case—among others—Morrison's *Jazz*. Marcel Reich-Reinicki summed up his unease with and ultimate dismissal of the novel by claiming that such literature is just too strange and alien for German readers (the same show discussed a novel of contemporary war experience without any show of similar alienation).

The second incident occurred when Toni Morrison was awarded the Nobel Prize for literature. The *Tagesthemen*, the best-known news show on German television, reported the news and obviously felt compelled to broadcast an expert's view. That expert, interviewed at the Frankfurt/Main book fair, turned out to be German Secretary of Defense Volker Rühe, whose qualification for being allowed to air his opinion was that he had once studied English literature. His statement amounted to the admission that even he, the expert, had never heard of Toni Morrison—the implication of course being that an extremely obscure writer had been honored—and the choice of commentator suggesting a lack of genuine interest in Morrison's work, to say the least.

I have quoted these two media events because they demonstrate that in the German mass media, literature by women of color is still considered marginal or exotic, a literature of otherness. The reviews, as telling in their silences as in their explicit observations, not only fail to realize the relevance of the writings

---

5. The editor's identity was not disclosed. *Rowohlt Revue*, January/February/March 1986, 12: "Der Feuilletonchef einer großen Zeitung, telefonisch gefragt, ob er vorhabe, zu Toni Morrisons Pressegespräch oder zu ihrer Lesung zu kommen, erklärt, solche Bücher fänden bei ihnen nicht statt." One can only speculate how much the arrogance of the influential editors prevented more profound analyses of African-American women's literature. Unless otherwise noted, all translations are my own.

of women of color, but they also overlook or distort the fundamental concerns of these fictions. In dealing with the literature of a group that is different in terms of race and/or gender, the reviewers do not feel the need to reconstruct the perspective of the other—to understand black women's literature against its cultural and literary background—but they take the validity of their own perspective for granted. That position, of course, is white and male. Such an "innocent" rejection or recuperation of otherness is less possible in reviews of the 1990s, where the debate on multiculturalism has filtered down. In these later years, we find either attempts to take the other perspective seriously (mostly based on interviews with black women writers) or rejections on the ground that other perspectives are just a political fad, overemphasized by political correctness.

In the early period (until about 1989/90) of dealing with black women's literature, some reviews are brief and confine themselves to plot summaries,[6] yet the more prestigious and influential newspapers and magazines, like *Die Zeit, Frankfurter Allgemeine Zeitung* and the Swiss *Neue Zürcher Zeitung*, also published more detailed analyses. These "early" contributions in the German media demonstrate an urge to deny the uniqueness and validity of a nonwhite American cultural and literary tradition. Part of that denial may stem from a lack of knowledge about black women's literature and black culture, but it is remarkable that the reviewers obviously feel comfortable in their state of ignorance. The idea emerges that this is a strange and distant culture we are dealing with—mostly only an implied idea, yet one reviewer makes that explicit: "These are reports from another country. That impression is not entirely off the mark: indeed, the culture of Black America is one of the least familiar for us. Especially the writers of Black America, and here again women writers, are still relegated to the footnotes of standard literary histories" (author's translation).[7] The observation that black women writers have been neglected especially by literary

6. See Elisabeth Bogarz, "Kaleidoskop einer Freundschaft" (on *Sula*), *Münchner Stadtzeitung*, 25 January 1985, 66; Helga Kotthoff, "Toni Morrison. Sehr blaue Augen" (on *The Bluest Eye*), *Emma*, March 1987, 48.

7. Adrian Wolfen, "Die dunklere Schwester. Alice Walker—Wege zum Verständnis," *ultimo*, February 1987, 22. "Es sind Berichte aus einem anderen Land. Dieser Eindruck ist übrigens so falsch nicht: Tatsächlich ist uns nämlich kaum eine Kultur so unbekannt wie die des schwarzen Amerikas. Gerade ihre Literaten, insbesondere auch die weiblichen Autorinnen, fristen immer noch eine Fußnotenexistenz in den gängigen Literaturgeschichten."

criticism is wrong—if anybody has dealt with black women's literature in Germany, it is academic criticism. Angela Praesent, the editor of Morrison's novels at Rowohlt, although usually quite hostile to academic criticism, claims as much.[8] By 1987, one book-length study of African-American women's literature and various articles had been published in Germany.[9]

The same review actually suggests that it might have been more difficult for Spielberg to direct the film version of a novel by a black woman than to come up with movies about extraterrestrials, implying that for white men, black women's literature might be more alien than aliens from outer space. Although the review from which the last two quotes are taken means to be critical of the attitudes of both academic criticism and Spielberg, the exaggerations seem to project the author's own unease—Spielberg, after all, has lived in a multicultural society, and it is hard to imagine that African-American culture is as alien to him as the author suggests. If distance and lack of information are identified as a problem, the most reasonable reaction might be trying to learn about African-American culture and literary tradition. However, since that lack of knowledge is not acknowledged, most reviewers choose to ignore what is "unknown" and "strange," i.e., different, about the other culture and assimilate it to white culture. Thus, the—always unstated—thrust of early German comments moves to recuperate multicultural literatures for a homogenous cultural ideal, to render otherness invisible. In the process of these reviews, difference is erased by its forceful integration into white paradigms.

There are two manifestations of this denial of multiculturalism that is typical of German media reactions to African-American women's literature: most reviews try to reclaim Morrison's and Walker's literature for a white "mainstream" tradition, and nearly all reviews are blind to gender as an essential part of Morrison's and Walker's work. Although Morrison's works were first published and marketed in Germany in the *rororo neue frau*, a series of women's literature, the reviewers never explore the gender implications of Morrison's work. There are, increasingly over the last years, references to the double oppression of black women, but never any attempts to enter into a

8. *Rowohlt Revue*, January/February/March 1986, 12: "Toni Morrisons Literatur ist in ihrer Bedeutung von den Literaturwissenschaftlern früher erkannt worden als von den Rezensenten; bei den meisten Autoren ist es umgekehrt."

9. Günter H. Lenz, ed., *History and Tradition in Afro-American Culture* (Frankfurt/Main, 1984); Anne Koenen, *Zeitgenössische Afro-Amerikanische Frauenliteratur* (Frankfurt/Main , 1985).

serious investigation of what the consequences of that position might be. It does not occur to a single reviewer to look for potential similarities with German women's literature (Christa Wolf comes to mind with her reconstruction of history) or Afro-German women's experience[10] of German reactions and denial of difference and otherness.

Instead that denial is extended to black women's literature of the United States, creating the impression that only one difference can be seen and dealt with at a time.

Thus, again, multiculturalism and multiplicity are ignored in favor of a secure position of white male hegemony. Reviewers reject Morrison's "feminist convictions" as "incongruous"[11] or feel relieved that Walker is not an *Emanze* (a women's libber), not an extremist with fanatical ideas.[12] Unlike the American public, serious confrontations of gender issues and feminism are extremely rare in the German media. The negative connotations of Emanze is one example; thus, one article identifies Walker as preaching the "feminist idea of free love" ("das feministische Bekenntnis zu freier Liebe"),[13] a ludicrous idea for anybody who has read Walker's novels. The same writer identifies *The Color Purple* as a "historischer Roman über schwarze Farmer im alten Süden"(a historical novel about black farmers in the old South),[14] as if gender were not at the center of the Walker's concerns as well. This blindness reflects a generally low level of awareness concerning gender issues in the German media, where the literary establishment is still firmly grounded in a traditional, male understanding of literary tradition.

As to the second point, race and black women's literature: misconceptions and mistakes abound in the reviews,[15] and they not only display a lack of basic information about ethnic and women's

10. May Opitz, ed., *Farbe bekennen* (1986).

11. Gerd Fuchs, "New York, New York," *Die Woche*, 7 April 1993, 26, in a review of Morrison's *Jazz:* "Eher aufgesetzt wirken auch die Elemente, die aus ihren feministischen Überzeugungen stammen, ..."

12. Elisabeth Braem-Kaiser, "Geschichten aus dem schwarzen Süden," *Die Zeit*, 22 February 1985, 53. See similarly Eva-Maria Lenz, "Paradies in Schwarz," *Frankfurter Allgemeine Zeitung*, 25 August 1986, 23, in which Lenz laments Walker's "feminist credo."

13. Rudolf Haas, "Zurück zu den Schatten," *Die Welt*, 11 August 1990, 21.

14. Peter Steinhart, "Lichtungen im Gestrüpp der Klischees," *Frankfurter Rundschau*, 19 August 1986, 17.

15. See for example an early review by Helmut Winter, "Sie schaffen sich ihre eigene Hölle," *Frankfurter Allgemeine Zeitung*, 7 May 1979, 24, which claims that in *Song of Solomon* mothers burn their children; obviously, this does not happen in *Song*

literatures, but are also a consequence of the reviewers' desire to recuperate these writings for mainstream literature and to create a frame of references that will supposedly make black women's literature accessible for white (male) readers. The most obvious sign of that movement for homogeneity is the ubiquitous comparison of Morrison with Faulkner, who is called "ihre literarische Wahlverwandtschaft"(her literary elective affinity).[16] Although an awareness of Faulknerian techniques can certainly be traced in Morrison's works, her commitment to deconstructing race and gender, to name only the most obvious points, radically differs from Faulkner's ideas.[17] The comparisons with Faulkner do not penetrate under the surface of shared features like historical period or setting, nor do they analyze the relevance of a black perspective—they are not interested in how Morrison fills the silences of Faulkner's work and exposes his use of blackness as "a metaphor to sustain the narrative."[18] Once even Shakespeare served as a reliably white Western predecessor of black women's literature, the claim being that black women still write in English: "Niemals wird sie sich aus dem Urgrund lösen können, der von der Sprache Shakespeares ... bestimmt ist" (She will never be able to free herself from the source, which is based on the language of Shakespeare).[19] Along the same lines, this reviewer explicitly rejects the idea that Morrison might have developed an African-American language, because he sees such a language as unintelligible for non-black readers and limited, comparing it with German and

---

of Solomon, but in *Sula.* He then claims that history is of no interest to Morrison, because all her female characters have a personal history of sexual abuse and so on.

16. "Sklavenglöckchen und Jazztrompeten," *die tageszeitung,* 8 October 1993, 1; Reinhard Görling, "Schwarz und Frau: doppelt unterdrückt," *Frankfurter Rundschau,* 8 October 1993, 8, places her in the tradition of Poe, Melville, Twain, and Faulkner. An exception in these early reviews is Maria Frisé, "Die honigbraune Nichte des Butlers," *Frankfurter Allgemeine Zeitung,* 29 March 1983, L5, who—like later reviewers—relies on information from Morrison herself and identifies Ellison, Wright, and Baldwin as context.

17. Morrison pursues the issue of "race" and its deconstruction most explicitly in "Recitatif," her only short story that places the two female protagonists at the intersections of race, gender, and class and undermines racial identifications. Faulkner, on the other hand, while seemingly trying to question "race" by using the motif of passing in *Light in August,* does revert to biologism; when Joe Christmas, the protagonist, is killed, the novel uses the racist trope of "black blood" in describing his wound.

18. Cornel West, *Prophetic Reflections: Notes on Race and Power in America* (Monroe, 1993), 129. See also Morrison's reflections in *Playing in the Dark: Whiteness and the Literary Imagination* (Cambridge/London, 1990).

19. Klaus Harpprecht, "Peace Next Time?" *Die Zeit,* 15 October 1993, 73.

Swiss dialects. Although black English is finally no longer falsely categorized as wrong English (the translations into German, however, often unintentionally repeat that mistake),[20] there is no awareness that language transports ideology, a central concern in the literature of—for example—Morrison, Silko, and Kingston, no insights into the significance of a "mother tongue," that is the relevance of oral traditions.

Recuperating black literature for white culture involves a familiarizing political and rhetorical strategy that constitutes a rejection of multiculturalism in setting up parameters that are entirely confined in white culture. In addition to using Faulkner as a point of reference, German reviewers invariably come up with Harriet Beecher Stowe's *Uncle Tom's Cabin*: the *tageszeitung* calls Morrison's female protagonists "Uncle Tom's Granddaughter,"[21] the *Heilbronner Stimme* says the same about Walker's protagonists,[22] yet another review refers to the protagonists in *Roselily* as "Uncle Tom's nieces."[23]

One might argue that this strategy is only intended to familiarize readers with black women's literature; one critic for example asks at the beginning of a review of *Jazz*: "What can a white European understand when black Americans tell stories to black Americans?"[24] But the dangers far outweigh any possible advantages of this strategy. Placing black women's literature only into an intertextual relationship with white writers like Faulkner, Stowe, and Mitchell implies reading it in isolation and out of context, ignoring literary kinship with writers like Zora Neale Hurston. As a result, Morrison is credited with being the first black writer who ever focused on the black community, as if Zora Neale Hurston had never existed. All early reviews lack awareness of a black (female) literary tradition; trying to praise Morrison by identifying her as the first black writer to focus on the black community instead of

20. See, for example, the critical comments in a review of the German translation of *The Color Purple*: Elisabeth Braem-Kaiser, "Geschichten aus dem schwarzen Süden," *Die Zeit*, 22 February 1985, 53; and in a review of the German translation of *Beloved*: Matthias Wegner, "Komm, sagt die Musik, komm und tue Böses," *Frankfurter Allgemeine Zeitung*, 30 March 1993, L8.

21. The same term is used by Wolfen, "Die dunklere Schwester," 22.

22. Gabriele Flessenkemper, "Aus dem anderen Amerika," *Heilbronner Stimme*, 29 November 1986, 7.

23. Anne Rose Katz, "Onkel Toms Nichten," *Süddeutsche Zeitung*, 18 June 1986, 42.

24. Fuchs, "New York, New York," 26; the question is never answered. See also Winter, "Sie schaffen sich ihre eigene Hölle," who states that a non-black reader of Morrison's *Song of Solomon* has to ask himself whether he can ever understand such a book.

concentrating on racial conflict, they cut her off from predecessors like Hurston and Gwendolyn Brooks: "For the first time, we find a Negro author who does not have to find his/her identity in the confrontation with whites."[25]

The strategy of recuperation culminates in the Germanification of black women's literature, and seems to stem from a foreboding that German readers cannot be bothered with perspectives from another culture; thus, the inside-cover description of the first German publication of *Sula* states that Morrison tells "our" story, although not a single white character is in the novel: "Sie erzählt von uns, auch wenn nicht eine weiße Figur auftritt."[26] And an early review in *Die Zeit* comments that basically the shared experiences between the (male) reviewer's childhood in Pommern and a childhood described by Morrison far outweigh the differences, even going so far as to equate *Jazz* with *Blasmusik*, a German folk music for brass instruments usually associated with more conservative contexts like the *Oktoberfest*: "The black families whom Toni Morrison portrays [in *Song of Solomon*] can be compared with the clans of German or Polish farmers who pushed into the cities of Western Europe after the abolition of serfdom. The parallels are amazing.... The author has uncovered fundamental patterns of human behavior, patterns that ruled reality here [in Germany] and there [the United States]."[27] Never mind racism and sexism, two categories that are ignored in a grand gesture in order to feel on common ground with Morrison's protagonists, or, to be more precise, to reclaim them for a white male position. In the process, Morrison's fundamental concerns—to expose the oppressive foundations of such a position—are thoroughly obscured. Discussions of Morrison's fictions identify history as a central concern as well, but not a single one of these earlier reviews feels challenged by Morrison's deconstruction of Western historiography in *Beloved*, her destabilizing a specifically Eurocentric construction of historical

25. Karl E. Keiner, "Auf den Spuren der Vergangenheit," *Neue Zürcher Zeitung*, 24/25 March 1979, 11: "Hier findet sich zum erstenmal ... eine Negerautorin, die nicht im Konflikt mit Weißen ihre Identität suchen muss...."

26. Harpprecht, "Peace Next Time?" 73.

27. Ibid., quoting—without revisions or corrections—an earlier review from 1977: "Die schwarzen Familien, die Toni Morrison schildert [in *Song of Solomon*] ließen sich mit den Sippen deutscher oder polnischer Kleinbauern vergleichen, die nach der Aufhebung der Leibeigenschaft in die Städte des europäischen Westens drängten. Die Parallelen sind erstaunlich.... Die Autorin hat Grundmuster menschlichen Verhaltens bloßgelegt, die hier wie dort die Realitäten bestimmten."

consciousness.[28] Major concerns of novels like *Beloved* are left
unstated when Morrison's challenging of Western world views
remains unnoticed; for example, the significance of a ghost as a
central protagonist in *Beloved* and the cultural ramifications and
implications of her haunting remain obscure. Similarly, Morrison's
and Walker's deconstruction of patriarchal notions like the priority of heterosexual relationships and romantic love go unnoticed
or uncommented.

Difference is ignored in order to create a universally human
approach—"Grundmuster menschlichen Verhaltens" (model of human behavior). In the same vein, a reviewer observes about Walker:
"The black authors have succeeded to articulate a universally human
problem in a novel focused on race and gender."[29] That universal
and just simply human problem is identified as "the dark continent
of the unconscious."[30] The article is *not* aware of the deeply ironic
implications of the dark continent reference in dealing with a novel
that actually confronts the meaning of the African heritage for
African Americans, is *not* aware of the ideological implications of a
body of metaphors that depend on blackness as "a signifier of the
id, or of chaos."[31]

In that context, we also find repeated assurances that Morrison
has always written for white readers as well, and that the writings
of black women do not espouse hostility toward whites. Both these
assurances miss the intentions of Morrison's work: writing primarily for a black audience, as she has stated again and again[32]
and confronting her white audience—who might expect realistic
and socially revealing literature—with her insistence on black culture vis-à-vis an instrumental rationality that she identifies as characteristically white. That insistence on black culture is not yet
another facet in a cultural pluralism where difference can be triv-
ialized and ultimately subsumed under white hegemony, but a

28. A later review by Paul Ingendaay, "Heraus aus der Hölle der Erinnerung,"
Frankfurter Allgemeine Zeitung, 8 October 1993, 33, however, explores this aspect.
29. Wolfen, "Die dunklere Schwester" : "Der schwarzen Schriftstellerin ist es gelun-
gen, mit einem auf Rasse und Geschlecht orientierten Roman eine allgemein men-
schliche Problemstellung zu artikulieren," 22.
30. Ibid.: "der dunkle Kontinent des Unbewußten," 23.
31. West, *Prophetic Reflections*, 129.
32. See, for example, Paula Giddings, "The Triumphant Song of Toni Morrison,"
Encore American & Worldwide News, 12 December 1977, 30; and Toni Morrison,
"Unspeakable Things Unspoken: The Afro-American Presence in American Literature," *Michigan Quarterly Review* 28, no. 1 (1989): 1–34.

subversive approach that questions the very foundations of the forces that oppress Blacks and women. Thus, black women's writing is placed in a white male tradition, ignoring both the tradition of women's writings and of African-American literature. As a side effect, white culture and literature can again be celebrated as a source of creativity, myths, and influential, if not exclusive, interpretations of reality.

The general thrust of such approaches to black women's literature becomes visible in the question of category, and the reviewers seem to consider it the utmost compliment to call Morrison an American writer instead of an African-American writer (a term Morrison identifies with), and to call her literature *universal* ("universaler Humanismus") and to praise her ability always to find the universal in the concrete.[33] The terms "women's literature" or—"even"—"black women's literature" are dismissed as too "colorless," meaning too narrow, in the case of a novel like *Beloved*.[34] The unintentional irony of calling black women's literature "colorless" betrays the desire to wish away the contributions of black/feminist criticisms that have uncovered the gender and race biases of mainstream literature and insisted on deconstructing these positions. Another reviewer even presumes to know Morrison's reaction to the publication of a protest of several authors in the *New York Times Book Review* in January 1988, authors who thought that she should have been awarded the National Book Award—namely, that this public support was Morrison's "most dangerous trial" and that Morrison was "deeply troubled" (tief beunruhigt), thus rejecting a "narrow" category herself.[35] That speculation is then bound to another insidious assumption: that a review by Michiko Kakutani was particularly relevant, because it was written by a woman who did not specialize in "so-called women's or minority literature."[36]

33. Keiner, "Auf den Spuren der Vergangenheit": "im konkreten Detail stets das Universale," 37.

34. Paul Ingendaay, "Lieber tot als versklavt?" *Frankfurter Allgemeine Zeitung,* 16 January 1990, 30: "Ein Etikett wie 'Frauenliteratur' oder gar 'schwarze Frauenliteratur' sieht besonders gegen ihren neuen Roman Menschenkind sehr blaß aus." Ingendaay also—with the same unintentional irony that characterizes his use of "pale/colorless" in this context—rejects such identification as "ghettoization" ("eine subtile Ghettoisierung").

35. Harpprecht, "Peace next Time?" 73: "Es könnte wohl sein, daß die gefährlichste Heimsuchung ... der offene Brief war...." The notion that an act of solidarity might have been a black woman's "most dangerous trial" on her (long) way to the Nobel Prize is too absurd to need comment.

36. Ibid., 73: "wog doppelt und dreifach, da die Verfasserin der Rezension keineswegs auf die sogenannte Frauen- und Minderheiten-Literatur spezialisiert war."

That last comment reflects a more recent development (from 1989/90 on) in the reception of black women's literature in German. In addition to the already described tendencies that continue to exist, we find a bifurcation of reactions to the debate on multiculturalism: one that acknowledges the validity of difference, the other a rejection of otherness on the grounds that without the movement of political correctness, nobody would be as interested in these voices, dismissing multiculturalism as a political fad. I do not want to imply that this is an attitude limited to Germany: in the United States, we find—in the context of the strong reaction against multiculturalism and political correctness— similar tendencies, as in Edwin M. Yoder's comments on the Nobel Prize for Morrison.[37]

Over the last five years, most German writings on Morrison's work have achieved a new quality.they are either closely based on interviews or show a familiarity with the issues of ethnic literatures. That recent readiness to confront the implications of Morrison's work feeds from two sources: the elevation of Morrison as a writer through the Nobel Prize and the willingness to listen (specifically to listen to Morrison herself). Increasingly, reviews and articles express an awareness that the voices of black women writers are neither marginal nor irrelevant.[38] A review of *Beloved*, for example, mentions different lines of tradition in black men's and women's literature, pointing out the shared features of Hurston's and Morrison's fictions.[39] Especially the reviews following the Nobel Prize place Morrison's work in a context of black women's writings, both fictional and theoretical; for example, Andrea Böhme uses Mary Helen Washington's ground-breaking essays as a frame of reference (in addition to the contributions in "Reading Black, Reading Feminist" and the fictions of Zora Neale Hurston, Ann Petry, Toni Cade Bambara, Gloria Naylor, and Terry McMillan).[40] Other articles discover and discuss

37. Edwin M. Yoder, "An Eccentric Selection from the Nobel Folks," *International Herald Tribune*, 13 October 1993, 9: "Since I read too little current fiction, I turned for an opinion of Toni Morrison's work to discerning readers who do not base their evaluations on the irrelevant factors of sex, race, or political identity. By them, Toni Morrison is a regarded as a gifted writer whose earlier novels showed some promise but who has lately drifted toward what one of them calls an oracular voice. Were she a white man rather than a black woman, they ask, wouldn't critics from Boston to Bombay be scratching their heads in mystification?"

38. See Wolfgang Binder, "Harlem in den Zwanzigern," *Nürnberger Zeitung*, 6 March 1993, 13.

39. Stefana Sabin, "Die unerträgliche Leichtigkeit des Leidens," *Neue Zürcher Zeitung*, 3 March 1989, 40.

40. Andrea Böhm, "Niemals auf Nummer Sicher," *die tageszeitung*, 9 October 1993, 19.

aspects like Morrison's use of the fantastic in re-memorizing black history,[41] the relevance of oral tradition for black (women's) literature,[42] and Morrison's interest in gender. However, these articles as well tend to discuss Morrison's work in isolation, not in a context of multicultural literatures, although the context and tradition of black literature is increasingly acknowledged[43] and universalism no longer considered the ultimate compliment.[44]

The only serious approach to an understanding of the complex processes and dynamics of multiculturalism I could detect is a survey of postcolonial literature in a *Spiegel* article, "Die Schale wird zum Kern,"[45] a title that could be loosely translated as "from margin to center." Here, we find the hint that a multicultural legacy might be considered an empowering potential rather than a disabling experience: "The younger writers no longer see their status of not belonging to only one culture as a disadvantage, but rather as an advantage: they see more, know more, and often are better than those writers who grew up in a mono-culture."[46]

While these reviews and essays point to an awareness of Morrison's work and its significance, other comments on Toni Morrison's work in the 1990s are in the context of the debate about political correctness and seem to feel compelled to express a profound skepticism, rejecting the idea of political correctness.[47] After quoting

41. A later review by Ingendaay, "Heraus aus der Hölle der Erinnerung," 33, however, explores this aspect. Ingendaay had rejected the category "black woman writer" in an earlier review of *Beloved* (1990); his later essay, like other writings on Morrison in the 1990s, refers to interviews with Morrison.

42. Ibid. See also Fridolin Furger, "Auf der Suche nach der schwarzen Identität," *Der kleine Bund,* 11 December 1993, Kulturbeilage, 1.

43. See, for example, Barbara von Bechtolsheim, "Doppeltes Anderssein," *Süddeutsche Zeitung,* 7 December 1989, 76; Elisabeth Wehrmann, "Blick zurück im Schmerz," *Die Zeit,* 22 December 1989, 51, for a review of *Beloved* that refers to James Baldwin; Maya Hostettler, "Um ihre eigene(n) Geschichte(n) kämpfen," *Tages-Anzeiger,* 3 April 1991, 11–12, a review-essay of Morrison's and Walker's books that draws on a wide variety of background information. Hostettler and Bechtolgsheim have taught American literature in Germany, Switzerland, and the United States. See also Binder, "Harlem in den Zwanzigern," who refers to Hurston as well as to Claude McKay, dos Passos, and Doctorow.

44. See Susanne Schötelburg, "Der platte Lauf der Welt," *Die Zeit,* 1 February 1991, 67.

45. "Die Schale wird zum Kern," *Der Spiegel* 48 (1993): 232–38.

46. Ibid.: "Ihren Chamäleon-Status [of belonging not only to one culture] sehen die Jüngeren [ethnischen Schriftsteller] eher als Zugewinn denn als Nachteil: Sie wissen mehr, kennen mehr, können oft mehr als Schriftsteller, die in einer Monokultur herangewachsen sind."

47. Political correctness has been trashed in the German media, although it has hardly had an impact on the German public (the use of the English instead of a

enthusiastic voices in praise of Morrison's work, a *Frankfurter Allgemeine Zeitung* writer claims: "Opinions about Toni Morrison always contain some diplomatic caution. The author is black."[48] The writer does not need to make his suspicion explicit—that Morrison gets better reviews than she deserves because she is black, that reviewers are "diplomatic" and circumspect because Morrison is black, that she owes her reputation to political correctness. Where ethnicity is concerned, however, most commentators feel a certain reluctance to denounce political correctness—there has been a growing awareness of the relevance of cultural difference based on ethnicity.

The unease about political correctness is more directly related to questions of gender, a totally blind spot in male writers' comments on Morrison's work that corresponds with a general reluctance in Germany to see gender as a part of multiculturalism. Symptomatic in that respect is an unintended dialogue between two texts in *Die Zeit*. On the one hand, Rowohlt has a huge advertisement celebrating Morrison's work and the Nobel Prize award, while on the other, an article by a male writer from East Germany rejects the notion that something like a feminine perspective might have any validity. "Not so long ago, I would have dismissed the verdict, 'You talk like a man,' as absurd; it is a verdict that cuts off further discussion, because it would require a sex-change. In spite of all recent indoctrination in the West, I still cannot see how such a primary distinction might improve our view of reality."[49] While the ludicrous essentialism of the comment with its reference to a sex-change reveals an extreme reluctance to even consider a gendered perspective, the absolute and unreflected confidence in the validity of masculine interpretations of reality seems to me an unchallenged stronghold of German media beliefs.

German term is a hint): see Gert Mattenklott, "Frauenrechte, Herrenwitze," *Der Tagesspiegel* 8, December 1994, 29, who explicitly refers to the rejection of "Negro" and the insistence on "black American" as "opportunistic" and a subversion of art.

48. Wegner, "Komm, sagt die Musik, komm und tue Böses," L8: "Das Urteil über Toni Morrison enthält immer eine Prise diplomatischer Vorsicht. Die Autorin ist von schwarzer Hautfarbe"; Harpprecht, "Peace Next Time?" also invokes political correctness, claiming that it results in "negative racism" (what would positive racism be, one wonders?) and "dangerous separatism."

49. Wolfgang Engler, "Die Grenzen des Diskurses," *Die Zeit*, 10 December 1993, 61:"Das jede weitere Äußerung abschneidende, weil einen Geschlechswandel voraussetzende Verdikt: 'Sie sprechen ja wie ein Mann!' wäre mir früher schlechtweg absurd erschienen. Trotz aller Schulung (die ich diesbezüglich seither im Westen erfuhr) will mir der Realitätsgewinn dieser Primärunterscheidung nicht recht einleuchten."

Thus, in the early stage, listening to different voices is only a superficial posture, since the reviewers only hear what they want and expect to hear; there is no sense that African-American women's literature challenges our understanding of American culture. In a second stage, most reviewers realize the relevance of the new perspectives that have emerged. Attempts to deal with these voices are most successful when they let the voices speak for themselves (as in interviews with Morrison).[50] The other reactions dismiss reflections on difference as irrelevant and imply that only an exaggerated sense of political correctness would elevate writers who insist on a discussion of power and difference to importance.

50. Articles based on interviews are: Annette Schlichter, "Als zweites Wort lernten sie 'Nigger'" (a translation of an interview originally published in *Time*, 22 May 1989), *die tageszeitung*, 28 July 1989, 16; Bechtolsheim, "Doppeltes Anderssein"; Paul Ingendaay, "Heraus aus der Hölle der Erinnerung"; Elisabeth Wehrman, "Klischees unserer zivilisierten Weltanschauung," *Die Zeit*, 8 October 1993, 51; Fridolin Furger, "Auf der Suche nach der schwarzen Identität." Schlichter and Bechtolsheim teach American literature at German universities.

Part III

AMERICAN STUDIES IN GERMANY—GERMAN STUDIES IN AMERICA

7. Multiculturality in the German Democratic Republic and the Reception of African-American Literature

Friederike Hajek

Multiculturality in East Germany was based on the notion of *Völkerfreundschaft* (friendship between peoples), which, again, was conceived as an important aspect of proletarian internationalism. The latter, supposedly, was the instrument of universal emancipation of mankind. The reception of African-American history and culture was included in that notion. Therefore, early reception of black writers in East Germany was predetermined by cultural politics that had a particular interest in movements that contained characteristics of a working-class movement or were viable at least for a working-class alignment. The black liberation movement of the 1960s seemed to have some such potential. This appeared all the more so as the black population in the United States was estimated as 95 percent working-class at the time. There was, moreover, already a history of black and white working-class alliance that had become most vital in the "Red Decade" of the 1930s. Some of the best-known African-American writers like Richard Wright, Ralph Ellison, and John Oliver Killens had started their writing careers in connection with the John Reed Clubs of the Communist Party. James Baldwin, too, had his own however "brief days as a socialist,"[1] as he said. The impact of the black liberation struggle in the United States

---

1. James Baldwin, *Notes of a Native Son* (London, 1965), 6. In the following, my focus will be more or less consistently on Baldwin; he was the most consistently read and most controversially discussed black author in the G.D.R. for two decades.

and the national liberation movements in Africa during the 1950s and 1960s was such as to nourish hopes for an effective black and white working-classes alignment with a revolutionary, that is, socialist perspective.

Among the first publications of African-American literature were Shirley Graham, *Your Most Humble Servant* and Loyd L. Brown, *Iron City* in 1952; Oliver Killens, *Youngblood* in 1956; Alice Childress, *Like One of the Family*; and Paul Robeson, *Here I Stand* in 1958.[2] The publication of Robeson's autobiography was significant. For a great many people, literary or not, African-American culture was exemplified in his personality and in his singing. He was the ambassador of Völkerfreundschaft and international solidarity, and also the personification of the struggle for the freedom of his people. Yet, the case of Paul Robeson also exemplifies the limitations of the concept of Völkerfreundschaft. For the Germans, multiculturality largely meant reception and even celebration of the traditional folk elements in the other culture. Numerous groups of young as well as older people practiced national and international folk dance, music, and song. For many years, their public performances were quite popular and drew large audiences. Likewise, there were many groups who engaged themselves in Native-American history and traditional lifestyle. They camped out in tepees or wigwams, collected clothes and all kinds of equipment supposedly *indianisch* (Native-American). Very few of all these activities were grounded in actual experience with real people. It was all very literary and imaginative. The cultural "other" was like an item in a museum, something at which to wonder. The experience was intellectual, aesthetic, or emotional, or all three at the same time, but hardly ever real. The other did not become part of one's own culture. It remained outside, excluded, strange, impersonal, somewhat abstract, and even sterile.

Another equally important factor was the literary situation in the G.D.R. itself. Literary theory was, up to the late 1960s, quite strictly defined by the concept of realism that had been developed in the aesthetic debates of the early 1930s. Its leading expert and basic authority was the Hungarian-Marxist Georg Lukacs. He was convinced that realism based on Hegelian aesthetic principles (dialectic unity of essence and appearance) and on Marx's philosophical concept of historical progress was the single method for the realization of a literature aimed at general human progress. Historical

2. For easier reading in English, I leave out the German titles here; as the latter are fairly literal translations of the original, no information is lost.

models were the great realistic novels of the nineteenth century as well as Thomas and Heinrich Mann, Maxim Gorki, and for the United States, Theodore Dreiser. According to Lukacs, the greatness of realistic achievement depended on the author's ability to make the individual character representative of and within a social totality. By representing the individual in his/her manifold relations to reality, the author would be able to invent characters representative of more general tendencies of historical development. The not-so-tacit implication was that capitalism was in a state of general decline and no longer capable of giving new impulses either to historical progress (strictly conceived in terms of linearity) or to artistic creativity. Accordingly, Lenin's theory of the two cultures in capitalist society—one of which was the dominant one, and the other, the new democratic culture developed by the oppressed and the exploited—was applied in such a way as to devalue any literary mode different from realism by branding it "formalism," and formalism was synonymous with decadence (*volkfremde Dekadenz*).[3] Thus, any kind of formal innovation was likely to be considered formalism and therefore rejected. Obviously, criticism of formalism was a good deal formalistic itself.

Lenin's thesis of the two cultures also defined the reception of African-American literature during the first twenty years of the G.D.R. As this literature was produced by a suppressed minority, it was seen as part of the "second culture,"[4] closely connected with the struggle against racism and against capitalist exploitation in general. Models of this reception included authors like W.E.B. Du Bois and Langston Hughes, and novels like John Oliver Killen's *Youngblood*, and Richard Wright's *Uncle Tom's Children* and *Native Son*. These authors represented the continuity of the proletarian revolutionary heritage of the 1930s; they were made to function as yardsticks against which all the younger authors were measured. Not without justification in the 1960s, black people were seen as the one social force struggling for revolutionary change in the United States.

The development of black cultural and political nationalism in the 1960s raised mixed responses: solidarity with respect to the right to self-definition and the struggle against cultural and social suppression, on the one hand, and concern about the implications of an unselective negation of all whites, on the other. In a benevolent,

---

3. Cf. Werner Mittenzwei, *Der Realismusstreit um Brecht. Grundriss der Brecht-Rezeption in der DDR 1945–1975* (Berlin and Weimar, 1978), 54.

4. Eberhard Brüning, "Probleme der Rezeption amerikanischer Literatur in der DDR," *Weimarer Beiträge* 16, no. 4 (1970): 182–183.

but somewhat patronizing tone, the fact that the younger generation of black writers were not yet able to fully recognize the class
character of the race problem was deplored.

A black writer com-
mitted to the liberation struggle of his or her people was expected
to fictionalize ways that would help to instigate an alliance of the
exploited of all colors to overcome racist discrimination and exploitation as part of a worldwide struggle for a (communist) millennium of universal brotherhood.

In this perspective, it was extremely puzzling, if not irritating, for
a critic like Heinz Wüstenhagen to find, in the 1960s, a brilliant
black author like James Arthur Baldwin—who had proven his loyalty
to his people by returning from the safety of his Paris exile to participate in the dangerous turmoil of Alabama civil rights marches—
advocating in his essays "love and acceptance," expressing skepticism
about "causes" that he considered "notoriously blood thirsty," suggesting that "all theories are suspect," suspecting even "the finest
principles" to be in need of modification and—perhaps worst of
all—to find Baldwin heavily attacking the "protest literature" exemplified by Richard Wright's *Native Son* and Harriet Beecher-Stowe's
Uncle Tom's Cabin. Instead, Baldwin was choosing "one's own moral
center" for the highest authority "hoping that this center will guide
one aright." None of these statements of Baldwin's seemed compatible with what Wüstenhagen considered the social responsibility of a
writer who was a representative of a suppressed and discriminated-
against people, and who was himself deeply involved in the liberation struggle of that people. Wüstenhagen explained Baldwin's
statements by finding that the author was surely "irrational," and
"extremely individualistic" if not "anarchistic."[5] The characteristics
assigned to Baldwin carried strong notions of official ideological dis-
approval. Yet the critic is well aware of the power of Baldwin's language, of his brilliant style, and of his capacity to represent the race
problem with a deeply humane understanding and great sensibility.
Wüstenhagen also acknowledges the author's honesty and serious
engagement. He remains, however, critical of the latter's "psychoanalytical" method, which, though most skillfully handled, seems to be
insufficient for a thorough grasp of the complexities of black-white
American reality, namely its economic-political-social-interrelations.

5. Heinz Wüstenhagen, "James Baldwins Essays und Romane. Versuch einer
ersten Einschätzung," *Zeitschrift für Anglistik und Amerikanistik* 13, no. 2 (1965):
119–122. A modified view on Baldwin is expressed in Wüstenhagen's book *Krisenbewußtsein und Kunstanspruch. Roman und Essay in den USA seit 1945* (Berlin, 1981),
97–124. Unless otherwise noted, all translations are my own.

Baldwin's "narrow" interest in emotional and irrational spheres supposedly also accounted for his emphasis on sexuality. Clearly, questions of literary authority are involved here. If a literary discourse gains authority almost exclusively from a proletarian and/or antiracist movement, it becomes difficult, if not impossible, for the literary critic to see any issues beyond these movements. For example, in Baldwin's love story between a black and white man in their Paris exile in *Giovanni's Room*, the critic cannot find anything more than a well-written, thrillingly extravagant, but basically very questionable and even "decadent" piece of fiction—a private tragedy without the power of a general message. In the G.D.R., sexuality, in spite of Marx, was tacitly considered a private affair as long as it was not directly connected with social issues as in *Blues for Mister Charlie*. Yet even that play had to be "freed of its sexual overtones" in order to get its "real" message across to the public, so as to not divert the audience from the true message, when it was staged in Rostock as well as in Leipzig in 1968.[6]

How much the reception of almost any literature in East Germany was influenced by the tradition of the social protest novel of the 1930s and by the aesthetic concept of Lukacs can perhaps best be exemplified by a statement by Karl-Heinz Wirzberger, who was dean of American Studies in the G.D.R. at the time: Baldwin's three novels—*Go Tell It on the Mountain*, *Giovanni's Room*, and *Another Country*—are proof enough "that there are hardly any bridges that connect Baldwin to the tradition of black literature up to the Second World War."[7] Accordingly, the great African-American novel that could be considered on par with *Native Son* and could continue the tradition of the 1920s and 1930s had yet to be written. Ironically, criticism of this sort had an unintended effect; it led other, mostly younger scholars to explore Baldwin's original texts and come to their own, different conclusions, just as it was common practice for theater-goers to interpret harsh criticism in the leading daily *Neues Deutschland* as a clue that they should rush to see what was likely to be an interesting performance before it was banned.

The all-inclusive synecdoche of East Germany and socialism in general was the notion of the historic mission of the proletariat, which would, in a linear historical process, eventually lead to universal freedom. As its realization, naturally, was located in the future, the

6. Brüning, "Probleme der Rezeption," 184.
7. Karl-Heinz Wirzberger, "Probleme der Bürgerrechtsbewegung in der amerikanischen Prosaliteratur der Gegenwart," in *Vom Cooper bis O'Neill. Beiträge zur USA-Literatur*, ed. idem (Berlin, 1979), 174.

all-inclusive paradoxically turned into an instrument of exclusion—
an exclusion of otherness that did not seem to contribute to this
goal. Utz Riese once called this the 'failure of synecdoche.' To my
mind, the burden of synecdoche on the minds of the people who
were supposed to carry it through was a fatal ideological burden.
For a long time many of us accepted and carried this burden, until
we learned to recognize it for what it was and began to shift it, if not
drop it altogether. Slowly and cautiously, changes toward broader,
more inclusive conceptions of realism and social and cultural reality came forward.

In his afterword (writing afterwords for literary publications was
a common and accepted, even desired, practice in the G.D.R.) for
the 1968 publication of *Go Tell It on the Mountain*, Karl-Heinz Schönfelder defended the novel against earlier criticism by explaining it
as a "realistic portrayal" of the life of a black family in the first three
decades of this century.[8] Interestingly enough, he also accepted the
female characters as victims both of racial and sexual oppression.
Eberhard Brüning, in his introduction of *American Dramas of Five
Decades* in 1968, describes plays by Baldwin, LeRoi Jones (Amiri
Baraka), Lorraine Hansberry, and other black writers as "a source
of genuine vital and dramatic impulses ... since what they bring
onto the stage is nothing invented, accidental, or individualistically
divertive [*sic*] but sober and even terrible reality."[9]

More complex changes in critical literary reception were related
to new developments in the literary discourse at the beginning of
the 1970s. There were, among others, scholars from the Central
Institute for Literary History in Berlin like Werner Krauss, Robert
Weimann, Manfred Naumann, and Werner Mittenzwei, who engaged themselves in the development of new theories that ap-
proached literature in terms of dialectics, such as Weimann's
notion of "past significance and present meaning," of the changing
historical function of literature, and of reader response. These
efforts resulted in the liberation from older dogmatic standards
and allowed for more inclusive approaches to literary texts. A climate developed in which realism was not only redefined in such a
way as to embrace a far wider specter of literary techniques, but also

8. Karl-Heinz Schönfelder, "Nachwort," in *Gehe hin und verkünde es vom Berge*, J.
Baldwin (Berlin, 1968), 319, 322.

9. Eberhard Brüning, "Einleitung," in *Amerikansche Dramen aus fünf Jahrzehnten*,
ed. idem (Berlin, 1968), 14. See also Bernhard Scheller's analysis of the 1968 productions of *Blues for Mister Charlie*, in *Studien zum amerikanischen Drama nach dem
zweiten Weltkrieg*, eds. E. Bruning, K. Köhler, and B. Scheller (Berlin, 1977), 259–264.

to include a much more complex and diversified notion of reality than was perceived before. It became possible to seriously discuss avant-gardism as well as naturalism and modernism, and, a little later in the 1980s, even postmodernism, as "adequate" modes of writing. In general, literature was studied more in its historical, functional, and communicative aspects. The reception of black writers did not remain outside of these developments. Baldwin's basic concept of love and acceptance, for example, was no longer rejected as irrational mysticism. Acceptance became seen as the awareness of a historical process in the course of which Africans had become African Americans. This awareness, again, was seen as a prerequisite in a search for strategies to change the unacceptable reality that was the outcome of that process. For, in Baldwin's words: "To accept one's past—one's history—is not the same thing as drowning in it, it is learning how to use it."[10] (How true for so many of us today.) Equally, his notion of love was recognized as a concept closely connected with "responsibility" *(A Rap on Race)*, a responsibility to restore human community as Martin Luther King, Jr. argued, and also as the moving force in all his novels. Baldwin's idea of a genuine humanism was then much more compatible with the general trend toward ideological and cultural differentiation in East Germany. Baldwin's most intense internalization and individualization of social and cultural conflict eventually became recognized as an expression of his struggle to come to terms with an oppressive reality. Similarly, the problem of identity, which moves much of his work, in the 1980s raised sympathetic responses. In fact, an increasing number of G.D.R. citizens saw themselves confronted with problems of identity and were therefore able to identify with an author like Baldwin.

Significantly, Baldwin's two novels with the largest readership in the 1980s were *Another Country* and *Giovanni's Room*. They were first published in East Germany in 1977 and 1981 respectively; in contrast to *If Beale Street Could Talk* (published in 1976), both novels had second printings. As the availability of printing paper was severely limited, second printings implied postponement or even cancellation of other publications and were therefore hard to achieve. In the

10. James Baldwin, *The Fire Next Time* (Harmondsworth, 1965), 71. A first attempt toward a more constructive understanding of Baldwin's texts was made by Friederike Hajek, *Das Identitätsproblem im Befreiungskampf der afroamerikanischen USA-Bürger und seine Widerspiegelung in Selbstzeugnisssen der sechziger Jahre* (Ph.D. diss., Universität Potsdam, 1974). The dissertation was under the guidance of H. Wüstenhagen; although my analysis clearly contradicted his own, he did nothing to discourage me.

case of *Giovanni's Room,* a second edition of forty thousand, which was very large for a population of only sixteen million, sold out within a few weeks time. Baldwin was appreciated for his highly sensitive yet reckless will to explore the most intimate, most vulnerable, and most tabooed regions of human relations, particularly for his fictional treatment of sexuality, and specifically homosexuality as a valid manifestation of human love. Bernhard Scheller, in his afterword on *Giovanni's Room,* was able to eventually do justice to this formerly much criticized aspect of Baldwin's work,[11] as had Norbert Krenzlin, though more cautiously, in his afterword on *Another Country* some years before.[12]

Equally well-received were a number of other black authors, mostly women, all during the 1980s when questions of gender became more widely discussed: Toni Morrison, Alice Walker, Paule Marshall, Ntozake Shange, Ernest J. Gaines, and others. Publication and reception of African-American literature—and of foreign literature, including American literature, in general—had moved, in the 1970s and 1980s, far beyond its earlier dogmatic restrictions. Along the way, the notion of multiculturality had—in practice, if not in official propaganda—abandoned its narrow definition in terms of proletarian internationalism. The publication of Richard Wright's *The Outsider* or *American Hunger,* or of Ralph Ellison's *Invisible Man,* however, would have to wait another five years or so before political changes in the publication industry would allow for the publication of clearly anti-communist writing.

Interestingly, after the fall of the Wall, reader interest changed considerably. Before, reading foreign literature was, for many people, a sort of substitute for traveling. It was a way of imaginative traveling to a world outside the narrow confines of Eastern Europe. It had the fascination of a spiritual experience of otherness. Almost immediately after the opening of the Wall, people started to look for travel literature, exotic cookbooks, and the like. In other words, they were ready to grab the long-desired opportunity to go and see for themselves, to turn from imaginative traveling to the real experience of multiculturality. Needless to say, such experience is a necessary prerequisite to replace self-righteous provincialism with a broader, more sophisticated, and more receptive acceptance of otherness in our not yet well-developed multicultural society of the new Germany.

11. Bernard Scheller, "Stichwörter statt eines Nachworts," in *Giovannis Zimmer,* J. Baldwin (Leipzig, 1981), 161–186.
12. Nobert Krenzlin, "Nachwort," in *Eine andere Welt,* J. Baldwin (Berlin, 1977), 509–519.

8. American Studies East and West: A Multicultural Project?

Catrin Gersdorf

The nonacademic realities in both Germany and the United States are full of cultural, political, social, and economic conflicts which demand a sound and sober discussion in a conference on "Multiculturalism in Transit," rather than an apparently vain self-reflexive discourse on the unification of an academic field. However, the concept of multiculturalism includes the discussion of intracultural as well as intercultural aspects. Assuming that forty years of different political, economic, and social developments in East and West Germany have finally led to previously unthought of cultural differences such as mentality, behavioral patterns, language practices, etc., the project of German unification is not only a political and economic experiment but also a multicultural project. Part of this project was (and still is) the adaptation of East German schools to the West German educational system, including, of course, the academic system. "Adaptation," according to the American Heritage Dictionary, being defined as "change in behavior of a person or group in response or adjustment to new or modified surroundings" has been dominating the East German experience.

In 1989/90 East Germany opted for adaptation to democratic capitalism rather than to democratic socialism out of fear of exclusion from the material wealth of Western consumerism, which is certainly a sign of the political and cultural indifference of consumerist desires. But is this representative of an overall cultural indifference? Does that mean that forty years of economic and political differences have had no effect whatsoever on other realms of society? For instance, does the fact that East and West Germans share 99 percent of the German lexicon mean that they speak the same language? In light of the subject of this paper the question reads: is there a specifically East German tradition of academic discourse(s)? Has East German American Studies developed a unique language different from contemporary West German American Studies? These are the questions that inspired the following argument. According to Charles Taylor, a "discourse of recognition"[1] is the precondition for identity formation in a truly multicultural society. Therefore, I would like to provide with this essay a venue for a discourse of recognition of forty years of American Studies in the G.D.R. In a larger context, this might shed some light on what looks like the almost unconditional surrender of East Germany to economic, social, and political structures, which are themselves debatable.

My thesis is that East Germany lacked an *institutionalized* intellectual power, which could have functioned as an effective corrective to the immense political, social, and cultural strains of unification. American Studies cannot exclude itself from a critical retrospective of East Germany's intellectual past even though the field was a negligible factor in the equation between state politics and the academia. Although the exclusion of large parts of the East German academic community from the institution cannot be undone, the critical memory of forty years of academic endeavors behind the "Iron Curtain" can help those who remained in the institution (and here I speak about East *and* West Germans) to at least partly undo the process of mere adaptation to the West German system. I say partly because the adaptation to academic structures has been finished by now, but the adaptation of the histories of the various academic fields can still be substituted by a process of integration in the best sense of the word. This is certainly not an easy task, especially since it cannot be the purpose of such a venture either to point at the failure of individual men or women (all East German intellectuals who had kept their places in academic institutions have arranged themselves with the system) nor to fall into to the trap of a collective self-justifying gesture ("after all, we haven't done so bad").

This contribution does not advocate the preservation of an ideologized version of Marxism. It will rather point to the fact that the erosion of the presumed solidity of Marxist theory and its decrystallization as the only legitimate methodological basis for institutionalized criticism had begun long before the implosion of socialism. It

1. Charles Taylor, *Multiculturalism and "The Politics of Recognition"* (Princeton, 1992), 37.

has repeatedly been argued that the inability or the unwillingness (or rather a combination of the two) to modernize and decrystalize Marxist thinking was one of the major reasons for the disappearance of a distinct East German academia. My argument (and my contribution to the discourse of recognition) will be that the condition of the field as a whole has been marked by a methodological dilemma during the last fifteen years or so before unification. A short review of the history of the field will explain further.

American Studies in the G.D.R. was part of the ensemble of the Marxist-Leninist *Literaturwissenschaften*. The conventional translation of that German term into English as "literary criticism or theory" does not work here because it would blur the underlying ideological implication. A scientific *Weltanschauung* based on Marxism-Leninism was the educational doctrine. Science delivered the model for how the "socialist personality" was to conceive the world. In this context the arts and the sciences had more or less the same social function: both had to picture "objective reality," in other words, the expected result of both endeavors was the *Abbild* (the mimetic rendition) of reality. According to these premises the major task for "literary science" was to reveal the laws of this production process and evaluate a work of art according to its success or failure to depict social processes. Translated into the realm of American Studies, this meant the concentration on so-called progressive aspects of the literature, culture, and history of the United States. This included—to name just one not so obvious historical example—the discussion of the antifeudal, anti-British War of Independence and the writing that prepared and accompanied it, but also the discussion of the literature and culture of the so-called "other" America (working-class literature, black-American literature under the premise that black Americans are a suppressed class), and—last but not least—the discussion of the realist tradition in American literature.[2] The limits of such an approach are obvious and need no further discussion, because it would only add to the all too well-known stereotype of G.D.R. academia as a completely ideologized, monolithic bloc. A short mentioning of that early stage of East German American Studies was, however, necessary not only to appreciate the project of including otherwise neglected authors (such as for instance Albert Maltz) or historical phenomenons (such as the 1930s drama

2. I owe these insights to Robert Weimann, "Literaturwissenschaft und historisch-materialistische Theorie: Aktuelle Fragen der Entwicklung der Literaturtheorie und Methodologie in der Anglistik-Amerikanistik," *Zeitschrift für Anglistik und Amerikanistik* 1 (1980): 12–31.

and the impact of the writers congresses of the 1930s) into the text of American literary history, but first of all to fully grasp the complicated attempt of East German Americanists to expand the methodological terrain of Marxist theory (in other words to modify its prescriptive implications and reestablish it as an analytical instrument). I daresay that this process began as early as 1974, and it was not yet finished on the third of October 1990. Let me explain. The year 1974 marks the political and diplomatic recognition of the G.D.R. by the United States, an event that had a tremendous impact on the self-definition of East German American Studies. At this point of my argument, it is again Charles Taylor and his discussion of "the importance of external recognition" in the praxis of multiculturalism who provides the terminology. It is Taylor's conviction that the recognition of "the equal value of different cultures" does not only grant their survival but also the acknowledgment of "their *worth*."[3] Granted that culture is not only defined as an artistic representation of certain historical, political, and social realities, but a discursive process that is rooted in those realities, Taylor's definition can also be applied to *different political* cultures. Thus, the politics of recognition and the East-West dialogue that began to determine the political arena in the early 1970s increased the sense of identity and stability of East Germany (and presumably all other Eastern European countries).

Of course, that recognition did not change the political and ideological framework for academic work overnight, but it certainly had an impact on public discourse. The official image of the United States as the ultimate incarnation of imperialism and hence evil continued to be the leitmotif of the official discourse. On the occasion of the twenty-fifth anniversary of the foundation of the G.D.R. on 7 October 1974, Leonid Brezhnev stated that "the G.D.R., situated on the border between the two systems, is particularly exposed to the damaging influence of imperialism."[4] In this situation, the critical discussion of the literature of the United States was, according to Maurice Mendelson, one of the leading Soviet Americanists (and thus a legitimizing authority for his East German colleagues), an appropriate means to counteract the supposed devastating influence of imperialism. In order to detect the political, ideological, and cultural weaknesses of the other system, the field was opened up

3. Charles Taylor, *Multiculturalism*, 64.
4. As quoted in Maurice Mendelson, "Einige Bemerkungen zur Amerikanistik in der DDR," *Zeitschrift für Anglistik und Amerikanistik* 3 (1975): 190. Unless otherwise noted, all translations are my own.

to those authors and phenomenons outside a proletarian and/or realistic literary tradition, such as the literary traditions of the American renaissance and modernism/postmodernism.

Yet despite the continued skepticism towards all things nonsocialist, the external recognition of socialism's worth as a partner in a diplomatic dialogue allowed for the presumption (or should I rather say illusion?) by one critic of a "higher level of the social and individual consciousness"[5] among the people. This belief, in turn, was seen as the precondition for the ability of individual East German readers to establish a critical distance to works of art rooted in totally different social structures and ideological positions. Whether this presumption, stated in an article on the topic of "U.S.-American literature in the G.D.R. since 1965," should be read as an expression of ideological opportunism by its author or as an intellectual gimmick, for which the author used the official language of the powerful, is hard to determine today. In any case, it speaks of the attempt to open the gate for a wider range of academic work and to include "works from a different social structure and ideological position"[6] into the canon of American literature that could be published, read, and taught in the G.D.R. Writers as diverse as Henry David Thoreau, William Faulkner, Henry Miller, Gertrude Stein, F. Scott Fitzgerald, Jack Kerouac, Ken Kesey, Charles Bukowsky, Joyce Carol Oates, James Baldwin, John Updike, Joseph Heller, Susan Sontag, Thomas Pynchon, Leslie Marmon Silko, and Toni Morrison give evidence of the multiple voices that could be heard behind the now semipermeable Iron Curtain.

This multilayered list speaks of the introduction of other cultural expressions, different aesthetic concepts, and new philosophical ideas to the East German reading public; a process that was certainly encouraged and supported by Americanists in the academy (most of whom cooperated with publishers as editors, authors of afterwords, or even translators). The process was accompanied by theoretical innovations (or rather modifications) in the writings of East German American Studies. In an article entitled "Literaturwissenschaft und historisch-materialistische Theorie," published in 1980, Robert

---

5. Eberhard Brüning, "U.S.-amerikanische Literatur in der DDR seit 1965," *Zeitschrift für Anglistik und Amerikanistik* 4 (1980): 293–94.

6. Ibid., 293–94. The full passage reads: "Das höhere Niveau des gesellschaftlichen wie individuellen Bewußtseins ermöglichte zudem nicht nur die differenzierte Erfassung der eigenen, komplizierter gewordenen Umwelt, sondern förderte auch die Fähigkeit zur kritischen Distanz und klassenmäßigen Wertung von Werken ganz anderer sozialer Strukturen und ideologischer Positionen."

Weimann considered the emerging interest in social theory in the West (triggered by the protest movements of the 1960s and 1970s) ample reason for a sound examination and reevaluation of the theoretical framework of East German literary criticism (especially, of course, the criticism of English and American literature). His main point was to modify the critique of the mimetic function of literature and integrate its communicative function into the theoretical discourse of Marxist literary criticism. The literary work was no longer to be seen as a mere reflection of a sociohistorical status quo, rather it was to be conceived of as an object and agent of aesthetic education and communication. Even though this was the farewell to a rather static view of literature, its sociopolitical and ideological function was still implied as the most important evaluative criterion.[7] Now, what impact did this modification of Marxist literary theory as demanded by Robert Weimann in 1980 have on the praxis of literary criticism in East German American Studies? As far as I can see, two major tendencies can be identified.

First, some critics continued to emphasize literature's epistemological function as more important than its aesthetic and communicative functions. They examined American literature with regard to its social and historical content. In this vein, literature was merely seen as the reflex of "objective reality," and, in turn, the examination of the sociohistorical context in which a work of literature was produced granted the understanding of a literary text as well as the text of literary history. In order to differentiate between naturalism and realism, one critic argues, it does not help just to read the two literary modes in opposition to tendencies of "sentimentalism and pseudoromanticism" in late nineteenth-century literature.[8] It is also necessary to "recognize the working-class movement as the true basis of social movements" and thoughts of the time.[9] Against this

7. Robert Weimann, "Literaturwissenschaft und historisch-materialistische Theorie: Aktuelle Fragen der Entwicklung der Literaturtheorie und Methodologie in der Anglistik-Amerikanistik," *Zeitschrift für Anglistik und Amerikanistik* 1 (1980): 12–31. The passage that I paraphrased reads: "Dennoch hat die Kritik an der Widerspiegelungstheorie wie an der geschichtsphilosophischen Ästhetik einen produktiven Aspekt: Sie unterstreicht die Tatsache, daß der mimetische Aspekt der literarischen Tätigkeit nur die eine Seite (und nur ein Gegenstand) literaturhistorischer Arbeit ist, worüber der soziale und kommunikative Funktionszusammenhang, in dem die Texte stehen, sowie ihr Systemcharakter nicht ins Hintertreffen geraten dürfen."

8. Heinz Wüstenhagen, "American Literary Naturalism and the Anti-Imperialist Movement and Thought," *Zeitschrift für Anglistik und Amerikanistik* 4 (1983): 345–47.

9. Ibid., 345.

background, realism and naturalism can be read as a literary response "to the [social] spirit of the decade [the 1890s]." The logical conclusion of this argument is that since American literary naturalism can be "considered as the first broad movement to express strong anti-imperialist sentiments in a generalized and innovative aesthetic manner," it can be interpreted as a "literary expression of revolutionary class consciousness."[10] This argument is a fine example of how the deterministic fatalism of the naturalists is given a revolutionary twist and thus has been appropriated for a socialist reception. It also shows the relative vitality of a modified *Abbildtheorie*.

Another example may illustrate my argument from a somewhat different angle. In 1986, *Zeitschrift für Anglistik und Amerikanistik* published an essay entitled "The Productivity of Native American Myths in Gerald Vizenor."[11] This essay is certainly to be appreciated for its attempt to introduce to academic discussion the complex web of Native-American mythology and contemporary literature. But still, the analysis and interpretation of Gerald Vizenor's writings is legitimized by the author's political and social activism within and by the influence of the black civil rights movement on the Native-American renaissance. The "productivity" of American-Indian mythology is not interpreted as a cultural and aesthetic productivity rooted in the spiritual and mnemonic strength of mythological texts, but rather as a productivity rooted in the sociopolitical involvement of its protagonists. For example, the function of Nanabush, the trickster figure, is quoted as meaningful, because "he always came to the assistance of the oppressed and the weak."[12] The essay does not analyze narrative strategies nor the breakup of realist traditions in the postmodern novels by one of the most prominent Native-American writers.

As to the second tendency: if it were possible to relate (or reduce?) the aesthetics of naturalism/realism and the ethno-aesthetic aspects of Native- (and black) American literature to social aspects of literary production and reception, this interpretative strategy became more and more difficult for those critics dealing with the aesthetic impact of modernist/postmodernist narrative strategies and theories on the literature of the 1960s, 1970s, and 1980s. As compared to the novels of the 1950s, one critic detects "sharper

10. Ibid., 347.
11. Helga Lumer, "Die Produktivität indianischer Mythen bei dem Chippewa-Autor Gerald Vizenor," *Zeitschrift für Anglistik und Amerikanistik* 1 (1986): 60–64.
12. Basil Johnson, *Ojibwa Heritage* (Toronto, 1979), in Lumer, 61.

social contours"[13] in the novel of the 1960s and 1970s. Although the novels of that period give away "an intensely critical engagement of the writers" and "appeal to human understanding, love, and human decency," they also "reveal a deep sense of helplessness." This is—according to the critic—"an essentially abstract form of humanism." And the conclusion of this analysis: "if social change as a prerequisite to achieving a tolerable situation for the individual and self-realization are implied at all, then only in very vague and abstract terms."[14]

The article attempts an unconditional recognition of the essential "otherness" of American literature and aims to rescue a literature that does not fit into the normative prerequisites of Marxist ideology for the general reading public in the G.D.R. The following sentence from the same essay may serve as an example for the discursive tightrope walking of East German American Studies in the 1980s and further illustrates my point. Referring to the counterculture, its literary explorations are described as "essentially emotional, individualistic, but radical in their challenge of the Establishment," and they are seen as "issued from an earnest quest for self-fulfillment and a harmonious life in love and happiness."[15] In the vein of Marxist ideology, the "emotional" and "individual" are questioned as an acceptable means to cause social change; yet the nonrational and the noncollective are recognized as "a radical challenge of the Establishment."[16] In this context, it is not surprising that the author, Ken Kesey, is given a highly sympathetic treatment by the critic. McMurphy's (the main character in Kesey's novel *One Flew Over the Cuckoo's Nest*) "individuality and anarchic resistance to Big Nurse and the combine" are highly praised, but the author is accused of ending up "playing power games" and thus "diverting many from meaningful social action."[17]

Here we have what can be called the classical dilemma of late socialism's intellectuals: the textual representations of individualism and anarchy are (cautiously) admired, but they are presented as devoid of meaning which—in contrast—can only be found in social action. In other words, *meaning* is not recognized as the product of linguistic and/or cultural activities, rather only of social activities.

13. Eva Manske, "Individual and Society in Contemporary American Fiction," *Zeitschrift für Anglistik und Amerikanistik* 4 (1980): 322.
14. Ibid.
15. Ibid.
16. Ibid., 323.
17. Ibid., 326.

The same kind of sympathetic criticism can be detected in a reading of Northrop Frye's *Anatomy of Criticism*, published in 1988.[18] Frye's retreat from the historicity of literature and literary theory into metahistorical, timeless myths and archetypal symbols is heavily criticized, but at the same time the article concedes to Frye's theory that literative yearns for a transcendence of a fragmented and atomized world and the attempted establishment of a holistic vision of the world.[19] The article's ideological critique of Northrop Frye is not only supplemented by a psychologically sanctioned comment but, in a way, neutralized by it.

These articles show quite clearly the theoretical as well as the social dilemma of East German American Studies in the 1980s. On the one hand, they reveal a great deal of sympathy for the literature and theories discussed. On the other hand, they speak of a more and more obvious collision of the critical praxis of Marxism with its own theoretical prerequisites. Although praxis is—according to Marxist theory—the field where a theory has to prove its validity, literary theory in East Germany did not take the next step and question the practicality of Marxist categories for the interpretation of a reality totally different from Marx's late nineteenth-century experience. The limitation was always seen within the literature, the literary text, or the author and not with one's own theoretical premises. More and more, East German Americanists found themselves caught in a paradoxical situation. It was the same paradox that Robert Weimann had criticized in Northrop Frye's differentiation between the theorist of literature and the consumer of literature who are "not the same at all, even when they co-exist in the same man"[20] (or woman, as a few colleagues would have added even then). What

18. Marianne Müller, "'A self-contained universe': Zur mythologisch-archetypischen Literaturbetrachtung von Northrop Frye," *Zeitschift für Anglistik und Amerikanistik* 3 (1988): 227–34.

19. Müller, "'A self-contained universe,'" 232. The passage in question: "Aus der Krisenhaftigkeit der gesellschaftshistorischen Entwicklung des Imperialismus, aus der Erschüterung des Ideals bürgerlicher Demokratie—schockierend und bewußt geworden durch faschistische Diktatur und McCarthyism, 2. Weltkrieg und Indochinakrieg, Kommerzialisierung der Kultur und Mißbrauch der Sprache zur Bewußtseinsmanipulierung—erfolgt ein Rückzug aus der Geschichtlichkiet der Literatur und der Literaturwissenschaft in metahistorisch-zeitlose Mythen und Ursymbole. Die Hinwendung zur Mythologie offenbart zugleich die Sehnsucht nach Überwindung der fragmentierten und atomisierten Welt in einem ganzheitlichen Weltempfinden wie auch den Versuch der Auflösung des im New Criticism isolierten Literaturwerkes in einem einheitlichen 'mythological or imaginative universe.'"

20. Robert Weimann, *Literaturgeschichte und Mythologie: Methodologische und historische Studien* (Frankfurt/Main , 1977): 294.

Weimann criticizes in Frye's theorem is that he gives credit to theory over praxis, and to the critical system over the critical activity. The consequence of such rationalizing was a split between the social function of literary criticism and its theoretical function[21] and thus an affront to the Marxist theorem of the unity of theory and praxis. That it was exactly this split that Marxist literary criticism suffered from in late socialism is an irony of history and explains the silence of East German American Studies during the first five years of German postcommunist unity.

21. Weimann, *Literaturgeschichte und Mythologie*, 294. "Hier wird die Theorie gegen die Praxis, das kritische System gegen das wertende Tun abgesichert. Die Folge dieser Absicherung besteht in einer der bürgerlichen Gesellschaft des 19. Jahrhunderts unbekannten Aufspaltung zwischen den gesellschaftlichen und den wissenschaftlichen Funktionen der Literaturkritik."

9. Transnational American Studies: Negotiating Cultures of Difference— Multicultural Identities, Communities, and Border Discourses

Günter H. Lenz

Multiculturalism and the Culture Concept in German and U.S.-American Society: Comparative Perspectives

Since the 1980s, debates on multiculturalism and minority discourses have played a crucial role both in the general public and in academia in the United States. In recent years, the issues have also been taken up, though in a more subdued manner, in Germany. As a German scholar who has taught American Studies at German universities for more than two decades, I have had to realize, however, that the same terms that traveled from the United States to Germany have taken on different meanings, reacting to a different social and cultural situation and performing different functions in the discourse of cultural heterogeneity.[1] The recent controversies over the meanings of multiculturalism have revealed the strikingly different and conflicting understanding of the foundations and the boundaries of Western nation-states and cultures, of their ways of recognizing, accepting, or incorporating other cultures, and of

1. For a concise and pertinent analysis of the German discourse on multiculturalism as a case of "traveling theory," written from the perspective of cultural anthropology, see Gisela Welz, "Multikulturelle Diskurse: Topoi der Differenzerfahrung in Deutschland und den Vereinigten Staaten," *Amerikastudien/American Studies* 38 (1993), 265–72.

their ways of dealing with cultural heterogeneity within their societies. The question is—if I may propose a somewhat schematic opposition—if these nation-states define their "own" culture in clear contradistinction to "other" cultures and try to "keep them out," allowing only for selective acculturation by individuals and granting of citizenship, or if they conceive of their own culture as always having been constituted in a multicultural and intercultural manner.

A country such as Germany has traditionally defined its national culture as more or less homogeneous and—in contradistinction, however, to other European countries such as France—based its notion of the nation-state and the right to citizenship primarily on *ius sanguinis* (descent). During the nineteenth century a notion of ethnos as homogeneous cultural identity was used to legitimize a form of ethnic nationalism that was seen as transcending social differences and political conflicts and that—as a powerful unifying political ideology—turned heterogeneous or ethnically different groups of people living within the borders of the German nation-state, or entering its national territory, into (unwanted) "ethnic minorities" who were forced to assimilate or be expelled.[2] Therefore, the impact of global migrations, of successive waves of millions of foreign workers, and of people seeking asylum during the last decades, as well as the repercussions of the common labor market of the European Community, have forced Germans—in spite of strong opposition not exclusively from conservative quarters—to challenge and hopefully to reject this closed concept of culture and

2. For a historical account and critical analysis of the highly problematical implications of the German notion of the "ethnic nation-state" (*Volksnation*) or "ethnic nationalism" and a discussion of alternative foundations of a "politically constituted nation-state" (*Staatsbürgernation*) or "civic nationalism," see, e.g., Friedrich Heckmann, "Ethnos, Demos und Nation, oder: Woher stammt die Intoleranz des Nationalstaats gegenüber ethnischen Minderheiten?" in *Das Eigene und das Fremde*, ed. Uli Bielfeld (Hamburg, 1991), 51–78; Wolfgang Kaschuba, "Nationalismus und Ethnozentrismus: Zur kulturellen Ausgrenzung ethnischer Gruppen in (deutscher) Geschichte und Gegenwart," in *Grenzfälle: Über neuen und alten Nationalismus*, eds. Michael Jeismann and Henning Ritter (Leipzig, 1993), 239–73, 378–80; Claus Leggewie, "Ethnizität, Nationalismus und multikulturelle Gesellschaft," in *Nationales Bewußtsein und kollektive Identität: Studien zur Entwicklung des kollektiven Bewußtseins in der Neuzeit*, ed. Helmut Berding, vol. 2 (Frankfurt/Main, 1994), 46–65; and Dan Diner, "Nationalstaat und Migration: Zu Begriff und Geschichte," in *Politik der Multikultur: Vergleichende Perspektiven zu Einwanderung und Integration*, eds. Mechthild M. Jansen and Sigrid Baringhorst (Baden-Baden, 1994), 17–30 (Diner rejects the clean-cut opposition of *Demos* and *Ethnos* and distinguishes between *Ethnie*, as cultural memory of every people or nation, and *Ethnos*, as cultural homogeneity based on common descent.) Unless otherwise noted, all translations are my own.

fully acknowledge the reality of having become an immigrant country and of having to revise the restrictive notion of citizenship and face the problems of a multicultural society.[3] The strong emphasis on questions of citizenship and social policies concerning foreigners living in Germany that has dominated German debates on multiculturalism has often led, however, to a reductive understanding of the fundamental challenges to traditional notions of society that multicultural theory has tried to articulate in American cultural studies, anthropology, historiography, political studies, and minority discourses. Therefore, the discourse on multiculturalism in Germany should not be reduced to the problem of the integration of foreign workers (*Gastarbeiter/innen*) and their descendants born in Germany[4] or of other, foreign ethnic groups into the ethnically "homogeneous" German society, nor to the polemical rejection of multiculturalism as a fashionable exoticism in culinary or musical taste.[5] Nor should the emphasis on intercultural differences too quickly be read as simply a questionable culturalist displacement of social and political inequalities.

3. The public debate on multiculturalism in Germany has often been conducted in the political realm in terms of the question, if "we" *want* a multicultural society or not. A critical analysis of these debates and a proposal for realizing "a multicultural society in an emancipatory perspective" is offered by Axel Schulte in his essay "Multikulturelle Gesellschaft: Chance, Ideologie oder Bedrohung?" *Aus Politik und Zeitgeschichte* 23/24 (1990): 3–15. A more skeptical assessment of the foundations and the political potential (or dangers) of (the German versions of) multiculturalism (and the program of "multicultural or intercultural education") is Frank-Olaf Radtke's "Lob der Gleich-Gültigkeit: Zur Konstruktion des Fremden im Diskurs des Multikulturalismus," in *Das Eigene und das Fremde*, ed. Uli Bielefeld (Hamburg, 1991), 79–96. The most wide-ranging critical accounts of a politics of multiculturalism, or multicultural politics, are Claus Leggewie, *Multi Kulti: Spielregeln für die Vielvölkerrepublik* (Berlin, 1990); his essay "Vom Deutschen Reich zur Bundesrepublik—und nicht zurück: Zur politischen Gestalt einer multikulturellen Gesellschaft," in *Schwierige Fremdheit: Über Integration und Ausgrenzung in Einwanderungsländern*, eds. Friedrich Balke, Rebecca Habermas, Patrizia Nanz, and Peter Sillem (Frankfurt/Main, 1993), 3–20; and the comparative studies in Mechthild M. Jansen and Sigrid Baringhorst, eds., *Politik der Multikultur*. For the most wide-ranging and challenging critical discussion of the political implications of the multiculturalism debate in the United States, see Berndt Ostendorf's essay "The Costs of Multiculturalism," *Working Paper No. 50* (1992), John F. Kennedy-Institut für Nordamerikastudien, Freie Universität Berlin, 1–30.
4. See, e.g., the critical essays in Hermann Bausinger, *Ausländer—Inländer: Arbeitsmigration und kulturelle Identität* (Tübingen, 1986).
5. A brief analysis of the controversies in Germany for or against a *multikulturelle Gesellschaft* is given by Welz, "Multikulturelle Diskurse," 267–71. She also points out that in contradistinction to the United States, representatives of the "immigrant groups" or women rarely have taken part in the debate as yet.

The charge of culturalism is a valid critique of versions of multicultural theory that offer "cultural diversity" instead of structural change and that are based on closed concepts of culture characterized by stable, quasi-inherent traits in values and behavior of more or less homogeneous traditional ethnic groups.[6] But the critique of multiculturalism as a culturalist displacement of the "real" structural inequalities in society often tends to rely on a more or less clean-cut distinction among the various spheres of modern societies such as the economy, politics, and culture which are no longer adequate for conceptualizing the complex and heteronomous social processes, interactions, and representations in post-Fordist, postmodern Western societies that force us to reconceptualize the notions of culture and the political, of multicultural identities and communities in crucial ways. Multicultural discourse in Germany must deal with the questions of the social and political organization of cultural heterogeneity, of the constitution and the political repercussions (and also the potential) of intra- and intercultural differences, and of the dimensions and new manifestations of public culture. These are the inescapable consequences of recent globalizing, transnational, as well as localizing processes of economic, social, and cultural mediations, but they have taken on a specific urgency and a unique historical configuration in the difficult processes of "reunification" of West and East Germany after the demise of the German Democratic Republic.[7]

Obviously, the political, social, and cultural questions addressed in public and scholarly debates on the theory and the practical consequences of a multicultural society cannot be answered in the context of a nation-state or a national culture, but ask for a comparative, intercultural approach. The political as well as the theoretical issues of multiculturalism in the United States often have polemically been rephrased in terms of "inside" vs. "outside," in terms of "synthesis" or "core culture" vs. "fragmentation," or as an

6. For a powerful critique of "culturalism" as a displacement of social conflicts in current discourses of the humanities and social sciences as well as particularly dangerous "strategies of political instrumentalization" of notions of cultural "purity" and the "invention of ethnicity" for purposes of legitimizing political power and new "nation-states," see Wolfgang Kaschuba, "Kulturalismus: Vom Verschwinden des Sozialen im gesellschaftlichen Diskurs," in *Kulturen—Identitäten—Diskurse: Perspektiven Europäischer Ethnologie*, ed. idem (Berlin, 1995), 11–30.
7. An interesting reading of the problems of the "reunification" of Germany after 1989 in terms of the challenges of a "German-German multiculturalism" is offered by Dieter Thomä in his essay "Multikulturalismus, Demokratie, Nation: Zur Philosophie der deutschen Einheit," *Deutsche Zeitschrift für Philosophie* 43 (1995): 349–63.

instance of fashionable "postmodern" commodification. And, in its "affirmative" versions, multiculturalism has frequently been fixed in a simple reversal of valorization of the old oppositions and dichotomies of dualistic thinking. However, in its more radical and multifaceted positionalities and strategies, American multicultural discourse has offered, and continues to offer, challenging ways of reconceptualizing the social construction of the culture concept and its political implications in Germany.

American multicultural critique, in its most productive and provocative forms, i.e., forms of critical multiculturalism beyond liberal pluralism as well as beyond ethnic or racial absolutism and essentializing interest politics, is motivated by an *open* concept of culture and by a notion of a "civic nation-state" (*Staatsbürgernation* —M. Rainer Lepsius) that bases the right to citizenship, with some important qualifications, on *ius soli,* on the country of birth and/or extended residence. As argued and elaborated in minority discourses or in studies by American historians such as Joan W. Scott, David Hollinger, or Lawrence W. Levine, it attempts to account for the *inherent* diversity and complexity of what is called "American culture" (or American cultures in the plural) and for their social and political repercussions in the political culture(s) of the United States. However, it is crucial to realize that this exceptional complexity and diversity of American culture cannot be adequately grasped in a "nationalist" discourse limited to the boundaries of the United States—an attempt all too often found in contributions to the multiculturalism debate—but is in its very dynamic also inherently intercultural and has to be analyzed in an explicitly transnational perspective.

Multicultural critique in this sense can also help Germans to recognize that "German culture" is not only becoming increasingly multicultural and intercultural, but that it has always been much less stable and homogeneous and much more heterogeneous and internally differentiated by various dimensions of multiculturality than adherents of the German closed culture concept have been willing to concede. American Studies in Germany can play an important role in mediating multicultural discourse in the postmodern and post-Fordist United States and the revisionary critical discourse on the meanings of and the social and political role of cultural differences and social heterogeneity in a reunited Germany and an expanding European Community.

However, if we take the historical context of this mediating role of American Studies in Germany seriously, we will realize that it asks

us to give up the traditional comparative or cross-cultural approach
to the study of cultures that isolates and decontextualizes some cultural traits for comparison or that compares two or more "whole"
cultures as discrete and separate units according to general or seemingly universal common criteria.[8] In the context of an increasingly
globalizing and interdependent world, cultures cannot be seen any
longer as closed systems characterized by a unity of their own; they
have lost clearly definable boundaries (if they ever had them at all)
and are heterogeneous, ever changing, interactive, and mutually
(re-)defining each other. Therefore, "comparative consciousness,"
as cultural anthropologist Laura Nader argues, must try to "illumi-
nate connections—between local and global, between past and present, between anthropologists and those they study, between uses of
comparison and implications of its uses."[9] We will also have to question the Eurocentric way of thinking that starts from the premise of
a self-contained meaningful entity called Europe, or the West, and
then analyzes other cultures in relationship to this Western frame of
reference (projected as universal). Let me briefly indicate two historical case studies that can make us aware of the mutual implications of "our" culture(s) and "other" cultures in the construction of
the Western and non-Western world and that explore the interactions of European and American constructions of the public representation of the politics of culture: first, the European invention of
"Europe" and the "West" at the beginning of the modern age and its
later history, and, second the Americanization of Western European countries after World War II.

First, the Enlightenment "project of modernity" (Habermas) has
not only been blind to its inherent racism, but in its conception and
realization it has been dependent on "othering" cultures outside
Europe as exotic, inferior, or primitive. The very "idea of Europe,"
as Cornel West has argued, was based on colonialism, on conquer-
ing cultures in other parts of the world, on enslaving and eliminat-
ing their populations and exploiting their resources. Therefore,
our idea of Europe is inherently heterogeneous, hybrid, and intercultural. "Europe is always already multicultural; after Napoleon,

---

8. The problems and the potential of comparative approaches in cultural anthropology are critically analyzed in Gisela Welz's essay on the "The Uses of Comparison,"
in which she points out the importance of the work by Laura Nader and indicates
some implications of the revised understanding of a comparative consciousness in
anthropology for transnational cultural studies (this volume, chap. 1, pp. 9–11).

9. Laura Nader, "Comparative Consciousness," in *Assessing Cultural Anthropology*,
ed. Robert Borofsky (New York, 1994), 86.

multinational ..."[10] "Imperial concerns" have been "constitutively significant to the culture of the modern West," and modernist culture cannot be understood without recognizing the "external pressures on Western society and culture" by the processes of "decolonization, resistance culture, and the literature of opposition to imperialism."[11] These processes of othering were reproduced within the cultures of Europe, the cultures of the West themselves. The cultures of the nation-states that have developed over the centuries have always been implicated in other cultures by drawing and redrawing boundaries, by defining and redefining external (as well as internal) differences, not only among the various European cultures, but also—through slave-trade, commerce, colonialism— in the cultures of other continents. "Borders and all," writes anthropologist Mary Louise Pratt in her fascinating book *Imperial Eyes: Travel Writing and Transculturation* (1992), describing this dialectical interrelationship between Europe and its others, between "reinventing America" and "reinventing Europe," "the entity called Europe was constructed from the outside in as much as from the inside out."[12] In important ways, as Paul Gilroy has shown, the concept and the repercussions of race have been at the very heart of English (or British) culture and discourse: "[R]acial slavery was integral to western civilisation and . . . the master/mistress/slave relationship . . . foundational to both black critiques and affirmations of modernity."[13]

Moving to my second case study, the debate about the Americanization of twentieth-century or post-Second World War Europe has to be seen not only as the question of the influence of U.S. (mass and consumer) culture on traditional European cultures but also as one of the more recent chapters in a long history of the European invention of "America" as its utopian *or* its dystopian other. By inventing and re-inventing America as the other, Europe again and again re-invented and reconstructed itself. Nor was post-Second World War Americanization a process that worked in the same way in the various European countries. Obviously, in important respects

10. Cornel West, "Beyond Eurocentrism and Multiculturalism," in *Beyond Eurocentrism and Multiculturalism*, vol. 2: *Prophetic Reflections* (Monroe, 1992), 121, cf. 115, 118, 120.

11. Edward W. Said, *Culture and Imperialism* (New York, 1993), 66, 188, 243.

12. Mary Louise Pratt, *Imperial Eyes: Travel Writing and Transculturation* (New York and London, 1992), 6.

13. Paul Gilroy, *The Black Atlantic: Modernity and Double Consciousness* (Cambridge, 1993), x.

West Germany is a special case with the "democratic re-education programs" designed for its population. Yet at a closer look we discover that many of the postwar cultural phenomena and new developments, which we as Europeans immediately tend to isolate and define as living proof of Americanization, must be understood as results of—often belated—processes of social and economic modernization that have characterized, in different ways, industrialized and postindustrial societies and cultures all over the (Western or Western-dominated) world. By identifying these transformations and their often unwanted social and cultural consequences as results of a kind of U.S. cultural imperialism, Europeans constructed them as outside influences, othered them as not being part of their "genuine" cultural and social heritage and identity, which they vainly attempted to hold onto or to reinvent as some kind of "imagined community" and home, ignoring the often powerful liberating impact American culture had in West European countries such as the Federal Republic of Germany.[14]

What these two case studies show are the complex, intricate, and highly politically charged interactions among cultures on a (potentially) global scale that transcend the boundaries of the modern nation-states and that constitute and reconstitute (national) cultures as inherently intercultural, multicultural, and transnational. If Cultural Studies in Germany wants to mediate and "transfer" the dynamic of multicultural critique in the United States to the different German situation in order to redefine and refocus the public discourse on the notion of culture, the nation-state, and the specific political and cultural implications of a *multikulturelle Gesellschaft* (multicultural society), they have to be careful in (re-)positioning their own critical discourse in relation to the American context. The questions I ask in looking at American Cultural Studies in the United States as a German American Studies scholar interested in the "comparative," intercultural project I described above is to identify those

14. It would be interesting to study in detail the role of phenomena, processes, and notions of "Americanization" in the culture and society of the German Democratic Republic and the changes brought about after 1989. For a short discussion of the deeply ambivalent use of the terms "Americanism" and "Americanization" in twentieth-century Germany and a detailed case study of the intricate interactions, the refractions of American and German modernism in West German culture after World War II, see my essay "Refractions of Modernity —Reconstituting Modernism in West Germany after World War II: Jackson Pollock, Ezra Pound, and Charlie Parker," in *Demokratie und Kunst in Amerika—Democracy and Art in the U.S.A.: Festschrift zu Ehren von Martin Christadler,* eds. Olaf Hansen and Thomas Liesemann (Trieste, 1996), 183–208.

concepts and discursive strategies that explicitly address and elaborate (1) the meaning of multiple and intercultural identities and communities that have increasingly been seen as distinctive for the American multiculture and (2) the transnational, intercultural processes at work in the interplay of cultures in the United States, the "border discourses" that define American culture and situate it in a global historical context. These critical explorations will provide a basis for further studies of the forms and the social and political consequences of multiculturalist discourse in Germany.

Situating American Multicultural Critique: Intercultural and Transnational Dimensions

Cultural Studies in the United States has to respond in a critical and productive manner to the crucial revisions of the understanding of culture (or cultures in the plural) in more recent postmodern and postcolonial anthropology and in minority discourses (in the wider sense of Abdul JanMohamed and David Lloyd), which ask us to conceive of cultural critique as inherently self-reflective, multicultural, and intercultural.[15] They conceive of cultures as always contested and emergent, as being continuously, and discontinuously, de- and reconstructed in (politically charged) *processes* of the formation of identities (or identifications) and communities. A self-reflective critique of American culture must articulate in its discursive strategies a crucial doubleness or ambiguity in the use of the term "culture." On the one hand, cultural critics today are asked to see the various realms of a society (or culture), such as the social, the economic, and cultural realms, in a common focus or, better, address their interrelations and their differences as a network of complex and often conflicting interactions,

15. For detailed discussions of these issues see my essays "'Ethnographies': American Culture Studies and Postmodern Anthropology," in *Prospects* 16, ed. Jack Salzman (New York, 1991), 1–40; "Multicultural Critique and the New American Studies," in *Multiculturalism and the Canon of American Culture,* ed. Hans Bak (Amsterdam, 1993), 27–56; "American Studies as Multicultural Critique: Postmodern Culture, Interdisciplinarity, and Intercultural Identities," in *Anglistentag 1993 Eichstätt: Proceedings,* eds. Günther Blaicher and Brigitte Glaser (Tübingen, 1994), 269–86; and "*American Studies*: Multikulturalität und Postmoderne," in *Multikulturelle Gesellschaft: Modell Amerika?* ed. Berndt Ostendorf (Munich, 1994), 167–87. Cf. also Gisela Welz, "Die soziale Organisation kultureller Differenz: Zur Kritik des Ethnosbegriffs in der anglo-amerikanischen Kulturanthropologie," in *Nationales Bewußtsein und kollektive Identität,* ed. Helmut Berding (Frankfurt/Main, 1994), 66–81.

and not limit their analysis to the traditional sphere of culture in the narrower sense. On the other hand, it is exactly the seeming omnipresence of these processes of cultural mediation and the increasing economic, social, political, and public role cultural processes have acquired in American (and other Western and non-Western) societies over the last decades in the context of the post-Fordist economy of postindustrialism and of postmodernity that challenge cultural critics to reassert distinctions and differences and carefully analyze the *specific* historical modes of representation at work in the public sphere.

Multi*cultural*, in this sense, is *not* identical with multi*ethnic*. If some theoretically sophisticated and politically committed critics ask us to move "beyond multiculturalism," they usually refer to versions of multiculturalism based on a plurality of ethnic groups characterized by common descent and essentializing interest group politics within the borders of the American nation-state. The intellectually most demanding of these critiques, David A. Hollinger's *Postethnic America: Beyond Multiculturalism* (1995), offers, however, the vision of a cosmopolitan, postethnic perspective that explicitly recognizes and acknowledges multiple identities, internal diversity, and emphasizes voluntary affiliations over group identities by descent. Hollinger knows that the nation-state is under attack, but he finds anthropologist Arjun Appadurai's notion of "postnationality" premature and counters it with his version of a postethnic "civic nationality," of a plurality of "publics nested within a larger public that is the larger polity of the United States." Hollinger's vision of a "postethnic America" in several places acknowledges the multiplicity of differently constituted "we's," of overlapping and conflicting communities and voluntary affiliations, which would lead to a fundamental revision of the constitution of what he calls "ethno-racial blocks" (as they have been used in the American census). In his strong effort to save—in a revised form—the (postethnic) Euro-American nation-state, however, he may still be too Eurocentric and monological in his arguments.[16]

A critical multiculturalism rejects the wide-spread versions of a pluralist multiculturalism that use the display and representations of cultural diversity of ethnic cultures in their state of "authenticity" in order to displace social and economic conflicts and economic discrimination of immigrant groups, or *Gastarbeiter/innen*, and

16. David A. Hollinger, *Postethnic America: Beyond Multiculturalism* (New York, 1995), 106, 108, 134–36, 155.

minorities into the realm of public spectacle.[17] It also rejects multi-culturalism as a plurality of ethnic groups based on essentialist notions of group identity, while acknowledging the strategic use of "ethnicities" in the fight for political recognition and social agency.[18] Instead, a critical multiculturalism explicitly addresses the *interrelationships* among various, often conflicting dimensions of difference (differentiation) in a culture, such as gender, race, ethnicity, class, religion, language, or age. Instead of comparing cultures seen as more or less independent and stable units, an intercultural approach is distinguished by the insight that cultures reproduce, represent, and reshape within themselves multiple axes or fault-lines of difference that are energized by, and manifested and transformed in, transcultural interactions. It is at these points of intersection, of confrontation, and difference that "impure," multicultural identities and communities are envisioned, constructed, and reconstructed. Defined in this way, an intercultural approach attempts to account for the inherent hybridity and self-difference of cultures and transcultural interactions, opening up multicultural discourse to critical dialogues articulated from different, often conflicting perspectives.

This project of multi- and intercultural critique in the United States as a counterdiscourse defines an understanding of American society and culture alternative to the traditional or common models of a nation of nations, a melting-pot, cultural pluralism, as well as of fragmentation vs. synthesis or center vs. periphery. As a consequence of the fundamental redefinition of the concept of (multi-)culture, this alternative model radically reconceives the common notions of identity and community. It analyzes *multiple identities* as historically contextualized, evolving, and changing always contested and ambivalent subject-positions or identifications. It explores the potential of forms of communities without stable membership or common territory and of new, changing coalition politics and social movements across cultural differences in their specific historical locations and social spaces.

In feminist theory, these multicultural identities are powerfully argued by Joan W. Scott and by Teresa de Lauretis. Joan W. Scott

17. See Gisela Welz, *Inszenierungen kultureller Vielfalt: Frankfurt am Main und New York City* (Berlin, 1996).

18. On the strategic use of "essentialism" in the project of "subaltern consciousness," see Gayatri Spivak, *In Other Worlds: Essay in Cultural Politics* (New York and London, 1987), 205; and Lisa Lowe, *Immigrant Acts: On Asian American Cultural Politics* (Durham, 1996), 65, 82.

historicizes the question of identity, which leads her to the conclusion that "subjects are produced through multiple identifications, some of which become politically salient for a time in certain contexts and that the project of history is not to reify identity but to understand its production as an ongoing process of differentiation, relentless in its repetition, but also—and this seems to me the important political point—subject to redefinition, resistance, and change."[19] Teresa de Lauretis defines these multicultural identities as "ec-centric subjects," as historically specific discursive positions organized around several axes of difference or "power differentials." Identity or identification is defined as "a locus of multiple and various positions, which are made available in the social field by historical processes and which one may come to assume subjectively and discursively in the form of political consciousness."[20] For de Lauretis, in the same way, "community" is inherently unstable and contextual, the product of collective work and struggle. In her view, these notions and visions of identity and community in feminist theory are the result of the interventions of "women of color" and of lesbian critics that have situated feminist critique in a "postcolonial mode."[21] Identity and community in her argument are understood as critical positionalities, *not* as the privileging of some essentialist lesbian or race and gender experience, but as sites of discourse and points of articulation of resistance and agency.

We can find similar reflections on multicultural identities and communities in this sense in recent African-American cultural critique, which has moved beyond the concentration on working out specific and unique forms of "vernacular criticism" or "native theory" competing with poststructuralism and beyond the notion of a race-based black community. In the United States, the work of Hazel Carby, Cornel West, bell hooks, and, particularly in more recent years, of Houston Baker, Jr. or Henry Louis Gates, Jr. comes to mind. In his defense of a critical multiculturalism that overcomes a culturalist reductionism and the commitment to a notion of a "stable" identity, of primordial cultural authenticity, and any kind of essentialist identity politics, but is informed by a revisionary conception of racial difference, Henry Louis Gates, Jr. emphasizes its "anti-utopian" pluralism, rejecting "final solutions of all

19. Joan W. Scott, "Multiculturalism and the Politics of Identity," *October* 61 (Summer 1992): 19.

20. Teresa de Lauretis, "Eccentric Subjects: Feminist Theory and Historical Consciousness," *Feminist Studies* 16 (Spring 1990): 116.

21. Ibid., 131–139.

sorts."[22] Gates does not give up the vision of a society that recognizes the various, competing, and radically contingent dimensions of cultural difference, especially the effects of the social construction of race and its complex interrelationships with culture, but he can describe this kind of multicultural society only in negative terms as a place of "constrained disagreement" (Alasdair MacIntyre). This vision "lets us remember that identities are always in dialogue, that they exist . . . only in relation to one another, and that they are, like everything else, sites of contest and negotiation."[23]

In her essay, "The Multicultural Wars," Hazel Carby also addresses the political uses of a depoliticized notion of multiculturalism (as a code word for race) and attacks the mindless celebration of "difference" as an expression of essentialist cultural group identities or as a reinforcement of existing frameworks of ghettoization and segregation in society. She poses several important questions: "[D]o existing power relations remain intact and unchallenged by this discourse [of difference]? . . . Is the emphasis on cultural diversity making invisible the politics of race in this increasingly segregated nation, and is the language of cultural diversity a convenient substitute for the political action needed to desegregate?"[24] To her, a politics of difference must acknowledge that *all* people, not just members of minorities, are "racialized subjects" in our political imagination, and it must argue in terms of "structures of inequality and exploitation," of power, not of concepts of individual identity or of exclusionary discourses of difference, such as "women of color."[25]

But I think it is no accident that the most elaborate and penetrating work in this vein has been written by black critics in Great

22. Henry Louis Gates, Jr., "Beyond the Culture Wars: Identities in Dialogue," *Profession 93* (New York, 1994), 7. Black feminist cultural critic bell hooks points out that the outright, abstract rejection of identity politics appears threatening to oppressed peoples, as it again seems to deny them the validity of achieving an identity of their own, but she fully accepts "postmodern critiques" of "outmoded [essentializing] notions of identity." Instead, she asks for the construction of "selves that emerge from the meeting of diverse epistemologies, habits of being, concrete class locations, and radical political commitments," for a cultural critique that affirms "radical black subjectivities," "multiple black identities" rooted in "a process of decolonization that continually opposes re-inscribing notions of 'authentic' black identity." (*Yearning: Race, Gender, and Cultural Politics*, Boston, 1990), 19, 20, 28.

23. Ibid., 11.

24. Hazel V. Carby, "The Multicultural Wars," in *Black Popular Culture*, ed. Gina Dent (Seattle, 1992), 190. Cf. Cornel West's highly suggestive essay, "The New Cultural Politics of Difference," *October* 53 (Summer 1990): 93–109.

25. Ibid., 193–194.

Britain such as Stuart Hall, Paul Gilroy, or Kobena Mercer.[26] They articulate black identities in the context of what Paul Gilroy calls the transnational, intercultural "black Atlantic" and focus in their discussions of new social movements (in Great Britain) on the formation and the strategies of a "black" political movement that transcends the traditional definitions of race and seeks to unite minority people from Africa, the Caribbean, as well as Asia, in an oppositional coalition. I will return to some of this work later in the essay.

Now, it is crucial to realize that these notions of multicultural identities and communities do not only apply to minorities and underprivileged groups, but—in many different ways—are also characteristic of American society or other societies at large. Cultural identities in the modern and postmodern world are always multicultural, they are never complete and unified, do not exist as something to be recovered and reclaimed, but are distinguished by process, discontinuity, self-difference, and constituted and reconstituted in the historical discourses of cultures. And, this is a second implication, they take us beyond the boundaries of U. S. national culture into the decentered and multicentered analysis of *transnational* and *intercultural* relations. If we approach the more recent work in American Cultural Studies and the various efforts of rewriting American literary history, we realize that they are—in spite of their revisionary and innovative impulse and some gestures toward the multiple (oral and literary) origins of American literary history—all too often characterized by a parochial understanding of what is meant by "America." Therefore, Gregory S. Jay proposes the "end" of "teaching 'American' literature" and suggests that we construct "a multicultural and dialogical pattern for the study of writing in the United States," which sets out to question and subvert the "nation's identity" and establishes "courses and programs in North American Studies that would integrate the cultural history of the U[nited] S[tates] with those of Canada, Mexico, the near Latin American countries, and the Caribbean."[27] Yet Jay realizes that just extending the geographical scope of American Studies in a comparative vein can all too easily lead to a repetition of the ethnocentric and colonialist vision of "American national identity" on a larger scale.

---

26. We should not forget, however, that Hazel Carby was affiliated with the Birmingham Centre for Contemporary Cultural Studies for quite some time.

27. Gregory S. Jay, "The End of 'American' Literature: Toward a Multicultural Practice," *College English* 53 (March 1991): 264, 266, 268.

However, in our search for the construction of what black feminist critic Hortense Spillers calls "comparative American identities," we can draw on powerful self-consciously intercultural—and politically situated—strategies of multicultural critique that have been developed in Chicano/a Cultural Studies/Mexican-American Studies. When they talk about "America," it is neither simply the United States or Mexico nor a transhistorical myth or ideology, but the term refers to North, Middle, and South America, to intercontinental relationships (with Africa and Europe), to geographically and historically defined border societies and cultures that have been working out multicultural identities, what Alfred Arteaga has called "intercultural sel[ves]," and transnational discursive strategies. Critics and writers such as José David Saldívar, Norma Alarcón, Alfred Arteaga, or Gloria Anzaldúa and Rolando Hinojosa envision dialogical projects of "comparative American Studies" permeated by the awareness of common as well as different traditions and cultural representations. These projects are animated by what José David Saldívar calls a "distinctly post-colonial, pan-American consciousness" or what Gloria Anzaldúa refers to as a "new *mestiza* consciousness" that dramatizes the complex interplay and the conflictual interrelations of cultures in the American Southwest. "Being 'chicano,'" writes Alfred Arteaga, "is a process of continual remaking, a discursive process that is always negotiated within the context of the circumscribing discursive practices of the United States," a discursive context that is "inherently polyglot." Chicano/a writers and critics produce and analyze pan-American texts of multiple origins and read them intertextually, as José David Saldívar puts it, as "orchestration[s] of multivocal, cross-cultural exchanges occurring in politically charged situations."[28]

Again, these radical insights into intercultural, comparative American identities return us from the specific historical perspectives of a "minority discourse" to reconceptualizing the society and culture of the United States at large. It is a challenge to American

28. José David Saldívar, *The Dialectics of America: Genealogy, Cultural Critique, and Literary History* (Durham, 1991), xi, xii, cf. 4–5, 82–84; Alfred Arteaga, "An Other Tongue," in *An Other Tongue: Nation and Ethnicity in the Linguistic Borderlands* (Durham, 1994), 13, 16, 18, 30; Gloria Anzaldúa, *Borderlands/La Frontera: The New Mestiza* (San Francisco, 1987); Rame New Mestiza*Chicano Narrative: The Dialectics of Difference* (Madison, 1990); Héctor Calderón and José David Saldívar, eds., *Criticism in the Borderlands: Studies in Chicano Literature, Culture, and Ideology* (Durham, 1991); cf. José David Saldívar's critique of the homogenizing tendencies of what he calls the "postmodern cultural studies" of anthropologist Michael M. J. Fischer and others in "The Limits of Cultural Studies," *American Literary History* 2 (1990): 251–66.

Cultural Studies that Donald E. Pease's revisionary program in his introduction to the second special issue of *Boundary* 2 on the New Americanists, "National Identities, Postmodern Artifacts, and Postnational Narratives," begins to take up, when he clarifies the intricate connection of the construction of an American national identity and the repression of multicultural realities and counter-discourses in term of race, class, and gender: "When understood from within the context of the construction of an imagined national community, the negative class, race, and gender categories of these subject peoples were not a historical aberration but a structural necessity for the construction of a national narrative whose coherence depended upon the internal opposition between Nature's Nation and peoples understood to be constructed of a 'different nature.'" As these national subject peoples, "figures of race, class, and gender," refused to identify with the dominant national narrative and asserted their social and cultural agency, the notion of an American national identity became dislocated from its transhistorical position and recognized in its politically constructed, contested, and preliminary status. But, even more important, *postnational* narratives have become possible, which dramatizes, as Pease puts it, "New Americanists' multiple interpellations: their different identifications with the disciplinary apparatuses in the new American Studies, as well as with social movements comprised of the 'disenfranchised groups' already cited."[29]

Situating multicultural critique in this sense means recognizing the processes of globalization, of a developing Wallersteinian world system of a post-Fordist economy, of what Scott Lash and James Urry have called "disorganized capitalism," or of what Gayatri Spivak has referred to as "post-modernization," which have had deep social and cultural repercussions. Globalization as such is *not* a new process, as Stuart Hall has pointed out, but it has taken on new dimensions and a new transformative power.[30] The processes of economic globalization of the last decades, particularly in international

29. Donald E. Pease, "National Identities, Postmodern Artifacts, and Postnational Narratives," Special Issue on the New Americanists No. 2, *Boundary 2* 19 (Spring 1992), 3, 4, 6. Of course, the collection of essays only imperfectly illustrates the vision Pease sketches in his introduction. Unfortunately, there are very few contributions to these "postnational narratives" by representatives of the "figures of race, class, and gender" themselves in the volume.

30. Stuart Hall, "The Local and the Global: Globalization and Ethnicity," in *Culture, Globalization and the World System: Contemporary Conditions for the Representation of Identity*, ed. Anthony D. King (London, 1991), 19–39.

financial transactions, however, have not led to an annihilation of the local, of regionally definable centers, as critics had prophesied. "The global and the local" does *not* register a dualism or a fixed opposition, but the processes of globalization are always also processes of the re-emergence and the reconstitution of "localisms." Even though in the post-Cold War world the dynamics of capitalism seem to have taken on the power of a force of nature, globalization must *not* be understood as a unilinear, uncontestable process of the annihilation or reappropriation of differences; it produces its own kinds of contradictions and oppositions. Deterritorialization always produces forms of reterritorialization. As Saskia Sassen has discussed, these processes have established new "world cities" or "global cities," and often have reinvigorated former metropolitan cities and urban centers, a process of reinvigoration that changed the social structure of the cities fundamentally and produced what John H. Mollenkopf and Manuel Castells consider "dual cities," resulting in a glaring economic and social polarization of the population and a restructuring of urbanization and suburbanization and of social space.[31]

The economic processes of globalization also have important cultural dimensions and force us to redefine the range and meaning of culture, of public culture, and the cultural sphere. In spite of the increasing omnipresence of new electronic media and communication networks and of the products of American mass culture we do not simply find an all-pervasive sameness all over the world and fragmentation and annihilation of cultural differences; instead, the processes of globalization assert themselves through multiple strategies of differentiation, of producing and appropriating differences. The reemergence of cultural differences can thus be seen as a result of strategies of containment. But the new localisms, if they are not romanticized as per se less heterogeneous and as less affected by social processes of institutionalization and commodification, also have activated resistances. They have resulted in the reappropriation and transculturation of products of a globalizing (media) culture in Third World countries or by American minorities or immigrant groups, and have provided the basis for a new politics of difference,

31. See especially Saskia Sassen's books *The Global City: New York, London, Tokyo* (Princeton, 1991); *Cities in a World Economy* (Thousand Oaks, 1994); and her recent essay "Whose City Is It? Globalization and the Formation of New Claims," *Public Culture* 8 (1996): 205–23. For New York, see John H. Mollenkopf, Manuel Castells, eds., *Dual City: Restructuring New York* (New York, 1991); and for Los Angeles, see Mike Davis, *City of Quartz: Excavating the Future in Los Angeles* (New York and London, 1990).

of political agency, which challenges and potentially subverts the drive toward the conformity of a globalizing capitalism and confronts it with alternative models of cultural practice and community.[32] As Arjun Appadurai has argued, postcolonialism is a concept that has been proposed for situating and defining these processes and tensions between cultural homogenization and cultural heterogenization in a global historical political frame, working to elaborate their complex, ambivalent social and cultural consequences in their different specific contexts. In cultural terms, these complex and highly conflictual interactions of globalization and new localisms could be described as the project of a critical, multicultural postmodernism that reached its crucial stage only with the powerful and wide-ranging manifestations of the different minority discourses, and that attempts to reconstruct and remap the new dynamics of cultures as cultures of difference and of their interrelationships as they have developed in recent decades.[33]

Now, which concepts and critical discourses have been developed in Cultural Studies that enable multicultural critics, as defined, from different perspectives, to analyze these transnational processes, that explore and reflect these contacts, conflicts, and interactions of cultures on the global as well as on the local scene? How can they conceive of cultural differences without reducing them to Western ethnocentric standards and positionings *and* without reifying other cultures in their pure otherness? How can cultures, e.g., American multiculture, be analyzed in their complex— in crucial ways, intercultural and transnational—dynamics as negotiating multiple dimensions and positionalities of difference in their representations of identities and communities?

32. Obviously, the resurgence of *local politics* can also result in questionable or disastrous "invented" nationalisms and ethnic politics. For a vision of a "new cultural politics of difference" written from the perspective of an African-American intellectual see Cornel West, "The New Cultural Politics of Difference," 93–109. The dynamics of homogenization and heterogenization in the global cultural economy are most suggestively discussed in anthropologist Arjun Appadurai's essays "Disjuncture and Difference in the Global Cultural Economy," *Public Culture* 2 (Spring 1990): 1–24; and "Global Ethnoscapes: Notes and Queries for a Transnational Anthropology," in *Recapturing Anthropology: Working in the Present*, ed. Richard G. Fox (Santa Fe, 1991), 191–210. Appadurai's important essays have recently been collected in his book *Modernism at Large: Cultural Dimensions of Globalization* (Minneapolis, 1996). The processes of "global localizations" and the global/local synergy of the "transnational imaginary" are the topic of the various case studies collected in Rob Wilson and Wimal Dissanayake, eds., *Global/Local: Cultural Production and the Transnational Imaginary* (Durham, 1996).

33. See my essay "American Studies as Multicultural Critique," 269–86.

Border Discourses: Conceptualizing Cultures of Difference

The first concept of these "border discourses" is the project of cultural translation, of the translational, of processes of translation and retranslation from one culture to another culture with a signifying difference at the crossings of cultures (Henry Louis Gates, Jr., Houston Baker, Jr., Homi K. Bhabha). In his theory of postcolonial discourse, Homi Bhabha defines culture as "a strategy of survival ... both transnational and translational," constructed and enunciated in processes of the transfer and the transformation of complex forms of signification. Culture is

> transnational because contemporary postcolonial discourses are rooted in specific histories of cultural displacement, whether they are the 'middle passage' of slavery and indenture, the 'voyage out' of the civilizing mission, the fraught accommodation of Third World migration to the West after the Second World War, or the traffic of economic and political refugees within and outside the Third World. Culture is translational because such spatial histories of displacement—now accompanied by the territorial ambitions of 'global' media technologies—make the question of how culture signifies, or what is signified by *culture,* a rather complex issue. It becomes crucial to distinguish between the semblance and similitude of the symbols across diverse cultural experiences—literature, art, music, ritual, life, death—and the social specificity of each of these productions of meaning as they circulate as signs within the specific contextual locations and social systems of value.[34]

The theory of cultural translation is a position questioned by Third World feminist critics who insist on the "untranslatability" of Third World experiences into the First World.[35] The challenge is to translate other cultures without appropriating and domesticating their otherness in the framework of the dominating, ethnocentric discourse nor in a reductive manner renouncing the need for intercultural understanding and communication by identifying these efforts as inherently impossible or "violent."[36] As cultures are never

34. Homi K. Bhabha, "Postcolonial Criticism," in *Redrawing the Boundaries: The Transformation of English and American Literary Studies,* eds. Stephen Greenblatt and Giles Gunn (New York, 1992), 438.

35. Cf., e.g., Rey Chow, *Writing Diaspora: Tactics of Intervention in Contemporary Cultural Studies* (Bloomington, 1993), 38.

36. For a suggestive analysis of the debate about the "impossibility" of intercultural understanding see the essay by Lothar Bredella, "Multiculturalism between Assimilation and Segregation: The Debate on Multicultural Curricula in the United States

homogeneous or unified, but always "impure" and heterogeneous, they are always self-differentiated and permeated by other cultures. A hermeneutics of intercultural understanding and translation does not look for a (dis)solution of cultural differences, but sets out to recognize, dramatize, and negotiate the asymmetries, ambivalences, and mutual blind spots in inter- (and intra-)cultural encounters in historical contexts of often unequal power relationships and articulates the transformative potential in these encounters of cultural difference and otherness in open-ended, dialogical, multifocal critical discourses.

A second concept, "transculturation," was first developed by Cuban anthropologist Fernando Ortiz in the late 1930s and early 1940s, and is defined by his American colleague Mary Louise Pratt five decades later for a different context as a process of "how subordinated and marginal groups select and invent from materials transmitted to them by a dominant or metropolitan culture."[37] However, important as the emphasis on the perspective and the agency of subordinated, marginal, and colonized groups is, as it overcomes the serious limitations of the traditional diffusionist accounts of conquest and domination, transculturation is not a one-directional process, but describes dialectical and historical interactions between the "metropolitan culture" and the cultures of the colonies. Put differently, transculturation is "a phenomenon of the contact zone," which Pratt defined in an earlier essay as "social spaces where cultures meet, clash, and grapple with each other, often in contexts of highly asymmetrical relations of power, such as colonialism, slavery, or their aftermath as they are lived out in many parts of the world today."[38] The processes of transculturation are reconstructed from conflicting perspectives, not seen as processes of acculturation and deculturation projected from the viewpoint of the white dominant culture, but primarily as the results of the active, transformative, self-asserting responses of colonized or "subaltern" peoples to constructions of their otherness, responses and interactions that powerfully reshape the colonized cultures as well as the colonizing cultures themselves.

Closely related to transculturation is Gloria Anzaldúa and Alfred Arteaga's notion of "border cultures," the production of cultural meanings at the crossings of cultures, where cultures meet and get

and Germany," in *American Studies in Germany: European Contexts and Intercultural Relations*, eds. Günter H. Lenz and Klaus J. Milich (Frankfurt/Main, 1995), 226–61.

37. Mary Louise Pratt, *Imperial Eyes*, 6.

38. Ibid., "Arts of the Contact Zone," *Profession 91* (1992): 34.

transformed and continuously reconstituted. In these critical approaches, speaking of "border crossings" and the "revision and transcendence of boundaries" is not a matter of fashionable tropes of transgressive rhetorics, but relates to material referents in geographical, social, and cultural space and to processes of historical change where discourses have been produced and are being recreated in multiple interactions. If the border qua frontier has had a crucial place in the American historical and political imagination and has been declared the foundation of American democracy and the melting-pot, it was always seen from the perspective of "advancing civilization," of the white, Anglo-Saxon, mostly male conquest of the wilderness and of the "virgin land," a version of the encounter of cultures that presupposes that the others, the "savages" have to acculturate to the white advancing civilization, if they want to survive.

For Alfred Arteaga, the intercultural dynamics at play in constructing Chicano/a identity occurs "in the interface between Anglo and Latin America, on the border that is not so much a river from the Gulf of Mexico to El Paso and a wire fence from there to the Pacific but, rather, a much broader area where human interchange goes beyond the simple 'American or no' of the border check. It is the space to contest cultural identities more complex than the more facile questions of legal status or images in popular culture."[39] As Guillermo Gómez-Peña puts it:

> There is no such thing as a permanent, static, homogeneous sense of identity for Chicanos or for Mexican immigrants. In many ways, I can say that I am a Mexican in the process of Chicanization and that I am developing a multiple identity ... [But] there is a point at which you realize that to defend this monolithic concept of identity—la *Mexicanidad*—in a process of ongoing border crossings and reterritorialization and deterritorialization is absurd.[40]

The border as "discursive and existential fact" removes the discussion of the interplay of languages from the purely aesthetic realm, because, Alfred Arteaga writes, "the border is a space where English and Spanish compete for presence and authority," a "site of polyglossia, where multiple national languages interact."[41] Border

39. Arteaga, ed., *An Other Tongue*, 10.
40. Guillermo Gómez-Peña, "Bilingualism, Biculturalism, and Borders," in *English Is Broken Here: Notes on Cultural Fusion in the Americas*, ed. Coco Fusco (New York, 1995), 153.
41. Arteaga, ed., *An Other Tongue*, 11, 13.

discourse dramatizes the interactions from *both* sides of the border and therefore is not only inherently dialogical, but also asks us to move beyond the monological positioning of a self-reflexive cultural critic toward a critical dialogue (and confrontation) with critics positioned on a different side (or site) of the border.

If the first three concepts address processes of the construction (de- and reconstruction) of meanings in encounters between cultures and of the articulation of cultural difference and otherness, the following three critical notions elaborate the dimensions and implications of intercultural differences and intracultural self-difference constituting and reconstituting multiple, plurivocal cultural identities and communities.

Gloria Anzaldúa's notion of *Mestizaje* envisions a plurivocal, performative notion of identity, or identification and agency, which subverts all versions of essentialism and suspends the quest for a "real-life" fusion of multiple differences in a new synthesis (or *raza*). In her book *Borderlands/La Frontera: The New Mestiza*, Anzaldúa explores, in a complex collage and interplay of different discourses, genres, and linguistic codes, the destructive consequences, but also the cross-fertilization and revitalization of languages and assertions of identity and community, on the juncture of cultures at the U.S.-Mexican border. She dramatizes these processes in a project of a "new mestiza/mestizaje consciousness" of a "shifting and multiple identity and integrity." "The switching of 'codes' in this book from English to Castilian Spanish to the North Mexican dialect to Tex-Mex to a sprinkling of Nahuatl to a mixture of all of these, reflects my language, a new language—the language of the Borderlands." Thus it is not simply a question of combining or negotiating two national languages, English and Spanish, but the intercultural heteroglossia is both "multilingual" *and* "multivoiced." As Alfred Arteaga concludes, making use of Bakhtinian concepts: "The hegemony of Anglo-American representation and subjectification is dialogized by a mestizaje of heteroglot texts that assert Chicano heterogeneity and American heteroglossia."[42]

For Anzaldúa, the new mestiza consciousness has to negotiate and sustain different languages, cultural resources, and subjective positionalities (as to race, gender, sexuality, or class) and projects of nonstable, nonessentialized communities in situations of an unequal distribution of power. "As a *mestiza* I have no country, my homeland cast me out; yet all countries are mine because I am

42. Anzaldúa, *Borderlands/La Frontera*, Preface; Arteaga, ed., *An Other Tongue*, 14, 27.

every woman's sister or potential lover. (As a lesbian I have no race, my own people disclaim me; but I am all races because there is the queer of me in all races.)"[43] To live in the borderlands does not only locate you in contested, multicultural, and multilingual space, but defines your very identity, as she writes in one of her poems in the volume:

> In the Borderlands
> you are the battleground
> where enemies are kin to each other;
> you are at home, a stranger,
>
> To survive the Borderlands
> you must live *sin fronteras*
> be a crossroads.[44]

If Anzaldúa's notion of mestizaje is suffused by a dream of "healing the split that originates in the very foundation of our lives, our culture, our languages, our thoughts," of "a common culture," of a "new race," a "new gender," she does not think of a new harmonizing synthesis or unity in which, finally, the tensions and ruptures have disappeared. What she is envisioning is the enabling power of transcending the constricting dualities of traditional rationality and achieving what she calls a "new consciousness" or "divergent thinking" that sustains ambiguities and contradictions and transforms them creatively into reconstructive multicultural identities and communities open to change.[45]

Cultural hybridity is a term that has played a crucial role in recent Latin American critical discourse on the contacts and conflicts of cultures that have characterized the history of Latin America. As with the earlier term *mestizaje*, there are two versions of hybridity. *Culturas híbridas* as an explicit conceptualization of cultural heterogeneity in Latin America can be understood as a pluralist notion of the coexistence and the interplay of historically and ethnically different cultural "streams" that are (to be) united in the *totalidad conflictiva* of a national culture. Or it can be conceived as a multicultural, transnational, postmodern theory of cultural heterogeneity that considers

43. Anzaldúa, *Borderlands/La Frontera*, 80, cf. Preface and 3–5, 22, 54–59, 63, 67, 77–91, 194–95.
44. Ibid., 194–95.
45. Ibid., 79, 80, 87, 194. Cf. Norma Alarcón's recent essay "Anzaldúa's *Frontera*: Inscribing Gynetics," in *Displacement, Diaspora, and Geographies of Identity*, eds. Shmadar Lavie and Ted Swedenburg (Durham, 1996), 41–53, esp. 43f., 53.

cultural heterogeneity in Latin America as a decentralized structure and field of force of different cultural traditions and social and political arrangements. These arrangements are both convergent and divergent and cannot be united in a common logic and envisioned, in the end, as a cultural totality. It is this second version of culturas híbridas that best explains the hybridization of literary texts in the context of the colonial conflict between European literacy and indigenous Indian oral cultures. And it is in this second sense that José Joaquín Brunner and Néstor García Canclini have analyzed since the late 1980s cultural processes of migration, exile, the globalization of mass culture, new social movements, the derealization and transformation of social space, or the instability of meanings and the flow of discontinuous images and multivalent messages in the fragmented urban world of postmodernity. It is obvious that García Canclini's postmodern notion of culturas híbridas asks for new strategies of a transdisciplinary cultural critique that positions itself in the hybrid "in-between" of global transitory spaces, as Petra Schumm puts it.[46]

In the United States, hybridity as a theoretical concept in multicultural and transnational cultural critique has been most powerfully elaborated in Homi K. Bhabha's analysis of colonial and postcolonial discourse, which is informed by a critical reading of Foucault's reflections on power and discourse, a politicization of Freudian and Lacanian psychoanalysis, and a revision of Fanon's reflections on the dynamics of the interaction of the colonizers and the colonized. The colonial encounter has not only "silenced" the colonized other cultures and enforced various kinds of double-consciousness and hybrid discourses, but has also split the colonizers' discourse in its very substance. What is crucial to Bhabha's theory of hybridization of discourse and power is that it does not refer to a mixture of preexistent identities or essences and that it has to be distinguished from Hegel's master/slave dialectic, as well as from the psychoanalytical process of "inversion that would suggest that the originary is,

46. The whole paragraph about "culturas híbridas" in Latin America is heavily based on Petra Schumm's excellent essay "'Mestizaje' und 'culturas híbridas'—kulturtheoretische Konzepte im Vergleich," in *Lateinamerika denken: Kulturtheoretische Grenzgänge zwischen Moderne und Postmoderne*, ed. Birgit Scharlau (Tübingen, 1994), 59–80. The book also contains an essay by Hermann Herlinghaus on Brunner's postmodern theory of everyday culture and Carlos Rincón's critique of Garcia Canclini's book *Culturas híbridas: Estrategias para entrar y salir de la modernidad* (México, 1990), English translation *Hybrid Cultures: Strategies for Entering and Leaving Modernity* (Minneapolis, 1995). Rincón also points outs Garcia Canclini's use of Anglo-American theories of modernity and postmodernity.

really, the 'effect' of an *Entstellung* [distortion]."⁴⁷ Instead, this hybridization is "a *différence* produced within the act of enunciation as a specifically colonial articulation of those two disproportionate sites of colonial discourse and power: the colonial scene as the invention of historicity, mastery, mimesis or as the 'other scene' of *Entstellung*, displacement, fantasy, psychic defense, and an 'open' textuality."⁴⁸ Hybridity is always ambivalent, and by revealing ambivalence as inherent in discourses of power it also enables forms of resistance and subversion. For Bhabha, "colonial hybridity is not a *problem* of genealogy or identity between two different cultures which can then be resolved as an issue of cultural relativism. Hybridity is a problematic of colonial representation and individuation that reverses the effects of the colonialist disavowal, so that other 'denied' knowledges enter upon the dominant discourse and estrange the basis of its authority—its rules of recognition."⁴⁹

The crucial question Homi Bhabha has been asking in much of his work is "what the function of a committed theoretical perspective might be, once the cultural and historical hybridity of the postcolonial world is taken as the paradigmatic place of departure."⁵⁰ He investigates the historical inevitability of hybridity as a practice in the signification of the political, not in something like the special area of colonial and postcolonial discourse, but as an effort of "conceptualizing an *inter*national culture" based on the "inscription and articulation of culture's *hybridity*" at large in the contemporary world.⁵¹ Again, cultural difference is not a play of polarities and pluralities in a homogeneous field of a national community, but "a form of intervention" that articulates "the difference between representations of social life without surmounting the space of incommensurable meanings and judgements that are produced within the process of transcultural negotiation."⁵² The concept of cultural difference, in contradistinction to cultural diversity, recognizes that "the problem of the cultural emerges only at the significatory boundaries of cultures, where meanings and values are (mis)read or signs

47. Homi Bhabha, "Signs Taken for Wonders: Questions of Ambivalence and Authority under a Tree Outside Delhi, May 1817," *Critical Inquiry* 12 (Autumn 1985): 156.

48. Ibid., 150.

49. Ibid., 156.

50. Homi Bhabha, "The Commitment to Theory," *New Formations* 5 (Summer 1988): 7.

51. Ibid., 22.

52. Homi Bhabha, "DissemiNation: Time, Narrative, and the Margins of the Modern Nation," in *Nation and Narration*, ed. Homi Bhahba (New York and London, 1990), 312.

are misappropriated."[53] Cultural identity is always cultural difference in this sense. Therefore, Bhabha defines interdisciplinarity as "the discursive practice of cultural difference" that in its hybridity, in minority discourse, articulates the insight that "all forms of cultural meaning are open to translation because their enunciation resists totalization."[54]

The postcolonial perspective forces the recognition of the complexities at the boundaries of conflicting political and cultural spheres, of "the transnational as the translational," as Bhabha writes in his wide-ranging essay "Postcolonial Criticism," reprinted as 'The Postcolonial and the Postmodern: The Question of Agency" in his book *The Location of Culture* (1994).[55] It is from this hybrid location of culture that the cultural and literary critic qua postcolonial intellectual attempts to elaborate a historical and critical project that explores the "possibilities of a cultural hybridity that entertains difference without an assumed or imposed hierarchy."[56]

Bhabha's theoretical reflections on cultural hybridity have grown out of the specific experiences and constellations of colonialism and postcolonialism in India. He has convincingly been criticized for his tendency to generalize this specific situation as representing the colonial and postcolonial condition and discourse per se and for a tendency to replace political conflict in the colonial and postcolonial world by their discursive effects.[57] If, in some sense, all cultures are hybrid cultures, the dialectics of hybridization seems to have most clearly unfolded in the colonial situation of the British Empire in the interactions between the colonizers and the colonized.

However, if we set out to explore the specific cultural and political repercussions of hybridity in the United States, we face a very different and much more complex historical situation that cannot be adequately analyzed by simply taking up Bhabha's dialectical model of (post)colonial hybridization. As Ruth Frankenberg and Lata Mani argue convincingly in their highly suggestive essay, "Crosscurrents, Crosstalk: Race, 'Postcoloniality,' and the Politics of Location" (1996), the concept of "postcoloniality" cannot be applied

53. Bhabha, "The Commitment to Theory," 19.

54. Bhabha, "DissemiNation," 314.

55. Homi Bhabha, "Postcolonial Criticism," 439, cf. Homi Bhabha, *The Location of Culture* (New York and London, 1994), ch. 9.

56. Bhabha, *The Location of Culture*, 4.

57. The most forceful critique of Bhabha's work is offered by Benita Perry in her essay "Signs of Our Times: Discussion of Homi Bhabha's *The Location of Culture*," *Third Text* 28/29 (Autumn/Winter 1994): 5–24.

indiscriminately to all countries and continents, but has to be redefined and complemented according to the specific politics of location. For the United States, the term tends to obscure crucial historical, political, social, and cultural differences among various minority, immigrant, or ethnic groups. Frankenberg and Mani tentatively propose the term "post-civil rights" instead, used broadly to refer to "the impact of struggle by African-American, American Indian, La Raza, and Asian American communities that stretched from the mid-1950s to the 1970s," a term to be used, however, in conjunction with another term "that would name the experience of recent immigrants/refugees borne here on the trails of U.S. imperialist adventures, groups whose stories are unfolding in a tense, complicated relation—at times compatible, at times contradictory—with the post-civil rights United States." Drawing on critics such as Chela Sandoval, Norma Alarcón, and Teresa de Lauretis, they find this "conjuncturalist approach" most powerfully developed in the discourses of U.S.-Third World feminism.[58]

"There are no pregiven or singular models of hybridity guaranteed to be 'politically correct,'" Smadar Lavie and Ted Swedenburg write in their Introduction to *Displacement, Diasporas, and Geographies of Identity*. Yet, as hybridity should not just be used for any kind of the intermixture of cultures, it has to be seen as "a construct with the hegemonic power relations built into the process of constant fragmented articulation" and as a form of agency that "subversively appropriates and creolizes master codes."[59] The more distinctive New World manifestations and discourses of hybridity have powerfully been articulated, for different groups and cultures, in their different sociocultural historical contexts, by Stuart Hall and Lisa Lowe. Stuart Hall, who grew up in Jamaica before coming to England, has addressed the processes of cultural hybridization in his work on Afro-Caribbean identities and related them to the concepts of "diversity," "difference," "creolization," and "diaspora," a conception of cultural identity "which lives with and through, not despite difference; by *hybridity*."[60]

58. Ruth Frankenberg and Lata Mani, "Crosscurrents, Crosstalk: Race, 'Postcoloniality,' and the Politics of Location," in *Displacement, Diaspora, and Geographies of Identity*, 273–93; 274f., 287, 291. For a trenchant analysis of the politics of location and the discourses of displacement in contemporary cultural theory see Caren Kaplan, *Questions of Travel: Postmodern Discourses of Displacement* (Durham, 1996).

59. S. Lavie and T. Swedenburg, eds., *Displacement, Diaspora, and Geographies of Identity*, 8–10.

60. See, e.g., Stuart Hall's essay "Cultural Identity and Diaspora," in *Identity: Community, Culture, Difference*, ed. Jonathan Rutherford (London, 1990), 235.

Lisa Lowe, in her book *Immigrant Acts: On Asian American Cultural Politics*, distinguishes her use of hybridity from "linguistic mixing" or "ambivalence" and defines it as a "material form that expresses the sedimented traces of a complex history of violence, invasion, exploitation, deracination, and imposed rule by different colonial and neocolonial powers."[61] In her analysis of the specific constellations of heterogeneity, hybridity, and multiplicity characteristic of the historically and geographically very different Asian-American groups and their cultures, she elaborates the social and political problems and potentials of her materialist concept of hybridity as conveying that "the histories of forced labor migration, racial segregation, economic displacement, and internment are left in the materialist concept of 'hybrid' cultural identities." Lowe emphasizes the political urgency and ambivalence of these processes of cultural hybridization. They can always be appropriated and commodified by commercial culture and become part of a pluralist version of multiculturalism that diffuses the demands of material differentiation and levels of contradictions within and among racial and ethnic minority groups through the "homogenization, aestheticization, and incorporation of signifiers of ethnic difference." But, at the same time, these hybrid identities can be rearticulated by Asian-American groups as oppositional agency and in the creation of "resistance cultures." Hybridization is "the uneven process through which immigrant communities encounter the violences of the U.S. state, and the capital imperatives served by the United States and by the Asian states from which they come, *and* the process through which they survive these violences by living, inventing, and representing different cultural alternatives."[62]

The concept of creolization is another term of "impurity," of "mixing" that has been reappropriated, displaced, and redefined in minority discourses and Cultural Studies. As a critical term of transnational cultural theory it has most persistently been elaborated by Swedish anthropologist Ulf Hannerz in his social theory of contemporary complex societies and their cultures, cultures defined as "systems of meaning." Hannerz draws on the linguistic analysis of creolizing languages in order to describe global processes of the interactions of the cosmopolitan and the local, of the center (or core) and the periphery, of an urbanizing world culture marked by a re-assertion and an organization of diversity and differences rather

61. Lowe, *Immigrant Acts*, 210, cf. 67
62. Ibid., 82 (my italics), 86, cf. 42.

than by a total homogenization and a replication of uniformity, as he shows in his analysis of the transformation of American popular culture in Nigerian society. The critic of culture (or the anthropologist) has to acknowledge, and not to deplore, the observation that there are no "distinct cultures, only intersystematically connected, creolising Culture," as he writes in his essay "The World in Creolisation." Creole or creolizing cultures are the product of "multidimensional cultural encounters," of (global) migrations, of the confluence, the tensions, and the confrontation of widely separate, heterogeneous historical currents occurring most pronouncedly in the urban centers of the Third World and in postindustrial "world cities" of the West where Third World migrants assemble. They produce "hybridizing webs of meaning" in center-periphery relationships that increasingly allow "the periphery to talk back." Creolizing cultures are open-ended, complex, "a network of perspectives, or ... an ongoing debate" that has more and more become constitutive of *all* contemporary, postmodern societies.[63]

If in most of his work Ulf Hannerz explores the repercussions of cultural processes of creolization on a global scale, his theoretical project also is directly pertinent to an analysis of American culture, of culture(s) of, and in, the United States. The very title of his essay, "American Culture: Creolized, Creolizing" (1987), marks the two—interrelated—directions or dimensions of his understanding of American culture, as a culture that is inherently heterogeneous and creoli*zed*, and as a culture that has powerfully been creoli*zing* other cultures on a global scale. Any attempt in American Studies to understand the dynamics of "American culture" has to investigate the internal creolizing effects of transnational cultural processes as they have shaped the development of dominant culture as well as of all countercultures and their interactions in the United States.

It is this ever new diversity and fluidity of American culture "along the creolizing continuum" that has been its distinctive quality since its beginnings. But if American culture is multifaceted and socially differentiated, its meaning cannot be grasped unless its

63. Ulf Hannerz, "The World in Creolisation," *Africa* 57 (1987): 546–59; and his later book *Cultural Complexity: Studies in the Social Organization of Meaning* (New York, 1992), 261–67. Most of the important essays by Hannerz have recently been collected in his book *Transnational Connections: Culture, People, Places* (New York and London, 1996). For a critical analysis of Hannerz's efforts to come to terms with cultural mediation on a global scale, see the essay by Gisela Welz, "Anthropology, Minority Discourse, and the 'Creolization' of Cultures," in *Mediating Cultures: Probleme des Kulturtransfers*, ed. Norbert H. Platz (Essen, 1991), 22–28.

highly complex, often contradictory creolizing effects on all the
cultures of the world ("an American cultural hegemony") *and* their
creative and transformative response of decoding and reincoding
cultural meanings, their processes of transculturation, are recognized and become part of a revisionary project of American Studies that studies the interplay of American culture with the cultures
of the world.[64]

Diasporas and the Transnational Moment

Let me, finally, discuss a concept in more detail that has been taken
up and debated from different perspectives in recent years, the
notions of diaspora or of diasporic cultures, of diasporic identities
and communities that have been debated most provocatively in relation to transnational U.S. cultures. This notion can activate a powerful analytical potential in our context, drawing on the concepts
discussed in the third part of the essay, for it can be seen as one way
of explicitly addressing the tenuous and multiple relation of culture
and territory and, most importantly, the interactions, the tensions,
the dynamics, and dialectics of globalization and the redefinitions
and reassertions of localisms as they have become characteristic of
the contemporary, transnational, post-Fordist world today. James
Clifford has offered a penetrating account of the implications of
the diaspora concept which he defines against (1) the norms of
nation-states and (2) the claims of indigenous "tribal" peoples. He
points out that diaspora is not a term only to be applied to the Jewish people, to Armenians, or some other selected migrant peoples
who have lost their homelands, but that "in the late 20th century,
all or most communities have diasporic dimensions (moments, tactics, practices, articulations)."[65]

"Diasporas are the exemplary communities of the transnational
moment," Khachig Tölölian writes as the editor in the first issue of
the new journal *Diaspora: A Journal of Transnational Studies*, not
"epiphenomena of the nation-state or global capitalism."[66] Diaspora

64. Ulf Hannerz, "American Culture: Creolized, Creolizing," in *American Culture: Creolized, Creolizing and Other Lectures from the NAAS Biennial Conference in Uppsala, May 28–31, 1987*, ed. Erik Åsard (Uppsala University: The Swedish Institute for North American Studies, 1987), 7–30.
65. James Clifford, "Diasporas," *Cultural Anthropology* 9 (1994): 310.
66. Khachig Tölölyan, "The Nation-state and Its Others: In Lieu of a Preface," *Diaspora* 1, no.1 (1991): 5, as quoted in Clifford, "Diasporas," 302.

communities can be of different kinds and need not pursue the quest for a return to the original "homeland" in a literal way. On the contrary, we should add, in our postcolonial times the return to a homeland and the (re-)establishing of a "pure" nation-state of "one's own people" would only result in new displacements, in the production by power and violence of new diasporic experiences for other peoples. Clifford argues that "diasporic language appears to be replacing, or at least supplementing, minority discourse," as the transnational connections and interrelations "break the binary relation of *minority* communities with *majority* societies—a dependency that structures projects of both assimilation and resistance" and also transcends the common center-periphery model. He concludes: "Diaspora discourses reflect the sense of being part of an ongoing transnational network that includes the homeland, not as something simply left behind, but as a place of attachment in a contrapuntal modernity."[67] Clifford sides with Daniel and Jonathan Boyarin who argue that for Jews the homeland should not be identified with a specific place or state that brings the diasporic exile to its final end. Instead, it is to be held onto as a utopian perspective that keeps Jewish diasporic identity and culture alive and in process. "Cultures are not preserved"—as the Boyarins argue—"by being protected from 'mixing' but probably can only continue to exist as a product of such mixing. Cultures, as well as identities, are constantly being remade."[68]

Diasporic cultures are constituted by experiences of displacement and discrimination, but also contain a strong utopian dimension and dynamic of a struggle for emancipation and political and social equality. They articulate, Clifford writes, "alternative public spheres, interpretive communities where critical alternatives (both traditional and emergent) can be expressed."[69] In a similar vein, Stuart Hall, in his essay "Cultural Identity and Diaspora," defines the diaspora experience, drawing on his own biography of a childhood and adolescence in Jamaica and his adult life in England, "not by essence or purity, but by the recognition of a necessary heterogeneity and diversity, by a conception of 'identity' which lives with and through, not despite, difference; by *hybridity*. Diaspora

67. Clifford, "Diasporas," 311.

68. Daniel Boyarin and Jonathan Boyarin, "Diasporas: Generation and the Ground of Jewish Identity," *Critical Inquiry* 19 (Summer 1993): 721. For another careful discussion of these issues, cf. William Safran, "Diasporas in Modern Societies: Myths of Homeland and Return," *Diaspora* 1 (Spring 1991): 83–99.

69. Clifford, "Diasporas," 315.

identities are those which are constantly producing and reproduc-
ing themselves anew, through transformation and difference."[70]
The political implications of the modern and postmodern diaspora
experience and tradition and their role in a politics of representation are further explored by Cornel West who develops strategies of
a "demystificatory criticism" (what he calls "prophetic criticism")
that got its decisive push by the "powerful critiques and constructive explorations of Black diaspora women (i.e., Toni Morrison)"
and that tries to "construct more multivalent and multidimensional
responses that articulate the complexity and diversity of Black practices in the modern and postmodern world."[71]

A powerful use of this notion of diaspora and diasporic cultures
is made by Paul Gilroy in his book, *The Black Atlantic: Modernity and
Double Consciousness* (1993). Gilroy conceives of the black Atlantic as
a multicentered intercultural and transnational formation, as a
"counterculture of modernity." He attempts "to rethink modernity
via the history of the black Atlantic and the African diaspora into
the western hemisphere," which reveals the "internality of blacks to
the West," and to show that "racial slavery was integral to western
civilization" and that "the master/mistress/slave relationship ... is
foundational to both black critiques and affirmations of modernity." The book explores "the special relationship between 'race,'
culture, nationality, and ethnicity which have a bearing on the
[post-colonial] histories and political cultures of Britain's black citizens." It also introduces a second perspective, decentering the
common positionality and perspective of black America, of African
Americans (and destroying any notion of the essential black subject) by pursuing manifold crossings, travels, explorations, inter-
connections, experiences of exile of African-American writers,
intellectuals, and musicians. But Gilroy also acknowledges the
importance of these African Americans in conceiving a "global,
coalitional politics in which anti-imperialism and anti-racism might
be seen to interact if not to fuse." In showing "how the politics of
location and the politics of identity get inscribed in analyses of
black culture," he expounds the "fundamental antinomy of diaspora blacks" by extending Amiri Baraka's understanding of black
music in *all* its forms as the "changing same" to the different parts

70. Stuart Hall, "Cultural Identity and Diaspora," 235; cf. his essay "Old and New
Identities, Old and New Ethnicities," in *Culture, Globalization, and the World System*,
41–68. See also Keya Ganguly, "Migrant Identities: Personal Memory and the Construction of Selfhood," *Cultural Studies* 6, no. 1 (Jan 1992): 27–50.
71. Cornel West, "The New Cultural Politics of Difference," 104–105.

of the black Atlantic, particularly in popular culture, processes which he regards as the crucial test-case of hybridization of the black counterculture of modernity.[72]

In Richard Wright's later work the black American is seen as a central symbol in the psychological, cultural, and political system of the modern West as a whole.[73] If this politics of transfiguration reveals "the hidden internal fissures in the concept of modernity," this means that the common "periodisation of the modern and the postmodern [may have] to be drastically rethought."[74] In the final part of *The Black Atlantic*, Gilroy complements his spatial focus on the diaspora concept with a vision of "diaspora *temporality* and *historicity, memory* and *narrativity* that are the articulating principles of the black political countercultures that grew inside modernity in a distinctive relationship of antagonistic indebtedness."[75] In a penetrating analysis of the transfigurations of black music at the crossroads of a global cultural network or force field and of several recent African-American novels dealing explicitly with history, historiography, memory and remembrance of the middle passage, slavery, and its aftermath, Gilroy reaches the conclusion that the black Atlantic has been constituted by all these cultural practices as "a non-traditional tradition, an irreducibly modern, ex-centric, unstable, and asymmetrical cultural ensemble that cannot be apprehended through the manichean logic of binary coding." His study of the fundamental antinomy of the black diaspora "explodes the dualistic structure which puts Africa, authenticity, purity, and origin in crude opposition to the Americas, hybridity, creolization, and rootlessness" and offers an alternative reading of what is often called from a Western perspective "postmodern" culture.[76]

Both Gilroy and Clifford are well aware of the fact that their more general use of the concept of diaspora is a critical appropriation of its original meaning in describing the specific Jewish experience, and Gilroy explicitly expresses his commitment to improving the relations between the Jewish and the black diasporas. But they also make clear that the diaspora concept has always been, and will remain, a controversial one and that it can have very different implications in different contexts for various transnational cultures. If diaspora traditionally highlights the spatial and historical dispersion

72. Gilroy, *The Black Atlantic*, 3–5, 17–18, 30, cf. 36.
73. Ibid., 159, cf. 162, 173, 175, 186.
74. Ibid., 38, 42, cf. 45–46, 49, 70, 197—middle passage!
75. Ibid., 191 (my italics).
76. Ibid., 198–99.

of a people experienced and perceived as one, the postmodern and post-Fordist notion of diasporic cultures and communities must carefully avoid a covert reproduction and reaffirmation of an ethnically homogeneous, quasi-organic culture concept as if it were suspended in space and time until the return home in the future. It must articulate instead the dimensions and perspectives of intra- and intercultural diversity and hybridity.

As diasporic cultures—as well as cultures of hybridity, *mestizaje*, or creolization—are *not* per se oppositional or subversive, but are "fundamentally ambivalent," as Clifford puts it, their reconstructions, their representations, their critical discourses will always be contested and open to conflicting political interpretations and consequences. Kobena Mercer's political critique of Gilroy's vision of a black "populist modernism" and his own use of the concept of diasporas as "materially produced" in his book *Welcome to the Jungle: New Positions in Black Cultural Studies* is an important case in point.[77]

However, the focus in diasporic discourses on the complexities of black diasporas and their relationship to the Jewish diaspora prevents us from realizing that transnational American Culture Studies also have to confront and analyze other diasporic experiences, communities, and cultures that are constituted in very different ways. Rey Chow's political-ideological critique of the "lures of diaspora" for Third World intellectuals in her book *Writing Diaspora: Tactics of Intervention in Contemporary Cultural Studies* leads her to insist on the social, political, material situatedness of diasporic knowledges and cultural studies. Lisa Lowe's book *Immigrant Acts: On Asian American Cultural Politics* can be seen as a model study of transnational diasporic communities in the United States that situates the various groups of Asian Americans in their historically, socially, economically, and legally very different contexts. "'Immigrant acts,' then, attempts to name the *contradictions* of Asian immigration, which at different moments in the last century and a half of Asian entry into the United States have placed Asians 'within' the U.S. nation-state, its workplaces, and its markets, yet linguistically, culturally, and racially marked Asians as 'foreign' and 'outside' the national polity." The different contradictions of immigration and citizenship find expression in distinct formations of the racialization of Asian Americans: "the Chinese as alien noncitizens, the American citizen of Japanese descent as racial enemy, and the

---

77. Kobena Mercer, *Welcome to the Jungle: New Positions in Black Cultural Studies* (New York, 1994), 247.

American citizen of Filipino descent as simultaneously immigrant and colonized national."[78] The positioning of Asian Americans in the United States as "outsiders-within," in spite of their being stereotypically being praised as the "model minority," is seen by Lowe less as a sign of failed integration of Asians into the American cultural sphere, but as dramatizing a distance or an active distancing, from the national culture that preserves (or creates) "Asian American culture as an alternative formation that produces cultural expressions materially and aesthetically at odds with the resolution of citizens in the nation." If, as Lowe argues, "legal institutions *reproduce* the capitalist relations of production as *racialized gendered relations*," and if in the American political system "the state suppresses dissent by governing subjects through rights, citizenship, and political representation," it is in the cultural sphere, through "immigrant acts," through the agency of "immigrant cultures," that Asian Americans "conceive and enact new subjects and practices in antagonism to the regulatory *locus* of the citizen-subject" that question the system of government and project alternative forms of subjectivity, collectivity, and public life.[79]

Of course, Lowe is fully aware of the fact that in the United States national culture is assigned the role of resolving inequalities and social class conflict that cannot be resolved in the political and economic sphere, and she attacks versions of a pluralist multiculturalism. She does not propose to replace political practices by cultural struggles, but, again, she elaborates the dialectics of diasporic cultures, of a politics of identity and a politics of difference, when she engages in a critique of the term "Asian Americans" as a questionable labeling from outside that blurs crucial distinctions, but, at the same time, as a strategic program of political solidarity that enables Asian Americans to form coalitions across the boundaries of nationality and race and to open up perspectives for articulating the interactions among diverse transnational American diasporas. She writes: "The specific history of Asian immigration in relation to U.S. citizenship is different from the histories of other migrant or racialized groups, such as African-Americans, Native Americans, and Chicanos/Latinos, yet the Asian-American critique of citizenship generated by its specific history opens the space for such cross-race and cross-national possibilities."[80]

78. Lowe, *Immigrant Acts*, 8.
79. Ibid., 22.
80. Ibid., 35, cf. 153, 175.

Cultural Complexities and Cultural Studies

The critical debate about the use of diaspora or diasporic cultures highlights two important insights which we should also apply to the other critical concepts and discourses discussed. If diaspora is really historicized and contextualized in our critical discourse, it cannot and should not be turned into the "master trope" or new "master discourse" for the analysis of modern and postmodern identities and communities. None of the concepts or theoretical discourses of transnational cultural border crossings or hybridity can provide the code that explains everything. There cannot be a unifying theory of globalizing, transnational, and interculturally connected societies and cultures.

Still, in his important study *Cultural Complexity: Studies in the Social Organization of Meaning*, in which he addresses the cultural dimensions and repercussions of processes of globalization in communication and in the economy, Ulf Hannerz has provided a "*formal* sociology of cultural process" and a challenging multidimensional and multiperspective model of the forms and sites of contemporary creolizing cultures and their cultural flows in the interplay between world culture and the national and local cultures of the periphery and the processes of transculturation they produce.[81] He also addresses the difficult questions of the—often highly disparate and conflictual—transnational interrelationships between cultural asymmetries and economic and political asymmetries in the world system and their repercussions on the production and social organization of meaning in a postmodern, creolizing world beyond the old model of center and periphery. "In creole cultures, as I see them, as systems of meaning and expression mapped onto structures of social relations, there is also a continuous spectrum of interacting forms, along which the various contributing historical sources of the culture are differentially visible and active."[82]

Hannerz's analytical approach transcends the limitations of the modernization and world system theories. As his emphasis is on historical differences, on hybridity, internal divisions, and structural asymmetries, he realizes, however, that these multiple differences and interactions cannot be generalized in a kind of overarching global theory of cultural mediation, but take on different historical

81. Hannerz, *Cultural Complexity*, 55 (my italics).
82. Ibid., 264.

forms and meanings. Near the conclusion of his book he writes: "The asymmetries of cultural flow within market and state frameworks, taking their places within the spectrum, have different points of origin and different reach. Movements arise at different points, at different times. In relation to this, there is a built-in political economy of culture, as social power and material resources are matched with the spectrum of cultural forms."[83] Here, I think, anthropologist Arjun Appadurai's approach to the central problem of today's global interactions, "the tension between cultural homogenization and cultural heterogenization," his model of the (disjunction of the) five dimensions of global cultural flow (based on a wider notion of the culture concept) that attempts to account for the "new cultural economy" as a "complex, overlapping, disjunctive order" and sees ethnoscapes, mediascapes, technoscapes, finanscapes, and ideoscapes as perspectival constructs, "inflected by historical, linguistic and political situatedness of different sorts of actors," could further clarify the potential of the "poetics and politics" of transnational cultural analysis.[84]

Nor are the different concepts and theoretical discourses—and this is my second point—basically identical. They overlap in many ways, as we have seen, but they should not be turned into metaphors and used more or less interchangeably. All the terms have been elaborated in their theoretical potential and transcultural repercussions by cultural critics positioned and positioning themselves on the margins, in minority discourses, and have been worked out in their inescapable ambivalences and dialectics in specific historical and intercultural contexts. They conceptualize and dramatize conflictual cultures, cultural heterogeneity, and versions of cultural "impurity" and fragmentation, but these discourses of cultural difference and impure mixtures are also energized by reference to their invisible other, to the visions of a lost or utopian unity or a vision of an earlier or future state of purity. If these terms represented the negative other in earlier dominant cultural discourses, marks of oppression or victimization, and in some cases of the questionable claims of biologistic essentialism, minority discourses have radically deconstructed the positive other of these terms and de-essentialized, revalorized, transformed, transculturated their negative meanings, have

83. Ibid., 265.

84. Appadurai, "Disjuncture and Difference in the Global Cultural Economy," 5–7. See also his essay "Global Ethnoscapes: Notes and Queries for a Transnational Anthropology," in *Recapturing Anthropology*, 191–210.

de- and reterritorialized them, and subverted and transcended their original discursive frame of reference.

If these complex and contested processes of transculturation occur in specific historical and cultural contexts, the translation of one of these border discourses from one group and one situation to another group or context is a difficult, but also a vitally important and challenging task. We have to remind ourselves that the projection of multiple and intercultural identities and communities discussed in the first half of the essay and the various competing, heterogeneous, and complementary border discourses explored in the latter half of the essay do not only address problems of specific minorities or marginal positionalities. Instead, none of these discourses is isolated, independent. All of them are in some way interrelated to, or involved in, the others. Each of them highlights and engages some important dimensions and problems of contemporary societies and rearticulates the complex intercultural and intracultural dynamics of difference and otherness of their cultures at large that can help us, from different positionalities, to work out and to pursue transnational, intercultural (American) Culture Studies. American Culture Studies in Germany can enter, and has entered, the dialogue with these American critical discourses and contributes—from an *inter*cultural perspective, not so much from an "independent" "outside" position—to the critical project of transnational cultural studies. If the transnational border discourses developed in U.S. cultural critique cannot be "applied" or transferred directly to the task of conceiving and realizing a *multikulturelle Gesellschaft* in Germany, they provide a challenge that makes us realize that the German (and European) constitution and reconstitution of discourses of multiculturalism are always already implicated in globalizing processes, contexts, and interactions—with a (local) difference.

10. Multiculturalism and the European Connection: Theme Park or Dual Citizenship?

Frank Trommler

After the stormy ascent of multiculturalism as a concept in the 1980s and its institutionalization in the halls of academe in recent years, it might be timely to ask what it has done to the perceptions of Americans regarding other cultures. Can we understand the battles over the different definitions of culture, reflecting race and ethnicity, identity and otherness, as a sign of a new post-Cold-War international awareness? Is there a new sensitivity on this side of the Atlantic toward the increasingly interconnected, yet independent-minded cultures in other parts of the world? For teachers of foreign languages, literatures, and cultures, these questions are more than an academic exercise; for Europeanists they go straight to the rationale of their disciplines.

The following observations are meant to help rethink the close relationship which many Americans, especially the elites, used to have with the cultures of Europe and which appear to have entered a different stage under the auspices of multiculturalism, globalization, and, of course, the end of the Cold War. Numerous critics have argued that multiculturalism gained its momentum as an anti-Eurocentric movement. Others felt that such a view overestimates the role of Europe in American public discourse but has some validity if restricted to the universities, with their ingrained Euro-orientation and monocultural traditions. Others, again, took the cue from the battles over curricula at school boards and community councils and blamed multiculturalism, in the manner of

Arthur Schlesinger, Jr., for *The Disuniting of America.*[1] Many polemics later, there is reason to believe that the anti-Eurocentric stance should not be mixed up with the recognition of ethnic diversity as a base of American identity, but there is also reason to believe that at the end of the twentieth century, American identity is increasingly defined without reference to the European roots of its culture and democracy, even in denial or rejection of it.

This is nothing new, so it seems, if one looks back at waves of Americanization-cum-Europe-bashing that have swept the country throughout the nineteenth and twentieth centuries. What is new, however, is the extent to which anti-Eurocentrism has been made into an intellectual criterion that serves in the establishment of academic, even scholarly ventures, and the shaping of college curricula and university disciplines. Postcolonialism has gained much through the association with anti-Eurocentrism, but there are other isms which have gained intellectual profile in conjunction with the notion that they have freed themselves from the traditional European connections. David Hollinger, looking "Beyond Multiculturalism" in his recent treatise *Postethnic America*, has provided a genealogy of the sympathy of liberal intellectuals for ethnic minorities and immigration groups that stood in sharp contrast to "traditional Anglo-Protestant nativism."[2] What has been subsumed under the label "multiculturalism" since the 1980s, though, is a more drastic reorientation of academic elites than the earlier excursions into the exoticism of the underprivileged groups in the 1920s and 1930s. To claim, for instance, that *Unthinking Eurocentrism*, as a recent volume is called, "critiques the universalization of Eurocentric norms,"[3] and "configures an interdisciplinary field which has been gaining momentum but has barely been named and which we would call 'multicultural media studies,'"[4] is a novel enterprise. The book "is written in the passionate belief that an awareness of the intellectually debilitating effects of the Eurocentric legacy is indispensable for comprehending not only contemporary media representations but even contemporary subjectivities."[5] A passionate plea for the decolonization of global culture, the volume analyzes the representation of

1. Arthur M. Schlesinger, Jr., *The Disuniting of America: Reflections on a Multicultural Society* (New York, 1992).
2. David A. Hollinger, *Postethnic America: Beyond Multiculturalism* (New York, 1995), 97.
3. Ella Shohat and Robert Stam, *Unthinking Eurocentrism: Multiculturalism and the Media* (London and New York, 1994), 3.
4. Ibid., 6.
5. Ibid., 1.

the Third World in film and media for an oppositional aesthetic of multiculturalism.

Still, the continuities of recent debates and pronouncements with earlier concepts of diversity should not be overlooked. "America is a unique sociological fabric," Randolph Bourne wrote in his famous treatise against a homogenized nation, "Trans-National America," "and it bespeaks poverty of imagination not to be thrilled at the incalculable potentialities of so novel a union of men."[6] In a period of increasingly militant monoculturalism, Bourne held out the prospect of a multilayered, multicultured America with an eye on schools and universities. For Bourne, the failure of the melting-pot was complemented by the failure of the Anglo-Saxon elite to shape a genuine American culture. In his words:

> It is not uncommon for the eager Anglo-Saxon who goes to a vivid American university today to find his true friends not among his own race but among the acclimatized German or Austrian, the acclimatized Jew, the acclimatized Scandinavian or Italian. In them he finds the cosmopolitan note. In these youths, foreign-born or the children of foreign-born parents, he is likely to find many of his inbred morbid problems washed away. These friends are oblivious to the repressions of that tight little society in which he so provincially grew up. He has a pleasurable sense of liberation from the stale and familiar attitudes of those whose ingrowing culture has scarcely created anything vital for his America of today.[7]

Though dated by the focus on the Anglo-Saxon elite, Bourne's elated praise of alterity and diversity in the encounter with other cultures still rings an echo in the outbursts of intellectual creativity in the multicultural academy of the late twentieth century. Exploding the disciplinary doctrines regarding political institutions, national traditions, and white male intellectual supremacy, the emerging strata of minority professionals can be credited with creating a truly transnational set of intellectual practices that have transformed our sense of society and identity as well as our perceptions of the university as the seat of knowledge production.

Although Hollinger is right in pointing out that the concept of cultural pluralism that shaped the tradition of this thinking has been tame and compromising compared with the multicultural agenda of the 1980s, Bourne's self-critical reconsideration of America's cultural potential already goes beyond the integrationist culturalism that

6. Randolph S. Bourne, *War and the Intellectuals: Essays 1915–1919*, ed. Carl Resek (New York, 1964), 114.
7. Ibid., 118.

Horace Kallen promoted between 1915 and 1924.[8] Unperturbed by his own condemnation of European nationalism, Bourne defied the calls for an intellectual withdrawal; he even insisted on maintaining the cultural give-and-take with Germany when his teacher, John Dewey, embarked on Wilson's notion that only war was the answer to the provocations, producing the national homogeneity needed to decide the future of democracy in Europe.[9] In the period of World War I, Bourne took risks when he argued that cultural homogenization meant provincialism. He pointed out the dangers of a self-referential Americanism beholden to the interests of a special class. His legacy, encoding the relations of power and identity in cultural terms, is still called upon.

The sense of liberation, of unearthing voices, traditions, individual and group experiences that were buried under the homogenizing inventory of modern society, has received splendid impulses from multiculturalism, even though the latter has become "bureaucratized," as Cornel West opined. For the 1990s, West sees the problem in maintaining the momentum of this creativity: "The serious intellectual work must not stop once multiculturalism becomes institutionalized and we have courses in black writers and women writers and so on; we need the same kind of critiques that have been brought to bear on the earlier, more xenophobic canons."[10] In such a predicament, so the provocative comment, multiculturalism comes close to resembling another version of "colonialism, or of exotism, or of the sort of primitivism that 'saved' Western art in its modernist moment."[11] Indeed, as Western consumer culture has absorbed many of the unearthed vistas and voices as a boon to provocative advertising, the chronicling of the intellectual ruptures of recent decades can look like a rescue operation of a sliding territory. While many contemporaries would argue that multiculturalism has turned the territory into a slide, others would insist that the slide has been on, and this is the only way to keep us on top of it. Cornel West plays into the latter by extolling the creative powers of experiencing otherness: "The exotic is a tradition that will not go away, and it has to be interrogated over and over again. It becomes

8. Hollinger, *Postethnic America*, 92–96. See also Hollinger, "Ethnic Diversity, Cosmopolitanism and the Emergence of the American Liberal Intelligentsia," *American Quarterly* 27 (1975): 133–51.

9. Bourne, "A War Diary," in *War and the Intellectuals*, 36–47.

10. Cornel West and Bill Brown, "Beyond Eurocentrism and Multiculturalism," *Modern Philology* 90, Suppl. (1993): S154.

11. Ibid.

a way for students and teachers to feel good about their sense of liberal openness by being open to those who are exotic, primitive, and so forth, to feel as if these people—and when I say 'these people' I include myself—are closer to reality than were Shakespeare, Dante, Milton, to feel as if those people are more authentic."[12] This is, certainly, also the moment of rejection of the dead white European males which, in its rhetoric, has its own tradition within anti-Eurocentrism. Although confessional and part of identity politics, its place in education has been established through the transformation of many liberal arts curricula since the 1980s.

Another widely celebrated advancement of multiculturalism as a concept had a different impact on the conduct toward foreign, especially European cultures. It occurred in the political arena, not unrelated to the wars over political correctness which accompanied the academic institutionalization of multiculturalism, but transcending them with its internationalist intentions. Drawing its energies from a redefinition of the democratizing mission that had inspired the civil rights movement, multiculturalism in this context became the crucial code for the encounter with the decentering forces of a postindustrial, post-Cold-War society. Calling it "global multiculturalism" and anchoring it in the constitutionally guaranteed equal rights of the American democracy, Benjamin Barber summed it up in the assertion: "Multiculturalism has become the specter for Europe and the world beyond."[13] In light of the daily reports of the devastating warfare between Serbs, Croats, Bosnians, and other ethnic groups that tore apart multicultural Yugoslavia, such raising of the flag against the old European divisiveness seemed a natural reaction: "With such strife-ridden former nations as the Soviet Union, Afghanistan, Yugoslavia, Liberia, and Czechoslovakia offering their own pathogenic alternatives to American multicultural development, the experience of the United States as an embattled but relatively successful multicultural society cries out for careful attention in Europe."[14]

Ironically, it seems that academic elites, reassured of the usefulness of the democratic mission in the fight for moral supremacy, are more outspoken in waving the flag than the foreign policy establishment, which has used the argument but rarely translated it into an action agenda. Asking the question, "Why don't you get

12. Ibid.
13. Benjamin R. Barber, "Global Multiculturalism and the American Experiment," *World Policy Journal* 10 (1993): 47.
14. Ibid., 47f.

along, you Europeans, as we do on this side of the Atlantic?" yields more satisfaction for those who stake out a moral claim at the academy than those who conduct business across the Atlantic. At any rate, global multiculturalism, made in the U.S.A., has come to represent an important frame of reference for the debates about the status of immigrants in relation to native-born citizens that have shaken up parliaments in several countries since the 1980s. America, the classic immigration country, delivers expertise in structuring immigration and ethnic communality. Its multiculturalism is referred to as a guide for the building of a legal structure that provides equal rights to ethnic and other minorities all over the world.[15]

In his recent study on the evolution of the American nation, Michael Lind has argued that the period with the closest ties to Europe ran its course a long time ago. "Euro-America,"[16] as he calls it, followed "Anglo-America" in the 1870s and came to a close in 1957. Afterwards "Multicultural America" established itself. If Lind is right—and he argues his position well, as critics have conceded —one might ask why Europe still draws so much passion, even if in an often opposing and negating mode. Or does it? Is the frequent reference to Europe just a compensatory ploy for the opposition to the deeply ingrained doctrine of a gentrified America of which so many of the critics, male and female, are part? A detailed discussion of this suggestion, which cannot be delivered here, would probably help explain the tendency to keep a ready-made Europe for many of the more problematic features of cultural representation in public and academic life, something that already Thorstein Veblen, in *The Theory of the Leisure Class*, caustically situated on the other side of the Atlantic. What Veblen dismissed as a system of wasteful ceremonies intended to preserve a sense of hierarchy, seems to experience a resurrection as the antidote to the breeding of authentic cultures, to the new democracy of communal liberation. In other words: as the era of direct confrontation with, defense of, and concern about Europe recedes into history, the European phenomenon which has shaped innumerable rituals and reflexes is

---

15. As a representative volume, see Berndt Ostendorf, ed., *Multikulturelle Gesellschaft: Modell Amerika?* (Munich, 1994). About the differences of the notion of multiculturalism in France and Germany, see Nikolaus Werz, "'Multikulturelle Gesellschaft'—ein umstrittener Begriff: Zur Diskussion in Frankreich und Deutschland," *Dokumente* 47 (1991): 474–79.

16. Michael Lind, *The Next American Nation: The New Nationalism and the Fourth American Revolution* (New York, 1995), 55–95.

not easily abandoned, but rather reconstructed as a theme park, accessible at any time, and with the great feature of being right here on this continent.

A suggestion, no doubt. Yet it is one that finds its realization in many of the foreign language and literature departments which for decades have devoted themselves to the double mandate of bringing that foreign continent closer to home and of helping in the cultural reproduction of an America that is not just a big island, taken from the natives, but the mainland of the modern world due to its anchoring on both sides of the Atlantic. The proposed negativity of the otherness that runs through much of multicultural theory, takes on a decidedly positive and reassuring character in these departments, whereby the split between affirmative strategies on the college level and dissecting, even deconstructing strategies on the graduate level makes for a differentiated approach. This is no minor operation, if one thinks of the strategies with which a theme park like Busch Gardens near Williamsburg, Virginia, keeps its customers happily plunging into the sequence of England, Italy, France, and Germany. What is similar is the spoon-feeding approach to learning how to move around in that foreign territory of the other language, interspersed with rides and entertainment, prizes and accolades; what is different is the lack of roller coasters in the classrooms if one does not count among those the thrill ride of Parisian pronunciation or the fun house of German verbs.

Due to the low standing of the dollar with which affordable trips to Europe—the rule in the 1960s, when the enrollment soared—evaporated, due to the end of the military and ideological threat from the communist bloc, due to the breakdown of the Berlin Wall, and the onslaught of globalization which replaces the moral patronage system across the Atlantic and the Pacific, the cultural reproduction of America in its educational institutions[17] has been settled with the theme-park approach as a maintenance strategy for the transatlantic connection. The departments, threatened by increasing budget cuts across the universities and a further decline in language enrollments—while Spanish is not considered a foreign or European language anymore—find their monocultural

---

17. A comprehensive, superbly argued discussion of cultural reproduction in the era of multiculturalism can be found in Michael Geyer, "Multiculturalism and the Politics of General Education," *Critical Inquiry* 19 (1993): 499–533. See also Manfred Henningsen, "Der heilige Mauritius und der Streit um die multikulturelle Identität des Westens," *Merkur* 46 (1992): 834–45.

program picked on by multiculturalists, yet at the same time feel drawn to the practice of encoding America's place in the modern world in cultural terms. Little has been made of these contradictions, surprisingly little has been written about the fact that the multiculturalist agenda, liberating in Cornel West's sense, has seized the clash with and amalgamation of authentic otherness, an important stage in education, from the foreign language departments.

This is not a suggestion, this is a fact, though not an irreversible one. Recent institutionalizations hold sway over old installations of academe. There is a powerful intellectual drain toward the anthropology of the colonial, now the postcolonial. But it is by no means clear whether the absorption of the multicultural agenda within the American orbit does not itself create the conditions of a theme park if it intensifies the insularity instead of overcoming it.

In the mid-1980s political scientists, sponsored by the Carnegie Endowment for International Peace, tried to tackle a recurring phenomenon in the American encounter with the world. In view of the innumerable strings and connections with other countries they did not call it isolationism but rather *estrangement*.[18] The term registers the shock which the United States, regarding itself an anticolonial power, experienced when it found itself "regarded as an ally and extension of colonialism, rather than a society that offered inspiration for future development."[19] In his introduction to the book, editor Sanford Ungar asserted:

> The United States is estranged from that complex world—separate, aloof, more alone than even the most cynical or pessimistic observers might have predicted in the heyday of American postwar power.... Part of what makes today's world so uncomfortable for Americans is the perfectly understandable tendency to reject a new reality, especially strong in a society where self-confidence is part of the national ideology. 'Americans feel unqualifiedly that this is the best country in the world,' the pollster Danial Yankelovich has observed. They are taught to believe that from their earliest days in school, and any politician who disputes this fundamental truth ... is severely punished for his heresy. 'The dark side of this attitude is that we don't believe we can be wrong,' Yankelovich went on; 'we're not looking at the world from anybody else's point of view.'[20]

18. Sanford J. Ungar, ed., *Estrangement: America and the World* (New York, 1985).
19. Ibid., 13.
20. Ibid., 14 f.

Echoed in the articles of the book,[21] the indictment aimed beyond the jitters of the foreign policy establishment—at the ignorance of Americans about the world, seen as the real source of the estrangement. A decade later one might counter the indictment by calling on the success of multiculturalism which, in its American definition, is being heralded as a boon to the post-Cold-War world. There can be no doubt about the importance of this contribution, which draws on a contemporary interpretation of American democracy. And yet, despite its traceable traditions, this redefinition is itself embedded in the hegemonic insularism analyzed in the Carnegie volume. Otherwise the efforts of UNESCO in the 1980s to produce an agreement about protecting indigenous cultures from the leveling effects of international media monopolies would have been welcomed in the United States; American academic elites would have noticed that most countries in the Third World and Europe had been engaged since the 1970s in important battles over a new world information order that was to help emerging nations create their own public spheres.[22] Aside from rumblings among media specialists and watchful journalists, there was no outcry in this country in 1984 when the United States took the unprecedented step and left the foremost organization of international cultural exchange, UNESCO, because it felt disadvantaged by other peoples' insistence on maintaining their cultural identities.[23] Playing down the resentment in other countries as the usual compensatory anti-Americanism, the United States fought an economic and diplomatic battle against any infringement on its communication monopoly.

Besides the American human rights policy, which has drawn much admiration since it is upheld at the expense of American business interests, the notion of "peoples' rights," for which the international communications legislation is the measuring stick, should not go unnoticed. It delineates the extent to which other countries are enabled to retain control of their public sphere. The free circulation of information is a great principle under American tutelage,

21. "Americans are brilliant communicators but bad listeners. Because Americans can communicate effectively, the rest of humanity is, to some extent, becoming Americanized. But because Americans are bad listeners, they have resisted being humanized, in the sense of learning to respond to the needs and desires of the rest of the world." Ali A. Mazrui, "Uncle Sam's Hearing Aid," in *Estrangement: America and the World*, 181.

22. See George Gerbner and Marsha Siefert, eds., *World Communications: A Handbook* (New York, 1983), esp. 14–36, 192–216.

23. Jean Broward Shevlin Gerard, "Pourquoi les Etats-Unis ont du quitter 1 'U.N.E.S.C.O.," *Revue des Deux Mondes* 25 (June 1984): 513–21.

but it also represents the principle on which the American communications and entertainment industries overwhelm the world.

This is where European notions of cultural diversity clashed—and still clash—with American cultural monopolies, reaffirming the estrangement from undue vilification of the United States. As leaders on behalf of European and Third World countries, the French have been singled out for ridicule in their fight for keeping cultural boundaries under their own control. In 1983, the French government brought together in a conference at the Sorbonne "women and men of culture," writers, artists, historians, economists, sociologists, and industrialists, from all over the world. In the presence of President Mitterand, the two-day conference "Creation et developpement" was designed to lay down the principles of an international cultural policy whose objectives, according to Culture Minister Jacques Lang, should be "to prevent market mechanisms and the economic power struggle from imposing stereotyped, culturally meaningless products on individuals of other nations."[24] The participants agreed to complement the notion of cultural identity with that of cultural democracy, aware of the fact that cultural self-expression has a great potential for economic gains or can, at times, compensate for insufficient economic gains. The fact that ethnicity was not in the limelight does not make this realization less stringent. Where Americans are likely to argue race and ethnicity, Europeans point to social and class issues, and in this case at multiculturalism as a compensatory strategy for the dismantling of social responsibilities in the United States.

There is obviously more at stake than the fight of the French government against Hollywood on behalf of the French film industry. The battle is about different practices of global multiculturalism. It pits the preservation of local, regional, and national cultures against the workings of the international media and entertainment monopolies which carry the label "Made in the U.S.A.," if not "Made for the U.S.A." Stephen Langley has illuminated the relationship with American multiculturalism:

> The great irony about America's belated attention to its multicultural makeup is that it occurred just when the electronic media and technology are perfecting our ability to obliterate diversity. Historically, cultural assimilation has been accelerated by mass migrations, crusades,

24. Chantal Cinquin, "President Mitterand Also Watches *Dallas*: American Mass Media and French National Policy," in *The Americanization of the Global Village: Essays in Comparative Popular Culture*, ed. Roger Rollin (Bowling Green, 1989), 19.

wars, colonization and, more recently, by emigration, air travel and the increasing economic interdependence of nations. Yet, these have all had only moderate influence on the global psyche compared with the growing impact of telecommunications. How many cultures will be able to maintain their identities once they are fully 'wired?' If cultural Darwinism is part of the dynamic, then cultures that cannot adapt and evolve will not survive. People who would promote a multicultural society should perhaps focus their attention less on each other and more on the phenomenon that threatens to absorb all traditional cultures into a synthetic marketplace of consumers.[25]

Highlighting technoculturalism as the true challenge of the late twentieth century, Langley contextualizes multiculturalism "as the last significant opportunity for the human race to celebrate its diversity beyond the comparatively superficial differences imposed by skin color, national boundaries, and cultural imperialism."[26] The two developments, multiculturalism and technoculturalism, have to be seen together in the present contest between cultural conformity and cultural diversity. Langley suggests "that objections to our 'Eurocentric' society merely obscure the fact that our real cultural base is now capitalist-technological America—or, at least, what we still own of it."[27]

Recognizing this fact need not lead to technopessimism, which has its own tradition in recent history. Walter Benjamin's maxim of the 1930s, that the means of technological reproduction should not be discarded as the end of art but rather used for the political enlightenment of the masses, still has its significance. The newest tools of technological communication can be put in the service of multiculturalism. Who else but the American entertainment industry has fostered in television, film, and pop music at least a glimpse of multiculturalism as an enlightening feature for the contemporary world?[28] Who else should be swayed to do more of it? And yet, it is a thorny issue, as John Rockwell stated in the *New York Times*

25. Stephen Langley, "Multiculturalism versus Technoculturalism: Its Challenge to American Theatre and the Functions of Arts Management," in *The American Stage: Social and Economic Issues from the Colonial Period to the Present*, eds. Ron Engle and Tice L. Miller (Cambridge, 1993), 279f.

26. Ibid., 280. For a broader discussion of cultural imperialism, see John Tomlinson, *Cultural Imperialism: A Critical Introduction* (Baltimore, 1991), esp. the chapters "Media Imperialism" and "Cultural Imperialism and the Discourse of Nationality."

27. Ibid.

28. For the interwar period, see Ruth Vasey, "Foreign Parts: Hollywood's Global Distribution and the Representation of Ethnicity," *American Quarterly* 44 (1992): 617–42.

when he published a collection of international reactions to American popular culture and concluded that its overwhelming dominance in the world breeds insensitivity to other cultures' fears about the loss of their values.[29] The insensitivity is enhanced by the fact that current media priorities keep American viewers in a "cocoon,"[30] insulated from a broad understanding of people in other countries.

Thus, it is hard to have faith in a new sensitivity among Americans toward other cultures, a possibility suggested at the outset of this article. Multiculturalism has been institutionalized as an American venture with a problematic relationship to the multiculturalism of other countries and continents. It has had a great momentum, but this is hard to maintain without letting its most poignant manifestations be roped into the public relations departments of international companies or eclipsed by the leveling forces of the entertainment, media, and tourist industries. Critics have stressed the usefulness of this concept for business elites at a time of a widening rift between rich and poor and many signs of a fracturing of the middle class.[31] Even the moral satisfaction behind the American export of multiculturalism is not exempt from criticism. Benjamin Schwarz dismantles it in his proposition that political elites pursue this export from a feeling of insecurity rather than self-assuredness. Americans, he muses, realize that they do not get along well without the Anglo elites:

> The apparent success of our own multiethnic and multicultural experiment might have been engendered not by tolerance but by hegemony. Without the dominance that once dictated, however ethnocentrically, what it meant to be an American, we are left with only tolerance and pluralism to hold us together. Unfortunately, the evidence from Los Angeles to New York, from Miami to Milwaukee, shows that such principles are not so powerful as we had believed and hoped. Afraid to face our problems directly, we look elsewhere, and encourage other countries to prove to us that more pluralism and more tolerance are all that are needed to reunite divided societies.[32]

29. John Rockwell, "The New Colossus: American Culture as Power Export," *New York Times*, 30 January 1994, 30–31.

30. Kathryn J. Olmstead, "Breaking the Cocoon: Cultural Journalism in a Global Community," *Journal of Popular Culture* 25, no. 2 (1991): 153–65.

31. Michael Lind, "To Have and Have Not: Notes on the Progress of the American Class War," *Harper's Magazine*, June 1995, 35–47.

32. Benjamin Schwarz, "The Diversity Myth: America's Leading Export," *Atlantic Monthly*, May 1995, 67.

How far away has Europe moved? Looking at English departments in academic institutions, one cannot be sure. The fortress of Anglo culture has integrated, against many odds, gender studies, ethnic studies, postcolonial and cultural studies, offering the stomping grounds for both the initiated and uninitiated to engage in reading the canon and discussing the "other." The engagement is multifaceted and intellectually stimulating, has revitalized a stale curriculum and made the English major attractive again. In response to the interest in multiculturalism, the departments have institutionalized it. Multiculturalism has become a drawing card of a department that does not teach a foreign language. It assumes competence in teaching many works of foreign cultures in English. The engagement with the other occurs on safe ground.

A reason for concern? Under the current decrease of funding for education, this curricular agglomeration in one department is welcomed by administrators. Keeping multiculturalism under an English roof reflects the national disposition. The decline of foreign language departments where the engagement with other cultures tends to involve another language is linked both to this disposition and the steep decrease in public funding for universities. There can be no doubt that government sponsoring, from the GI Bill to Title IV allocations, have helped sustain the work of foreign language departments through most of the Cold War. Simply put, public funding usually means public recognition. The current reprivatization of the university relieves it of many obligations that have made the linkup with Europe a two-way street. Reprivatization drains funds away from the teaching of all languages, not just from Russian or less commonly taught languages. What Michael Geyer calls "the Atlanticist cultural formation"[33] framed an important part of the publicly supported curriculum; the reprivatized university tends to frame its goals according to the needs of intellectual and commercial pressure groups. Multiculturalism fits into the latter as it "seems to offer the prospect of using intellectual discourse no longer as a means of dominant acculturation or international administration, but rather as the articulation of alternative points of view represented in the persons of the intellectuals themselves."[34]

The question is to what extent the latter agenda will be absorbed by the venerable American tradition of self-help and individualism which always had a strong grounding in the general education

33. Geyer, "Multiculturalism," 510.
34. Chicago Cultural Studies Group, "Critical Multiculturalism," *Critical Inquiry* 18 (1992): 541.

philosophy of the college. This tradition is not without an European-oriented component which since the nineteenth century has responded to a broad constituency of second-, third-, and even fourth-generation immigrant cultures and identities. If in doubt, one studies the language that reconnects with some aspects of identity. It is worth mentioning that the ethnic revival of the 1960s and 1970s was a predominantly European-oriented phenomenon. The notion of the "Invention of Ethnicity,"[35] as the theoretical basis of most contemporary research in this area, has been a mediation of American identity primarily through European diversity. Its reality can be observed in the foreign language classroom in the college, where the Italian, German, Russian, or even French heritage of an assumed ethnicity translates into a grassroots internationalism that makes many students into bicultural professionals. While the assumption that ethnicity leads to these language contacts might often be true, the opposite is at least as frequent: that ethnicity as an assumed secondary identity is a result or by-product of this kind of learning. Only the French connection is built mainly on the traditional educational status formula, although its drawing power is vanishing. Also mentioned should be the numerous incentives that reinforce the European connection for the identity building of Jewish students—beyond the specifics of national cultures.

Although these practices contribute to a less idiosyncratic approach to educational self-definition, they tend to be seen as a hold-out rather than an up-to-date mandate. Their vulnerability was amply proven by the curriculum wars about Western Civilization and the "great books" courses in the 1980s. It was confirmed in the mid-1990s when previous proclamations that had been formulated by Republican conservatives were eclipsed in the big sweep with which Newt Gingrich declared an end to, among others, the government's responsibility for social welfare and the coordination of public education. The ease with which the commitments to the humanistic and social values of Western tradition were canceled in the confirmation of American economic individualism and capitalist elitism, is the true marker of vulnerability, even though the undertaking remained stalled, in a confirmation of the experience that Americans, after watching the pendulum swing far out, tend to guide it back to a middle ground.

35. For an overview of the discussion, see the special forum in *Journal of American Ethnic History* 12, no. 1 (1992): 3–63, esp. Kathleen Conzen et al.,"The Invention of Ethnicity: A Perspective from the U.S.A.," 3–41.

In order to gain from the advances of multiculturalism and post-colonialism, and in light of the increasing orientation of the country toward the Pacific, a rethinking of this middle ground has to make use of the traditions that favor such a middle in the first place. Although a "sense of balance" is not exactly a clear measure for political and social programs, it might not be without significance in the educational realm, where the reproduction of knowledge mediates between the general and the specific, between self and other, past and present. It might even have its bearing on the disassociation from Europe and its consequences for the maintenance of American ideological leadership. At any rate, the correlation between the Atlanticist ties and the ability of the United States to overcome parochialism—also in the realm of self-confirmation—is an old truth. It should be challenged by every generation. It has been challenged by this generation.

If it is still appropriate to refer to tradition, it might be worthwhile to return once more to Randolph Bourne who not only articulated this truth but also looked for remedy when he observed the country's first attempt to assume moral leadership as an international power in World War I. Bourne addressed the problems of insularity with a suggestion which, under the auspices of today's world-wide communication network, holds even more promise than in his troubled years. He spoke of "some form of dual citizenship" which, as an intellectual, "cultural" concept, should be established despite "so much articulate horror among us." "Dual citizenship we may have to recognize as the rudimentary form of that international citizenship to which, if our words mean anything, we aspire."[36] Bourne mentions as an illustration the dual citizenship that France permitted its citizens; today one would refer to the Europeans who enjoy the dual citizenship both of their country and of Europe, thus advancing their self-definition beyond the confines of their national identity. The American, for example, who is enamored of France, "finds that this expansion involves no shameful conflict within him, no surrender of his native attitude."[37]

Thanks to current computer technology which wires the home to the world, the outreach to the other continent is not confined to the traditional channels. While privatization has its negative effects on the academic pursuit of foreign languages, it can compensate in this area. Individual computer connections allow different forms of intercontinental communication. It can help promote comparative

36. Bourne, "Trans-National America," *War*, 119.
37. Ibid., 120.

perspectives on a myriad of issues that cut across national boundaries, from the social welfare system to sports accidents and drug rehabilitation, from piano repairs to many questions within education. As the recent battles over the viability of area studies have shown,[38] comparison is a practice that reaches beyond a strictly intellectual endeavor. It yields its best results if it is also *experienced* in contact with a specific culture, a different form of everyday pursuits, leading to a humane application of globalization. Whether the computer can provide enough of the experience—and can address the language question creatively—is, however, another matter. It seems that the university still has more resources for the institutional practice of such a dual or multiple citizenships.

38. Jacob Heilbrunn, "The News from Everywhere: Does Global Thinking Threaten Local Knowledge? The Social Science Research Council Debates the Future of Area Studies," *Lingua Franca* (May/June 1996): 49–56. The Social Science Research Council is an important agenda setter in European Studies. See the *European Studies Newsletter*, and for a recent overview: Peter A. Hall, "The State of European Studies," *Lingua Franca* 24, no. 5/6 (1995): 6–16.

11. Inventing the Nation: Literary Study As a Discipline of Identity

Hinrich C. Seeba

The national discourse in nineteenth-century Germany clearly preceded the academic discipline called *Germanistik*. The question what it means to be German, or—in Ernst Moritz Arndt's famous words of 1813—"Was ist des Deutschen Vaterland?"[1] was discussed long before serious efforts were made to explore such meaning in political or academic institutions. It was not before 1846 that Jacob Grimm borrowed the name of *Germanisten* from legal studies, the study of Germanic (rather than Roman) law, to embrace three disciplines devoted to defining and reaffirming German identity. Grimm saw jurisprudence, history, and philology bound together by "der begriff der deutschheit, worauf der name hinweist" (the term Germanness, which is reflected by the name [Germanisten]).[2] The very name of Germanistik meant the study of what constitutes Germanness, which in turn was widely understood to exclude alterity on ethnic grounds. This, of course, raises the question implied in the planning of this panel: what was the role of Germanistik in suppressing multiculturalism? As the terms "multiculturalism" and "multiethnicity" are often used interchangeably, I would rather pose the question as follows: what role have various disciplines of cultural studies played in shifting the definition of national identity from a multicultural to a mono-ethnic constituent?

1. Ernst Moritz Arndt, "Des Deutschen Vaterland" (1813), in *Gedichte*, 2nd ed., (Berlin, 1865), 233–35.

2. Jacob Grimm, "Über den Namen der Germanisten" (Rede auf der Frankfurter Germanisten-Versammlung 1846), in *Recensionen und vermischte Aufsätze*, (Berlin, 1884), vol. 4, 568. Unless otherwise noted, all translations are my own.

The issue here, it seems to me, is not as much "nationalizing the discipline," which would presuppose the primacy of the discipline over the national discourse, as it is, if we remain within the word game of this panel, "disciplining the nation," i.e., reigning in, demarcating, and defining what was believed to be the national identity, in what we would call today an interdisciplinary effort. It is this commitment of interacting disciplines to the primary concern—*Deutschheit*—that determined the early history of Germanistik. The institutionalized study of German language and literature was the *result* of, rather than the *cause* for, the quest for a German national identity. The concept of nation as an "imagined community" (in the sense of Benedict Anderson)[3] was invented first as a literary image before it could be studied in the university and pursued as a political purpose.

This sequential model of disciplinary history is, of course, widely known,[4] but it needs to be remembered today, when Germany once again seems to be involved in another invention of national identity, even in an attempt at rewriting, if not remythologizing, the historical narrative. With German unification to be completed only one day later, Frank Schirrmacher claimed in the *Frankfurter Allgemeine Zeitung* on 2 October 1990 that postwar German literature now had outlived its purpose and its *Gründungsmythos* (foundational myth) needed to be replaced with another myth of origin which, as it turns out, recalls the German realism of Bismarck's *Gründerzeit*.[5] The pressure to debunk old myths of origin and to help create new ones, which would help restore, in spite of the Third Reich, a sense of continuity, could be seen in light of the reversed title of this panel as an attempt to shape the national discourse with the help of literary

3. Cf. Benedict Anderson, *Imagined Communities: Reflections on the Origin and Spread of Nationalism* (London and New York, 1983), 13: "My point of departure is that nationality, or, as one might prefer to put it in view of the word's multiple significations, nation-ness, as well as nationalism, are cultural artifacts of a particular kind."

4. Cf. Hinrich C. Seeba, "'Zeitgeist' und 'deutscher Geist': Zur Nationalisierung der Epochentendenz um 1800," in *Deutsche Vierteljahrsschrift für Literaturwissenschaft und Geistesgeschichte: Von der gelehrten zur disziplinären Gemeinschaft* (Sonderheft, 1987), eds. Jürgen Fohrmann and Wilhelm Vosskamp (Stuttgart, 1987), 188–215; and idem, "Nationalbücher: Zur Kanonisierung nationaler Bildungsmuster in der frühen Germanistik," in *Wissenschaft und Nation. Studien zur Entstehungsgeschichte der deutschen Literaturwissenschaft*, eds. Jürgen Fohrmann and Wilhelm Vosskamp (Munich, 1991) vol. 1, 57–71.

5. Frank Schirrmacher, "Abschied von der Literatur der Bundesrepublik. Neue Pässe, neue Identitäten, neue Lebensläufe: Über die Kündigung einiger Mythen des westdeutschen Bewußtseins," *Frankfurter Allgemeine Zeitung*, 2 October 1990, Literaturbeilage, 1.

imagination no longer justified with the moral impetus of the post-national generation after 1945. Looking at the literary implications of identity formation in the nineteenth century, it thus seems, is not at all a merely historical exercise in antiquarian notions.

With regard to identity formation, as with almost anything requiring models of explanation, there are two schools of thought, represented by the "essentialists," on the one hand, and the "constructivists," on the other. While the first would argue that there really is an inherently different German character created by an act of God, the second would contend that what is perceived as a German identity is the result of a collective effort to engage in the construction of such imagined character. While both schools, as we know, are at opposite ends of the spectrum, they both rely on highly fictionalized texts of collective memory to which they assign only a different status of significance. While the essentialists, among them many popular authors of nineteenth-century historiography, read the history of German literature as an *expression* of the primary unfolding of the *deutscher Geist* (German spirit), the constructivists see it as the privileged *medium* for inventing such national spirit. While the essentialists concentrate on the myth of origin from which the German persona sprang, the constructivists critically look at—and sometimes creatively engage in—the rhetorical strategies that are necessary to shroud the origin of identity in mythological mystery and, yet, to personify it with an heroic subject.

The most obvious, now almost forgotten genealogical myth of the essentialist kind is "Teut," presented in Theodor Heinsius's extensive, five-volume exploration of German identity in a handbook for teaching German, simply entitled *Teut* (1807–11). In this etymological fantasy based on the name of the Germanic tribe, the Teutons, who were defeated by the Romans in the battle of Aquae Sextae in 102 B.C., Teut was introduced as the Germanic god from whom *die Deutschen* derived their name and thus their god-given right to exist as an autonomous community. Obviously engaged in a cultural crusade against Napoleon's military dominance, Heinsius was the first to call the literary period from Haller to Klopstock and Lessing "das Zeitalter klassischer Literatur" (the age of classic literature).[6] In thus claiming literary classicism as a weapon in mythological identity

6. Theodor Heinsius, *Teut*, 2nd ed. (Berlin, 1818), vol. 4., 471f., 492, 519 ff., quoted from Eva Becker, "'Klassiker' in der deutschen Literaturgeschichtsschreibung zwischen 1780 und 1860," in *Zur Literatur der Restaurationsepoche 1815–1848. Forschungsreferate und Aufsätze*, eds. Jost Hermand and Manfred Windfuhr (Stuttgart, 1970), 355.

formation, Heinsius lay the ground for the politically inspired concept of national literature. As Ludwig Wachler, one of its first advocates, suggested in 1818, the study of such national literature promised "Rückkehr zu teutscher Gesinnung, zu teutschem Glauben, zu teutscher Frömmigkeit" (return to German sensibilities, to German faith, to German piety).[7] In this antiquated spelling reminiscent of Heinsius's renowned title, the desired return to "teutscher Gesinnung," of course, is another etymological attempt at restoring a lost national paradise, the triadic invention of a mythological origin evoking the past splendor of the Holy Roman Empire, which was defeated at the hands of Napoleon in 1806.

Another case in point, better known today and based on a much longer tradition of identity formation, is Hermann who defeated the Romans in A.D. 9. This Germanic tribesman and renegade officer in the Roman army, whose historic name until the sixteenth century was Arminius, was ideally suited to take on the role of the heroic subject with whom many generations of disadvantaged Germans could identify to uplift their spirits in times of national misery.[8] Hermann's role as hero of identity was celebrated in two historic moments: first, during the Reformation when Hermann came to serve as a symbol of Protestant opposition to "Rome," which in Luther's time meant the papacy, and, second, during the emerging nationalism of the nineteenth century when Hermann came to symbolize the anti-French sentiment and the German resolve to achieve national unity, if necessary, militarily. In both instances Hermann personified the ethnic opposition between Germanic and Romance cultures.

The underlying opposition between German and Latin had been at the very root of the word "deutsch." For deutsch, which is derived from Old High German "diot" (people), meaning the language of the people, signifies the linguistic separation from the dominance of Latin as the universal language in medieval Europe, a claim to autonomy in the name of the less educated people and, one might say, of popular culture. Ironically, the first evidence of the word deutsch, written in 786 by Charlemagne's chaplain Wigbold reporting on a bilingual synod, is in its Latinized version: "tam latine,

7. Ludwig Wachler, *Vorlesungen über die Geschichte der teutschen Nationallitteratur*, 2nd ed. (Frankfurt/Main, 1834), vol. 1, 3.

8. On the national myth of Hermann, cf. Hinrich C. Seeba, "Schwerterhebung. Zur Konstruktion des heroischen Subjekts / Raising the Sword: On the Construction of the Heroic Subject," *Daidalos. Architektur-Kunst-Kultur* 49 (15 September 1993): 36–51.

quam theodisce, quo omnes intelligere possent."[9] The reason, thus, for introducing German as a second language, which would increasingly compete with the universal Latin, was to give localized attention to the diversity of people who needed to understand what was negotiated on their behalf. It was at least as much recognition of such popular diversity as it was a move toward national unity which motivated also Luther's translation of the Bible.

Against this background the following—admittedly very hypothetical—suggestion may be less surprising. For the sake of argument I submit that it was such localized attention to cultural diversity that was also at the center of much of the national discourse in late eighteenth-century Germany. Multiculturalism, which, according to popular belief, is the antinomy of nationalism, may very well have constituted its very core—until the discourse of political unity eventually replaced the notion of cultural pluralism. Following Montesquieu's climatological studies in difference, in his 1748 *Esprit de lois*, and Herder's repeated plea for the historicization of culture, there was a sense of interconnection, if not outright causality, between the increasing awareness of cultural pluralism and the emerging need to define and defend one's own allegiance to national identity within the larger picture of cultural relativity. Characteristically for enlightened multiculturalism, the Swiss-born popular philosopher, Johann Georg Zimmermann, wrote his 1758 essay "Vom Nationalstolz" both *against* chauvinist prejudice, ignorance, and intolerance and, as if to anticipate Ernest Gellner's argument for the role of nationalism in modernization,[10] *for* genuine collective self-respect as a political virtue.[11] Seen in the context of the enormous differentiation of knowledge, the efforts by many Enlightenment writers to define and propagate national identity and to base it on literary tradition may no longer sound like calls for exclusive homogeneity so characteristic of nineteenth-century nationalism. Friedrich Carl von Moser in his brochure "Vom Deutschen Nationalgeist" (1765), Leonard Meister in his anonymous sketch of national literature, *Beyträge zur Geschichte der teutschen Sprache und National-Litteratur* (1777),[12] and especially Justus Möser in his response to King Frederic's II

---

9. Friedrich Kluge, *Etymologisches Wörterbuch der deutschen Sprache*, 19th ed. (Berlin, 1963), 129.

10. Ernest Gellner, *Nations and Nationalism* (Ithaca, 1983).

11. Johann Georg Zimmermann, *Vom Nationalstolz. Über die Herkunft der Vorurteile gegenüber anderen Menschen und Völkern* (1758), reprint of 4th ed. of 1768 (Zürich, 1980).

12. [Leonhard Meister], *Beyträge zur Geschichte der teutschen Sprache und National-Litteratur* (London, 1777), vol. 1.

attack on German literature, "Über die deutsche Sprache und Literatur" (1781)—all of them address cultural diversity as constituting German identity, not as much to lament it as friction and alienation during the final years of the declining Holy Roman Empire, but to celebrate it, as Justus Möser proudly does, as cultural variety which is particular to German identity: "es bleibt doch wohl eine unstreitige Wahrheit, daß tausend Mannigfaltigkeiten zur Einheit gestimmt mehr Würkung tun, als eine Einheit, worin nur fünfe versammlet sind" (it is an undeniable truth that a thousand pieces working as one unit are more powerful than a unit that is only made of five smaller pieces).[13] The privileging of diversity over unity may be somewhat out of place in the conventional national discourse as we know it, but it certainly offers an historical alternative to the dominant models of national tradition which are being surmised today in the search of a new German identity.

Against this background, even a nationalist hymn such as Ernst Moritz Arndt's "Was ist des Deutschen Vaterland?" takes on a different meaning. Even though the intended answer to the question, in the last line, is rather predictable: "Das ganze Deutschland soll es sein!" (It should be all of Germany!), in the enumeration of all the regions, which by themselves cannot comprise the nation ("O nein! nein! nein!"), there is an implicit recognition of the fact that German identity is based on regional, cultural diversity: Preußen, Schwaben, Rheinland, Schleswig, Bayern, Steiermark, Mark Brandenburg, Pommern, Westfalen, Schweiz, Tirol, Österreich are only a few regions listed for their particular cultural identities, all of which are to be integrated according to the dictum "e pluribus unum." As with most of the early advocates of national identity, from Johann Heinrich Campe in 1807 to Jacob Grimm in 1854, Arndt's common denominator for integrating "das ganze Deutschland" is, of course, the German language: "[s]o weit die deutsche Zunge klingt" (as far as the German tongue is heard).

Inventing the nation, so it seems, is an act of linguistic creation, a speech act. In order to grant a figment of imagination the status of political reality, this invention relies heavily on the dogged pursuit of national literature.[14] Literary study thus became the favored

---

13. Justus Möser, "Über die deutsche Sprache und Literatur. Schreiben an einen Freund" (1781), in *Anwalt des Vaterlands. Wochenschriften, Patriotische Phantasien, Aufsätze, Fragmente* (Leipzig and Weimar, 1978), 409.

14. Cf. Jürgen Fohrmann, *Das Projekt der deutschen Literaturgeschichte. Entstehung und Scheitern einer nationalen Poesiegeschichtsschreibung zwischen Humanismus und Deutschem Kaiserreich* (Stuttgart, 1988).

discipline of identity formation. But a decade after he had adopted the name of Germanistik to promote the study of Deutschheit, Jacob Grimm was compelled to lament the fictionality of his own claim to national identity: "was haben wir denn gemeinsames als unsere sprache und literatur?" (What do we have in common other than our language and literature?)[15] Obviously, the diversity prevailed over the textualized claim to unity—until the political unification of 1871, achieved with military rather than verbal strength, signified a powerful move toward ethnically based homogeneity. Only then multiculturalism, no longer a sign of desirable diversity, came to be considered a threat to centralized power. This is only one more reason why the *Gründerjahre*, whose pride in national diversity, with its as yet undeveloped respect for alterity, gave way to increasingly enforced claims to uniformity, do not serve well as a historical model. One hundred twenty years later, any attempts to once again invent a nation would be unified only in the desire to downplay difference.

15. Jacob Grimm, "Vorwort" (2 March 1854), in *Deutsches Wörterbuch*, eds. Jacob und Wilhelm Grimm (Leipzig, 1854), vol. 1, column III.

Part IV

MULTICULTURALISM IN THE TRANSATLANTIC SPHERE

12. Geographies of Memory: Protocols of Writing in the Borderlands

Azade Seyhan

Es warteten auch andereTürken an der Deutschland-Tür. Ein Mann mit dem Schaf, ein Hodscha mit seinem Minarett. Ein illegaler Arbeiter verkleidete sich als Fußballer, so hoffte er durch die Grenzkontrolle nach Deutschland durchzukommen. Der Bauer und sein Esel warteten auch. Sie warteten und warteten. Die Deutschland-Tür ging auf und gleich wieder zu. Es kam ein türkischer Toter, seinen Sarg tragend.[1]

(Other Turks were also waiting at the Gate to Germany. A man with his sheep, a hodja with his minaret. An illegal worker masqueraded as a soccer player hoping to get through the border patrol into Germany. The farmer and his donkey waited, too. They waited and waited. The Gate to Germany opened and then immediately closed. A dead Turk came out carrying his coffin.)

— *Emine Sevgi Özdamar*

To cross the linguistic border implies that you decenter your voice. The border crosser develops two or more voices. This is often the experience of Mexican writers who come to the United States. We develop different speaking selves that speak for different aspects of our identity.[2]

— *Guillermo Gómez-Peña*

---

1. Emine Sevgi Özdamar, "Karagöz in Alamania. Schwarzauge in Deutschland," in *Mutterzunge* (Berlin, 1990), 61. All translations are my own.
2. Guillermo Gómez-Peña, "Bilingualism, Biculturalism, and Borders." Conversation with Coco Fusco, in *English Is Broken Here: Notes on Cultural Fusion in the Americas*, ed. Coco Fusco (New York, 1995), 156.

This century, now in its final countdown to closing the door on a millennium, will probably go down in demographic history as an era of mass migrations of unprecedented magnitude, cutting across national, ethnic, religious, cultural, class, urban, and rural lines. "To the forcibly induced migrations of slaves, peasants, the poor, and the ex-colonial world that make up so many of the hidden stories of modernity," writes Iain Chambers, "we can also add the increasing nomadism of modern thought.... Our sense of belonging, our language and the myths we carry in us remain, but no longer as 'origins' or signs of 'authenticity' capable of guaranteeing the sense of our lives."[3] The mythic formulations of our originary communities now manifest themselves "as traces, memories and murmurs that are mixed with other histories, episodes, encounters."[4]

The last two decades have witnessed the widespread displacement and resettlement of a multiplicity of populations as a result of war, economic necessity, labor migration, brain drain from countries of the Third World, search for political asylum, or the dissolution of one-time national borders, such as the unification of Germany and the demise of the Soviet state. The various ethnic, religious, and national groups that have left their traditional homelands voluntarily or under threat of death, torture, poverty, or imprisonment surge in endless streams toward the gates of more affluent and politically stable countries of North America and Europe. The reception of these groups often takes place in an arena of contestatory and confrontational politics and is imbricated in the larger debates calling for "traditional national identities" or in "proposals for new forms of transnational community, and assertions of regionalized corporate identities."[5]

An active European site of fiery debates, where stakes involving issues of labor migration, immigration, patriation, and national and ethnic identity politics are very high, is the reunified German state. At this historical juncture, approximately six million foreigners, including the so-called *Gastarbeiter* (guest workers), refugees, various political and economic exiles, writers, artists, and professionals are permanently living in Germany. In the embattled Europe of the post-Cold War era, Germany with her economic stature, political power and stability, generous welfare system, and what

3. Iain Chambers, *Migrancy, Culture, Identity* (London, 1994), 18.
4. Ibid., 19.
5. Gisela Brinker-Gabler and Sidonie Smith, "Introduction," in *Writing New Identities: Gender, Nation, and Immigration in Contemporary Europe*, eds. idem (Minneapolis, 1997), 1.

until recently were very flexible asylum laws, has become, perhaps quite unwillingly and unwittingly, a new diaspora for an eclectic body of displaced peoples. However, since Germany is officially not a country of immigration, foreign-born residents of the German state who have lived, worked, and paid taxes there for decades and their German-born children cannot claim citizenship and the rights and privileges pertaining thereto.

In order to meet the labor needs of its postwar industrial growth, West Germany began importing workers from the countries of the Mediterranean basin. The first treaty to recruit short-term workers was signed in 1955 with Italy. Bilateral agreements with other countries followed in quick succession. Under the terms of the treaty signed with Turkey in 1963, the first crew of 100,000 Turkish workers arrived in West Germany. Although initially only poor Anatolian farmers joined the army of recruits, eventually artisans, civil servants, teachers, and small business owners, all increasingly frustrated by the economic hardship that was eroding the middle class, boarded the train to Munich. In 1973, when the need for workers had stabilized, recruitment was frozen (*Anwerbestopp*). However, whenever the economy demanded additional labor force, employers devised ways of letting more foreign workers in through the loopholes in the system.

In the course of time, a great number of Turkish workers and their families decided to stay. During the last two decades, many political refugees from Turkey also sought asylum in Germany, bringing the number of Turkish residents there close to three million. Most Germans are, at best, oblivious to this culture in their midst and, at worst, openly hostile to it. Although the Turkish community in Germany has been transformed from a migrant labor force into an ethnic minority, it has virtually no political representation. The nationalistic passions that swept Germany after the reunification brought the citizenship debates to a halt and "created a climate in which resident non-Germans were equated to asylum seekers and tarred with the same brush of illegitimacy."[6]

The German concept of citizenship is based on blood ties and birth place—*ius sanguinis*—and not residency, acculturation, language, and circumstance—*ius soli*. Consequently, the Turks of Germany are consigned, physically and figuratively, to a life of detention at the border. The literary works of many Turkish-German writers represent, in naturalistic, parodistic, or allegorical genres, the waking

6. Eva Kolinsky, "Conclusion," *Turkish Culture in German Society Today*, eds. David Horrocks and Eva Kolinsky (Providence, 1995), 185.

life of the Turkish subject as an uninterrupted nightmare of applying and reapplying for passports, visas, and residence and work permits. Caught in the interstices of geographical and cultural borders, the Turkish residents of Germany embody an essentialist "foreignness" marked by a hybridity of speech, custom, mannerism, and style. In tones resonant of the lament of the eternally "foreign" Turk, the Chicana poet, novelist, and critic Ana Castillo writes in her essay, "A Countryless Woman," that she is commonly perceived as a foreigner wherever she is, including the United States and Mexico.[7]

Guillermo Gómez-Peña, a Mexican writer, critic, and performance artist, who now lives and writes in America but is not (yet) a Chicano, maintains that living the history of border crossings, deterritorialization, and reterritorialization shreds the fiber of monolithic national or ethnic identities. Gómez-Peña sees himself as a Latin American, a Mexican, and a Mexican in the process of Chicanization. In America, he does not have a grasp of Chicano slang, in Mexico, his speech betrays patterns of *pocho* idiom, in Spain, he is called *Sudaca*, and in Germany, he is mistaken for a Turk.[8] Like Castillo, who eloquently expresses Lukács notion of the "transcendent homelessness" of the *mestiza* and Gómez-Peña, who has settled into the permanence of transition, the Turkish Germans, neither Turkish nor German, wander forever along the Möbius strip of cultural borderlands. Their social, cultural, and linguistic nomadism and struggles have produced a literature of powerful resonance at the periphery of German society.

The cultural activism of Turkish and other non-German writers, artists, and academics is both a response and a form of resistance to the social intolerance and injustice that daily confront the many foreign residents of Germany. In spite of the high degree of critical sophistication that the works of nonnative German writers have attained, their writing is still not stripped of the label *Migrant (In)enliteratur* (migrant literature). Like the term *Gastarbeiter*, this designation diminishes the impact and distorts the parameters of the significance of this body of writing. The word *Migrant* houses connotations of impermanence, instability, detachment, and lack of social commitment, and eschews empowering notions of adaptability, resilience, and synthesis. In order to examine more fully the critical and historical implications of this literature, I would

---

7. Ana Castillo, *Massacre of the Dreamers: Essays on Xicanisma* (Albuquerque, 1994), 21.
8. Gómez-Peña, "Bilingualism," 153.

like to draw on the transitive momentum of the concept of borderlands writing. This theoretical metaphor marks a turning point in contemporary cultural criticism, for it transforms the notion of a geographical space to include a historical place. It generates a conceptual field where word and act, different idioms, intellectual heritages, and cultural memories are engaged in exchange, confrontation, and renegotiation.

Although the topos of border originated in an actual topography, at a geographical border, it has since traveled to sites where borders mark passages not necessarily in space but rather in time, history, and memory. It is the challenge posed to individual and collective memory during the passage through the borderlands that lends the writing of dislocated peoples its poetic urgency. The writers of the modern diaspora can claim neither the homeland nor the host land as theirs. They need another place, a third space, often a place of writing which belongs to the geographies of language, memory, and myth. Memory is an essential component of individual, ethnic, or national identity. For the displaced people of modern diasporas, however, collective memory is often jeopardized. The reductive strategies of politicization or ideologization further challenge the endurance of cultural legacies in diaspora. Therefore, the necessity for remembrance and its realization in writing, or (more precisely) re-writing, often take on the function of a sacred ritual. In this context, writers become "speakers" of memory par excellence. Literature emerges as an institution of memory, the topos of subjective and historical agency in a time of emotional loss. What was lost, forgotten, erased, or occluded, is recovered in figurative discourse. Unlike official histories, literature can accommodate alternative memories and contestatory scripts of the past.

"To make themselves the master of memory and forgetfulness," writes Jacques Le Goff in *History and Memory*, "is one of the great preoccupations of classes, groups, and individuals who have dominated and continue to dominate historical societies."[9] When those minority groups that are often perceived as personae non gratae, such as Arabs in Europe and the United States, Mexicans in the southwest United States, Turks in Germany, and Koreans in Japan become objects of critical, academic, and media scrutiny, they suffer further disenfranchisement, as their own stories and histories are rewritten and reinterpreted in a way that erases their past and

9. Jacques Le Goff, *History and Memory*, trans. Steven Rendall and Elizabeth Claman (New York, 1994), 54.

confiscates their present. Individual and collective memories in the works of immigrant writers of the United States and Germany, who are the subjects of my recent research, constitute a vast complex of social history that represents what Le Goff considers its own "counterweight" or response to the one-sided flow of representation and information generated for the defense of certain interests. In what follows, I shall attempt to illustrate how memory recovers history, retells, reinvents, and repossesses it for individual and collective empowerment in the tales of two writers, Gloria Anzaldúa, a Chicana/*tejana* poet and critic from the United States side of the U.S.-Mexican border and Emine Sevgi Özdamar, a Turkish writer living in Germany. Their writing illustrates the critical development that is changing preconceived notions about so-called minority literatures.

I think it is no longer feasible to map in a seamless way either an American or a German identity. Both the United States and, more recently, Germany have come to represent the modern diaspora for growing numbers of people who leave their homelands for political and economic reasons. The choice of writers in this comparative reading was suggested by the border situation of their respective cultures with regard to the concept of a Eurocentrically defined history. Turkey is at the eastern border of Europe, and Mexico exists at a double border, that is, on the southern margin of the United States as well as on the western margin of Europe. Historically, both the Mexicans in the United States and the Turks in Germany constituted the backbone of imported (and often unskilled labor), although the history of Turkish labor in Germany is a much more recent phenomenon dating only from the 1960s. Both groups have faced the most extreme forms of economic exploitation and have traditionally been considered undesirable aliens. Though economically indispensable, they represent the personae not gratae among immigrant groups in their respective host countries.

Whereas the Asian American, for example, is generally regarded as ambitious, industrious, and academically gifted (the stereotypical science or math whiz), the Chicano is often represented as a wetback and a temporary or seasonal laborer. Turks in Germany are represented in almost identical terms. Since Turks are a predominantly Muslim, though a secular and Westernized people, they are considered culturally inferior to other "guest workers" from a Christian culture, such as Greeks or Italians. The juxtaposed reading of these two literary traditions of exile is not motivated by a mere comparatist impulse and is not meant to detract from the complex particularities of either one. Rather, it aspires to enhance both their uniqueness and their universal appeal by mutual reflection and by generating an awareness of the implicit dialogue that connects them. The work of a "conscienticized" writer, in the words of Ana Castillo, is "to be open to the endless possibilities of associations,"[10] whether by using cultural metaphors familiar to the intended reader or borrowing from other cultural traditions.

The works of Gloria Anzaldúa and Emine Sevgi Özdamar portray their historical and personal destinies as gendered and ethnic subjects and their positioning between different languages, idioms, and generational and cultural terms. Women of Turkish and Mexican descent, traditionally confined to home and hearth in self-aggrandizing patriarchal family structures, struggle to reinvent, without the benefit of historical precedent, a legitimate identity in yet another foreign idiom. And above and beyond their linguistic and narrative experimentation, the works of Anzaldúa and Özdamar should perhaps be recognized as a memorial to family and collective histories that are being forced into oblivion by our high-tech modernity. Computers, fax machines, the Internet, the World Wide Web overwhelm us with stored memory and a never-ending flow of information that is impossible to sort out and process. The ubiquitousness of this information overload has ironically led to a demand for human memory which has come to represent "the attempt to slow down information processing,... to recover a mode of contemplation outside the universe of simulation and fast-speed information and cable networks, to claim some anchoring space in a world of puzzling and often threatening heterogeneity ..."[11]

On the whole, the transfigurations and transplantations at cultural borders have developed in three successive and sometimes synchronic states. The first phase in emergent ethnic literatures tends to be confessional, comprising mostly personal and collective stories of passage and immigration. These are often in the form of interpretive chronicles of a group and written in the native language. The second phase is in the language of the country of immigration and takes in its purview an aesthetically inscribed field of social observation and critique. The critically transformative third stage is a borderland of different languages, rites of passage, and negotiations between myth and reality, memory and presence, madness and reason, and factual account and revolutionary experimentations in language and style. Since these stages may emerge

10. Castillo, *Massacre of the Dreamers,* 170.
11. Andreas Huyssen, *Twilight Memories: Marking Time in a Culture of Amnesia* (New York, 1995), 7.

both diachronically and synchronically depending on immigration histories and patterns, they cannot be classified in a strictly historical order but rather are characterized by various transformations of personal and collective memory, which "is sometimes retreating and sometimes overflowing."[12]

The critical interest of this discussion centers on memory as an act of construction initiated and reinforced by subject positions, pedagogical imperatives, critical training, and a dialectic of fragmentation and unity. Memory is always a re-presentation, making present again that which no longer is present. And representation is inherent to language. The theory debates of the poststructuralist era have shown us that concepts of race, ethnicity, and gender are socially and culturally constructed and are shaped by specific historical conditions. Language is the primary tool for these constructions. Therefore, literary texts become a critical forum for understanding the conditions for the production of prejudice, discrimination, sexism, and xenophobia. The work of Anzaldúa and Özdamar is informed by a critical consciousness of how language creates dichotomies of mastery and loss, and legitimizes structures of power. Through a sustained archeology and reconstruction of the lost continents of their respective cultures, these writers produce a discursive territory conducive to the creation of new forms of cultural community in exile.

Though not intended as a theoretical blueprint, Gloria Anzaldúa's *Borderlands/La Frontera: The New Mestiza* illustrates how ethnic individuals and groups can situate themselves sequentially and simultaneously in contesting or overlapping positions of cultural memory. Anzaldúa, a self-proclaimed new *mestiza*, produces a text in the tradition of German romanticism's *Mischgedicht* (mixed poem). A poetic performance of its own critical message and a crosssover of various genres, her book presents its story in a collection of poems, reminiscences, personal and collective histories, and critical combat. Thus, the text itself emerges as a *mestizaje*, a cross-fertilization of ideas, images, mourning, and memory. It resists generic limitations that may be geographical, historical, or cultural. The act of inscription at the borders establishes a position of questioning and challenge: "The U.S. Mexican border *es una herida habierta* where the Third World grates against the first and bleeds. And before a scab forms it hemorrhages again, the lifeblood of two worlds merging to form a third country—a border culture.... A borderland is a vague

12. Le Goff, *History and Memory*, 54.

and undetermined place created by the emotional residue of an unnatural boundary. It is in a constant state of transition."[13]

The border sites constitute zones of perpetual motion, confrontation, and translation. In writing and re-collection, the concepts of home and border become transportable, carried around in the form of political commitment and critical vision, "in leaving home, I did not lose touch with my origins.... I am a turtle, wherever I go, I carry 'home' on my back."[14] As a lesbian poet/writer/critic of color, Anzaldúa sees herself always transgressing/trespassing at border sites. In one of the last poems of the book: "To live in the Borderlands means you," she writes: "To survive the Borderlands/you must live *sin fronteras*/be a crossroads."[15] Anzaldúa's account is not just another postmodern self-reflexive analysis. It provides a critical space not only for political contestation and cultural clashes, but also ultimately for a new narrative of dialogic understanding. "I am participating in the creation of yet another culture," she writes, "a new story to explain the world and our participation in it, a new value system with images and symbols that connect us to each other and the planet."[16] Nevertheless, this new culture needs to preserve the memory of other languages and situate itself at polyglot borders. Anzaldúa's writing is uncompromisingly bi- and trilingual—English, Spanish, Spanglish—all inflected by the memory of the ancient accents of Nahuatl, the language of *Aztecas del norte*, the Chicanos who believe their homeland to be Aztlán. This defiant retreat from high tech to Aztec is a passionate expression of the human need to live in the comforting and accommodating diachronic structures of our histories, in the reassuring flow of continuity.

In the preface, Anzaldúa refers to her work as the representation of her "almost instinctive urge to communicate, to speak, to write about life on the borders...."[17] Indeed, the book is a testimony to the uncompromising power of a language forged at borders—of space, time, and memory—in legitimizing identity. She is relentlessly critical of those that have belittled hybrid languages born of sociohistorical necessity. "Even our own people, other Spanish speakers *nos quieren poner en la boca.* They would hold us

13. Gloria Anzaldúa, *Borderlands*/La Frontera. *The New Mestiza* (San Francisco, 1987), 3.
14. Ibid., 21.
15. Ibid., 195.
16. Ibid., 81.
17. Ibid., preface.

back with their bag of *reglas de academia.*[18] Subjecting the Spanglish speaker to the rules of academia and forcing locks on her mouth constitutes a full-fledged insensitivity to and misreading of the role of "border" languages. *"El lenguaje de la frontera,"* the border idiom, is a living, relevant product of change. "Change, *evolución, enriquecimiento de palabras nuevos por invención o adopción* have created variants of Chicano Spanish, *un nuevo languaje. Un languaje que corrosponde a un modo de vivir."*[19] This vibrant idiom, born of invention and adoption, records a diversity of social and linguistic registers.

Border culture with its valorization of many languages, dialogues, and sites of translation incorporates and expands theoretical insights developed elsewhere, most notably in Bakhtinian notions of dialogism and heteroglossia. The dialogic mode prevents monologism. Every speech form interacts with another and is subject to change and transformation. The dialogic imagination governs the generation of knowledge in the sphere of heteroglossia. Heteroglossia designates a certain configuration of physical, social, and historical forces which cannot be replicated at a different juncture in time and space. The concepts dialogism and heteroglossia highlight and validate the dynamic flow of change, crisis, and transformation that informs human language and discourse at all cultural levels. Bakhtin argues, for example, that the various genres simultaneously employed in the novel (diary, letter, confessions, aphorisms) relativize "linguistic consciousness in the perception of language borders—borders created by history and society, and even the most fundamental borders (i.e., those between languages as such)—and permit expression of a feeling for the materiality of language that defines such a relativized consciousness."[20] The conversation between languages and voices at the heteroglot site takes on concrete form in the borderlands, where linguistic cultures clash and harmonize in social speech forms of varying currency. Borderlands accommodate many variants of inofficial, hybrid, and carnivalesque speech forms, languages for which there are no official dictionaries, which switch "from English to Castilian Spanish to the North Mexican dialect to Tex-Mex to a sprinkling of Nahuatl to a mixture of all these."[21]

18. Ibid., 54.

19. Ibid., 55.

20. M.M. Bakhtin, in *The Dialogic Imagination,* trans. Caryl Emerson and Michael Holquist, ed. Michael Holquist (Austin, 1981), 323f.

21. Anzaldúa, preface to *Borderlands.*

Anzaldúa's richly accented, heteroglossic text is an eloquent response to the repeated charges directed at her tongue: teachers who punished her for speaking Spanish during recess, speech classes at college designed to get rid of her accent, the communal culture that denied women the right to talk back, purists and Latino/as who ridiculed her "mutilated" Spanish. "I am my language,"[22] Anzaldúa declares with justified pride, for she embodies the fluency of dialogic moves, "the confluence of primordial images" and "the unique positionings consciousness takes at these confluent streams."[23] In the final analysis, in an age of shifting centers and borders, living multilingually is the best revenge. The heterogeneous reality we participate in "is not a mere crossing from one borderline to the other or that is not merely double, but a reality that involves the crossing of an indeterminate number of borderlines, one that remains multiple in its hyphenation."[24]

Speaking for the artists creating at a time when "we witness the borderization of the world," Guillermo Gómez-Peña declares that they "practice the epistemology of multiplicity and a border semiotics" and engage in "the creation of alternative cartographies and a ferocious critique of the dominant culture of both countries" and share a common enthusiasm in their "proposal of new creative languages."[25] In yet another borderlands, thousands of miles away from the Texas border, another corps of migrant scribes, Turkish woman writers in Germany, similarly participate in a border semiotics, negotiate the use of conflicting cultural languages, reinvent self, geography, and genealogy in memory and imagination, and execute a relentless critique of both home and host cultures. Through an identification with or rejection, reconsideration, reacceptance, borrowing, and extension of their own native myths and literary traditions as well as those of the host country, these writers rewrite cultural memory. Like their fellow Chicana writers, *Türkinnen deutscher Sprache* (Turkish women of German) write in an idiom that resists easy understanding, for it represents the conflicting and contestatory voices and the hopelessly fragmented collective memory of their ethnic/expatriate communities. The reinterpretation

22. Ibid., 59.
23. Ibid., preface.
24. Trinh T. Minh-ha, *When the Moon Waxes Red: Representation, Gender, and Cultural Politics* (New York and London, 1991), 107.
25. Guillermo Gómez-Peña, "Documented/Undocumented," in *The Graywolf Annual Five: Multi-Cultural Literacy,* trans. Rubén Martínez, eds., Rick Simonson and Scott Walker (Saint Paul, 1988), 130.

of native myths and national epics in their tales provide an allegorical insight into their present multiple identities.

One of the most accomplished performers of the new German borderlands writing is Emine Sevgi Özdamar, a crossover artist, film and theater actress, dramatist, theater director, and writer. She was born in 1946 in one of Turkey's eastern provinces, Malatya, another border site where Turkish, Kurdish, and Arabic are spoken and the legitimacy of the non-Turkish cultures is officially ignored and denied—Kurdish, which is an Indo-European language is claimed to be a mere aberrant dialect of Turkish, a Turkic language. At nineteen, she crossed several borders and cultural and time zones and arrived in Germany. After an early stint as a factory worker, she studied drama in the former East Berlin, landing roles in many theater plays and feature films. Her dramatic training reveals itself in her conception of language as a performance art. Her writing validates and celebrates language in its various forms as speech, script, ritual of everyday life, cultural transaction and negotiation, and game of survival and mastery. Özdamar's first book *Mutterzunge* (mother tongue) is a collection of autobiographical sketches, meditations on language, and fantastic satires that unfold in verbal images resembling a surrealistic film. In 1991, she was awarded the coveted Ingeborg Bachmann prize in literature for her then unpublished novel *Das Leben ist eine Karawanserei hat zwei Türen aus einer kam ich rein aus der anderen ging ich raus* (Life is like a caravanserai has two doors through the one I went in and through the other I went out).

The first two stories of *Mutterzunge*, "Mutterzunge" and "Großvaterzunge" (grandfather tongue), illustrate how history and memory, geography and genealogy inhabit language. "In meiner Sprache heißt Zunge: Sprache" (in my language, tongue means language), reads the first sentence of "Mutterzunge," "Zunge hat keine Knochen, wohin man sie dreht, dreht sie sich dorthin" (the tongue has no bones; it turns wherever you turn it).[26] By deploying at the very onset of her tale a visibly organic metaphor of speech, Özdamar underlines the latitude of language, its acrobatic skill of expression, and its possibilities of articulation and action. "Zunge drehen" (twisting the tongue) is a literal translation of the Turkish idiom *dili dönmek*, often used in the negative as *dilim dönmüyor* (I cannot say or pronounce). The narrator then refers to herself as one with a "gedrehten Zunge " (twisted tongue),[27] someone capable of mastering

26. Özdamar, *Mutterzunge*, 7.
27. Ibid., 7.

difficult sounds. After her long sojourn in Germany, she feels that when she thinks of "mother sentences" spoken by her mother in her mother tongue, they sound like a foreign language she had mastered well.[28] The memories of the sounds of her language intricately linked to the sights of her homeland were fading away. Once when she asked her mother why Istanbul had become so dark, the mother replied: "Istanbul hatte immer diese Lichter, deine Augen sind an Alamanien-Lichter gewöhnt" (Istanbul has always been lighted like this, your eyes have become accustomed to the Alamanian lights.)[29]

In order to reclaim her mother tongue, she needs a detour through her "grandfather tongue." This grandfather tongue is Ottoman Turkish, a hybrid language of the Ottoman court and the educated classes which was mostly made up of Persian and Arabic loan words and structures held together by Turkish connectors. Like Anzaldúa, who ventures into the memories of Nahuatl that recall the glory of a preconquest civilization, Özdamar excavates the lost accents of a language evocative of a long bygone era of power. By reclaiming this history and expanding the memorial territories of their respective languages, both writers defy the low status assigned to Chicano Spanish in the United States and Turkish in modern Germany, a Turkish that is no longer the sign of nostalgia for the Orient. As Roland Barthes once remarked, "[h]ow remote it seems, that period when the language of Islam was Turkish and not Arabic! This is because the cultural image is always fixed where the political power is: in 1877, the 'Arab countries' did not exist; though vacillating ... Turkey was still, politically and therefore culturally, the very sign of the Orient."[30]

Before 1928, Turkish used the Arabic script. In the twenties, Kemal Atatürk, the founder and first president of the Turkish Republic, undertook a series of reforms designed to transform the new republic into a totally secularized and Westernized state. The Arabic writing system was replaced by a Latinized alphabet that corresponded ideally to the sounds of Turkish, thus radically raising the rate of literacy. Özdamar's narrator cannot read the Arabic script, and her grandfather never learned to read the Latin alphabet. If she and her grandfather were to lose their speech and had to communicate in writing, "they could not tell each other stories" ("könnten

28. Ibid., 6.
29. Ibid., 7.
30. Roland Barthes, *New Critical Essays*, trans. Richard Howard (New York, 1980), 116.

wir uns keine Geschichten erzählen").[31] She, therefore, decides to take Arabic lessons from "the great master of the Arabic script," Ibni Abdullah. Thus begins her commute from her residence in East Berlin to Ibni Abdullah's small apartment in West Berlin. This site of learning language(s) is located at multiple borders. Berlin before the fall of the Wall is a city divided, at the border of a country divided geographically, historically, and ideologically. The single room of the apartment is divided with a curtain into living and learning quarters, where Ibni Abdullah gives lessons to students of Oriental languages. The narrator and her Arabic teacher have both crossed several linguistic and cultural borders, before settling in Berlin. They now engage in an effort to find common borders of language and culture. This is, among other things, a love story told in German and framed by conversations between Arabic and Turkish, the religious and the secular, the spiritual and the carnal, and the old and the new. Like Anzaldúa, Özdamar's narrator experiences the semiotic memory of language as an act of inscribing on her body. "Cradled in one culture, sandwiched between two cultures, straddling all three cultures and their value systems," writes Anzaldúa, "*la mestiza* undergoes a struggle of flesh, a struggle of borders, an inner war.... The coming together of two self-consistent but habitually incompatible frames of reference causes *un choque*, a cultural collision."[32]

The narrator's experience of language and love in her body also marks a celebration of Arabic calligraphy. Since Islam forbade the representation of images, calligraphy became the dominant visual art form in Arabic and Ottoman culture. The narrator's love of the picture alphabet and her desire for Ibni Abdullah intermingle and dominate her body and soul. One day he leaves her to complete her reading assignment on her own. Although he is gone, "his watchmen, his words stood in the room, some sat firmly over their legs" ("Seine Wächter, seine Wörter standen im Zimmer, manche saßen fest über ihren Beinen").[33] She tries to "read" the inscribed images: "Ein Pfeil ging aus einem Bogen raus. Da steht ein Herz, der Pfeil ging, blieb stehen im Herz, ein Frauenauge schlug mit den Wimpern. Jetzt hat sie ein Auge von einer Blinden, ein Vogel fliegt und verliert seine Federn über dem Weg, wo der Pfeil gegangen ist. (An arrow goes off from a bow. A heart stood there. The

---

31. Özdamar, *Mutterzunge*, 12.
32. Anzaldúa, *Borderlands*, 78.
33. Özdamar, *Mutterzunge*, 42.

arrow gets stuck in the heart, a woman's eye bats her eyelashes. Now she has the eye of a blind woman, a bird flies and loses his feathers on the way the arrow has flown.)[34] As the letters come out of the narrator's mouth, she likens some to birds, some to hearts, some to caravans; still others remind the narrator of trees scattered in the wind, sleeping camels, running snakes, evilly raised eyebrows, eyes that cannot sleep, or the fat ass of a woman sitting on a hot stone in a Turkish bath.[35] This is a picturesque script, indeed, generously embellished by the speaker's imagination. The letters speak with one another "without a pause in different voices" ("ohne Pause mit verschiedenen Stimmen")[36] and wake the sleeping animals in her body. She tries to close her eyes, but the voice of love tortures her body which splits up like a pomegranate. An animal emerges from the bloody gap in her body and licks her wounds. She sees stones abandoned by the receded ocean waters under her feet. In the endless landscape, stones cry out for water. A sea flows from the animal's mouth, raising her body high, and she falls asleep on the body of water and wakes up rejuvenated. She is like "a newborn wet bird" ("ein neugeborener nasser Vogel").[37]

The symbolism of the split body healed in water, an element that knows no borders and boundaries is duplicated in Anzaldúa's text. The barbed wire of the U.S.-Mexican border is like a "1,950 mile long open wound" in her body, the memory of the rape and plunder of her culture; it splits her, chops her up, mutilates her "*me raja me raja.*" But the sea whose "tangy smell" "seeps"[38] into her "cannot be fenced;" "*el mar* does not stop at borders."[39] Standing at the edge between earth and ocean, her "heart surges to the beat of the sea." With the ease that the ocean touches the earth and heals, the narrator switches codes, a gesture that in this narrative consistently acts as a panacea for the torn tongue, "*Oigo el llorido del mar, el respiro del aire*" (I hear the cry of the ocean, the breath of the air).[40] Like the body of Özdamar's narrator, her body effortlessly becomes a bridge of language between two geographies and histories, between the world of the gringo (*gabacho*) and the wetback (*mojado*), the past and the present. Like body cells that are always renewed, words are

34. Ibid., 42.
35. Ibid., 16.
36. Ibid., 24.
37. Ibid., 25.
38. Anzaldúa, *Borderlands*, 2.
39. Ibid., 3.
40. Ibid., 2.

born, grow, mature, change, die, and are reborn. By employing such regionalisms and colloquialisms as *gabacho, mojado, pa'* (for) and shifting and purposefully misplaced accents, Anzaldúa smuggles the variegated fabric of Chicano Spanish into Spanish and English.

Thus a new language and identity, free of national borders, is celebrated in the borderlands: "Deep in our heart we believe that being Mexican has nothing to do with which country one lives in. Being Mexican is a state of soul—not one of mind, not one of citizenship. Neither eagle nor serpent, but both. And like the ocean, neither animal respects borders."[41] And neither does the bird, the image Özdamar's narrator transforms herself into. Image, metaphor, and metonomy re-member bodies of language, culture, and their inhabitants dismembered by imperialism, war, conquest, colonization, poverty, and violence. They restore them not only to memory but also invest them with a kind of material reality. Karen Remmler sees in "the prevalence of metonymical references to displaced bodies, body parts, and conditions in postmodern theoretical discourse" the anxiety emerging from "a significant increase in the number of displaced persons across political, cultural, and economic borders since World War II."[42] Names, identities, and histories that expired along with passports and visas can now only be brought back to life through the potent medicines of memory: language, image, script.

But what if that script is forgotten? "In der Fremdsprache haben Wörter keine Kindheit" (In the foreign language, words have no childhood),[43] observes Özdamar's narrator. She tries desperately to correct this loss by looking for the history of her language in Arabic and by a narrative revis(ion)ing of the hybridity characteristic of Ottoman Turkish. She celebrates the visual poetry of Arabic letters. During the lessons in Ibni Abdullah's house, her Turkish and Arabic sentences, lyrics to Turkish songs, and Koran recitations by other students are simultaneously spoken, clashing and harmonizing at once. Many Turkish words have Arabic roots, and by going to the roots, the narrator can trace branches of lyric, lore, and legend intertwined in the two linguistic cultures. She recites for her teacher Turkish words of Arabic origin: "Leb-Mund" (mouth), "Mazi-Vergangenheit" (past), "Yetim-Waise" (orphan). Bemused, he remarks

41. Ibid., 62.

42. Karen Remmler, "Sheltering Battered Bodies in Language: Imprisonment Once More?" in *Displacements: Cultural Identities in Question*, ed. Angelika Bammler (Bloomington and Indianapolis, 1994), 218f.

43. Özdamar, *Mutterzunge*, 42.

that they sound strange when spoken with a Turkish accent. "Bis diese Wörter aus deinem Land aufgestanden und zu meinem Land gelaufen sind, haben sie sich unterwegs etwas geändert" (As these words got up, left your land, and ran to mine, they've somewhat transformed themselves on the way),[44] she replies.

In the final analysis, this unusual love story transcends the boundaries of a meditation on language. It also tells a veiled political history complicated and sometimes compromised by the universal enforcement of Atatürk's hasty Westernization reforms. Atatürk has been held accountable and criticized by the left and the right alike for the collective forgetting of Turkey's cultural past, her Islamic Ottoman heritage. Stranded in this historical lacuna, modern Turks feel frustrated in their struggle to define a cultural identity. "Ich habe zu Atatürk-Todestagen schreiend Gedichte gelesen und geweint, aber er hätte die arabische Schrift nicht verbieten müssen" (on Atatürk's death anniversaries, I have loudly recited poetry and cried, but he should not have had to ban the Arabic script), remarks the narrator, "Dieses Verbot ist so, wie wenn die Hälfte von meinem Kopf abgeschnitten ist. Alle Namen von meiner Familie sind Arabisch" (It is as if this ban has cut my head in two. All the names of my family members are Arabic).[45] Once again the loss of language is symbolized by the loss or mutilation of body parts.

Nevertheless, the narrator considers herself fortunate to belong to a generation that has grown up with many Arabic words, a generation at the interstices of the past and the present of its language. For the most part, modern Turkish intellectuals overtly prefer to speak and write *öz Türkçe* (authentic or pure Turkish). The movement to reconstruct a form of pre-Ottoman proto-Turkish was initiated with Atatürk's founding of the *Türk Dil Kurumu* (Turkish Language Association). This association publishes a great number of books, professional journals, and dictionaries aimed at settling the debts of modern Turkish language to Arabic and Persian (and, more recently, to European languages such as English and French) and expanding its lexical possibilities through derivations of new words from root forms of modern and ancient Turkic languages. The ideology of reclaiming an "essential" Turkish language stripped of its history and organic development has come under attack, for it entails a practice of denying, forgetting, and erasing vital cultural heritages. Özdamar implicitly maintains that she can have much easier access to the knowledge of Arabic in Germany than in Turkey

44. Ibid., 27.
45. Ibid.

where her desire to reclaim her "grandfather tongue" could be construed as a politically reactionary gesture in the context of the secularist ideology that underwrites modern Turkish education. Like the Spanish academics who shudder at Anzaldúa's bastardized language, Turkish intellectuals protect their speech and script that is segregated from hybridized constructs, be they the legacies of the past or the necessities of the present.

Özdamar's narrative often resists translatability, although she translates Turkish expressions literally into German. Like most languages with a long oral tradition, Turkish is an impossibly metaphorical and imagistic language that defies ready comprehension. Özdamar challenges the reader by expressions that border on the absurd, when not explicated. A reference to alleged revolutionaries who have been tortured reads: "Man hat ihnen die Milch, die sie aus ihren Müttern getrunken haben, aus ihrer Nase rausgeholt" (They made them puke through their nose the milk they drank from their mothers).[46] A fairy tale begins "Es war einmal, es war keinmal" (Once upon a time there was, once upon a time there was not),[47] the Turkish version of "once upon a time," a turn of phrase that does justice to that rich ambiguity of the past. Referring to her paralysis when faced with Abdullah's seizure, she says: "ich konnte ihn nicht fassen, meine Hände lagen wie Buchstaben ohne Zunge auf meinen Knien" (I could not contain him; my hands lay on my knees like letters without a tongue).[48]

Turkish is, furthermore, marked by numerous expressions that signify the body in pain. During her first visit to Abdullah's apartment the narrator tells him that if her father had delivered her to his door for Arabic lessons, he would have said: "Ja, Meister, ihr Fleisch gehört Ihnen, ihre Knochen mir, lehre sie, wenn sie ihre Augen und Gehör und Herz nicht aufmacht zu dem, was Sie sagen, schlagen Sie, die Hand der schlagenden Meister stammt aus dem Paradies, wo Sie schlagen, werden dort die Rosen blühen" (Yes master, her flesh belongs to you and her bones to me, if she does not open her eyes, ears and heart to what you say, hit her, the hand of hitting masters hails from paradise, where you hit, there roses will bloom).[49] Without further explanations—in our postfeminist age—this statement can easily be interpreted as one man giving another the right to inflict violence on his own daughter's body. Here Özdamar mixes several

46. Ibid., 12.
47. Ibid., 31.
48. Ibid., 22.
49. Ibid., 13.

Turkish sayings and proverbs. When parents deliver their children (male or female) to a teacher, they say "eti senin, kemigi benim" (her/his—Turkish does not have a gendered third person singular form—flesh is yours, bones are mine). This expression illustrates the great faith put in teachers in Turkish culture. A teacher is believed to play a more important part than the parent in the formation of the child. "Dayak cennetten cikmadir" (spanking hails from paradise) is a proverb that sanctions the necessity of punishing children who misbehave. The third expression is one about roses blooming where the master touches.

Why does Özdamar not explain her unusual expressions and risk misinterpretation? Both Anzaldúa and Özdamar present the reader with a text, like a map full of blank spaces. Anzaldúa switches from English to Spanish to Spanglish and writes whole poems and paragraphs in Chicano Spanish without providing a translation. Özdamar provides everything in German translation but bombards the reader with the most unheard of turns of phrase that make no sense to a German (or any non-Turkish) speaker. Both writers expect the reader to engage in a more informed and conscientious way with another discursive practice. Multicultural citizenship requires not only the admission of not knowing the other but also a willingness to learn about the other. Following Özdamar's lead, I am reminded of a Turkish proverb that illustrates this statement better than any critical formulation: "Bilmemek degil, ögrenmemek ayip" (Not to know is no reason to be ashamed, but not to learn is). Anzaldúa echoes Özdamar's unspoken sentiment in her preface, when she declares that she will make no apologies for the unique language of her people. "[W]e Chicanos no longer feel that we need to beg entrance, that we need always to make the first overture," she states, "to translate to Anglos, Mexicans and Latinos, apology blurting out of our mouths with every step. Today we ask to be met halfway."[50]

Anzaldúa and Özdamar do not interpret their mission as storytellers to be one of mere entertainment. They aim to instruct and guide the reader, the Anglo, the Mexican, the Latino, the German, and the Turk in crossing the border into other cultural times and domains and in decoding the borderized text of the Chicana and the Turkish-German woman. As immigrants, "minorities," and women, they had to undertake the labor of self-translation, always sparing their "hosts" that arduous task. Their writing is a new challenge for the reader to join a conversation of genuine cultural bilingualism. It

50. Anzaldúa, preface to *Borderlands*.

is an effort to reverse the one-sided perceptions of lesser known, "non-status," often misunderstood and misrepresented cultures. Like many other Chicana and Turkish-German woman writers, they create their literary traditions not only from their own cultural memories but also from the literary communities they enter in exile and immigration. In this way, they free cultural production from its adherence to the notion of an "ethnic" aesthetics and urge both the producers and consumers of these emergent literatures to become conversant in a multicultural idiom.

13. The Transatlantic Ties of Cultural Pluralism—Germany and the United States: Horace M. Kallen and Daniel Cohn-Bendit

Alfred Hornung

There does not seem to be a common basis between Germany and the United States as far as cultural pluralism is concerned. In terms of the development of nation-states, the two countries could hardly be more different. Historically, Germany has always been a rather monolithic nation with a closely knit, more or less uniform population, protecting the purity of the race by exclusion and extermination. The United States, on the other hand, is the classic country of immigration, ranging from the migration of the Native Americans 50,000 years ago across the Bering Strait to the North American continent, through the settlement by Europeans and the forced immigration of Africans, to the massive immigration waves in the nineteenth and early twentieth centuries.[1]

The formula of creating *e pluribus unum*, of uniting different peoples from different parts of the world in the metaphorical melting pot were political persuasions that in principle worked by inclusion and integration. After World War I, however, the situation changed in the United States, as it did in Germany after World War II. In the 1980s and 1990s, both countries were faced with the phenomenon of economic migration. The Federal Republic of Germany suddenly

1. Cf. Roger Daniels, *Coming to America: A History of Immigration and Ethnicity in American Life* (New York, 1991); and Nell Irvin Painter, *The Great Migration in Historical Perspective: New Dimensions of Race, Class, and Gender*, ed. Joe William Trotter, Jr. (Bloomington, 1991), viii.

became the land of hope for many people from underdeveloped countries—as the United States had been ever since the turn of the century—and saw waves of migration which followed each other with accelerated speed. Both countries had to face the new situation. First the United States in the 1920s, when the American government passed immigration laws to regulate the flow of foreigners to the country; then Germany in the 1980s, when the Bundestag voted for a change of the constitutional guarantee of asylum for persecuted aliens (the famous Article 16 of the *Grundgesetz* [Basic Law]).

While the political actions of the American and the German parliaments in the 1920s and the 1990s might be compared, the cultural and philosophical implications are still different. The political lag in terms of curbing immigration and controlling migrant workers between the United States and Germany is due to the different origins of the two countries and their historical developments into open and closed societies. The openness of the American continent for the persecuted of the world was part of a liberal policy ingrained in the American consciousness, as expressed in immigrant Emma Lazarus's poem "The New Colossus" embossed on the Statue of Liberty:

> Give me your tired, your poor,
> your huddled masses
> yearning to be free,
> The wretched refuse
> of your teeming shore,
> Send these, the homeless,
> tempest-tossed, to me:
> I lift my lamp
> beside the golden door.[2]

This liberal policy of immigration promising a haven for the persecuted of the world changed under economic political pressure in the United States. For much the same reason, German politicians felt they had to change the liberal Article 16 of the Grundgesetz guaranteeing asylum for the politically persecuted of the world, an article expressly created by its drafters, some of whom had enjoyed asylum abroad during the Nazi regime. While there might be some similar political and economic features about granting or restricting

2. See John Higham's classic study about immigration to the United States, which derives its title from this poem: *Send These to Me: Jews and Other Immigrants in Urban America* (New York, 1975); rev. ed. *Send These to Me: Immigrants in Urban America* (Baltimore, 1984).

immigration, German community in the Berlin с the exception of the internationa. parable to the American spi 930s—has never had anything comparable to the American spi 930s—has never had anything comparable foreigners. In spite of all discrimilation and incorporation of tory, particularly with regard to theory actions in American history, particularly Americans, the country and its inhabita Americans and African efforts to integrate and accept cultural di ave made tremendous auspices of the new ethnic consciousness of i nce. It is under the that the cultural program of multiculturalism was 1980s and 1990s concrete repercussions in politics and society. While Germany and other European nations could learn a lot from the United States in dealing politically with newcomers and foreigners, they could learn even more from the American capacity for forming a population of difference. In short, Germans could learn the lessons of multiculturalism and adopt the Americans' multicultural competence.[3]

Unfortunately, there does not seem to be a basis for a multicultural network in Germany yet. Because of their different historical pasts, Germany developed as one of the classical nation-states in Europe with a monocultural paradigm, as opposed to the early recognition in the United States of a conglomeration of different ethnic groups as the basis of a federal republic. In recent debates, the idea of the nation-state and of national unions has been contested and found obsolete. Instead, we have to reckon with a variety of concurrent cultures presently engaged in coming out and working out their differences, defying the former pushes and pulls of assimilation and homogeneity. It is due to their embattled status that the different cultural groups are wary of the conventional metanarratives of national union. Rather than rallying around the flag, more and more people organize along ethnic heritage or religious creed. A combination of ethnic and religious ideas seems to underlie some of the theoretical formulations of multicultural concepts.

This seems to be most obvious with regard to Jewish culture and the proposals by Jewish intellectuals for the multicultural organization of modern societies. Moreover, I would like to suggest that it is this ethnic and religious component of the Jewish cultural heritage which could be seen as a transatlantic tie of multicultural concepts. In line with the overall topic of multiculturalism in transit between

3. See my "The Making of Americans: Mary Rowlandson, Benjamin Franklin, Gertrude Stein, Maxine Hong Kingston," *American Studies in Germany: European Contexts and Intercultural Relations*, eds. Günter H. Lenz and Klaus J. Milich (Frankfurt/Main and New York, 1995) 96–117; esp. 113. See also Berndt Ostendorf, ed., *Multikulturelle Gesellschaft: Modell Amerika* (Munich, 1994).

Germany and the United States, like to concentrate on two figures of German-Jewish des..ept prominent in the debate past and present: Horace Kallen first cept of cultural pluralism in the United States developed..iences decades of this century and Daniel Cohn-Bendit's democracy —in theory and practice—with forms of a multicul.. in today's Federal Republic of Germany. Althou.. o direct ties exist between these two cultural critics, there st.. eem to be similar occasions and motivations out of which the. thinking and actions arose.

Horace Kallen's concept of cultural pluralism is well-known and has received new attention in our time.[4] The most important biographical details for my purposes are his birth in Berenstadt, Silesia, in 1882 as the son of a rabbi, the emigration of his family to the United States when Kallen was five, and his education at Harvard University. They are the decisive factors which eventually determine his evolution from a foreigner, to an assimilated American, to an American of German-Jewish descent. This evolution also implies his rejection of the ideology of the melting pot for the sake of the recognition of different cultural backgrounds.[5] This personal evolution is part of what one could call an American *Kulturkampf* at the turn of the century, in which the convergent forces of an Americanization movement[6] were pitted against the divergent manifestations of different ethnic cultures. With the influx of new immigrants, especially

4. Cf. Ira Eisenstein, "Dialogue with Dr. Horace M. Kallen," in *What I Believe and Why – Maybe: Essays for the Modern World*, ed. Alfred J. Marrow (New York, 1971); Michael Walzer, "Pluralism: A Political Perspective," in *Harvard Encyclopedia of American Ethnic Groups*, ed. Stephan Thernstrom et al. (Cambridge, 1980), 781–87; Werner Sollors, "A Critique of Pure Pluralism," in *Reconstructing American Literary History*, ed. Sacvan Bercovitch (Cambridge, 1986), 250–79; Milton R. Konvitz, ed., *The Legacy of Horace M. Kallen* (Rutherford, 1987); Susanne Klingenstein, *Jews in the American Academy, 1900–1940: The Dynamics of Intellectual Assimilation* (New Haven, 1991); Sarah Schmidt, "Horace M. Kallen and the Americanization of Zionism," (Ph.D. Thesis, University of Maryland, 1973); and her recent *Horace M. Kallen: Prophet of American Zionism* (Brooklyn, 1995).

5. For the ideology of the melting pot, see the play of the same title, performed in New York in 1908, by the British writer of Russian-Jewish descent, Israel Zangwill, which, due to its American setting, can overcome the religious differences between Russian Americans of Jewish and Christian backgrounds. See also Willi Paul Adams, "Die Assimilationsfrage in der amerikanischen Einwanderungsdiskussion 1890–1930," *Amerikastudien/American Studies* 27, no. 3 (1982): 275–91; and Volker Bischoff and Marino Mania, "Melting Pot-Mythen als Szenarien amerikanischer Identität zur Zeit der New Immigration," in *Nationale und kulturelle Identität: Studien zur Entwicklung des kollektiven Bewußtseins in der Neuzeit* (Frankfurt/Main, 1991), 513–36.

6. For a recent assessment, see Dietrich Herrmann, *"Be an American!" Amerikanisierungsbewegung und Theorien über Einwandererintegration* (Frankfurt/Main, 1996).

from Eastern and Southern Europe, the process of acculturation in the United States changed insofar as the process of becoming an American turned into a total assimilation to the American way of life and the exclusion of the so-called unassimilable aliens, i.e., Eastern-European Jews and Southern Italians. The definition of an American was henceforth modeled after the belief system of the white Anglo-Saxon Protestants.

The closing of the frontier in 1890, the bad economic situation after the depression of the 1890s, and the insistence on the superiority of the Anglo-Saxon race were the factors of a new nativism which led to the foundation of the Immigration Restriction League in 1894, the establishment of the Bureau of Immigration and Naturalization in 1906, and the institution of the Dillingham Commission in 1907 to investigate the consequences of unchecked immigration.[7] The simultaneous migration of African Americans from the South to the Northern cities compounded the ethnic and racial situation and brought about racist activities, most visible in the resurgence of the Ku Klux Klan, which encapsulated the racist ideology directed against blacks, Jews, and Catholics.[8] Thomas Dixon's racist novels about the Reconstruction period in the South, especially *The Clansman* (1905), which became the basis for David W. Griffith's film *The Birth of a Nation* (1915), bespeak the mood of a nation which, in the wake of the United States's entry into World War I, transformed nativist sentiments into the demand for one-hundred percent patriotism. In this sense, the idea of the birth of a white Anglo-Saxon Protestant nation encapsulates the ideological warfare about an exclusive definition of Americanness and brings with it the idea of the birth of a multicultural nation first indirectly formulated by Horace Kallen.[9] It is my assumption that it is Kallen's rediscovery of his Jewish background at Harvard and his experience of the changed American times which were essential for his concept of cultural pluralism.

The first stage in the rediscovery of his Jewish heritage occurred during his sophomore year at Harvard College in 1902 when his English professor Barrett Wendell acquainted him with the importance of "Hebraic elements in American political and literary thought

7. For a summary survey of these developments, see Berndt Ostendorf, "Einwanderungspolitik der USA: Eine historische Skizze," in *Multikulturelle Gesellschaft*, 15–31.

8. See the introductory essay, "Postscript—To Be Read First: Culture and the Ku Klux Klan," *Horace M. Kallen's Culture and Democracy in the United States: Studies in the Group Psychology of the American Peoples* (New York, 1924), 34.

9. See my "The Birth of a Multicultural Nation: Horace M. Kallen's Cultural Pluralism," *Transatlantic Encounters: Studies in European-American Relations*, eds. Udo J. Hebel and Karl Ortseifen (Trier, 1995), 347–58.

and institutions."[10] In an interview with Sarah Schmidt, Kallen recalls "how Wendell had emphasized the role of the Old Testament in defining a certain perspective and way of life": "He [Wendell] showed how the Old Testament has affected the Puritan mind [and] traced the role of the Hebraic tradition in the development of the American character.... And so I developed the interest in what you might call the Hebraic, the secular, the non-Judaistic component of the entire heritage and that naturally linked with what I knew about Zionism, the Herzl movement."[11]

The rediscovery of his own cultural heritage in the Puritans' reliance on the Biblical and Hebraic tradition, as well as in the social structure of their colonial lives as the basis of the American idea of a democratic society, meant the recognition of a mundane form of Judaism in the form of Zionism. It was by embracing Zionist ideas that Kallen could reconcile his thinking with his concept of the American idea.

> After 1902, Kallen began to construe the Old Testament as the source of the American idea, the basis of the Declaration of Independence and of the Bill of Rights. Instead of being the embodiment of the rituals of Jewish theology, the Old Testament became the catalyst that had encouraged the formation of a free society with notions of equal liberty to all individuals and to all groups, no matter how different.[12]

In spite of the important role of his English professor, Kallen—having read Spinoza at home—felt drawn to the philosophy of William James, who directed his thesis on the nature of truth. This turn to James and philosophy, and Kallen's instrumental role in the foundation of the Menorah Society at Harvard in 1906 mark the second stage of his evolution. This decisive reorientation in the thinking of an intellectual who is rediscovering his Jewishness is summarized by Henry Hurwitz, the society's founder, in a later editorial of the *Menorah Journal*:

> The Menorah is a spiritual quest, an enterprise of research and enlightenment, a passion for creative Judaism. As such a movement, it must be constantly developing, never standing still, achieving one stage in its program only to go on to the next, changing its forms of organization and activities as its progress requires. From its beginning the Menorah has been a pioneering and creative endeavor. It arose twenty years ago

10. Milton R. Konvitz, "Horace Meyer Kallen (1882–1974): In Praise of Hyphenation and Orchestration," in *The Legacy of Horace M. Kallen*, 17.
11. Sarah Schmidt, "Horace M. Kallen and the Americanization of Zionism," 77.
12. Ibid.

in the Harvard of Eliot and William James, Royce and Santayana. In an atmosphere of exalted intellectual adventuring. At a time, moreover, when a new type of Jewish student set foot in the Yard – the sons of the most recent immigration from Eastern Europe. They were possessed by an intense Jewish consciousness which, interlocked with their remorseless intellectualism and passionate acceptance of Western culture, demanded a fresh appraisal of the Jewish heritage and of present-day Jewish aims in terms of the new environment.[13]

A third and last step in Kallen's professional evolution was his embrace of a vitalist philosophy of flux, derived from Henri Bergson's *élan vital* through William James's pragmatism. James had corresponded with Bergson since the 1890s and included a section on Bergson's philosophy in his lectures at Oxford in 1908. Kallen himself had a fellowship at Oxford in 1907-08 and went to see Bergson in Paris. In 1909, when James's lectures appeared as *A Pluralistic Universe*, Kallen published an essay entitled "Hebraism and Current Tendencies in Philosophy" in which he opposed the Greek's striving for "structure, harmony, order immutable, eternal" with the Hebraic view of the world in flux.[14] As further evidence of this paradigmatic change, Kallen cited Darwin's evolutionary biology, which he traced in the pragmatic philosophy of the American William James with its emphasis on epistemology and ethics as well as in the metaphysics of "Henri Bergson, a Jew of France."[15] In Kallen's mind, this new pluralist and processual thinking provided the best approach for coping with the new American reality at the beginning of the twentieth century. Along with William James's pluralist concept of a "multiverse"[16] rather than a universe, Kallen advocated an inclusive and dynamic model of society as opposed to the static WASP model.

Although Kallen later claimed to have first begun formulating "the notion of cultural pluralism"[17] in 1905 in connection with the

13. Henry Hurwitz, "Watchmen, What of the Day?" *The Menorah Journal* 12 (1926): 18f.

14. See Horace M. Kallen, "Hebraism and Current Tendencies in Philosophy," *Judaism at Bay: Essays Toward the Adjustment of Judaism to Modernity* (New York, 1972), 9.

15. Ibid., 12. The elective affinities between James and Bergson, expounded in Kallen's 1914 study on the two philosophers, *William James and Henri Bergson: A Study in Contrasting Theories of Life* (Chicago, 1914), date back to their correspondence from 1896 on and James's visit to Bergson in Paris in 1905. The popularity of Bergson's new life philosophy reached its culmination with the philosopher's visit to the United States where he gave several lectures at Columbia University (cf. Tom Quirk, "Bergson in America," *Prospects* 11 (1987): 453–90).

16. See William James, *A Pluralistic Universe* (1909); *Writings 1902–1910* (New York, 1987) 625–819; here, 778.

17. Sarah Schmidt, "Horace M. Kallen and the Americanization of Zionism," 49.

discrimination against the African American Alain Locke in his class and as a fellow exchange student at Oxford, the writing of his influential two-part essay, "Democracy *versus* the Melting Pot: A Study of American Nationality,"[18] in 1915 was a reaction to the changed political situation at the outbreak of World War I when his German and Jewish origin came under attack and as a refutation of racist ideas about the singularity of Anglo-Americans who opt for the assimilation of all differences or the exclusion of the "unassimilable aliens."[19] Taking up William James's idea that "[t]he pluralist world is ... more like a federal republic than like an empire or a kingdom,"[20] Kallen states that "Democracy involves, not the elimination of differences, but the perfection and conservation of differences."[21] In opposition to the closely knit European nations, he sees the American people not as such a nation-state but as "a mosaic of peoples" and sees "'American civilization'" as "a multiplicity in a unity, an orchestration of mankind" whose main goal is not the oneness of union but the harmony of the many.[22]

Kallen's regained Jewishness, which formed the evolution of his thought and became the basis of this "multiplicity in a unity," later termed "cultural pluralism" in his 1924 *Culture and Democracy in the United States*,[23] also figures prominently in his multicultural theory. Twice he cites the special role of Jewish immigrants in his crucial essay "Democracy *versus* the Melting Pot." Possibly in line with the Hebraic influence on Puritan culture, Kallen likens the Jewish

18. Kallen's essay was first published in *The Nation*, 18 and 25 February 1915, and later reprinted in his *Culture and Democracy in the United States: Studies in the Group Psychology of the American Peoples* (New York, 1924) 67–125.

19. Ludwig Lewisohn, a German-Jewish immigrant from Berlin, in 1890 at the age of eight underwent a similar evolution away from the coercive influence of the Anglo-American model of self-definition, through the painful experience of the rejection of his assimilated Americanness, to the recognition and final acceptance of his Jewish difference from both the inherited German descent and the coveted American consent. "... at the age of fifteen," he writes in his autobiographical novel *Up Stream*, "I was an American, a Southerner and a Christian," *Up Stream* (New York, 1922), 77; cf. also my "The Making of (Jewish) Americans: Ludwig Lewisohn, Charles Reznikoff, Michael Gold," in *Ethnic Cultures in the 1920s in North America*, ed. Wolfgang Binder (Frankfurt/Main, 1993), 115–34. See also Jane Addams's analysis of American patriotism as a "process of elimination": "Immigration: A Field Neglected by the Scholar," *The Commons* 10 (Jan. 1905); quoted from *Immigration and Americanization: Selected Readings*, ed. Philip Davis (Boston, 1920), 11.

20. William James, *A Pluralistic Universe*, 776.

21. Kallen, *Culture and Democracy*, 61.

22. Ibid., 58, 124.

23. Ibid., 11.

migration to America to the Puritan flight from persecution and disaster in Europe.[24] Like the Puritans, the Jews "have thus far looked to America as their homeland, and seem, with all their Zionism, likely to continue to do so."[25] Later he claims a special status for the Jews, different "from that of other immigrant nationalities. They [the Jews] do not come to the United States from truly native lands, lands of their proper *natio* and culture. They come from lands of sojourn where they have been for ages treated as foreigners, at most as semi-citizens.... They come with the intention to be completely incorporated into the body-politic of the state."[26] Lacking a clearly defined national origin, the old Jewish tradition and culture have worked as a strong communal bond creating one of the most group-conscious peoples.

The democratic basis of the American system effectively facilitates the easy assimilation of Jewish people, for once "the Jewish immigrant takes his place in American society a free man ... and an American, he tends to become rather the more a Jew."[27] Of course, the racial pride behind these formulations is quite obvious and the correlation of the Puritan settlement and the Jewish immigration can be seen as an unconcealed aspiration to the cultural elite status of the New England descendants. But at the same time, these phrases also reveal his fundamental belief, instilled by the teachings of Professor Wendell and expressed in his 1909 essay, "Hebraism and Current Tendencies in Philosophy," about the modernness of Hebraic thought as opposed to Greek thinking and its proximity to the American idea. In the final analysis, Kallen's cultural pluralism hence appears as the principle for the harmonious coexistence of different groups enlightened by Hebraism.[28] In the same sense in which the Puritan organization of life was governed by Hebraic ideas, modern American society must be guided by a similar belief system.

24. See Mary Antin, *The Promised Land: The Autobiography of a Russian Immigrant* (1912) for a similar analogy between modern immigration and the Puritan settlement.

25. Kallen, *Culture and Democracy*, 77.

26. Ibid., 111f.

27. Ibid., 113. See also Sarah Schmidt, *Horace M. Kallen: Prophet of American Zionism*, xiii: "Zionism thus was able to fulfill two functions for Kallen: It allowed him to retain his Jewish identity and to become, thereby, a better American."

28. For the racist and romantic underpinnings of Kallen's cultural pluralism see Higham, *Send These to Me*; Philip Gleason, "American Identity and Americanization," *Harvard Encyclopedia of American Ethnic Groups*, 31–58; Sollors, "A Critique of Pure Pluralism," 268–73, and Michael Walzer, "Multiculturalism and Individualism," *Dissent* (Spring 1994): 185–91.

Like Kallen, other Jewish intellectuals discovered the world of Zionism as an alternative to American society. Next to Ludwig Lewisohn, Randolph Bourne was the most prominent one. Bourne developed his vision of a "trans-national America" as a truly cosmopolitan community in an address to the Harvard Menorah Society on Jewish-American culture. In a lecture entitled "The Jew and Trans-national America," he "endorsed the Zionist movement as the embodiment of his own dream of transnationality. Zionism allowed American Jews to weigh the claims of 'cultural allegiance and political allegiance,' with their Jewish national identity transcending the political boundaries of the American state."[29] Although Kallen stopped being a "Zionist activist" after 1921 over disputes with "unrealistic and irrational passions" of fellow Zionists and abandoned his advocacy of cultural pluralism between the wars, he "remained a Zionist at heart"[30] and took up his model of a pluralist society in the 1950s when again American democracy was threatened by monocultural constraints.

In the spring of 1954, Horace Kallen was invited to give a couple of lectures on cultural pluralism at the Center for Human Relations at the University of Pennsylvania intended as the basis for a discussion among scholars about Kallen's ideas, a dialogue later published as *Cultural Pluralism and the American Idea* (1956). This discussion of cultural pluralism again coincides with a time of turmoil termed the "'age of anxiety'" with "instant excitements of these days over communists and atom bombs, espionage and mccarthyism, cold war and Third World War...."[31] Hence Kallen's formulations are a renewed attempt to launch his model of the acceptance of difference at a time of imposed uniformity. "No institution of any civilization," he argues, "ever gathers enough power to impose an everlasting submission and servitude upon the different, or to suppress differentiation within the same."[32]

Based on Kallen's understanding of culture as the opposite of vocation, as the activities of the individual after work, in the evening, at night, weekends, he associates it with the idea of "reverie" and attributes the idea of free play and liberation to it. This is a "pattern

29. Casey Nelson Blake, *Beloved Community: The Cultural Criticism of Randolph Bourne, Van Wyck Brooks, Waldo Frank and Lewis Mumford* (Chapel Hill, 1990), 119.

30. See Gary Gerstle, "The Protean Character of American Liberalism," *The American Historical Review* 99, no. 4 (1994): 1064.

31. Horace M. Kallen, *Cultural Pluralism and the American Idea: An Essay in Social Philosophy* (Philadelphia, 1956), 56.

32. Ibid., 27.

of interpersonal and intergroup communication," which he sees at work in the arts and sciences and wishes to apply to politics. Hence the repeated image of the "ongoing self-orchestration of individuals" within a society whose "unity tends to be sustained by voluntary commitment to union...."[33] The unifying bond is the American idea which has motivated the American experience from the very beginning and all immigrants thereafter. "Thus, Americanization seeking a cultural monism was challenged and is slowly and unevenly being displaced by Americanization, supporting, cultivating a cultural pluralism, grounded on and consummated in the American idea."[34] The religious overtones become quite obvious when Kallen speaks of books which contain this American idea as "the Bible of America": the Declaration of Independence, the Constitution, Lincoln's Gettysburg Address, the works of Emerson, Thoreau—in short, the classic canon of good books.[35]

Idealism and the concept of a transnational bond such as the Jewish culture, as well as his own personal and political experiences, might also be behind Daniel Cohn-Bendit's engagement with cultural pluralism in a multicultural democracy. Born in 1945 in Montauban, France, of German-Jewish parents who had fled Nazi Germany, he first associated with the far left and became one of the political activists in the student demonstrations of the 1960s, first in France and then, after his expulsion from France, in Germany. If he seems more settled lately, he nevertheless has preserved his independent and critical individualism and his opposition to all forms of repression. His embattled and relatively independent position within the Green Party gives him a range of freedom which he uses along with the ideals of the student revolution in Paris in May 1968 and one of its pervasive slogans: "l'imagination au pouvoir."[36] His job as an honorary director of the office for multicultural affairs in the city of Frankfurt/Main, which was created in the 1989 negotiations of a red-green coalition and which he held until May 1997, also stressed the idealistic drive of his engagement. The fifteen members in his office represented fifteen different languages.

This initiative of the Green Party was an attempt to recognize not only the multicultural reality of the city of Frankfurt, which has

33. Ibid., 30.
34. Ibid., 97.
35. Ibid., cf. 87, 96.
36. See his recollective account of the revolutionary days, *Wir haben sie so geliebt, die Revolution* (Frankfurt/Main, 1987) and his contributions to the leftist journal *Frankfurter Pflasterstrand*.

close to thirty percent non-German inhabitants, but also the political reality of Germany as a country of immigration and to give it an institutional backing. Cohn-Bendit's seat as a representative of the Green Party in the European Parliament in Strasbourg can equally be seen as part of his overall idealistic endeavors, determined not so much by concrete political actions, but by the belief in the idea of a European union. This combination of an idealistic vision and a cultural mission, grounded in historical research and concrete political experiences, is at the basis of *Heimat Babylon: Das Wagnis der multikulturellen Demokratie*, which he co-authored with Thomas Schmid, a freelance writer and councillor at the office for multicultural affairs in Frankfurt.[37]

The authors open their book with the thesis of Germany as a country of immigration opposing the official policy of the German government:

> Germany is an immigration country, and therefore multicultural. We are not celebrating that fact, just stating it. Where it is multicultural, it is confusing. Multicultural society: It is, in this light, only another word for the diversity and disunity of all modern societies, which want to be open societies. This trend is not reversible. And it has two sides: one is advantageous and one causes fear.[38] (Author's translation)

The anxiety and fear of Anglo-Saxons in the United States at the turn of the century of losing their racial purity have been dominant feelings of German citizens not only in the twentieth century. These feelings of anxiety found and find their political equivalent in protective or repressive political measures to stem the tide and to assuage the fears of worried citizens. By basing their deliberations on the political, but not officially recognized, reality of Germany as a country of immigration, Cohn-Bendit and Schmid are primarily concerned with mediating between the fears of Germans and non-German residents by pointing to the advantages to be derived from

37. Daniel Cohn-Bendit and Thomas Schmid, *Heimat Babylon: Das Wagnis der multikulturellen Demokratie* (Hamburg, 1992). I am aware that—for the sake of my argument—I am focusing on Cohn-Bendit and his Jewish cultural background at the expense of co-author Thomas Schmid.

38. Ibid., 11. "Deutschland ist ein Einwanderungsland, und auch dadurch multikulturell. Wir feiern das nicht, wir stellen es nur fest. Wo es multikulturell zugeht, geht es auch unübersichtlich zu. Multikulturelle Gesellschaft: Das ist, so gesehen, nur ein anderes Wort für Vielfalt und Uneinheitlichkeit aller modernen Gesellschaften, die offene Gesellschaften sein wollen. Diese Tendenz ist nicht umkehrbar. Und sie hat zwei Seiten: eine vorteilhafte und eine, die angst macht." Unless otherwise noted, all translations are my own.

a multicultural society, advantages which—in their minds—by far compensate for the fears. In this sense their usage of the term *multikulturelle Gesellschaft* does not correspond to the one used in the present discussion of multiculturalism in the United States, where it seems to refer less to a political than to a cultural debate in academia concerned with the crisis in "general education" and its economic, political and ideological reasons.[39]

Schmid and Cohn-Bendit much rather seem to connect with Horace Kallen's concept of cultural pluralism, the harmonious orchestration of individuals of different cultural backgrounds. Although the authors clearly make political statements and proposals for an official recognition of the reality of Germany as a country of immigration, such as separating the issue of immigration from that of political asylum, or granting citizenship based on the American *ius soli* (citizenship based on residency) instead of the German *ius sanguinis* (citizenship based on blood), they remain within the spectrum of peaceful coexistence of all cultural groups. Accordingly, the Frankfurt office for multicultural affairs functions (certainly for lack of funding) mostly as a sort of a clearinghouse to negotiate individual hardships. Hence one could argue that Cohn-Bendit's point of departure is—in his own words—the recognition of a *"Weltunordnung"* (unorder of the world) in modern, or better still, in postmodern and postcolonial times, which needs a new principle of organization.

Here again, the authors have learned from the model of the United States, *the* country of immigration. The plea for a new order recalls Horace Kallen's evocation of the principles of the American founding fathers, who embossed into the seal of the new republic the Latin words *"Novus Ordo Seclorum"* as an expression of their

39. See Berndt Ostendorf's "Einführung," to *Multikulturelle Gesellschaft,* 8; and the contributions to that volume by Hans-Jürgen Puhle, "Multikulturalismus und der amerikanische *consensus*," 77–93, and Günter Lenz, "*American Cultural Studies:* Multikulturalismus und Postmoderne," 167–87. For the German debate, see Claus Leggewie, *Multi Kulti: Spielregeln für die Vielvölkerrepublik* (Frankfurt/Main, 1993); his article "Ethnizität, Nationalismus und multikulturelle Gesellschaft," in *Nationales Bewußtsein und kollektive Identität: Studien zur Entwicklung des kollektiven Bewußtseins in der Neuzeit,* 2nd ed., ed. Helmut Berding (Frankfurt/Main, 1994), 46–65; as well as his description of nativism and the conservative revolution in the United States: *America First? Der Fall einer konservativen Revolution* (Frankfurt/Main, 1997). The specifically pedagogical aspect of the debate in Germany is the topic of Franz Hamburger's collected essays, *Pädagogik der Einwanderungsgesellschaft* (Frankfurt/Main, 1994); and of Lothar Bredella's article, "Multiculturalism between Assimilation and Segregation: The Debate on Multicultural Curricula in the United States and Germany," in *American Studies in Germany,* 226–61.

belief that this new nation would ban anarchy and tyranny forever and would be "the beginning of a 'new order of the ages,' an order which establishes and fulfils the intent of *e pluribus unum*."[40] This new order, this new orchestration of peoples, is meant to defuse the "age of anxiety" which Kallen experienced in the 1920s and 1950s and which Cohn-Bendit and other concerned intellectuals register just now. Given the long history of Kallen's cultural pluralism in the United States, it is not surprising that Cohn-Bendit and Schmid find their sources in episodes of immigration in America with references ranging from Benjamin Franklin and Thomas Jefferson all the way to the Los Angeles riots of 1992.[41] Although they also discuss the contributions of eminent American historians and sociologists on multiculturalism, e.g., Robert Ezra Park's 1950 study about Chicago, *Race and Culture*, or John Higham and Michael Walzer,[42] they seem to be primarily interested in finding a guiding idea, a mental concept for the identification of people of different ethnic backgrounds, along Kallen's formulation of the American idea.

This search for a common bond in a unifying idea, which takes on religious dimensions in Kallen's concept, can be realized best in a republic and a shared value system.[43] Hence Cohn-Bendit evokes time and again the republican value system as the basis of a multicultural society: "Demokratie ergibt sich *nicht* umstandslos aus der multikulturellen Situation. Demokratie braucht ein gemeinsames Verständnis verbindlicher Werte, über die Einigkeit hergestellt werden muß."[44] (Democracy does not develop naturally out of a multicultural reality. Democracy needs a common understanding about binding values, about a unity that must be founded.) This seems to be the common challenge which citizens and politicians face today.

40. Kallen, *Cultural Pluralism*, 69.

41. The authors also recognize the important work of German Americanists on immigration and migration such as Christiane Harzig, Wolfgang Helbich, Walter D. Kamphoefner, Günter Moltmann et al.

42. For relevant excerpts, see Werner Sollors, ed., *Theories of Ethnicity: A Classical Reader* (New York, 1996).

43. Jane Addams, a like-minded social worker, whom Kallen also quotes, tried to establish such a bond among the residents at her community project at Hull-House in Chicago by promoting "a culture which will not set its possessor aside in a class with others like himself, but which will, on the contrary, connect him with all sorts of people by his ability to understand them as well as by his power to supplement their present surroundings with the historic background." Idem., *Twenty Years at Hull-House* (1910), reprint (New York, 1961), 300. See also my "Social Work and Modern Art: The Autobiographies of Jane Addams and Gertrude Stein," *Anglistentag 1989 Würzburg: Proceedings*, ed. Rüdiger Ahrens (Tübingen, 1990), 207–18 and 217f.

44. Cohn-Bendit and Schmid, *Heimat Babylon*, 319.

This persuasion determines Cohn-Bendit's position in general and in particular. Within the Green Party he distances himself from the "unsägliche Fraktion der Antifaschischten" and their talk about the anti-democratic tradition in Germany.[45] He also criticizes the intransigent ideological attitude of the Social Democratic Party (SPD) of the 1980s and early 1990s as responsible for its vanishing influence among the working class whom he sees as "Modernisierungsverlierer" (the losers of modernity).[46] Following his independent mind, he rather seems to side with the positions of Heiner Geißler and his Christian Democratic Party (CDU) friends about quotas of immigration for economic reasons and a modification of the law of asylum: "Es ist daher nicht sinnvoll, den Artikel 16, Absatz 2, Satz 2 für sakrosankt zu erklären. Die Asylpraxis muß zugleich enger und weiter gefaßt werden."[47] (It is therefore not sensible to declare Article 16, Paragraph 2, Line 2 sacrosanct. The asylum practice must be defined more narrowly and broadly at the same time.) While this article has been changed in the meantime with the help of a changed SPD, Cohn-Bendit's hope that Heiner Geißler would be the first director of a future federal office to be instituted for questions of political asylum was not fulfilled.[48]

Daniel Cohn-Bendit's sense of mission as well as the idealistic and religious dimension of his form of multiculturalism, which I see as a variation on Kallen's cultural pluralism and equally informed by a Jewish cultural heritage, are evident in his most spectacular event while in office, as well as from the title and the ending of his book. On 17 June 1990, the former "Tag der Deutschen Einheit" (Day of German Unity) before the reunification of the two Germanies, Cohn-Bendit organized in Frankfurt the "Fest der Farben" (Concert of Colors), a very popular rock concert which brought young people of different ethnic backgrounds together. Common musical taste and the lure of youth culture effectively transcended ethnic differences in a sort of (mystical) community spirit. While the performance at this rock concert allowed for the formation—in Kallen's words—of "a mosaic of peoples" and "a multiplicity in a unity, an orchestration of mankind," the ending of Cohn-Bendit's study on multicultural democracy stresses the freedom of the ethnic individual from a community.

45. Ibid., 276.
46. Ibid., 325.
47. Ibid., 344.
48. Ibid., 345.

Elaborating on John Higham's reference to Harry Houdini, the son of a Hungarian immigrant and rabbi whose forced migration the son voluntarily imitated in the United States and eventually turned into the magic of escape art,[49] Cohn-Bendit recognizes in this practice the flight of the individual from patterns of assimilation through a multiplication of identities.[50] The mystic dimension of the multicultural community at the Fest der Farben and the magic dimension of the escape artist's multiplied identity seem to point to a transcendent spiritual dimension evident in the title of the book: *Heimat Babylon*. Referring once more to the anxiety about a multicultural democracy, Cohn-Bendit explains in the introduction:

> This is what is meant by 'Homeland Babel.' Hoyerswerda, Hünxe, Rostock: that was only Babel. In these cases, 'all the languages of the world were jumbled'; the strict refusal to understand and to speak, was programmatic. That foreigners were present is part of the modern confusion.[51] (Author's translation)

The correlation of the confusion brought about by the confusing array of different languages at Babel with the situation of a multicultural society permeates the whole study. The authors take care to compare the Biblical situation with the sociological situation at the end of the twentieth century and to quote the relevant passage from the Bible in full length.[52] Human pride to build "a city and a tower, whose top *may reach* unto heaven" and to make a name "lest we be scattered abroad upon the face of the whole earth" (Gen. 11. 4) is not only the beginning of a confusion of languages but also the start of worldwide migration. Although it seems to be impossible to reverse this proliferation of languages and people across the earth, the dream of the original state of grace when "the whole earth was of one language and of one speech" (Gen. 11. 1) resonates not only in Daniel Cohn-Bendit's multiculturalism. It is the dream of *e pluribus unum* and maybe of a European idea.

49. See John Higham, *Send These to Me* (rev. ed. 1984), 27.

50. Cohn-Bendit and Schmid, *Heimat Babylon*, 346ff.

51. Ibid., 11. "Das ist mit 'Heimat Babylon' gemeint. Hoyerswerda, Hünxe, Rostock: Das war *nur* Babylon. Hier war 'die Sprache aller Welt verwirrt'; die strikte Weigerung, zu verstehen und zu reden, war Programm. Daß Ausländer anwesend sind, ist Teil der modernen Unübersichtlichkeit."

52. "Go to, let us go down, and there confound their language, that they may not understand one another's speech. So the Lord scattered them abroad from thence upon the face of all the earth: and they left off to build the city. Therefore is the name of it called Babel; because the Lord did there confound the language of all the earth: and from then did the Lord scatter them abroad upon the face of all the earth" (Gen. 11, 7–9).

14. Wong Kim Ark and the Determination of United States Citizenship

Brook Thomas

The central thesis of this presentation is that a brief look at United States Supreme Court determinations of citizenship in the nineteenth century reveals that the tradition of the United States' openness to heterogeneity is complicated by the issue of race. The United States has, indeed, been a land of immigration, one open to people from a variety of cultures. But it has not always been one open to people from a variety of races.

My thesis has comparative interests for two important reasons. First, it raises a question about the meaning of the term "multicultural." It seems to me that in the American context the term is a code word for multiracial and that most advocates and detractors are fully aware of this code.[1] If I am correct, three questions are of vital importance: (1) What does this displacement of "race" by "culture" tell us about the status of race in the United States today and the unwillingness of people in the country, including some advocates of multiculturalism, directly to address the issues that it raises, which may continue to be as much economic and political as cultural? (2) Since, as most of us here would agree, race is in part a cultural construction, what is the relation between race and culture, and is that relationship different in the United States and Germany? (3) Does "multicultural" have the same meaning in Germany as in the United States, or in Germany does it tend more often to have its

---

1. See a number of the contributions in *Mapping Multiculturalism*, eds. Avery F. Gordon and Christopher Newfield (Minneapolis Press, 1996).

literal meaning? If there is a different meaning of the term in the two countries, why? Furthermore, if it does have different meanings, I would argue that not all multicultural societies will look the same; the ideal vision of multicultural advocates in the United States, for important historical reasons that need to be considered, will be different from the ideal vision of its advocates in Germany.

The second point of comparative interest is more concrete. It is commonplace to compare German determination of citizenship by *ius sanguinis* (a child's citizenship is determined by the citizenship of the parents—by blood) with the United States' determination by *ius soli* (a child's citizenship is determined by where it is born—by soil). But it was not until 1898 that the United States Supreme Court definitively ruled in favor of ius soli, and it did so against the desires of the executive branch. Until that ruling, people of Asian ancestry, especially Chinese, had fewer constitutional rights than those of Turkish ancestry in Germany today. The situation of Vietnamese workers in the former G.D.R. is perhaps more comparable. Native Americans had an even more complicated status. One lesson that can be drawn from the brief history that I am about to sketch is that changes in the legal determination of citizenship are indeed possible and that they are important for creating the conditions for a multicultural society. At the same time, I will end with a few speculations that raise questions about the role of national citizenship in our increasingly global society.

Perhaps the most important Supreme Court case defining citizenship before the Civil War was the infamous *Dred Scott* case (1857). Called one of the Court's "self-inflicted wounds"[2] by a later chief justice of the Supreme Court, *Dred Scott* considered, among other things, whether or not people of African ancestry living in the United States were American citizens. Because citizenship was not defined in the Constitution, Chief Justice Roger B. Taney offered his own definition that linked United States citizenship to the famous phrase "We, the people of the United States." "The words 'people of the United States,' and 'citizens,'" Taney wrote, "are synonymous terms, and mean the same thing. They both describe the political body, who, according to our republican institutions, form the sovereignty, and who hold the power and conduct the government through their representatives. They are what we familiarly call the 'sovereign people,' and every citizen is one of this people, and a constituent member of this sovereignty." Taney's definition, therefore, confirmed the republican theory of government in which there is only one class of

2. Charles Evans Hughes, *The Supreme Court of the United States* (New York, 1928), 50.

citizens and citizens are those who constitute the sovereignty of the country. But Taney used his definition to deny citizenship, not only to slaves, but to all people residing in the United States of African descent. Since there is only one class of citizens, he argued, the "deep and enduring marks of inferiority and degradation" implanted on blacks excluded them from the community that originally constituted the sovereign people of the nation.[3]

Taney's definition was in part necessitated by the federal system of the United States that allows a distinction between state and national citizenship. Since it was clear that some northern states included blacks as citizens, Taney had to claim that a citizen of a state was not automatically a citizen of the United States. "We must not confound the rights of citizenship, which a state may confer within its own limits, and the rights of citizenship as a member of the Union. It does not by any means follow, because he has all the rights and privileges of a citizen of a State, that he must be a citizen of the United States."[4] Since at the time of the ruling naturalized citizens were limited to those of European descent, Taney's exclusion of blacks as citizens effectively meant that only whites could be United States citizens.

When the South lost the Civil War and slavery was abolished by the Thirteenth Amendment, neither former slaves nor free blacks were explicitly granted citizenship. Thus one of the primary intentions of the Fourteenth Amendment was to overturn *Dred Scott* and guarantee citizenship to all of African descent born in the country. That guarantee is accomplished in the amendment's first sentence: its citizenship clause. "Section 1. All persons born or naturalized in the United States, and subject to the jurisdiction thereof, are citizens of the United States and of the State wherein they reside...."[5] Since almost all of African descent living in the United States had been born here, this clause undid the harm done by Taney's decision. Indeed, within two years Congress changed its laws to allow people from Africa to become naturalized citizens.

But the story is not yet over. In fact, the main part of my story has just begun, even if it is a story not often told. The events that I have related are familiar ones to students of American history, but an issue left unresolved by the Fourteenth Amendment is rarely acknowledged: what about the citizenship rights of other groups not

3. *Dred Scott v. Sandford*, 19 How. 393, 404 and 416 (1857).
4. Ibid., 19 How. 393, 405 (1857). In *Dred Scott* Taney contradicts his earlier ruling that "every citizen of a State is also a citizen of the United States." 7 How. 283, 492.
5. U.S. Constitution, amend. 14, sec.1.

of European descent, also implicitly excluded by Taney? Blacks born in the United States prior to the Civil War were rarely subjects of another country, but, depending on how the phrase "subject to the jurisdiction thereof" is interpreted, it could be argued—and was argued—that Chinese people were subject to the jurisdiction of China. Exactly how this crucial phrase in the citizenship clause should be interpreted was not decided by the Supreme Court until thirty years after the Fourteenth Amendment was passed, in a case involving the Wong Kim Ark of my title. But before turning to that important, complicated, and neglected case, I want at least to touch on the status of Native Americans in the nineteenth century.

The leading case is *Elk v. Wilkins* (1884). Native Americans who retained tribal loyalty were, under existing laws, clearly not United States citizens because they were subject to their own jurisdiction. What was not clear, however, was the status of someone, like Elk, who renounced his tribal loyalty and claimed citizenship because he was born in the United States. In its decision the Court denied Elk automatic citizenship by birth, because at the time of his birth he was, it argued, subject to a foreign—that is tribal—jurisdiction.[6]

The issue facing the Court in *United States v. Wong Kim Ark* (1898) involved someone of Chinese descent born in this country to parents who were still subjects of China. The facts of the case were as follows. In 1873, Wong Kim Ark was born in San Francisco of Chinese parents. In 1890, his parents moved back to China, and Wong Kim Ark visited them, returning to San Francisco on 26 July 1890. In 1894, he again visited China. Returning in August 1895, he was denied entrance by the United States government under existing Chinese exclusion acts that barred almost all Chinese from entering the country. An exclusion act was in force in 1890. But in 1890 the San Francisco customs officer considered Wong Kim Ark a native-born citizen of the United States; the 1895 officer did not. One reason for this changed ruling was a new administration in Washington, D.C. In 1892 the Democrat Grover Cleveland had been elected president. Democratic support in California depended upon Representative Geary, who earlier in the year had sponsored the Geary Act, which both extended the first exclusion act of 1882 and added some harsher measures. The Cleveland administration ruled that someone of Chinese parents born in the United States was a subject of China, not a citizen of the United States. Wong Kim Ark claimed that he was a citizen by birth under the citizenship clause of the Fourteenth Amendment.

6. In 1924 an act of Congress made all Native Americans automatic citizens.

At stake was how to interpret the first sentence of the Fourteenth Amendment: "All persons born or naturalized in the United States, *and subject to the jurisdiction thereof,* are citizens of the United States and the State wherein they reside." The argument for granting Wong Kim Ark citizenship was that the United States had taken over the common law doctrine that all people born in the king's realm were subjects of the king, and that the crucial phrase in the amendment simply reinforced that doctrine. The argument against granting citizenship claimed that "subject to the jurisdiction thereof" did not mean subject to the territory thereof, but to the country the person owes allegiance. Since at the time of his birth Wong Kim Ark's father owed allegiance to China, he was born a subject of China, not the United States. The issue facing the Court, in other words, was does the United States determine citizenship according to ius soli or ius sanguinis?[7]

Because I suspect that the sentiment of most of us here is in favor of ius soli, I want to spend most of my time explaining the interpretation justifying ius sanguinis in order to emphasize how easily the Court could have argued in favor of the United States government. The government's case was that the intention of the language of the Fourteenth Amendment was to bring United States' law in conformity with the international law of citizenship stated by Vattel: "The true bond which connects the child with the body politic is not the matter of an inanimate piece of land, but the moral relations of his parentage...."[8] The government had strong

7. The issue was frequently debated in law journals in the late nineteenth century. See, for instance, George D. Collins, "Are Persons Born within the United States Ipso Facto Citizens Thereof?" *American Law Review* 18 (1884): 831–838; John A. Hayward, "Who Are Citizens," *American Law Journal* 2 (1885): 315–319; Henry C. Ide, "Citizenship," *American Law Journal* 2 (1885): 3–6; Simeon E. Baldwin, "The Citizen of the United States," *Yale Law Journal* 2 (1893): 85–94; George D. Collins, "Citizenship by Birth," *American Law Review* 29 (1895): 385–395; Simeon E. Baldwin, "Comment," *Central Law Review* 42 (1896): 299–300; Henry C. Ide, "Citizenship by Birth—Another View," *American Law Review* 30 (1896): 241–252; Marshall B. Woodworth, "Citizenship of the United States under the Fourteenth Amendment, *American Law Review* 30 (1896): 535–555; Boyd Winchester, "Citizenship in Its International Relation," *American Law Review* (1897): 504–513; Simeon E. Baldwin, "Comment," *Yale Law Journal* 7 (1898): 366–36; Simeon E. Baldwin, "Citizenship of Children of Alien Parents," *Harvard Law Review* 12 (1898): 55–56 (Reprinted in *Central Law Review* 46 (1898): 498); Marshall B. Woodworth, "Who Are Citizens of the United States? Wong Kim Ark Case—Interpretation of Citizenship Clause of Fourteenth Amendment," *American Law Review* 32 (1898): 554–561; and Simeon E. Baldwin, "The People of the United States," *Yale Law Journal* 8 (1899): 159–167.

8. Quoted by Chief Justice Fuller, in dissent, *United States v. Wong Kim Ark*, 169 U.S. 649, 708 (1898).

textual evidence to support its case. For instance, the 1866 Civil Rights Bill, passed two months before the same Congress proposed the Fourteenth Amendment, states: "That all persons born in the United States and *not subject to any foreign power,* excluding Indians not taxed, are hereby declared to be citizens of the United States"[9] (emphasis added). Furthermore, in the *Slaughter House Cases* (1873), the first important interpretation of the Fourteenth Amendment, Justice Miller in the opinion of Court added the dictum: "The phrase, 'subject to its jurisdiction' was meant to exclude from its operation children of ministers, consuls, and citizens or subjects of foreign States, born within the United States."[10] Since this interpretation was not crucial for the outcome of the case, the dictum was not binding, but no one, not even the dissenters, took issue with it.

The government also drew support from Congress's failure to include Asians when it extended the right of naturalization to Africans in its 1870 law. It was inconsistent, it argued, for the same Congress that denied all members of a group citizenship by naturalization to grant it automatically to children of that group by birth. In addition, it pointed out that to grant a child automatic citizenship while acknowledging, as the Court had, the government's power to deport aliens would potentially result in the separation of families. Moreover, to grant Wong Kim Ark citizenship would raise the problem of dual citizenship, which international law under Vattel had tried to avoid.

Another argument of the government was that the United States had not simply adopted common law doctrine. Common law doctrine, it demonstrated, has its origins in feudal practices. Those practices were not appropriate for a republic like the United States. If a feudal society is made up of subjects and lords, a republic is made up of equal citizens.[11] Common law referred to a king's subjects, not the citizens of a republic. It also declared that a subject's loyalty was indissoluble. The United States, however, was founded on the right to alter allegiance. Indeed, although it did not cite this piece of evidence, the government could have pointed out that the War of 1812 was fought over right of expatriation. What it did point out was that

9. Ibid., 719–720.

10. *The Slaughter House Cases*, 16 Wall. 36, 73 (1873).

11. The majority cites Chancellor Kent to dispute the importance of a distinction between citizens and subjects. "Subject and citizen are, in a degree, convertible terms as applied to natives; and though the term *citizen* seems to be appropriate to republican freemen, yet we are, equally with the inhabitants of all other countries, *subjects,* for we are equally bound by allegiance and subjection to the government and law of the land." *United States v. Wong Kim Ark,* 169 U.S. 649, 665 (1898).

the United States explicitly acknowledged the right of expatriation in a law passed by Congress on 27 July 1868, in other words, the same year that the Fourteenth Amendment was adopted. This acknowledgment suggested that the United States was making a clear break with common law doctrine.

At this point the government could have reinforced the distinction between subjects and citizens by referring to *Dred Scott.* That it did not do so is probably a sign of the difficulty that this case presented to those trying to get out from under its influence while still holding onto views of white supremacy. In any case, there was no question that under *Dred Scott* slaves were subject to the jurisdiction of the United States. But they were also clearly not citizens. Since it was universally granted that the purpose of the Fourteenth Amendment was to overturn *Dred Scott*, it seemed that in granting citizenship to former slaves, the Fourteenth Amendment signaled the United States' break with feudal practices of subjection, including the common law doctrine associated with them. The standard practice for countries to move from feudal practices to republican ones was to determine citizenship by descent. Thus it made sense to argue that with the Fourteenth Amendment the United States followed that practice.

To be sure, opponents argued that the United States had traditionally granted automatic citizenship to children born to immigrants. But the government responded that it granted it only to parents *permanently* domiciled in the country. Permanently domiciled here, they had indicated their intention to abandon subjection to the country from which they came. This option was not available to those of Chinese descent. First, a Chinese subject who renounced allegiance was subject to beheading. Second, because Chinese could not become naturalized citizens and because they had not assimilated into United States culture, the government considered them "sojourners" in the land.

Despite these arguments, the Court decided in favor of Wong Kim Ark and ius soli. According to the majority opinion, the phrase "subject to the jurisdiction thereof" created no new restrictions on citizenship. It simply confirmed that the United States had adopted common law doctrine. Thus the only exceptions were common law exceptions: the children of diplomats and the children of those in hostile occupation of territory during war. Wong Kim Ark was, therefore, a citizen by birth. Nonetheless, it is important to note that there were two dissenters: Chief Justice Fuller and Justice Harlan, who two years earlier was the lone dissenter in *Plessy v. Ferguson*, the case justifying "separate but equal" laws based on race.

As a consequences of this ruling, "The right of citizenship [in the United States] never *descends* in the legal sense, either by the common law, or under the common naturalization acts. It is incident to birth in the country, or it is given personally by statute."[12] Or as Gary Jacobsohn puts it, "Henceforward the ability of the native born to share in the aspirational content of American national identity was formed only by one's relation to the physical boundaries of the United States."[13]

With this decision my story ends, for even though the United States continued its restrictive immigration policy for those of Asian descent for many years—indeed, even tightened restrictions—once this ruling occurred, the legal definition made it virtually impossible to have a legal determination of citizenship by race. As two commentators have noted, "Persons within a given territory must inevitably and intensively interact with and affect one another, thereby creating a common life that ordinarily shapes their interests. Hence, defining political membership territorially expresses a recognition that all persons who share a specific locale over a period of time form an organic community, regardless of their inherited legal statuses."[14] But rather than close with such a tidy ending, I prefer to leave us with a few speculations to ponder.

The Fourteenth Amendment, which made possible what we can call this potentially multicultural (or should I say multiracial?) definition of United States citizenship, is the one most often appealed to to protect minority rights. But in *Santa Clara County v. Southern Pacific Railroad* (1886) the Court also granted corporations various Fourteenth Amendment rights. To be sure, corporations could not become citizens, but because corporations are, through a legal fiction, persons in the eyes of the law, they do come under its due process clause. By 1911, 607 Fourteenth Amendment cases had reached the Supreme Court; more than half involved corporations; only about thirty involved minority rights.[15]

This statistic might lead us to believe that corporate interests had co-opted the original intention of the amendment. But the situation is more complicated. Justice Field, who wrote a circuit court

---

12. *United States v. Wong Kim Ark*, 169 U.S. 649, 665 (1898).

13. Gary J. Jacobsohn, *Apple of Gold: Constitutionalism in Israel and the United States* (Princeton, 1993), 92.

14. Peter H. Schuck and Rogers M. Smith, *Citizenship without Consent* (New Haven, 1985), 39.

15. With slight adjustments, I take these statistics from Charles Wallace Collins, *The Fourteenth Amendment and the States*, (Boston, 1912), 183.

decision that was the model for *Santa Clara*, was closely aligned to corporate giants, such as California's "big four," who controlled the Southern Pacific Railroad. That corporation benefitted greatly from cheap Chinese labor, and it often lent financial and legal support for some of the cases brought by Chinese to protect their rights. Indeed, when the Supreme Court decided in favor of Wong Kim Ark, although Justice Field was no longer on the bench, the majority relied on a ruling that he had made in circuit court concerning the citizenship clause and the Chinese. This connection should make us at least consider the possibility that, while not identical, corporate and multicultural interests at some points overlap, especially as multinational corporations realize, as railroad giants over a century ago realized, that they can maximize profit by supporting a multicultural work force.[16]

I suspect that the situation in Germany is somewhat different. There is, for instance, no Fourteenth Amendment that brings together definitions of citizenship and the protection of both minority and corporate rights. Nonetheless, it might be worth exploring whether in both countries the move toward multiculturalism is linked, even if differently, to a globalization of the market and the work force that corporations have a better handle on than some of the academics participating in multicultural debates.[17] If so, we would also have to explore precisely what role definitions of national citizenship have to play in such a world, whether they are determined by ius soli or ius sanguinis.

---

16. Jon Cruz suggests that we "look at multiculturalism as part of a *social logic* of late capitalism and as a cultural feature at the intersection of economic globalization and the fiscal-domestic crisis of the state." "From Farce to Tragedy: Reflections on the Reification of Race at the Century's End," in *Mapping Multiculturalism*, 19.

17. See, for instance, Pierre Case, *Training for the Multicultural Management of People* (Washington, D.C., 1982).

15. The Discourse of Differentiation: German Political Membership

Gregg O. Kvistad

This essay will argue that a significant debate over political membership has occupied policy makers and a diverse group of political activists in the Federal Republic of Germany since the late 1960s. Specific episodes like the conflict over the *Radikalenerlass* (Radicals Decree) in the 1970s, the entrance of the Greens into the federal parliament in 1983, the bitter experience of amending the asylum law in the early 1990s, and recent efforts to reform citizenship law all share a profound questioning of what it means to enter and be a member of the German political community. Two main ways of answering that question have historically informed German political discourse. One, which is quite familiar and has been the subject of considerable recent attention in the Federal Republic and elsewhere, is the ethnocultural differentiation of German political membership. The other, less explicit but no less powerful, is the statist differentiation of political membership.

This essay will argue that German ethnocultural differentiation has historically been a crucial legal device for sorting "Germans" from "non-Germans" by deploying the principle of *ius sanguinis*, or law of blood. But if German political membership is to be fully understood, we must look not only at how Germans differentiate themselves from non-Germans, but also at how Germans differentiate themselves from one another. For that, it is necessary to incorporate into our analysis the statist ideological discourse that has historically sorted Germans along a vertical dimension, locating the hortatory political actor in the realm of the state "above" the proto-anarchic societal agent in society. Only then will it become clear that the current intensified debate in the Federal Republic over political membership is not only about the identity "non-German," but more centrally about what it means to be a member of the German political community. Indeed, it will be suggested that the recent reforms in naturalization law in the Federal Republic have been directly informed by the shift in the past thirty years in German political discourse about what it means to be a German political actor.

Differentiating German Political Membership

Historically, two main criteria for differentiating German political membership have appeared in German political discourse. First and most prominent, an ethnocultural differentiation identifies the German community as an ethnic and cultural nation.[1] Second and less explicit, a political statism vertically dichotomizes a set of state actors existing in a plane above ordinary citizens and subjects in the realm of society.[2] We shall first discuss ethnocultural differentiation and then turn to the statist mode. In the Federal Republic, the post-Nazi deracialization of German ethnocultural identity has left this differentiation primarily as a "horizontal" categorization of German political membership. The ethnocultural categorization has been specified since 1913 in Germany by the principle of ius sanguinis, or law of descent, which defines the nature of the German citizenry. Citizenship can generally be viewed as a sorting mechanism for modern nation-states to determine who is "in" and who is "out." From the legal perspective of citizenship in the nation-state, "insiders" constitute a single status, typically entailing residence rights, the right to enter the nation-state, and some level of political participation, but also obligations like compulsory military service. "Outsiders," in contrast, are a more variegated group: all are foreigners, some are temporary visitors, some are resident aliens (both long- and short-term), and some are more ambivalently "denizens," or foreigners with nearly fully guaranteed residence status, some with particular political rights.[3] "Outsiders" to a nation-state's citizenship are vertically differentiated by legal rights and obligations (denizens typically have the most, and temporary visitors have the least), while "insiders" as

---

1. Werner Conze, *The Shaping of the German Nation* (New York, 1979), 19–21.

2. Kenneth H. F. Dyson, *The State Tradition in Western Europe* (New York, 1980), 51–58.

3. Herbert Kitschelt, *The Logics of Party Formation: Ecological Politics in Belgium and West Germany* (Ithaca, 1989), 30–33.

legal citizens inhabit a "region of legal equality." According to Rogers Brubaker, "[to] be defined as a citizen is not to qualify as an insider for a particular instance or type of interaction; it is to be defined in a general, abstract, enduring, and context-independent way as a member of the state."[4]

From the legal perspective of the nation-state, outsiders are legally differentiated from insiders horizontally, in the sense that citizen and noncitizen are exclusive classes of rights- and duties-bearing persons. Noncitizens of one nation-state are virtually always citizens of another, and the metaphorical wall that separates these two classes is, from a global nation-state perspective, legally separating level territory —regardless of the views of particular migrating individuals. Since 1913, the German "region of legal equality" has been populated with "ethnic Germans" who occupy that location on the basis of descent, not location of birth or residence.[5] While the ethnoculturalist position may easily be deployed for hierarchical and racist purposes, it may also service the ethnopluralist who welcomes the vision of a "salad-bowl" society.[6] Differentiation is retained, but in a more complicated manner than suggested by the axes of vertical and horizontal. For purposes here, however, we will understand the ethnocultural differentiation of German political membership as primarily a horizontal one that differentiates a German "realm of legal equality" from other non-German realms.

A second means for differentiating members of the German political community is provided by the rich ideology of German statism. This is a tool for vertically differentiating political membership not by national or ethnocultural means, but rather in reference to some notion of a rational public interest. Generally compatible with German liberalism—both the richly differentiated nineteenth-century variety and that of the postwar Federal Republic—German statism is ultimately rooted in the Prussian General Code of 1794, a body of laws that placed the idea of the state above all persons in Prussia, including the monarch who, as a legal personality, was only

4. Rogers Brubaker, *Citizenship and Nationhood in France and Germany* (Cambridge, 1992), 21, 29.
5. Here, "ethnic German" refers not to the official "Vertriebene," or expellees, from East-Central Europe, but rather to all German citizens who hold that status because of their "ethnicity." See Brubaker, *Citizenship*, 206–207, note 19; Barbara Marshall, "German Migration Policies," in Gordon Smith, et al, eds., *Development in German Politics* (Durham, 1992), 250–51.
6. Sabine von Dirke, "Multikulti: The German Debate on Multiculturalism," *German Studies Review* 17 (1994): 522–23.

the state's "first servant."[7] The most important inhabitants of this realm of the state are civil servants who are loyally dedicated to serving an impersonal, secular, and universalistic political entity, "the well-being or power of which," according to Leah Greenfeld, "meant the common well-being."[8] As is so clearly represented in the history of German liberalism, however, the common well-being in this ideology is not some "will of the people" that percolates up from below, from a society of ordinary citizens and subjects.[9] It is, rather, a "public interest" elevated above all societal interests that are regarded, by definition, as egoistic and particularistic and hence politically less "rational" than what is represented by the idea of the German state.[10] This means of differentiation does not explicitly separate Germans from non-Germans either legally or ideologically, but rather differentiates hortatory and legitimate political actors in the domestic German context from those who are not.

The differences between these modes of traditional German political differentiation are important. First, the ethnocultural differentiation informs a robust and clear-cut principle for the attribution of German citizenship in the form of ius sanguinis. The statist differentiation, in contrast, is part of a more diffuse discourse of German politics, but one which is historically very powerful and of which we still find lingering institutional traces in the Federal Republic.[11] Second, the ethnocultural differentiation is a rather crude tool for separating Germans from non-Germans, regardless of place of birth or residence, compared to the more finely textured and ideological instrument of German statism. German statism cannot only internally differentiate Germans from one another for institutional employment, but it can also provide a more informal, yet powerful, means

7. Ernst Rudolf Huber, *Deutsche Verfassungsgeschichte seit 1789: Bd. II, Der Kampf um Einheit und Freiheit 1830–1850* (Stuttgart, 1968), 16–19; Kurt G. A. Jeserich, "Die Entstehung des öffentlichen Dienstes 1800–1871," in K. Jeserich, H. Pohl, G. C. v. Unruh, eds., *Deutsche Verwaltungsgeschichte, Bd. 2: Vom Reichsdeputationshauptschluss bis zur Auflösung des Deutschen Bundes* (Stuttgart, 1983), 304–5; Reinhart Koselleck, *Preussen zwischen Reform und Revolution: Allgemeines Landrecht, Verwaltung, und soziale Frage von 1791 bis 1848* (Stuttgart, 1967), 399.

8. Leah Greenfeld, *Nationalism: Five Roads to Modernity* (Cambridge, 1992), 286.

9. James J. Sheehan, *German Liberalism in the Nineteenth Century* (Chicago, 1978), 35–50.

10. Robert Berdahl, *The Politics of the Prussian Nobility* (Princeton, 1988), 312; Bernd Wunder, *Geschichte der Bürokratie in Deutschland* (Frankfurt/Main, 1986), 67.

11. Nevil Johnson, *State and Government in the Federal Republic of Germany: The Executive at Work* (Oxford, 1983), 1–21; Gregg O. Kvistad, "Radicals in the State: The Political Demands on West German Civil Servants," *Comparative Political Studies* 21(1988): 95–125.

of opprobrium and valorization of political actors and their actions in modern German politics, especially in periods of political stress.[12]

Third, and important for our discussion here, German ethnoculturalism is a construct of political particularism. In its most benign form, it allows the horizontal differentiation of Germans from non-Germans according to specific nonrational cultural and ethnic criteria.[13] It regards people as imbedded cultural and ethnic agents unable or unwilling to reach meaningfully beyond their particular societal identities. German statism, in contrast, identifies a universalistic realm of state political action focused on the embodiment of a rational public interest—not a peculiarly national German interest, as such, but rather one that, ideologically at least, exists above all societal, cultural, and ethnic particularity. The discourse of membership in the German ethnocultural community has meant having a particularism define one's identity. The discourse of membership in the German statist community has meant, in contrast, transcending all particularity to serve the universalistic idea of the German state. As will be discussed, these contrasting differentiations of German political membership have profoundly affected political debates over who has public significance in the Federal Republic and why. An enumeration of those debates over the last thirty years is first required.

Democratization in the Federal Republic

Debates over the nature of political membership in the Federal Republic in the past thirty years have been informed by a civic culturalization of the West German public that began in the late 1960s. Most schematically, that has involved the development of a growing political interest among West German citizens, a greater respect for the Federal Republic's democratic institutions, and a growing sense of individual political efficacy.[14] While Nazi Germany demonstrated

12. Gregg O. Kvistad, "The 'Borrowed Language' of German Unification: State, Society and Party Identity," *German Politics* 3 (1994): 206–21.

13. Laura M. Murray, "Einwanderungsland Bundesrepublik Deutschland? Explaining the Evolving Positions of German Political Parties on Citizenship Policy," *German Politics and Society* 33 (1994): 38–39.

14. David Conradt, "Changing German Political Culture," in Gabriel Almond and Sidney Verba, eds., *The Civic Culture Revisited* (Boston, 1980), 212–72; Ronald Inglehart, "New Perspectives on Political Change," *Comparative Political Studies* 17 (1985): 485–532; Kendall Baker, Russell Dalton, and Kai Hildebrandt, *Germany Transformed: Political Culture and the New Politics* (Cambridge, 1981).

that a modern concern for political membership could be completely disconnected from the democratization of a citizenry, the public debate over political membership in the Federal Republic since the 1960s has been demonstrably mediated by a "revolutionary" democratization of political culture and the challenges of that for some of Germany's most deeply rooted political traditions.[15] That democratization posed a direct challenge to what Karl Jaspers indicted in 1966 as the German political consciousness of

> respect for the government as such, whatever that government might be; need for honoring the state in the form of representative politicians as a replacement for emperor and king; feelings of subjecthood with regard to authority in all of its manifestations, including toward the counter clerk at the most insignificant state office; readiness for blind obedience; trust that the government will get it right; in short: political consciousness [*Staatsgesinnung*] is often among us still subject consciousness, not the democratic consciousness of the free citizen.[16]

By the late 1960s and early 1970s, Jaspers's "subject-consciousness" was being rejected in the Federal Republic's universities, on the streets of its large cities, and most broadly in the early 1970s, in the vibrant West German citizens' initiative movement.[17] These sites saw the rejection of both the form and content of traditional German political agency. In this transformation to what Habermas called "the politics of the first person," *Staat* and *Regierung* (state and government) became less trusted by German citizens to act in their interest;[18] and the "inherited expectations" of what counted as politically relevant shifted from economic worries about inflation and unemployment to include a "postmaterialist" focus on all manner of the "quality of life."[19] In short, the relative material satisfactions and security delivered to West Germans by a Keynesian welfare state managed from above by political and economic elites were no longer sufficient for the generation maturing in the late 1960s and early 1970s.[20]

15. Dennis L. Bark and David R. Gress, *A History of West Germany: From Shadow to Substance: 1945–1963*, Vol. 1 (Cambridge, 1989), xliii.

16. Karl Jaspers, *Wohin treibt die Bundesrepublik?* (Munich, 1988 [originally 1966]), 146.

17. P. C. Mayer-Tasch, *Die Bürgerinitiativbewegung: Der aktive Bürger als rechts- und politikwissenschaftliches Problem* (Reinbek bei Hamburg, 1976), 9–73.

18. Jürgen Habermas, "New Social Movements," *Telos* 49 (1981), 37.

19. Ronald Inglehart, *The Silent Revolution: Changing Styles among Western Publics* (Princeton, 1977); Ronald Inglehart, *Culture Shift in Advanced Industrial Society* (Princeton, 1990).

20. Claus Offe, *Contradictions of the Welfare State* (Cambridge, 1984), 147–61.

Following Habermas, two types of political mobilization appeared in the Federal Republic as part of this democratization process: "defensive" movements of "resistance and retreat [that] seek to stem or block the formal, organized sphere of action in favor of communicative structures," and "emancipatory" movements "deeply rooted in the acknowledged universalist foundations of morality and legality."[21] "Defensive" movements in this period were informed primarily by issue concerns: the environmental and peace movements that appeared in the 1970s and 1980s did vaguely offer their own agency to challenge that of traditional West German political and economic elites, but the primary concern of these activists was not acquiring public significance but rather halting and reversing environmental degradation and the risks of nuclear war.[22] As such, these movements were broadly global or European and did not primarily pose challenges to the membership criteria of the German political community as such.

"Emancipatory" movements in the Federal Republic, in contrast, have been mainly concerned with political agency in two senses: they have been struggles for rights to participate in the German political community, on the one hand, and struggles to end discrimination in and by that community, on the other.[23] These two concerns about agency are linked, but are not synonymous. The movement to open up the German civil service to a broader variety of German citizen, for instance, or to devolve the traditional political power of that institution to the citizenry, is more participatory in nature than the multiculturalist movement to halt xenophobia and appreciate cultural diversity in the Federal Republic. Yet when the multiculturalist movement demands local voting rights for foreigners, an expansion of political participation is the focus. Because these and other emancipatory movements are more directly mediated by German institutional traditions, laws, and social/cultural mores than by "defensive" movements, they are relatively more context specific and thus more relevant for this discussion of German political membership.

The two main tools for differentiating political membership in the Federal Republic—ethnoculturalism and statism—may be applied to defensive issue mobilizations in the last thirty years, but that will not be attempted here.[24] This essay will instead link these two modes of political differentiation to different emancipation movements that

21. Habermas, "New Social Movements," 34–35.
22. Kitschelt, *The Logics*, 2–3.
23. Habermas, "New Social Movements."
24. See, however, Kitschelt, *The Logics*, 75–97.

more specifically address the constraints within the German context. The ethnoculturalist differentiation is a horizontal tool for separating Germans from non-Germans, or more precisely ethnic Germans from ethnic non-Germans. Underlying the differentiation is the principle of ius sanguinis, which has informed German citizenship and naturalization policy since 1913. This ethnoculturalist differentiation has also been manifested in the recent discourse of xenophobia and violence against foreigners.[25] Then the horizontalist and relatively benign differentiation acquires a vertical dimension, as "nature" and not "culture" becomes the key distinction among civilizations and ethnoculturalism descends into blatant racism.[26]

The statist differentiation, in contrast, is a vertical tool for ideologically segmenting German political membership. In the statist tradition, "difference" is coded never as a relationship between relative equals and thus relatively benign, but always as what distinguishes a "higher" and more hortatory realm of political belief and action from a "lower" and less legitimate realm. Unlike the ethnoculturalist differentiation, however, the hierarchical statist differentiation does not turn ideologically on a question of Germanness and ancestry, but rather on a question about the approximation of consistency between political belief and action and a universalistic "public interest" that is "above" the egoism, particularism, and illegitimacy of sectionalized societal politics.[27] These modes of differentiation—ethnoculturalism and statism—have thus included and excluded according to very different criteria.

Democratic Challenges to Ethnocultural Differentiation

Ethnoculturalism as a sorting device for German political membership has helped to construct a variety of oppositional emancipatory movements and discourses in the Federal Republic since the early 1980s. They range from the "multicultural movement," which first appeared in 1980 in response to the treatment of migrant

---

25. Michael Schmidt, *Heute gehört uns die Strasse* (Düsseldorf, 1993), 29–168.

26. Thomas Faist, "How to Define a Foreigner? The Symbolic Politics of Immigration in German Partisan Discourse, 1978–1992," *West European Politics* 17 (1994): 63; see, however, Claus Leggewie: "Rassist ist, gleich ob er genetisch, historisch, ethnisch oder kulturell argumentiert, wer die Menschen einzig von ihres Herkunft her zu bestimmen ..." in von Dirke, "Multikulti," 522.

27. Kenneth Dyson, "The Ambiguous Politics of Western Germany: Politicization in a 'State' Society," *European Journal of Political Research* 7 (1979): 375–96.

laborers in the Federal Republic, to more recent calls for the reform of the ius sanguinis-based German citizenship law. These movements have rejected ethnocultural and ancestry criteria for differentiating political membership in the Federal Republic. At the same time, however, the multicultural movement retains room for, and calls for the positive appreciation of, cultural difference. According to Sabine von Dirke, the first *Tag des ausländischen Mitbürgers*, or Day of Foreign Residents, organized by Catholic and Protestant churches in 1980, "wanted to focus attention on [foreign workers] in a more comprehensive way and perceived the concept of culture as the appropriate point of departure. Instead of viewing the foreigners only in terms of their problems and their economic value, the German population should recognize the various foreign cultures which the migrant workers had brought with them as an enrichment of German culture."[28] The offer of a multicultural "enrichment" for Germans and their culture, which migrant workers might embody, requested a positive appreciation of cultural diversity in a context where a single culture had defined legal political membership for nearly seventy years.

While broadening, the multicultural alternative to German ethnoculturalism is thus built on the preservation and not transcendence of a cultural discourse of German political membership. On the one hand, German multiculturalism has a defensive moment of emancipation in its noble attempt to prevent German ethnocultural discourse from descending to naturalistic and racialist positings of difference. On the other hand, German multiculturalism's positive moment of emancipation is primarily directed at Germans who are beckoned to enrich their own cultural identities with the cultures of others. Put more pointedly, the latter can and has sanctioned a German new middle-class glorification of the exotic, a consumption of the cultural "other," and a voyeuristic participation in the "Oriental."[29] The multicultural "mirror-image" of ethnocultural differentiation can ignore, as Thomas Faist argues, a whole series of positive emancipatory issues for foreigners like concrete housing and workplace restrictions that have nothing to do with German enrichment.[30] By universalizing particularism without attempting its transcendence, multiculturalism in its most benign form reduces cultural discrimination for foreigners and becomes a bonus for ethnic Germans to consume.

28. Von Dirke, "Multikulti," 516.
29. Ibid., 519.
30. Faist, "How to Define," 66–67.

The citizenship reform effort of the 1990s is also defined by the ethnocultural differentiation of political membership in Germany. But unlike the multiculturalism movement, this emancipatory drive rejects the ethnocultural differentiation of German membership as a proper marker of public significance. Instead of reversing the normative values of ethnocultural discourse, it argues for the transcendence of that discourse for defining German citizenship. Jürgen Fijalkowski argues,

> a modernized understanding of citizenship and nation ... could be based only on the rejection of an ethnonational understanding of citizenship. It would represent a turn toward an understanding of nation as a self-governing society formed by heterogeneous citizens. The nation of common ethnic descent would be transformed into a postnational society characterized by the will of citizens to live together under the common law of constitutional democracy irrespective of race, gender, ethnicity, descent, origin, social group, religion, and political thinking, looking to the future rather than to the past.[31]

The Federal Republic as a "postnational society" would remove ethnicity and culture as legitimate terms in the discourse of German political membership. Practically, that would entail the introduction of *ius soli*, or residential, elements into German citizenship law. As a republican and universalist response to German ethnocultural political differentiation, this reform movement seeks to ground membership in the Federal Republic in political participation and not a particularistic ethnic or cultural identity.[32] But what kind of universalistic response is this? German political ideology has historically been profoundly informed by the Enlightenment's discourse of universalism. That has not, however, been republican in nature. We discover this when we return to Germany's other major mode of differentiating political membership: the ideological tradition of German statism.

Democratic Challenges to Statist Differentiation

German statism has historically sanctioned a hierarchic differentiation of a politically hortatory realm of reliable and loyal civil servants acting in the name of a universalistic public interest above a societal realm of ordinary citizens allegedly capable only of particularistic,

31. Jürgen Fijalkowski, *Aggressive Nationalism, Immigration Pressure, and Asylum Policy Disputes in Contemporary Germany* (Washington, D.C., 1993), 26–27.
32. Faist, "How to Define," 69; Murray, "Einwanderungsland," 38.

conflictual, and self-interested political agency. The historical
strength of the professional civil service in German politics, the relatively late development of political parties, the statist dimensions of
German liberalism, the historical denigration of parliamentary politics, and even the need politically to legitimize catch-all political
parties in the Federal Republic as constituting a *Parteienstaat,* or
party-state, are but a few of the many indicators of the robust statist
tradition of German political discourse. Two recent emancipatory
mobilizations around the question of German political membership
have rejected this deep tradition of German statism. Each, with varying directness, has rejected not a particularistic Germanness, but
rather a German statist universalism. Each ultimately redefines the
statist and universalistic public interest to a citizen-defined, more
open-ended, temporary, and concrete agreement on particular
political choices. While this resembles Faist's "postnational" alternative to the ethnocultural political differentiation—both in the form
of ius sanguinis-informed citizenship and in the form of the multiculturalism movement—unlike that alternative, it more concretely
addresses Germany's unique Enlightenment legacy of statist political discourse. These recent "emancipatory" mobilizations and subsequent reforms are thus less about the abstract "rights of man" than
the purported rationality of the German state. We turn now to these
mobilizations: the battle over the *Radikalenerlass* (Radicals Decree)
in the 1970s, and the movement to reform the Federal Republic's
naturalization law in the early 1990s.

The Radicals Decree appeared in January 1972 as a federal-level
agreement among *Länder* (states) minister-presidents and the federal chancellor who, adopting a standing Interior Ministers Conference recommendation, called on each state employee to "guarantee
that he would intervene on behalf of the free democratic basic order
at all times." Such a "guarantee" was positive in nature: if doubts
about the candidate's ability to embody this surfaced, the burden of
proof rested on the candidate to expunge them. Furthermore, this
guarantee was to be demonstrated during work and nonwork hours,
and it was to be determined not only by the actions, but also by the
beliefs of state employees and applicants. Though "each individual
case" was to be decided on its own merits, "membership" in organizations "hostile to the constitution" (*verfassungsfeindlich*) would "as a
rule" (*in der Regel*) justify either dismissal or denial of employment.[33]

33. For the text of the decree, see "Dokument Nr. 43: Beschluss der Regierungs-
chefs des Bundes und der Länder vom 28. Januar 1972," in Ehard Denninger, ed.,
Freiheitliche demokratische Grundordnung, Bd. II (Frankfurt/Main, 1977), 518–19.

The decree followed on the heels of a similar measure in Hamburg and was regarded by its signatories, including Federal Chancellor Willy Brandt, to be "no new law" but only an effort to "unify implementation" of standing civil service law at the Länder and federal levels.[34] This "no new law," however, appeared in a highly politicized environment that was informed by two important phenomena: first, the massive political mobilization of German university students and intellectuals that began in 1967 with the APO (*Ausserpolitische Organisation*), continued in 1968 with the anti-Emergency Laws demonstrations, and was encouraged by the so-called *Machtwechsel*, or power shift, of the Social Democratic Party (SPD)/Free Democratic Party (FDP) coalition coming to power in 1969; and second, the new government's active efforts to jump-start *Deutschlandpolitik* and *Ostpolitik* (West Germany's policies toward East Germany) immediately after forming the federal coalition.[35] The first threatened a "march through the institutions," in Rudi Dutschke's memorable phrase,[36] and the second drove the SPD to attempt to detach the historical opprobrium of unreliable "*vaterlandslose Gesellen*," or young men without a fatherland, from the party's identity by a series of *Abgrenzungen*, or lines of demarcation, that needed to be drawn to demonstrate especially to the opposition Christian Democratic Party (CDU)/Christian Social Party (CSU) that the SPD would also govern as an anti-communist post-Bad-Godesberg party.[37]

Both contextual determinants—the radicalization of the political culture by university students and intellectuals and the extraordinary "normalization" of relations with communist Eastern Europe—posed the question of the political reliability and loyalty of citizens of the Federal Republic. Indeed, the legitimacy of the political agency of ordinary German citizens was questioned in two senses: as participants in this universalistic institution of the German state civil

34. "Demokratie und Sicherheit: Interview des Bundeskanzlers," *Bulletin* 55 (15 April 1972), 773.

35. See Arnulf Baring and Manfred Görtemaker, *Machtwechsel: die Ära Brandt-Scheel* (Stuttgart, 1982); Klaus Hildebrand, *Geschichte der Bundesrepublik Deutschland, Bd. 4: Von Erhard zur Grossen Koalition, 1963–1969* (Stuttgart, 1984); and Wolfgang Jäger, "Die Innenpolitik der sozial-liberalen Koalition 1969–1974," in Karl-Dietrich Bracher, Wolfgang Jäger, and Werner Link, *Geschichte der Bundesrepublik Deutschland, Bd. 5/I: Republik im Wandel, 1969–1974* (Stuttgart, 1986).

36. Kurt Sontheimer, *Die verunsicherte Republik* (Munich, 1979), 27.

37. Baring, *Machtwechsel*, 358; for a perceived linkage between the decree and foreign policy, see Willy Brandt, "… wir sind nicht zu Helden geboren" (Zürich, 1986), 133; for an earlier denial of that linkage by the same actor, see Willy Brandt and Helmut Schmidt, *Deutschland 1976: Zwei Sozialdemokraten im Gespräch* (Hamburg, 1976), 48.

service, and as challengers to the legitimacy of ideologically elevating that institution above the political participatory experience of ordinary German citizens.[38] Producing one of the most divisive political conflicts in the history of the Federal Republic to that date, the decree experienced multiple revisions and amendments appearing at both the federal and state levels in the late 1980s and early 1990s (often characterized as "corrections" of the "mistaken implementation" of the decree), and the controversy over the Radicals Decree gradually abated.[39] A powerful political challenge was embodied in the furor over the Radicals Decree to hasten its slow and uneven demise. Vast numbers of mobilized West Germans from all parties, religious denominations, and countless interest groups rejected the traditional segmentation of German public life into politically "reliable" state civil servants with hortatory beliefs and actions, on the one hand, and politically "unreliable" ordinary citizens, on the other.

With unification in 1990, the question of the political loyalty of civil servants once more pressed itself on to the political agenda as the G.D.R. acceded to the Federal Republic. The civil service policy that was adopted in the unification treaty of 1990 for state employees from the ex-G.D.R. was substantially more liberal than what appeared in the Federal Republic in the 1970s. Only the employment of former Stasi members in unified Germany's civil service was categorically regarded as "unreasonable." Adopting the so-called single-case test, neither Communist party membership nor previous employment in the state service of the G.D.R., as such, was a disqualification for state employment in the unified Federal Republic.[40] Various explanations can account for this relatively liberal treatment and the Federal Republic's gradual move away from the strictures of the Radicals Decree. But all of them should incorporate the dynamics of the German democratization process in the last thirty years that have increasingly rejected statism as a sorting device for German political membership. That rejection has implicitly questioned the very construct of one definable rational public interest

38. See Gerard Braunthal, *Political Loyalty and Public Service in West Germany* (Amherst, 1990); and Kvistad, "Radicals and the State," 95–125.

39. Peter Graf Kielmansegg, "The Basic Law—Response to the Past or Design for the Future?" *Forty Years of the Grundgesetz* (Washington, D.C., 1989).

40. *Texte zur Deutschlandpolitik*, Reihe III/Band 8a-1990, ed. Bundesministerium für innerdeutsche Beziehungen (Bonn, 1991), 7–17; Gregg O. Kvistad, "Accommodation of 'Cleansing': Germany's State Employees from the Old Regime," *West European Politics* 17 (1994): 52–73.

for an entire society as well as the ascribed agency of state bureaucrats for constituting and protecting the German political order. The second challenge to the statist differentiation of German political membership appeared in the reform of naturalization law in the early 1990s. During the 1980s, foreigners became German citizens through naturalization at an average annual rate of less than one-tenth of what occurred in France, with its combination of ius soli and ius sanguinis.[41] A rather high wall for naturalization applicants thus existed in the Federal Republic. Part of that height was constructed, until the early 1990s, by the rigorous formal demands made on the political beliefs and actions of naturalization applicants. Because the principle of pure ius sanguinis made residence irrelevant, long-term residents of the Federal Republic needed positively to demonstrate a number of extraordinary political characteristics to qualify for German citizenship—characteristics not legally required of lifetime Germans of the Federal Republic, ex-East German *Übersiedler*, or "ethnic German" *Aussiedler* from Eastern Europe and the ex-USSR.[42] Most generally, these were captured in what was referred to as a "positive attitude toward German culture." Specifically, these included a long period of permanent residence and adequate accommodation in the Federal Republic; a good reputation; the capability to make a living for self and dependents without reliance on welfare; spoken and written German language fluency; a "voluntary attachment" to Germany; a basic knowledge of Germany's political and social structures; no criminal record; and a positive commitment to the Federal Republics "free democratic basic order."[43]

Until the early 1990s, naturalization in the Federal Republic remained entirely discretionary, controlled by state authorities whose job it was to determine the public interest in naturalizing any particular applicant. No private legal right to citizenship existed among ethnic non-Germans, regardless of place of birth or residence. In 1989, a law professor and Administrative Appeals Court judge in Baden-Württemberg argued: "To my mind, it is perfectly reasonable to require loyalty to the basic principles of the constitution as long as a clear distinction is made between fundamental constitutional principles and the existing political regime." He continued, "Political activities in emigrant organizations are usually

41. Brubaker, *Citizenship*, 82.
42. Fijalkowski, *Aggressive Nationalism*, 19.
43. Kai Hailbronner, "Citizenship and Nationhood in Germany," in William Rogers Brubaker, ed., *Citizenship in Europe and North America* (Lanham, MD, 1989), 68–69.

taken as evidence against a permanent attachment to Germany.
Activities in extremist or radical organizations justify, in general, the
conclusion that the applicant is not committed to the democratic
order of the Federal Republic."[44] This requirement of heightened
demonstrable political loyalty—and not mere political legality—is
virtually the same as what, until the 1980s, was traditionally required of German applicants to the state civil service. In each case,
the outcome of applications to these different venues of German
political membership—the naturalized citizenry and the civil service—turned on the ability of a person to transcend his or her specific particularism as a societal actor and embody a rational public
interest in the form of a positive and constant support for the "free
democratic basic order" of the Federal Republic.

The reform of naturalization law in the Federal Republic in
1991 and 1993 considerably lowered the political hurdles to acquiring naturalized German citizenship. The 1991 law stated that
a "legal eligibility for naturalization" was granted to foreigners who
had renounced their previous citizenship and met a number of
conditions. For foreigners between ages sixteen and twenty-three,
those conditions included legal residence and school attendance
in the Federal Republic for six years; for foreigners over the age of
twenty-three, they included legal residence for fifteen years, a permanent address, a means of maintenance that did not include welfare and unemployment benefits, and no convictions for a criminal
offense.[45] Gone was the explicit ethnonational demand to demonstrate an attachment and "positive attitude toward German culture"
and the statist demand to demonstrate positively the readiness to
uphold the free democratic basic order at all times.

Remaining in the 1991 law was, however, a continued reliance
on bureaucratic discretion—*Ermessen der zuständigen Behörden*—for
determining the public interest in granting German citizenship to
any particular naturalization applicant. While that was to be granted
"*in der Regel*" in 1991, no right to German citizenship was possessed
by these "eligible" foreigners. In 1993, however, the 1991 principle
of legal eligibility (*Regelanspruch*) was replaced by a legal right
(*Rechtsanspruch*) for the naturalization of foreigners who met the

44. Ibid.
45. Karsten Schröder and Hermann Horstkotte, "Foreigners in Germany," Sozial-
Report 2 (1993): 4; "Bericht der Beauftragten der Bundesregierung für die Belange
der Ausländer über die Lage der Ausländer in der Bundesrepublik Deutschland,
1993," *Mitteilungen der Beauftragten der Bundesregierung für die Belange der Ausländer*
(1994): 84.

necessary residential requirements listed above.[46] A significant de-politicization of German political membership thereby occurred. State bureaucratic discretion to determine whether the naturalization of a long-term foreign resident was in the public interest was removed, and in the process, the German statist delegitimation of ordinary legal life in society as prima facie a politically "lower" and inadequate experience for German political membership. In short, ordinary legal life in German society was elevated to constitute legitimate German political agency. A statist-universalist public interest was exchanged for the open-ended agency of ordinary citizens.

Conclusion

German political membership has historically been differentiated according to two criteria: ethnocultural and statist. Ethnoculturalism is primarily a horizontal sorting device to separate the legal realm of equality of ethnic Germans from that of ethnic non-Germans. Ethnoculturalism is consistent with the principle of ius sanguinis that has served as the basis for defining German citizenship since 1913. Since the democratization of Western German political culture in the 1960s, powerful oppositional and emancipatory movements to expand and/or redefine political membership in Germany have appeared which have incorporated and/or specifically responded to this ethnocultural sorting device. Two such emancipatory efforts have been the multicultural movement since the 1980s, and the citizenship law reform movement since the early 1990s.

This essay has argued that the multicultural movement in the Federal Republic has problematically retained the traditional German ethnocultural markers it apparently seeks to transcend: a good deal of multiculturalism in the Federal Republic involves the "exotic" consumption of the cultures of eternally foreign "others" by the new middle class. The movement to reform citizenship law from its exclusive reliance on ius sanguinis, in turn, specifically acknowledges the history of ethnocultural sorting for political membership in Germany, but it attempts to transcend that sorting with a very abstract invocation of the "rights of man" and continental republicanism. In its attempt to transcend the particularism of culture for a "republican" universalism, this emancipatory effort does not recognize the power of German statism and its history of

46. "Bericht der Beauftragten der Bundesregierung," 85.

positing a universalism that has absolutely nothing to do with republican citizenship.

Statism as a sorting device in German politics, in contrast, has traditionally defined a hortatory politics of state action in accord with a public interest that is "above" and categorically different from the "lower" actions and beliefs of ordinary citizens and subjects in society. Two democratic challenges to this statist device for sorting German membership were treated in this essay. The broad meaning of the challenge to the Radicals Decree of the 1970s and its subsequent reform was a diminution of the power and status of the German state bureaucracy as a political agent and its replacement with an open-ended citizen-based political agency. Similarly, the broad meaning of the reform of naturalization law in 1991 and 1993 was a removal of traditional statist criteria for German political membership, specifically, heightened demands on political loyalty. In their place appeared the ordinary political, social, and economic—and legal—experiences of long-term residents in the Federal Republic expressing a will to become naturalized citizens.

If we are to understand the current politics of membership in the Federal Republic, we must thus incorporate not only the readily accessible and obviously problematic ethnocultural reliance on ius sanguinis for citizenship law, but also the more diffuse and ideological "logic" of German statism. A focus on ethnoculturalism alone limits our vision to the multiculturalist alternative in the Federal Republic, on the one hand, and the abstract republican transcendence of ethnoculturalism with a "postnational" citizenship, on the other. An incorporation of German statism as a traditional sorting device, however, allows the positioning of the politics of German political membership within the transformative debate over what it means to be a German political actor that has consumed the Federal Republic since the 1960s.

16. Multiculturalism, Nationalism, and the Political Consensus in the United States and in Germany

Hans-Jürgen Puhle

Let me try to address the problems in nine points, dealing first with the different concepts involved like multiculturalism, citizenship, nation, state, and nationalism, and looking further on into the different constellations of multiculturalism, nationalism, and the political consensus in the United States and in Germany comparatively.

Concepts

Multiculturalism

Understood as a program as opposed to multicultural realities of different dimensions, scope, and mix, multiculturalism is a (revolutionary or reformist) radical project that is not just about culture: at its base it is about inclusion and exclusion, it has an anti-exclusionary direction and hence is about power and domination. Its program is that the mechanisms of exclusion should be abolished, or at least reduced, and the number of those included increased. Programmatic radical multiculturalism is about material opportunities: it is a call for change, and, in the end, for a different society, asking for legislation and institutions in order to facilitate the inclusion of the oppressed, the have-nots, and the previously excluded, particularly structural and power minorities of all kinds (including, of course, women). A multicultural program hence affects the lines that have been drawn legally or traditionally by different older concepts like those of *citizenship* or (in the American case) *ethnicity*.[1]

Citizenship

Citizenship is a universal and tendentially egalitarian principle within a given society, but it also has its exclusionary mechanisms: noncitizens are categorically excluded from the benefits of citizenship. In most modern states, particularly democratic ones, citizenship has been the basis for individual rights and access to political participation. According to the different traditions and legal institutions of modern societies, a person can become a citizen of a given country in different ways: by birth, by a voluntary act of the individual and acceptance from the authorities (mostly in new or revolutionized states), or by complying with a number of additional prerequisites and requirements along the lines of *ius sanguinis* (citizenship based on blood) or *ius soli* (citizenship based on residency) (or both), as they have been established in the German *Staatsangehörigkeitsrecht* (requiring a certain descent from German ancestry), or in a number of residence or capital requirements we can find in the United States or in Switzerland.[2]

Citizenship by definition is limited. The history of the modern states and nations has, however, been a history of a continuous extension of citizenship in terms of political and social rights. In the United States, citizenship was extended first to the low-taxed or propertyless white males, later to blacks, Chinese, women, and Native Americans. In Western Europe, after equal suffrage and suffrage for women, in long trajectories through the short "social democratic" twentieth century, citizenship, in addition to its legal and political dimensions, has been awarded a more developed third dimension: social citizenship in terms of T.H. Marshall.[3] In

1. For more details see H.J. Puhle, "'Multikulturalismus' und der amerikanische consensus," in *Multikulturelle Gesellschaft: Modell Amerika?* ed. B. Ostendorf (Munich, 1994), 77–93; "Vom Bürgerrecht zum Gruppenrecht? Multikulturelle Politik in den USA," in *Die multikulturelle Herausforderung*, ed. K.J. Bade (Munich, 1996), 147–66; "Unabhängigkeit, Staatenbildung und gesellschaftliche Entwicklung in Nord- und Südamerika," in *Lateinamerika am Ende des 20. Jahrhunderts*, ed. D. Junker et al. (Munich, 1994), 27–48.

2. See e.g., R. Brubaker, *Citizenship and Nationhood in France and Germany* (Cambridge, 1992).

3. T.H. Marshall, *Class, Citizenship, and Social Development* (Chicago, 1964). On the mechanisms of inclusion and exclusion, see M. Minow, *Making All the Difference: Inclusion, Exclusion, and American Law* (Ithaca, 1990); J. Habermas, *Die Einbeziehung des Anderen* (Frankfurt/Main, 1996), particularly 128–84.

the United States the civil rights movement of the 1960s and 1970s operated along the lines of citizenship. The civil rights activists still believed that the extension and the enforcement of civil rights, i.e., citizenship rights would be a sufficient device to secure the citizens' share in material opportunities and in political participation.

Beyond Citizenship

However, when people think that they will not achieve certain material opportunities through the extension of citizenship alone, and that there are structural inequalities built in society, which cannot be removed by following the principles of equal citizenship, they try to find additional vehicles. They may find political vehicles in reforms, revolutions, or in projects aiming at an extension of the rights of individuals or groups, as well as institutional vehicles in the establishment of special rights, in empowerment for special groups, or in guidelines for multiculturalism. These additional devices can be operated either within the institutional set of liberal democracy, or they can go beyond the institutions of liberal democracy. An example of the former would be quotas for women or blacks, equal opportunity employment, affirmative action programs, mechanisms and institutions of consociationalism, or additional levels of participation, be it in circumscribed territorial units or in selected *curiae* of different cultural orientations along the lines of the personality principle of the Austro-Marxists. The latter type can be found in institutional inequalities like giving some people more votes than others, reserving half of public offices (or more) for special groups, granting a politically defined empowerment to one group at the cost of other groups, establishing a "secondary citizenship" (Schmitter)—if not granting it for all citizens—or additional institutions of corporate or *berufsständische* participation.[4]

Nation, Nation-State, Nationalism

Since the American and the French Revolutions, the nation-state has increasingly become the most common form of societal organization to which most nations without a state, ethnic groups, or tribes have aspired. The concept of the nation-state is the modern mechanism bringing together and relating the two different types

4. See the discussion in J. Jennings, *The Politics of Black Empowerment* (Detroit, 1992); A. Phillips, "Must Feminists Give Up on Liberal Democracy?" *Political Studies* 40 (1992): 68–82; P.C. Schmitter, "Corporative Democracy: Oxymoronic? Just Plain Moronic? Or a Promising Way Out of the Present Impasse?" (MS Stanford, 1988).

of democratic legitimation: the sovereign people united as a nation in a state made up by a community of citizens. The concept of the nation has been always defined with reference to a state—existent, lost, or desired—no matter whether or not the nationals had a state of their own, and always according to the particular characteristics of the relationship between the particular nation and the particular state. The concepts of a nation and of a national "identity" have varied through time and space, mostly between two opposite poles: the subjective, voluntary, and political principle of the revolutionary West, Renan's *plébiscite de tous les jours*, and the more "objective," cultural concept of the East, where most nations, when they came into existence, did not have a state of their own. This applies to processes of integration (like in Germany or Italy), as well as to processes of dissociation of a nation from a multinational empire (like the Austro-Hungarian monarchy or the Ottoman Empire), or from a unitary state that may have ignored the multinational character of its society for long (like Spain or Great Britain).

What a nation is depends on the constellations of the society behind it. In most cases it may be a construct, a fiction, or an invention, in any case an act of "deliberate crafting."[5] Because national identity is just one identity among many that an individual or a number of individuals has at the same time, it usually requires an adequate trigger in order to give priority to and stress national identity. The criteria defining the nation also seem to require a certain amount of plausibility: we have many examples pointing to the fact that, in most cases, people seem to want more tangible criteria for exclusion and inclusion than just citizenship or *Verfassungspatriotismus* (constitutional patriotism). So far the most popular criteria have been definitions of the nation along the lines of linguistic, cultural, and ethnic prerequisites (which Eric Hobsbawm and others have eventually called "proto-national") of religion, color, or race. Even in France, where the revolutionaries had established an open, subjective, and political concept of the nation, a certain amount of linguistic and cultural connotations has already proliferated since the Napoleonic Wars. And the more one moved east in Europe, the more the "objective" criteria took over for the simple lack of state-ness of the national groups involved. Beginning with Germany, Central Europe and Eastern Europe for a long time have

---

5. J.J. Linz, "State Building and Nation Building," *European Review* 1 (1993): 364; for the context, see also H.J. Puhle, *Staaten, Nationen und Regionen in Europa* (Vienna, 1995).

been mobilized by the motto "Ein Volk, soweit die Zunge reicht" (One people, as far as the language reaches).[6]

United States

The United States As a Nation

The United States, in a way, is one of the most abstract nations in the world, however easy it may be for an American to explain his or her national identification. They may, however, tend to add some further hyphenated qualification (like Afro-, Italian-, or Hispanic-). The American nation was new, established in a revolutionary act, and so its original definition had to be completely on the subjective and voluntary side, even more so than in France. All the rest, and particularly the "identification" had to be crafted in an open and tendentially egalitarian society (in spite of a high amount of social inequality) without many corporatist, *ständisch*, or authoritarian residua and prone—in a way doomed—to be democratic. As the protonational (or ethnic) ingredients of the American nation became increasingly diversified, and the United States turned into a land of immigrants and highly mobile westward migrants during most of the nineteenth and the first two decades of the twentieth century, national integration and identification could be achieved only through the three classical mechanisms of American nation building: (1) through acceptance of and identification with the hard core of American institutions as they have been provided by the Constitution, (2) through participation in the labor market and market-related individual achievements, and (3) through the mechanisms of consensus and ideology guiding social interaction and conformity (which began with the exclusive use of the English language in public). Even if some groups were categorically excluded for a long time, like blacks, Chinese, women, and Native Americans, many others, regardless of their backgrounds, were accepted and integrated.[7]

The American consensus basically was Louis Hartz's Lockeian consensus of the propertied male WASPs in a relatively open society. In

6. Cf. J. Breuilly, *Nationalism and the State*, 2nd ed. (Manchester, 1993); E.J. Hobsbawm, *Nation and Nationalism since 1870* (London, 1990); E. Gellner, *Nations and Nationalism* (Ithaca, 1983). Unless otherwise noted, all translations are my own.

7. For more details, see H.J. Puhle, "Soziale Ungleichheit und Klassenbildung in den USA," in *Klassen in der europäischen Sozialgeschichte*, ed. H.-U. Wehler (Göttingen, 1979), 233–77; and the "classics": S.M. Lipset, *The First New Nation* (Garden City, 1967); R.N. Bellah, "Civil Religion in America," *Daedalus* 96, no. 1 (1976): 1–21.

this society, the market mechanisms prevailed over regulation and the interests of the social groups prevailed over the State, and the political rights to participate—in the beginning—were conditioned by property rights.[8] The framework of the Constitution, the economic basis providing political and economic citizenship, and the Lockeian consensus were complemented by a whole set of standardized ideological mechanisms as embodied in the "American dream," the "American myth," the convenient legend of the "melting pot," the American creed, and the belief that the market mechanisms would see to it that the virtuous and laborious individual would achieve his or her economic and social fulfillment. The American consensus along those lines, which can only be characterized in a rather sketchy way here, has served as a vehicle of nation building in the United States, and it has, in that function, been more explicit and more important than any mechanisms of consensus have been in Europe. This is basically because there has been an institutional identification from the beginning on and, in addition, the development of a multiethnic society. With the political and economic success stories of the nineteenth and twentieth centuries and, more in particular, the advent of social Darwinism since the last third of the nineteenth century, American nationalism has become closely associated with American imperialism. This imperialism usually proclaims a hemispheric or worldwide "mission" of the United States and respective policies of interventionism that are justified by an assumed superiority of American institutional and political traditions, economic and cultural achievements, or just by the American way of life.

Citizenship, Ethnicity, Multiculturalism, and the U.S. Consensus

The American constellations have established the classical relationship between (1) the institutions and the legal system, (2) the consensus, the idea of a "nation," and the American ideology, and (3) the social reality as it is reflected in class formation and "ethnicity" mechanisms. Ethnicity has been a typical American device designed to cope with the cultural diversity of those who comprised the nation because they were citizens. It usually indicated historical and cultural differences between Americans who had more important things in common, among them citizenship and a consensus.[9]

8. L. Hartz, *The Liberal Tradition in America* (New York, 1955).
9. See S. Steinberg, *The Ethnic Myth: Race, "Ethnicity," and Class in America* (New York, 1981); W. Sollors, *Beyond Ethnicity: Consent and Descent in American Culture* (New York, 1986).

The ethnic factor had its place at a level below politics and the legal system. The price for the life and glory of the colorful and often powerful ethnic subcultures (of the Irish or the Italians) was the recognition of the binding constellations of the American system, its institutions and consensus, and of the use of the English language in public. The term ethnic has also been mostly limited primarily to European immigrants and did not refer to the categorically excluded. White immigrants from Europe usually did not think of the revolutionary term, which later came to be called multiculturalism, but rather of the affirmative and potentially integrating term of ethnicity, as they could be sure that they would have their chances for material opportunities when moving upwards through the ranks, first economically and later also politically and socially.[10] It should be noted, however, that the ethnic subcultures cannot be understood as being cultures in the demanding and emancipatory sense of multiculturalism. The acceptance of the functioning of the subculture milieu under the predominant and encompassing umbrella of citizenship has not led to the recognition of any collective rights of ethnic groups. Whatever their ethnicity, American citizens could only participate in the political process as individual citizens, at least until some of the stronger minorities started to organize political pressure and to voice more radical demands.

Compared to the concept of ethnicity, the aspirations of radical multiculturalism might appear as being highly "un-American" and subversive like Pandora's box. The multiculturalists are asking for a categorical inclusion of those who are outside, in material opportunities and in politics; they are asking for the "rightful" share for blacks, women, Hispanics, Native Americans, and others. Even if this seems to be a revolution from the traditional forms of the American consensus, it may only be one in appearance: the multicultural aspirations demand a further extension and enforcement of citizenship beyond the scope of the present legal form of citizenship and beyond the traditional consensus as it stands now. They invoke, at the same time, the fact that the American consensus has always been flexible and that its history over the decades and centuries has also been a history of continuous extensions. *First* we had the progressive reforms, preceded and eventually triggered by the populist campaigns; they established new mechanisms of state interventionism and enlarged political participation. *Second* came the New Deal reforms which deepened, intensified, and institutionalized

10. Cf. S. Lubell, *The Future of American Politics*, 2nd ed. (Garden City, 1956).

government interventionism, mostly along progressive lines, and set the stage for full-fledged organized capitalism or neocorporatist intermediation including organized labor. In a *third* wave, the civil rights legislation of the 1960s and what remained of the Great Society programs further developed institutional guarantees for an enlarged political participation and acknowledged and implemented, to an extent, what Marshall has called the social dimensions of citizenship: citizens' claims to social and welfare payments and an obligation of the government to promote and protect the equality of material opportunities.[11]

In spite of a number of backlashes in every one of these reform packages, all of them have had a decisive and continuous impact on American society. In all three cases it was impossible to go back to the constellations as they had been before. The multicultural aspirations of the present seem to be part of a *fourth* wave of reforms, which is aiming at putting the recognized rights into practice—passing from negatively defined rights to positively defined rights—and asking the government to deliver the theoretically guaranteed economic and social opportunities systematically and comprehensively to everybody including those who so far have been structurally underprivileged. In contrast to the three earlier periods of reform, which have moved within the limits of what was considered to be the traditional American consensus, this time the demands go beyond. More precisely, they no longer respect the limitations and the biases of the American consensus in its male white Anglo-Saxon variant, which has finally been denounced as the ideology of those in power.

During the last three decades there has been a continuous process of erosion of the male white Anglo-Saxon cultural hegemony. It has been questioned, but it has not yet been destroyed or substituted with a new and different hegemony, like, e.g., one of multiculturalism. It has been weakened and it has been modified, due to a broad variety of means, from quotas, affirmative action, equal opportunity employment (EOE) programs, and government incentives, to the creation of new minority-conscious curricula and the campaigns for a "politically correct" speech, however exaggerated and problematic some of the latter may have been. Some of the exclusionary mechanisms have been softened, and by means of reformist politics (however limited) much has been achieved, particularly in the fields of education and public programs. Here, on many occasions, one has come back to the essentials of traditional interest intermediation.

11. For the context, see M. Weir et al., *The Politics of Social Policy in the United States* (Princeton, 1988).

Often, however, it has proven to be easier to begin with "culture" and not with hardcore material opportunities or tax legislation, and, in addition, the cultural aspect was emphasized by the mechanisms of "conscientization" and the eye-opener function of the debate.[12]

What happened has not broken but widened the American consensus beyond its particular, and, as it seems, historically outdated contents. Multiculturalism so far does not appear to go beyond the system and seems to be adaptable to its mechanisms—as "total emancipation" of the slaves was already for Thomas Jefferson when he wrote in 1785 that he "trembled for his country" when he reflected that God might be just.[13] The critics of multiculturalism have argued that the American system might be overstretched by its demands and could subsequently break. I do not think that this is likely to happen; there seems to be even a bit of evidence to the contrary: (1) So far the multiculturalists have usually worked in a two-tier system. The radicals and fundamentalists have addressed the eye-opening functions and launched the public debates, whereas the *politicos* later on started to work within the established institutions and have been much more moderate. (2) The capabilities of reformist politics still seem to be rather vigorous in the United States, particularly when it comes to the mechanisms of grassroots mobilization and of designing educational reform programs. (3) The constitutional framework and the institutional basis are uncontested, and (4) there is still a high capacity of the market for absorption and adaptation and valid rewards for economic success.

In the United States, multicultural politics, in a way, seem to be the logical next step after the end of the "social democratic" century, after the politics along the lines of an extension of citizenship have come to an end, yet people still want more of their shares. The multicultural aspirations may change some aspects and some constellations of the traditional American consensus as it has been known for so long. And there is a high probability that they will put less emphasis on its ideological side and more on its institutional and procedural side. On the whole, there is a good chance that multicultural programs in the end may become part of a new American consensus. In Germany this might be more difficult.

12. See the discussion in D. Johnson, *Multiculturalism: In the Curriculum, in the Disciplines, and in Society* (New York, 1992); P. Berman ed., *Debating PC* (New York, 1992); P. Aufderheide ed., *Beyond PC* (St. Paul, 1990); and D. Ravitch, "Multiculturalism: E Pluribus Plures," *The American Scholar* 59 (1990): 337–54; A.M. Schlesinger, Jr., *The Disuniting of America* (Knoxville, 1991); B. Ostendorf, "The Costs of Multiculturalism," J.F. Kennedy Institute Working Paper 50, Berlin 1992.

13. T. Jefferson, *Notes on the State of Virginia*, Query 18 (New York 1964), 156.

Germany

Traditional Constellations

In Germany almost everything has been different. It starts with the overall patterns of modernization. If, with a certain amount of simplification, we allow ourselves to reduce the factors intervening in the processes of Western modernization to three basic clusters: democratization, industrialization, and bureaucratization, then it can be said that the pattern of the American modernization has been characterized by a dominant combination of democratization, from the beginning on, with industrialization, since the 1860s, whereas bureaucratization entered late and was less important for a long time. The Prussian and German pattern, in contrast, was dominated by a mix of traditional comprehensive bureaucratization and (later) industrialization, whereas democratization came late and did not succeed before 1945. In Germany we had an authoritarian state; parliamentary democracy was long contained and even fought for. The traditions of absolutism, militarism, mercantilism, and bureaucratic regulation conditioned the long survival of premodern elites and premodern elements present after industrialization and subsequent social modernization had set in. State building was essentially achieved from above in the German territories and later on in the Reich given the hegemony of Prussia over the rest of Germany.[14]

In contrast to what happened in France, Great Britain, or the United States, the process of nation building in Germany, though it was belated as was the nation-state, was carried out from above and within the framework of an authoritarian state.[15] This accounts at least partly for the particular aggressiveness of German nationalism during the last decades of the nineteenth and the first half of the twentieth century. National identification and "belonging" were not defined in terms of citizenship or institutional allegiance, but in terms of cultural and ethnic heritage, and after the breakthrough of social Darwinism, even in terms of race. German nationalism at the end of the nineteenth century became highly imperialist, pan-Germanic, racist, and anti-Semitic.[16] And the

14. For the "long lines" of development, see H.-U. Wehler, *Deutsche Gesellschaftsgeschichte*, vols. 1–3 (Munich, 1987 and 1995).

15. Cf. M. Weber, "Parliament und Regierung im neugeordneten Deutschland," *Gesammelte Politische Schriften*, 3rd ed. (Tübingen, 1971), 306–443.

16. Cf. H.J. Puhle, *Agrarische Interessenpolitik und preussischer Konservatismus im Wilhelminischen Reich*, 2nd ed. (Bonn-Bad Godesberg, 1975); "Conservatism in Modern German History," *Journal of Contemporary History* 13 (1978): 689–720.

Reichsstaatsangehörigkeitsgesetz (citizenship law) of 1913 defined the lines of inclusion and exclusion along the lines of ius sanguinis and cultural ancestry. Being a German national became more important than being a German citizen.[17] The fact that Adolf Hitler was not a citizen of the Reich before 1932 was not detrimental to his popularity and political success.

Germany, by tradition, has not been seen as a country of immigrants, at least not in the American sense of immigration as a mass phenomenon. As we know, Germany since the breakthrough of industrialization has always been a country of immigrants (and, to a certain extent, also of emigrants).[18] The issue has, however, never been dealt with categorically and theoretically, and according to what we hear from the German government and the parliamentary majority, even today the Federal Republic is not considered to be a country of immigrants. On the other hand, even in the Reich there was only a limited concurrence between the nation and the state: there were many Germans in cultural terms left outside the Reich, particularly Austrians and Swiss, and a sizable number of non-Germans in cultural terms lived within the Reich, particularly in the state of Prussia which regarded its Polish and Danish subjects as Prussian nationals (or even citizens). The idea of the Prussian state was not an ethnic idea, and the mechanisms of integration, to a certain extent, functioned along similar lines as in, though not at the scale of, the United States.[19]

The myths, symbols, and ideologies of nation building and nationalism in Germany did not focus around the institutions, a way of life, the market, or individual economic achievement, as they did in America. In contrast, they focused on the national myth of the nineteenth century: they were anti-French, and that means anti-Western and anti-democratic; they were social Darwinist and fundamentalist, displaying an allegiance to an authoritarian system which was ideologically justified by the constellations of Germany's

17. See the contributions by J.J. Sheehan, D. Langewiesche, W.J. Mommsen, and H.A. Turner, Jr., in *Nation und Gesellschaft in Deutschland*, eds. M. Hettling and P. Nolte (Munich, 1996).

18. Cf. the work of K.J. Bade, particularly: *Vom Auswandererland zum Einwandererland? Deutschland 1880–1980* (Berlin, 1983); Bade, ed., *Auswanderer—Wanderarbeiter—Gastarbeiter* (Ostfildern, 1984); "German Emigration to the United States and Continental Immigration to Germany, 1879–1929, *Central European History* 13, no. 4 (1980): 348–77; Bade, ed., *Population, Labour, and Migration in 19th and 20th-Century Germany* (Leamington Spa, 1987).

19. See the contributions in H.J. Puhle and H.-U. Wehler eds., *Preussen im Rückblick* (Göttingen, 1980).

geopolitical situation—its "divergence from the West" (L. Krieger) and its ominous *Sonderweg*.[20] The German Kaiserreich, though it was full of multicultural realities and a variety of vigorous ethnic subcultures, particularly in Berlin, Frankfurt/Main, and other cosmopolitan centers, was not considered to be a multicultural empire like the Austrian-Hungarian monarchy or the Ottoman Empire. Instead, it cherished the idea of the cultural homogeneity of "Germanness," driving toward the nation-state and nationalism and, finally, toward the terror of the Nazis.

Germany after 1945

The end of the Second World War has put an end to the German Sonderweg, at least in West Germany. The Federal Republic has become a Western country and a parliamentary democracy, which, from the 1950s on, has continually become more open and more tolerant, particularly in its urban centers. The scope of labor migration from Southern Europe, Turkey, and Eastern Europe and the rise of relatively strong subcultures have essentially contributed to this process, even if occasional conflicts arose.[21] On the other hand, we still can find many of the old forms of national identification and self-assertion, not only after German unification, and of the old legal system which still defines German citizenship more or less along the lines of the Reichsstaatsangehörigkeitsgesetz of 1913.

Conclusion

The prospects of multicultural politics and programs seem to be much more difficult in Germany than in the United States, because German society still seems to be much less open than American society. Some German traditions, however, might even help to promote its chances: federalism, the cultural diversity within Germany and the differences between the North and the South and the East and the West, the traditions of religious tolerance, the shock of the Nazi regime, the Second World War and the Holocaust (or what has remained as their memories), and the relatively long process of

20. Cf. L. Krieger, *The German Idea of Freedom* (New York, 1957); J. Kocka, "German History before Hitler: The Debate about the German Sonderweg," *Journal of Contemporary History* 23 (1988): 3–16; C.S. Maier, *The Unmasterable Past* (Cambridge, 1988); Wehler, *Deutsche Gesellschaftsgeschichte*, vol. 3, 449–91.

21. See the discussion in D. Cohn-Bendit and T. Schmid, *Heimat Babylon* (Hamburg, 1992).

"Westernization" in West Germany. Other factors include the more recent trajectories of what can be called "Europeanization" and "globalization," i.e., all of the twentieth-century tendencies toward a convergence of the developmental patterns of the Western societies: "Americanization" in Europe; "Europeanization" in America; the "McWorld" everywhere; transnational economy, tourism, intermarriage, etc.[22]

Some caveats, however, might be appropriate: the process of Europeanization in the sense of European integration so far has been rather contained. In Western Europe the nation-states are still strong actors and certainly will determine the immediate future, and the concept of the nation and of national peculiarity is still very much there, even if West European societies may become more multicultural over the years. There is also no European citizenship (only an indirect, mediated one), and the traditional nation-states still seem to be the only agencies capable of protecting and securing civil and political rights, democracy, and the welfare state. Also globalization has its confining conditions and counter currents: there is widespread localism, regionalism, parochialism, and fundamentalism (Benjamin Barber's *Jihad*), and the overall culturalization of social conflicts as embodied in Sam Huntington's "clash of civilizations," though it may, to a certain extent, be a fashion of the fin de siècle where everything is considered to be somewhat "post," may also imply a certain fundamentalist undercurrent that might not be too helpful in making multicultural politics more popular in Germany.[23]

In addition, there are the obvious symptoms of the crisis of the economic and social system, and there is the problem of consensus. What is exactly the German consensus? Traditionally there has not been too much of it, if we do not count the more problematic approaches. In the nineteenth century there was more polarization than consensus—a heritage of authoritarianism as well as of Bismarckian politics. Then we had *völkisch* nationalism and social imperialism ("ich kenne keine Parteien mehr" [I don't know political parties any longer]), then anti-Versailles feelings, and finally the Nazi ideology, all of them fundamentally exclusionary on grounds

22. Cf. J.J. Sheehan, "Vorbildliche Ausnahme: Liberalismus in Amerika und Europa," in *Von der Arbeiterbewegung zum modernen Sozialstaat*, ed. J. Kocka et al. (Munich, 1994), 236–48; B. Barber, "Jihad or McWorld: Does Democracy Have a Global Future?" *The Atlantic* (1991).

23. Cf. S.P. Huntington, "The Clash of Civilizations," *Foreign Affairs* 72, no. 3 (1993): 22–49.

of culture, race, or even *Gesinnung* (convictions). After the war we had socialism and the G.D.R., which was not really convincing, and in West Germany we first had the *Wirtschaftswunder*, consumerism, and the *Deutschmark*, and later *Verfassungspatriotismus*, which so far does not appear to have developed into a full-fledged political consensus, with all the plausible ideology around it.[24]

Instead, we finally got the *Historikerstreit* and its G.D.R. equivalent (the *differenziertes historisches Erbeverständnis* [a differentiated understanding of the historical heritage]), which even before unification was often forgotten, both again directed toward nationalistic integration and exclusionary of others.[25] The problem is still there, and its solution has, of course, not become easier after unification: it consists in trying to integrate important elements of multiculturalism into a kind of incipient, weak, and diffuse political consensus of the republic, which whenever it has looked for reassurance and backing in the society, so far has come up with the parts of an old and counterproductive tradition along the lines of national self-assertion in cultural terms. This is not helpful, and it may take a longer time for the Germans to learn and to build institutions anew (e.g., in reforming the Reichsstaatsangehörigkeitsgesetz and framing an *Einwanderergesetz* [immigration law]). In the end they will have no choice, because the immigrants are there, many of them already in the third generation, the economic system needs them, they do not seem to be willing to leave, and they certainly will be asking for their share more and more convincingly.[26]

24. See K. von Beyme, "Deutsche Identität zwischen Nationalismus und Verfassungspatriotismus," in *Nation und Gesellschaft in Deutschland*, eds. M. Hettling and P. Nolte (Munich, 1996), 80–99; J. Habermas, *Faktizität und Geltung* (Frankfurt/Main 1992), 632–60.

25. Cf. R. Augstein et al., *Historikerstreit* (Munich, 1987); Maier, *Unmasterable Past.*

26. See *Das Manifest der 60. Deutschland und die Einwanderung*, ed. K.J. Bade (Munich, 1994); K.J. Bade, *Ausländer, Aussiedler, Asyl in der Bundesrepublik Deutschland* (Bonn, 1994).

List of Contributors

Timothy Brennan, Associate Professor of English and Comparative Literature at the University of Minnesota, Minneapolis

Dieter Dettke, Director of the Friedrich Ebert Stiftung, Washington, D.C.

Catrin Gersdorf, Assistant Professor of American Literature at the University of Leipzig

Friederike Hajek, Independent Scholar, Berlin

Renate Hof, Professor of American Literary, Cultural and Gender Studies at Humboldt University, Berlin

Alfred Hornung, Professor of American Literary and Cultural Studies at Johannes Gutenberg University, Mainz

Anne Koenen, Professor of American Literature at the University of Leipzig

Gregg O. Kvistad, Associate Professor of Political Science at the University of Denver

Sara Lennox, Professor of German at the University of Massachussetts, Amherst

Günter H. Lenz, Professor of American Literary and Cultural Studies at Humboldt University, Berlin

Klaus J. Milich, Assistant Professor of American Literary and Cultural Studies at Humboldt University, Berlin

Jeffrey M. Peck, Professor of German at Georgetown University, Washington, D.C.

Hans-Jürgen Puhle, Professor of Political Science at Johann Wolfgang Goethe University, Frankfurt/Main

Berndt Ostendorf, Professor of American Cultural Studies at Ludwig Maximilian University, Munich

Hinrich C. Seeba, Professor of German at the University of California, Berkeley

Azade Seyhan, Professor of German and Comparative Literature at Bryn Mawr College

Brook Thomas, Professor of English at the University of California, Irvine

Frank Trommler, Professor of German at the University of Pennsylvania

Gisela Welz, Professor of Cultural Anthropology at Johann Wolfgang Goethe University, Frankfurt/Main

References

Adams, Willi Paul. "Die Assimilationsfrage in der amerikanischen Einwanderungs-
diskussion 1890–1930." *Amerikastudien / American Studies* 27, no. 3 (1982).
Addams, Jane. "Immigration: A Field Neglected by the Scholar," *The Commons* 10
(Jan. 1905)
————. *Twenty Years at Hull-House.* 1910. Reprint, New York, 1961.
Adelson, Leslie. *Making Bodies, Making History: Feminism and German Identity.*
Lincoln, 1993.
————. "Racism and Feminist Aesthetics: The Provocation of Anne Duden's *Open-
ing of the Mouth.*" *Signs* 13, no. 2 (Winter 1988).
Alarcéon, Norma."Anzaldúa's *Frontera*: Inscribing Gynetics." In *Displacement, Dias-
pora, and Geographies of Identity,* ed. Shmadar Lavie and Ted Swedenburg.
Durham, 1996.
Anderson, Benedict. *Imagined Communities: Reflections on the Origin and Spread of
Nationalism.* London and New York, 1983.
Angelou, Maya. *I Know Why the Caged Bird Sings.* New York, 1969.
Anheier, Helmut K., Lester M. Salamon, and Edith Archambault. "Participating
Citizens: U.S.-European Comparisons in Volunteer Action." *Public Perspective*
5 (March– April 1994).
Antin, Mary. *The Promised Land: The Autobiography of a Russian Immigrant.* 1912.
Anzaldúa, Gloria. *Borderlands/La Frontera: The New Mestiza.* San Francisco, 1987.
Appadurai, Arjun. *Modernism at Large: Cultural Dimensions of Globalization.*
Minneapolis, 1996.
————. "Disjuncture and Difference in the Global Cultural Economy." *Public Cul-
ture* 2 (Spring 1990).
————. "Global Ethnoscapes: Notes and Queries for a Transnational Anthropol-
ogy." In *Recapturing Anthropology: Working in the Present,* ed. Richard G. Fox.
Santa Fe, 1991.
Arndt, Ernst Moritz. "Des Deutschen Vaterland." 1813. In *Gedichte,* 2nd ed.
Berlin, 1865.
Arteaga, Alfred. "An Other Tongue." In *An Other Tongue: Nation and Ethnicity in the
Linguistic Borderlands.* Durham, 1994.
Aufderheide, P., ed. *Beyond PC.* St. Paul, 1990.
Augstein, R., et al. *Historikerstreit.* Munich, 1987.
Bach, Robert. "Recrafting the Common Good: Immigration and Community." *The
Annals of the American Academy of Political and Social Sciences,* no. 530
(November 1993).
Bade, K.J. *Vom Auswandererland zum Einwandererland? Deutschland 1880–1980.*
Berlin, 1983.

————. "German Emigration to the United States and Continental Immigration to Germany, 1879–1929." *Central European History* 13, no. 4 (1980).

————. *Ausländer, Aussiedler, Asyl in der Bundesrepublik Deutschland.* Bonn, 1994.

————, ed. *Auswanderer—Wanderarbeiter—Gastarbeiter.* Ostfildern, 1984.

————, ed. *Population, Labour, and Migration in 19th and 20th-Century Germany.* Leamington Spa, 1987.

————, ed. *Das Manifest der 60. Deutschland und die Einwanderung.* Munich, 1994.

Baker, Kendall, Russell Dalton, and Kai Hildebrandt. *Germany Transformed: Political Culture and the New Politics.* Cambridge, 1981.

Baldwin, James. *Notes of a Native Son.* London, 1965.

————. *The Fire Next Time.* Harmondsworth, 1965.

Baldwin, Simeon E. "The Citizen of the United States." *Yale Law Journal* 2 (1893).

————. "Comment." *Central Law Review* 42 (1896).

————. "Comment." *Yale Law Journal* 7 (1898).

————. "Citizenship of Children of Alien Parents." *Harvard Law Review* 12 (1898).

————. "The People of the United States." *Yale Law Journal* 8 (1899).

Barber, Benjamin, "Jihad versus McWorld," *Atlantic* March, 1992.

————"Global Multiculturalism and the American Experiment." *World Policy Journal* 10, no.1 (Spring 1993).

Bark, Dennis L. and David R. Gress. *A History of West Germany: From Shadow to Substance: 1945–1963.* Vol. 1. Cambridge, 1989.

Baring, Arnulf and Manfred Görtemaker. *Machtwechsel: die Ära Brandt-Scheel.* Stuttgart, 1982.

Barthes, Roland. *New Critical Essays.* trans. Richard Howard. New York, 1980.

Bauer, Otto. *Die Nationalitätenfrage und die Sozialdemokratie.* Vienna, 1907.

Bausinger, Hermann. *Ausländer—Inländer: Arbeitsmigration und kulturelle Identität.* Tübingen, 1986.

Becker, Eva. "'Klassiker' in der deutschen Literaturgeschichtsschreibung zwischen 1780 und 1860." In *Zur Literatur der Restaurationsepoche 1815–1848. Forschungsreferate und Aufsätze,* ed. Jost Hermand and Manfred Windfuhr. Stuttgart, 1970.

Becker-Cantarino, Barbara. "Feministische Germanistik in Deutschland. Rückblick und sechs Thesen." In *Women in German Yearbook 8,* ed. Jeanette Clausen and Sara Friedrichsmeyer. Lincoln, 1992.

Bellah, R.N. "Civil Religion in America." *Daedalus* 96, no. 1 (1976).

Berdahl, Robert. *The Politics of the Prussian Nobility.* Princeton, 1988.

"Bericht der Beauftragten der Bundesregierung für die Belange der Ausländer über die Lage der Ausländer in der Bundesrepublik Deutschland, 1993." *Mitteilungen der Beauftragten der Bundesregierung für die Belange der Ausländer* (1994).

Berman, P., ed. *Debating PC.* New York, 1992.

Beyme, K.von. "Deutsche Identität zwischen Nationalismus und Verfassungspatriotismus." In *Nation und Gesellschaft in Deutschland,* ed. M. Hettling and P. Nolte. Munich, 1996.

Bhabha, Homi K. *The Location of Culture.* New York and London, 1994.

————. "Signs Taken for Wonders: Questions of Ambivalence and Authority under a Tree Outside Delhi, May 1817." *Critical Inquiry* 12 (Autumn 1985).

————. "The Commitment to Theory," *New Formations* 5 (Summer 1988).

————. "DissemiNation: Time, Narrative, and the Margins of the Modern Nation." In *Nation and Narration,* ed. Homi Bhabha. New York and London, 1990.

————. "Postcolonial Criticism." In *Redrawing the Boundaries: The Transformation of English and American Literary Studies,* ed. Stephen Greenblatt and Giles Gunn. New York, 1992.

References • 273

Bakhtin, M.M. *The Dialogic Imagination.* Trans. Caryl Emerson and Michael Holquist. Ed. Michael Holquist. Austin, 1981.

Bischoff, Volker and Marino Mania. "Melting Pot-Mythen als Szenarien amerikanischer Identität zur Zeit der New Immigration." In *Nationale und kulturelle Identität: Studien zur Entwicklung des kollektiven Bewußtseins in der Neuzeit.* Frankfurt/Main, 1991.

Blake, Casey Nelson. *Beloved Community: The Cultural Criticism of Randolph Bourne, Van Wyck Brooks, Waldo Frank and Lewis Mumford.* Chapel Hill, 1990.

Boetcher Joeres, Ruth-Ellen. "'Language Is Also a Place of Struggle': The Language of Feminism and the Language of American *Germanistik.*" In *Women in German Yearbook 8,* ed. Jeanette Clausen and Sara Friedrichsmeyer. Lincoln, 1992.

Borneman, John. "Time-Space Compression and the Continental Divide in German Subjectivity." *New Formations* 21 (Winter 1993).

Bourdieu, Pierre. "Narzißtische Reflexivität und wissenschaftliche Reflexivität." In *Kultur, soziale Praxis, Text. Die Krise der ethnographischen Repräsentation,* ed. Eberhard Berg and Martin Fuchs. Frankfurt/Main, 1993.

Bourne, Randolph S. *War and the Intellectuals: Essays 1915–1919.* Ed. Carl Resek. New York, 1964.

Boyarin, Daniel and Jonathan Boyarin. "Diasporas: Generation and the Ground of Jewish Identity." *Critical Inquiry* 19 (Summer 1993).

Braidotti, Rosi. "Feminism By Any Other Name." *differences* 6, no. 2/3 (1994).

Brandt, Willy and Helmut Schmidt. *Deutschland 1976: Zwei Sozialdemokraten im Gespräch.* Hamburg, 1976.

Braxton, Joanne M. and Andrée Nicola McLaughlin, eds. *Wild Women in the Whirlwind.* New Brunswick, 1990.

Braunthal, Gerard. *Political Loyalty and Public Service in West Germany.* Amherst, 1990.

Bredella, Lothar. "Multiculturalism between Assimilation and Segregation: The Debate on Multicultural Curricula in the United States and Germany." In *American Studies in Germany: European Contexts and Intercultural Relations,* ed. Günter H. Lenz and Klaus J. Milich. Frankfurt/Main, 1995.

Breuilly, J. *Nationalism and the State.* 2nd ed. Manchester, 1993.

Brinker-Gabler, Gisela. "Alterity-Marginality-Difference: On Inventing Places for Women." In *Women in German Yearbook 8,* eds. Jeanette Clausen and Sara Friedrichsmeyer. Lincoln, 1992.

Brinker-Gabler, Gisela, and Sidonie Smith, "Introduction." In *Writing New Identities: Gender, Nation, and Immigration in Contemporary Europe,* eds. idem. Minneapolis, 1997.

Brubaker, Rogers. *Citizenship and Nationhood in France and Germany.* Cambridge, 1992.

Brüning, Eberhard. "Probleme der Rezeption amerikanischer Literatur in der DDR." *Weimarer Beiträge* 16, no. 4 (1970).

———. *Studien zum amerikanischen Drama nach dem zweiten Weltkrieg.* Ed. E. Bruning, K. Köhler, and B. Scheller. Berlin, 1977.

———. "Einleitung." In *Amerikansche Dramen aus fünf Jahrzehnten,* ed. idem. Berlin, 1968.

———. "U.S.-amerikanische Literatur in der DDR seit 1965." *Zeitschrift für Anglistik und Amerikanistik* 4 (1980).

Buddin, Gerd, Hans Dahlke, and Adolf Kossakowski, eds. *Unfrieden in Deutschland.* Berlin, 1994.

Bulletin. "Demokratie und Sicherheit: Interview des Bundeskanzlers," 55 (15 April 1972).

Bundesministerium für innerdeutsche Beziehungen. *Texte zur Deutschlandpolitik.* Reihe III/Band 8a-1990. Bonn, 1991.

Butler, Judith. *Gender Trouble: Feminism and the Subversion of Identity.* New York, 1990.

———. "Contingent Foundations." In *Feminist Contentions: A Philosophical Exchange,* ed. Seyla Benhabib, Judith Butler, Drucilla Cornell, and Nancy Fraser. New York, 1995.

Calderón, Héctor, and José David Saldívar, eds. *Criticism in the Borderlands: Studies in Chicano Literature, Culture, and Ideology.* Durham, 1991.

Canclini, García. *Culturas híbridas: Estrategias para entrar y salir de la modernidad.* México, 1990.

Carby, Hazel V. "The Multicultural Wars." In *Black Popular Culture,* ed. Gina Dent. Seattle, 1992.

Case, Pierre. *Training for the Multicultural Management of People.* Washington, D.C., 1982.

Cassidy, John, "Who Killed the Middle Class? The Economy is Fine, but Most Americans Are Not ..." *New Yorker,* 16 October 1995.

Castillo, Ana. *Massacre of the Dreamers: Essays on Xicanisma.* Albuquerque, 1994.

Chambers, Iain. *Migrancy, Culture, Identity.* London, 1994.

Chow, Rey. *Writing Diaspora: Tactics of Intervention in Contemporary Cultural Studies.* Bloomington, 1993.

Cinquin, Chantal. "President Mitterand Also Watches *Dallas*: American Mass Media and French National Policy." In *The Americanization of the Global Village: Essays in Comparative Popular Culture,* ed. Roger Rollin. Bowling Green, 1989.

Clark, Charles S., "Religion in America." *CQ Researcher,* 25 November 1994.

Clausen, Jeanette and Sara Friedrichsmeyer. "WIG 2000: Feminism and the Future of *Germanistik.*" In *Women in German Yearbook 10,* ed. Jeanette Clausen and Sara Friedrichsmeyer. Lincoln, 1994.

Clifford, James. *The Predicament of Culture: Twentieth-Century Ethnography, Literature, and Art.* Cambridge and London, 1988.

———. "Diasporas," *Cultural Anthropology* 9 (1994).

Cohn-Bendit, Daniel and Thomas Schmid. *Heimat Babylon. Das Wagnis der multi-kulturellen Demokratie.* Hamburg, 1992.

Collins, Charles Wallace. *The Fourteenth Amendment and the States.* Boston, 1912.

Collins, George D. "Are Persons Born within the United States Ipso Facto Citizens Thereof?" *American Law Review* 18 (1884).

———. "Citizenship by Birth." *American Law Review* 29 (1895).

Conradt, David. "Changing German Political Culture." In *The Civic Culture Revisited,* ed. Gabriel Almond and Sidney Verba. Boston, 1980.

Conze, Werner. *The Shaping of the German Nation.* New York, 1979.

Conzen, Kathleen, et al. "The Invention of Ethnicity: A Perspective from the U.S.A."
Journal of American Ethnic History 12, no. 1 (1992).

Cruz, Jon. "From Farce to Tragedy: Reflections on the Reification of Race at the Century's End." In *Mapping Multiculturalism,* ed. Gordon, Avery F. and Christopher Newfield. Minneapolis Press, 1996.

Dahn, Daniela. *Westwärts und nicht vergessen.* Berlin, 1996.

Dahrendorf, Ralph. *Die angewandte Aufklärung. Gesellschaft und Soziologie in Amerika.* Munich, 1963.

Daniels, Roger. *Coming to America: A History of Immigration and Ethnicity in American Life.* New York, 1991.

Davis, Mike. *City of Quartz: Excavating the Future in Los Angeles.* New York and London, 1990.

Davis, Philip, ed. *Immigration and Americanization: Selected Readings.* Boston, 1920.
de Lauretis, Teresa. *Technologies of Gender: Essays on Theory, Film, and Fiction.* Bloomington, 1987.
———. "Eccentric Subjects: Feminist Theory and Historical Consciousness." *Feminist Studies* 1 (1990).
Denninger, Ehard, ed. *Freiheitliche demokratische Grundordnung.* Bd. II. Frankfurt/Main, 1977.
Derrida, Jacques. "Choréographies." Interview with Christie V. MacDonald. *Diacritics* 12 (1982).
Dettke, Dieter. "Amerika nach den Zwischenwahlen: Revolution von Rechts?" Occasional Papers, *Friedrich Ebert Stiftung.* 1995.
Diner, Dan. "Nationalstaat und Migration: Zu Begriff und Geschichte." In *Politik der Multikultur: Vergleichende Perspektiven zu Einwanderung und Integration,* ed. Mechthild M. Jansen and Sigrid Baringhorst. Baden-Baden, 1994.
Dirke, Sabine von. "Multikulti: The German Debate on Multiculturalism." *German Studies Review* 17, no. 3 (October 1994).
Dissanayake, Wimal and Rob Wilson, eds. *Global/Local: Cultural Production and the Trans national Imaginary.* Durham, 1996.
Dred Scott v Sandford, 19 How. 393 (1857).
Drucker, Peter. *Post-Capitalist Society.* New York, 1993.
———. "The Age of Social Transformation." *The Atlantic Monthly,* November 1994.
Duggan, Lynn and Nancy Folbre. "Women and Children Last: East Germany Did It Better." *New York Times,* 8 January 1994.
Dyson, Kenneth H. F. *The State Tradition in Western Europe.* New York, 1980.
———. "The Ambiguous Politics of Western Germany: Politicization in a 'State' Society." *European Journal of Political Research* 7 (1979).
Early, Gerald, ed. *Lure and Loathing: Essays on Race, Identity, and the Ambivalence of Assimilation.* New York, 1993.
Economist, The. "Slicing the Cake: The Rights and Wrongs of Inequality." 1 October 1994.
Economist, The. "Rich North, Hungry South." 5 November 1994.
Economist, The. "American Values." 5 September 1992.
Eisenstein, Ira. "Dialogue with Dr. Horace M. Kallen." In *What I Believe and Why – Maybe: Essays for the Modern World,* ed. Alfred J. Marrow. New York, 1971.
Ellmore, R. Terry. *Broadcasting Law and Regulations.* Blue Ridge Summit, 1982.
Erickson, Peter. "Seeing White." *Transition* 67, no. 5.3 (Fall 1995).
Fabian, Johannes. *Time and the Other: How Anthropology Makes Its Object.* New York, 1983.
Faist, Thomas. "How to Define a Foreigner? The Symbolic Politics of Immigration in German Partisan Discourse, 1978–1992." *West European Politics* 17 (1994).
Fijalkowski, Jürgen. *Aggressive Nationalism, Immigration Pressure, and Asylum Policy Disputes in Contemporary Germany.* Washington, D.C., 1993.
Fish, Stanley. *There's No Such Thing as Free Speech, and It's a Good Thing, Too.* New York and Oxford, 1994.
Fisher, Philip. "American Literary and Cultural Studies since the Civil War." In *Redrawing the Boundaries: The Transformation of English and American Literary Studies,* ed. Stephen Greenblatt and Giles Gunn. New York, 1992.
Fohrmann, Jürgen. *Das Projekt der deutschen Literaturgeschichte. Entstehung und Scheitern einer nationalen Poesiegeschichtsschreibung zwischen Humanismus und Deutschem Kaiserreich.* Stuttgart, 1988.
Foucault, Michel. *Die Ordnung des Diskurses. Inauguralvorlesung am Collège de France – 2. Dezember 1970.* Munich, 1974.
———. *History of Sexuality.* Trans. Robert Hurley, vol. 1. New York, 1978.

Frankenberg, Ruth and Lata Mani. "Crosscurrents, Crosstalk: Race, 'Postcolonial-ity,' and the Politics of Location." In *Displacement, Diaspora, and Geographies of Identity*. Durham, 1996

Fraser, Nancy and Linda Nicholson. "Social Criticism without Philosophy." In *Feminism/ Postmodernism*, ed. Linda Nicholson. New York, 1990.

Furger, Fridolin. "Auf der Suche nach der schwarzen Identität." *Der kleine Bund*. 11 December 1993, Kulturbeilage, 1.

Ganguly, Keya. "Migrant Identities: Personal Memory and the Construction of Self-hood." *Cultural Studies* 6, no. 1 (Jan 1992).

Garvey, John, "My Problem with Multi-Cultural Education." *Race Traitor* 1, no. 2 (Winter 1993).

Gates, Henry Louis, Jr. "Beyond the Culture Wars: Identities in Dialogue." *Profession 93* (1994).

Geertz, Clifford. "Thick Description: Toward an Interpretive Theory of Culture." In *Interpretation of Cultures: Selected Essays*. New York, 1973.

Gellner, Ernest. *Nations and Nationalism*. Ithaca,1983.

Gerard, Jean Broward Shevlin. "Pourquoi les Etats-Unis ont du quitter l 'U.N.E.S.C.O." *Revue des Deux Mondes* 25 (June 1984).

Gerbner, George and Marsha Siefert, eds. *World Communications: A Handbook*. New York, 1983.

Gerstle, Gary. "The Protean Character of American Liberalism." *The American Historical Review* 99, no. 4 (1994).

Geyer, Michael. "Multiculturalism and the Politics of General Education." *Critical Inquiry* 19, no. 3 (1993).

Gilroy, Paul. *The Black Atlantic: Modernity and Double Consciousness*. Cambridge, 1993.

Gleason, Philip. "American Identity and Americanization." In *Harvard Encyclopedia of American Ethnic Groups*, ed. S. Therstrom. Cambridge, 1980.

Gómez-Peña, Guillermo. "Documented/Undocumented." In *The Graywolf Annual Five: Multi-Cultural Literacy*, trans. Rubén Martínez, ed. Rick Simonson and Scott Walker. Saint Paul, 1988.

———. "Bilingualism, Biculturalism, and Borders." In *English Is Broken Here: Notes on Cultural Fusion in the Americas*, ed. Coco Fusco. New York, 1995.

Goodheart, Eugene. "Against Coercion." *New Literary History* 19, no. 1 (1987).

Gordon, Avery F. and Christopher Newfield, eds. *Mapping Multiculturalism*. Minneapolis, 1996.

Greenfeld, Leah. *Nationalism: Five Roads to Modernity*. Cambridge, 1992.

Grimm, Jacob. "Über den Namen der Germanisten." Rede auf der Frankfurter Germanisten-Versammlung 1846. In *Recensionen und vermischte Aufsätze*, vol.4. Berlin, 1884.

———. "Vorwort." In *Deutsches Wörterbuch*, vol.1, eds. Jacob und Wilhelm Grimm. Leipzig, 1854.

Habermas, Jürgen. *Faktizität und Geltung*. Frankfurt/Main 1992.

———. *Die Einbeziehung des Anderen*. Frankfurt/Main, 1996.

———. "New Social Movements." *Telos* 49 (1981).

Hacking, Ian. "Language, Truth and Reason." In *Rationality and Relativism*, eds. Martin Hollis and Steven Lukes. Cambridge, 1982.

Hailbronner, Kai. "Citizenship and Nationhood in Germany." In *Citizenship in Europe and North America*, ed. William Rogers Brubaker. Lanham, MD, 1989.

Haizlip, Shirlee Taylor. "Passing." *American Heritage* February/March 1995.

Hajek, Friederike. "Das Identitätsproblem im Befreiungskampf der afroamerikanischen USA-Bürger und seine Widerspiegelung in Selbst-zeugnisssen der sechziger Jahre." Ph.D. diss., Universität Potsdam, 1974.

Hall, Peter A. "The State of European Studies." *Lingua Franca* 24, no. 5/6 (1995).

Hall, Stuart. "Cultural Identity and Diaspora." In *Identity: Community, Culture, Difference*, ed. Jonathan Rutherford. London, 1990.

————. "The Local and the Global: Globalization and Ethnicity." In *Culture, Globalization and the World System: Contemporary Conditions for the Representation of Identity*, ed. Anthony D. King. London, 1991.

————. "Old and New Identities, Old and New Ethnicities." In *Culture, Globalization, and the World System: Contemporary Conditions for the Representation of Identity*, ed. Anthony D. King. London, 1991.

Hamburger, Franz. *Pädagogik der Einwanderungsgesellschaft*. Frankfurt/Main, 1994.

Hannerz, Ulf. *Cultural Complexity: Studies in the Social Organization of Meaning*. New York, 1992.

————. *Transnational Connections: Culture, People, Places*. New York and London, 1996.

————. "The World in Creolisation." *Africa* 57 (1987).

————. "American Culture: Creolized, Creolizing." In *American Culture: Creolized, Creolizing and Other Lectures from the NAAS Biennial Conference in Uppsala, May 28–31, 1987*, ed. Erik Åsard. Uppsala University: The Swedish Institute for North American Studies, 1987.

Haraway, Donna. *Primate Visions: Gender, Race, and Nature in the World of Modern Science*. New York, 1989.

————. *Simians, Cyborgs, and Women: The Reinvention of Nature*. New York, 1991.

————. "Situated Knowledges: The Science Question in Feminism and the Privilege of Partial Perspective." *Feminist Studies* 14 (Fall 1988).

Hartz, L. *The Liberal Tradition in America*. New York, 1955.

Harvey, David. *The Condition of Postmodernity*. New York, 1989.

————"Klassenbeziehungen. Soziale Gerechtigkeit und die Politik der Differenz." In *Multikulturelle Gesellschaft. Modell Amerika?*, ed. Berndt Ostendorf. Munich, 1994.

Hayward, John A. "Who Are Citizens." *American Law Journal* 2 (1885).

Head, Simon. "The New, Ruthless Economy." *The New York Review of Books*, 29 February 1996.

Heckmann, Friedrich. "Ethnos, Demos und Nation, oder: Woher stammt die Intoleranz des Nationalstaats gegenüber ethnischen Minderheiten?" In *Das Eigene und das Fremde*, ed. Uli Bielfeld. Hamburg, 1991.

Hegel, Ralf-Dietmar, Martin Müller, and Michael Wolf. *Die produktive Kraft der Unfreiheit: Eine empirische Studie zu ostdeutschen Biographien in der "Wendezeit"*. Milow, 1994.

Heilbrunn, Jacob. "The News from Everywhere: Does Global Thinking Threaten Local Knowledge? The Social Science Research Council Debates the Future of Area Studies." *Lingua Franca* (May/June 1996).

Heinsius, Theodor. *Teut*, 2nd ed. vol.4. Berlin, 1818.

Henningsen, Manfred. "Der heilige Mauritius und der Streit um die multikulturelle Identität des Westens." *Merkur* 46 (1992).

Herrmann, Dietrich. *"Be an American!" Amerikanisierungsbewegung und Theorien zur Ein wandererintegration*. Frankfurt/Main, 1996.

Herrnstein Smith, Barbara. *Contingencies of Value*. Cambridge, 1988.

Herz, Dietmar. "Republik und Verfassung. Die theoretischen Grundlagen einer liberalen Staatsordnung." Ph.D. diss., Sozialwissenschaftliche Fakultät, Munich, 1995.

Hettling, M. and P. Nolte, eds. *Nation und Gesellschaft in Deutschland*. Munich, 1996.

Higham, John. *Send These to Me: Jews and Other Immigrants in Urban America*. New York, 1975.

Hildebrand, Klaus. *Geschichte der Bundesrepublik Deutschland, Bd. 4: Von Erhard zur Grossen Koalition, 1963–1969*. Stuttgart, 1984.

Hirsch, Marianne and Evelyn Fox Keller. "Conclusion: Practicing Conflict in Feminist Theory." In *Conflicts in Feminism*, ed. Marianne Hirsch and Evelyn Fox Keller. New York, 1990.

Hobsbawm, Eric J. *Nation and Nationalism since 1870*. London, 1990.

Hollinger, David A. *Postethnic America: Beyond Multiculturalism*. New York, 1995.

———. "Ethnic Diversity, Cosmopolitanism and the Emergence of the American Liberal Intelligentsia." *American Quarterly* 27 (1975).

Holmes, Stephen. "The Community Trap." In The Anatomy of Antiliberalism. Cambridge, 1993.

hooks, bell. *Yearning: Race, Gender, and Cultural Politics*. Boston, 1990.

Hornung, Alfred. "Social Work and Modern Art: The Autobiographies of Jane Addams and Gertrude Stein." In *Anglistentag 1989 Würzburg: Proceedings*, ed. Rüdiger Ahrens. Tübingen, 1990.

———. "The Making of (Jewish) Americans: Ludwig Lewisohn, Charles Reznikoff, Michael Gold." In *Ethnic Cultures in the 1920s in North America*, ed. Wolfgang Binder. Frankfurt/Main, 1993.

———. "The Making of Americans: Mary Rowlandson, Benjamin Franklin, Gertrude Stein, Maxine Hong Kingston." In *American Studies in Germany: European Contexts and Intercultural Relations*, ed. Günter H. Lenz and Klaus J. Milich. Frankfurt/Main and New York, 1995.

———. "The Birth of a Multicultural Nation: Horace M. Kallen's Cultural Pluralism." In *Transatlantic Encounters: Studies in European-American Relations*, ed. Udo J. Hebel and Karl Ortseifen. Trier, 1995.

Huber, Ernst Rudolf. *Deutsche Verfassungsgeschichte seit 1789: Bd. II, Der Kampf um Einheit und Freiheit 1830–1850*. Stuttgart, 1968.

Hughes, Charles Evans. *The Supreme Court of the United States*. New York, 1928.

Hull, Gloria T., Patricia Bell Scott, and Barbara Smith. *All the Women Are White, All the Blacks Are Men, but Some of Us Are Brave: Black Women's Studies*. Old Westbury, NY, 1982.

Huntington, S.P. "The Clash of Civilizations." *Foreign Affairs* 72, no. 3 (1993).

Hurwitz, Henry. "Watchmen, What of the Day?" *The Menorah Journal* 12 (1926).

Huyssen, Andreas. *Twilight Memories: Marking Time in a Culture of Amnesia*. New York and London, 1995.

Ide, Henry C. "Citizenship." *American Law Journal* 2 (1885).

———. "Citizenship by Birth—Another View." *American Law Review* 30 (1896).

Inglehart, Ronald. *The Silent Revolution: Changing Styles among Western Publics*. Princeton, 1977.

———. *Culture Shift in Advanced Industrial Society*. Princeton, 1990.

———. "New Perspectives on Political Change." *Comparative Political Studies* 17 (1985).

Jacobsohn, Gary J. *Apple of Gold: Constitutionalism in Israel and the United States*. Princeton, 1993.

Jacoby, Russell. "Marginal Returns: The Trouble with Post-Colonial Theory." *Lingua franca* 5, no. 6 (September/October 1995).

Jäger, Wolfgang. "Die Innenpolitik der sozial-liberalen Koalition 1969–1974." In *Geschichte der Bundesrepublik Deutschland, Bd. 5/I: Republik im Wandel, 1969–1974*, Karl-Dietrich Bracher, Wolfgang Jäger, and Werner Link. Stuttgart, 1986.

James, William. *Writings 1902–1910*. New York, 1987.

Jansen, Mechthild M. and Sigrid Baringhorst, eds. *Politik der Multikultur*. Baden-Baden, 1994.

Jaspers, Karl. *Wohin treibt die Bundesrepublik?* Munich, 1988.

Jay, Gregory S. "The End of 'American' Literature: Toward a Multicultural Practice." *College English* 53 (March 1991).

Jefferson, T. *Notes on the State of Virginia.* Query 18. 1781.

Jennings, J. *The Politics of Black Empowerment.* Detroit, 1992.

Jeserich, Kurt G. A. "Die Entstehung des öffentlichen Dienstes 1800–1871." In *Deutsche Verwaltungsgeschichte, Bd. 2: Vom Reichsdeputationshauptschluss bis zur Auflösung des Deutschen Bundes,* ed. K. Jeserich, H. Pohl, G. C. v. Unruh. Stuttgart, 1983.

Joas, Hans. "Gemeinschaft und Demokratie in den USA. Die vergessene Vorgeschichte der Kommunitarismus-Diskussion." In *Gemeinschaft und Gerechtigkeit,* ed. Micha Brumlik and Hauke Brunkhorst. Frankfurt/ Main, 1993.

Johnson, Basil. *Ojibwa Heritage.* Toronto, 1979.

Johnson, D. *Multiculturalism: In the Curriculum, in the Disciplines, and in Society.* New York, 1992.

Johnson, Nevil. *State and Government in the Federal Republic of Germany: The Executive at Work.* Oxford, 1983.

Jones, Gayl. *The Birdcatcher,* New York, 1985.

Kaiser, Nancy. *Selbst bewußt: Frauen in den USA.* Leipzig, 1994.

Kallen, Horace M. *William James and Henri Bergson: A Study in Contrasting Theories of Life.* Chicago, 1914.

———. *Culture and Democracy in the United States: Studies in the Group Psychology of the American Peoples.* New York, 1924.

———. *Cultural Pluralism and the American Idea: An Essay in Social Philosophy.* Philadelphia, 1956.

———. "Hebraism and Current Tendencies in Philosophy." *Judaism at Bay: Essays Toward the Adjustment of Judaism to Modernity.* New York, 1972.

Kaplan, Caren. *Questions of Travel: Postmodern Discourses of Displacement.* Durham, 1996.

Kaschuba, Wolfgang. "Nationalismus und Ethnozentrismus: Zur kulturellen Ausgrenzung ethnischer Gruppen in (deutscher) Geschichte und Gegenwart." In *Grenzfälle: Über neuen und alten Nationalismus,* ed. Michael Jeismann and Henning Ritter. Leipzig, 1993.

———. "Kulturalismus: Vom Verschwinden des Sozialen im gesellschaftlichen Diskurs." In *Kulture— Identitäten—Diskurse: Perspektiven Europäischer Ethnologie,* ed. idem. Berlin, 1995.

Kielmansegg, Peter Graf. "The Basic Law—Response to the Past or Design for the Future?" *Forty Years of the Grundgesetz.* Washington, D.C., 1989.

Kitschelt, Herbert. *The Logics of Party Formation: Ecological Politics in Belgium and West Germany.* Ithaca, 1989.

Klingenstein, Susanne. *Jews in the American Academy, 1900–1940: The Dynamics of Intellec-tual Assimilation.* New Haven, 1991.

Kluge, Friedrich. *Etymologisches Wörterbuch der deutschen Sprache.* 19th ed. Berlin, 1963.

Koenen, Anne. *Zeitgenössische Afro-Amerikanische Frauenliteratur.* Frankfurt/ Main, 1985.

Kolinsky, Eva. "Conclusion." *Turkish Culture in German Society Today,* ed. David Horrocks and Eva Kolinsky. Providence, 1995.

Konvitz, Milton R., ed. *The Legacy of Horace M. Kallen.* Rutherford, 1987

———. "Horace Meyer Kallen (1882–1974): In Praise of Hyphenation and Orchestration." In *The Legacy of Horace M. Kallen,* ed. idem. Rutherford, 1987.

Kocka, Jürgen. "German History before Hitler: The Debate about the German Sonderweg." *Journal of Contemporary History* 23 (1988).

Koselleck, Reinhart. *Preussen zwischen Reform und Revolution: Allgemeines Landrecht, Verwaltung, und soziale Frage von 1791 bis 1848.* Stuttgart, 1967.
Kotthoff, Helga. "Toni Morrison. Sehr blaue Augen." *Emma,* March 1987.
Kroh, Wolfgang and Günter Küppers. *Die Selbstorganisation der Wissenschaft.* Frankfurt/Main, 1989.
Krenzlin, Norbert. "Nachwort." In *Eine andere Welt,* J. Baldwin. Berlin, 1977.
Krieger, L. *The German Idea of Freedom.* New York, 1957.
Kvistad, Gregg O. "Radicals in the State: The Political Demands on West German Civil Servants." *Comparative Political Studies* 21(1988).
————. "The 'Borrowed Language' of German Unification: State, Society and Party Identity." *German Politics* 3 (1994).
————. "Accommodation of 'Cleansing': Germany's State Employees from the Old Regime," *West European Politics* 17 (1994).
Langley, Stephen. "Multiculturalism versus Technoculturalism: Its Challenge to American Theatre and the Functions of Arts Management." In *The American Stage: Social and Economic Issues from the Colonial Period to the Present,* ed. Ron Engle and Tice L. Miller. Cambridge, 1993.
Lasch, Christopher. *The Revolt of the Elites and the Betrayal of Democracy.* New York, 1995.
Leavis, Frank Raymond. "Two Cultures? The Significance of C.P.Snow." *Richmond Lectures.* London, 1962.
Leggewie, Claus. *Multi Kulti: Spielregeln für die Vielvölkerrepublik.* Berlin, 1990.
————. *America First? Der Fall einer konservativen Revolution.* Frankfurt/Main, 1997.
————. "Vom Deutschen Reich zur Bundesrepublik—und nicht zurück: Zur politischen Gestalt einer multikulturellen Gesellschaft." In *Schwierige Fremdheit: Über Integration und Ausgrenzung in Einwanderungsländern,* ed. Friedrich Balke, Rebecca Habermas, Patrizia Nanz, and Peter Sillem. Frankfurt/Main, 1993.
————. "Ethnizität, Nationalismus und multikulturelle Gesellschaft." In *Nationales Bewußtsein und kollektive Identität: Studien zur Entwicklung des kollektiven Bewußtseins in der Neuzeit,* ed. Helmut Berding, vol. 2. Frankfurt/Main, 1994.
Le Goff, Jacques. *History and Memory.* Trans. Steven Rendall and Elizabeth Claman. New York, 1994).
Lennox, Sara. "Feministische Aufbrüche: Impulse aus den USA und Frankreich." In *Frauen Literatur Geschichte,* ed. Hiltrud Gnüg and Renate Möhrmann. Stuttgart, 1985.
Lenz, Günter H. "'Ethnographies': American Culture Studies and Postmodern Anthropology." In *Prospects* 16, ed. Jack Salzman. New York, 1991.
————. "Multicultural Critique and the New American Studies." In *Multiculturalism and the Canon of American Culture,* ed. Hans Bak. Amsterdam, 1993.
————. "American Studies as Multicultural Critique: Postmodern Culture, Interdisciplinarity, and Intercultural Identities." In *Anglistentag 1993 Eichstätt: Proceedings,* ed. Günther Blaicher and Brigitte Glaser. Tübingen, 1994.
————. "*American Studies:* Multikulturalität und Postmoderne." In *Multikulturelle Gesellschaft: Modell Amerika?,*ed. Berndt Ostendorf. Munich, 1994.
————. "*American Cultural Studies:* Multikulturalismus und Postmoderne," *Multikulturelle Gesellschaft: Modell Amerika?,* ed. Berndt Osendorf. Munich, 1994.
————. "Transnational American Studies: Conceptualizing Multicultural Identities and Communities—Some Notes." In *Fremde Texte verstehen. Festschrift für Lothar Bredella,* ed. Herbert Christ and Michael K. Legutke. Tübingen, 1996.
————. "Refractions of Modernity—Reconstituting Modernism in West Germany after World War II: Jackson Pollock, Ezra Pound, and Charlie Parker." In *Demokratie und Kunst in Amerika—Democracy and Art in the U.S.A.: Festschrift zu*

Ehren von Martin Christadler, ed. Olaf Hansen and Thomas Liesemann. Trieste, 1996.

——, ed. *History and Tradition in Afro-American Culture.* Frankfurt/Main, 1984.

Lewisohn, Ludwig. *Up Stream.* New York, 1922.

Lind, Michael. *The Next American Nation: The New Nationalism and the Fourth American Revolution.* New York, 1995.

——. "To Have and Have Not: Notes on the Progress of the American Class War." *Harper's Magazine,* June 1995.

Linz, J.J. "State Building and Nation Building." *European Review* 1 (1993).

Lipset, Seymour Martin. *The First New Nation.* Garden City, 1967.

——. *American Exceptionalism: A Double-Edged Sword.* New York, 1996.

——. "Malaise and Resiliency in America." *Journal of Democracy* 6, no. 3 (July 1995).

Lubell, S. *The Future of American Politics.* 2nd ed. Garden City, 1956.

Lumer, Helga. "Die Produktivität indianischer Mythen bei dem Chippewa-Autor Gerald Vizenor." *Zeitschrift für Anglistik und Amerikanistik* 1 (1986).

MacPherson, C.B. *Die politische Philosophie des Besitzindividualismus.* 2nd edition. Frank-furt/Main, 1987.

Madrick, Jeff. "The End of Affluence." *New York Review of Books,* 21 September 1995.

Magnarella, Paul J. "Justice in a Culturally Pluralistic Society: The Cultural Defense on Trial." *Journal of Ethnic Studies* 19, no. 3 (1996).

Maier, C.S. *The Unmasterable Past.* Cambridge, 1988.

Manske, Eva. "Individual and Society in Contemporary American Fiction." *Zeitschrift für Anglistik und Amerikanistik* 4 (1980).

Marcus, George E. and Michael M. J. Fischer. *Anthropology as Cultural Critique: An Experi- mental Moment in the Human Sciences.* Chicago and London, 1986.

Marshall, Barbara. "German Migration Policies." In *Development in German Politics,* Gordon Smith, et al. Durham, 1992.

Marshall, T.H. *Class, Citizenship, and Social Development.* Chicago, 1964.

Martin, Biddy. "Zwischenbilanz der feministischen Debatten." In *Germanistik in den USA: Neue Entwicklungen und Methoden,* ed. Frank Trommler. Opladen, 1989.

Martin, Biddy and Chandra Talpade Mohanty. "Feminist Politics: What's Home Got to Do With It?" In *Feminist Studies/Critical Studies,* ed. Teresa de Lauretis. Bloomington, 1986.

Matthes, Joachim. "'Zwischen' den Kulturen?" In *Zwischen den Kulturen. Die Sozial- wissen- schaften vor dem Problem des Kulturvergleichs,* ed. idem. Sonderband Soziale Welt 8. Göttingen, 1992.

Mayer-Tasch, P. C. *Die Bürgerinitiativbewegung: Der aktive Bürger als rechts- und politikwissenschaftliches Problem.* Reinbek bei Hamburg, 1976.

Mazrui, Ali A. "Uncle Sam's Hearing Aid." In *Estrangement: America and the New World,* ed. Sanford Ungar. New York, 1985.

Meister, Leonhard. *Beyträge zur Geschichte der teutschen Sprache und National-Litteratur.* vol.1 London, 1777.

Menand, Louis. "Blind Date: Liberalism and the Allure of Culture." *Transition* (Fall 1995).

Mendelson, Maurice. "Einige Bemerkungen zur Amerikanistik in der DDR." *Zeitschrift für Anglistik und Amerikanistik* 3 (1975).

Mercer, Kobena. *Welcome to the Jungle: New Positions in Black Cultural Studies.* New York, 1994.

Michaels, Walter Benn, "Race into Culture: A Critical Genealogy of Cultural Identity." *Critical Inquiry* 18, vol. 4 (Summer 1992).

Mills, Nicolaus. *Arguing Immigration: The Debate over the Changing Face of America.* New York, 1994.

Minh-ha, Trinh T. *When the Moon Waxes Red: Representation, Gender, and Cultural Politics.* New York and London, 1991.

Minow, Martha, *Making "All" the Difference: Inclusion, Exclusion, and American Law.* Ithaca, 1990.

Mittenzwei, Werner. *Der Realismusstreit um Brecht. Grundriss der Brecht-Rezeption in der DDR 1945–1975.* Berlin and Weimar, 1978.

Möser, Justus. "Über die deutsche Sprache und Literatur. Schreiben an einen Freund." (1781). In *Anwalt des Vaterlands. Wochenschriften, Patriotische Phantasien, Aufsätze, Fragmente.* Leipzig and Weimar, 1978.

Mollenkopf, John H., Manuel Castells, eds. *Dual City: Restructuring New York.* New York, 1991.

Moraga, Cherrie and Gloria Anzaldúa. *This Bridge Called My Back: Writings by Radical Women of Color.* New York, 1982.

Mohanty, Chandra Talpade, Ann Russo, and Lourdes Torres. *Third World Women and the Politics of Feminism.* Bloomington, 1991.

Morrison, Toni. *The Bluest Eye.* New York, 1969.

———. *Song of Solomon.* New York, 1977.

———. *Sula.* New York, 1973.

———. *Tar Baby.* New York, 1981.

———. *Beloved.* New York, 1987.

———. *Playing in the Dark: Whiteness and the Literary Imagination.* Cambridge/London, 1990.

———. *Jazz.* New York, 1993.

———. "Unspeakable Things Unspoken: The Afro-American Presence in American Literature." *Michigan Quarterly Review* 28, no. 1 (1989).

Müller, Marianne. "'A self-contained universe': Zur mythologisch-archetypischen Literaturbetrachtung von Northrop Frye." *Zeitschift für Anglistik und Amerikanistik* 3 (1988).

Muller, Thomas. *Immigrants and the American City.* New York, 1993.

Murray, Laura M. "Einwanderungsland Bundesrepublik Deutschland? Explaining the Evolving Positions of German Political Parties on Citizenship Policy." *German Politics and Society* 33 (1994).

Nader, Laura. "Comparative Consciousness." In *Assessing Cultural Anthropology,* ed. Robert Borofsky. New York, 1994.

Naylor, Gloria. *The Women of Brewster Place.* New York, 1982.

Nicholson, Linda. "Interpreting *Gender.*" *Signs* 20, no. 1 (Autumn 1994).

Nipperdey, Thomas. *Deutsche Geschichte 1800–1866: Bürgerwelt und starker Staat.* Munich, 1983.

Offe, Claus. *Contradictions of the Welfare State.* Cambridge, 1984.

Özdamar, Emine Sevgi. "Karagöz in Alamania. Schwarzauge in Deutschland." In *Mutterzunge.* Berlin, 1990.

Olmstead, Kathryn J. "Breaking the Cocoon: Cultural Journalism in a Global Community." *Journal of Popular Culture* 25, no. 2 (1991).

Ostendorf, Berndt. *The Costs of Multiculturalism.* Working Paper no. 50, J. F. Kennedy Institut. Berlin, 1992.

———. "Der Preis des Multikulturalismus. Entwicklungen in den USA." *Merkur* (Sept./Oct. 1992).

———, ed. *Multikulturelle Gesellschaft: Modell Amerika?* Munich, 1994.

———. "Einwanderungspolitik der USA: Eine historische Skizze." In *Multikulturelle Gesellschaft,* ed. idem. Munich, 1994.

———. "Identitätsstiftende Geschichte: Religion und Öffentlichkeit in den USA." *Merkur* (May 1995).

Painter, Nell Irvin. *The Great Migration in Historical Perspective: New Dimensions of Race, Class, and Gender*. Ed. Joe William Trotter, Jr. Bloomington, 1991.

Pease, Donald E. "National Identities, Postmodern Artifacts, and Postnational Narratives." Special Issue on the New Americanists No. 2, *Boundary 2* 19 (Spring 1992).

Perry, Benita. "Signs of Our Times: Discussion of Homi Bhabha's *The Location of Culture*." *Third Text* 28/29 (Autumn/Winter 1994).

Petry, Ann. *The Street*. New York, 1982.

Phillips, A. "Must Feminists Give Up on Liberal Democracy?" *Political Studies* 40 (1992).

Plessner, Helmut, *Die verspätete Nation. Über die politische Verführbarkeit bürgerlichen Geistes*. Stuttgart, 1959.

Portes, Alejandro and Min Zhou. "Should Immigrants Assimilate?" *The Public Interest* (Summer 1994).

Pratt, Mary Louise. *Imperial Eyes: Travel Writing and Transculturation*. New York and London, 1992.

———. "Arts of the Contact Zone." *Profession 91* (1992).

Prize Selection Committee. "Prize Citation." Presidential Address. San Diego Convention Center. 28 December 1994.

Puhle, Hans-Jürgen. *Agrarische Interessenpolitik und preussischer Konservatismus im Wilhel minischen Reich*. 2nd ed. Bonn-Bad Godesberg, 1975.

———. *Staaten, Nationen und Regionen in Europa*. Vienna, 1995.

———. "Conservatism in Modern German History." *Journal of Contemporary History* 13 (1978).

———. "Soziale Ungleichheit und Klassenbildung in den USA." In *Klassen in der europäischen Sozialgeschichte*, ed. H.-U. Wehler. Göttingen, 1979.

———. "Multikulturalismus und der amerikanische *consensus*." In *Multikulturelle Gesellschaft: Modell Amerika?*, ed. Berndt Ostendorf. Munich, 1994.

———. "Unabhängigkeit, Staatenbildung und gesellschaftliche Entwicklung in Nord- und Südamerika." In *Lateinamerika am Ende des 20. Jahrhunderts*, ed. D. Junker et al. Munich, 1994.

———. "Vom Bürgerrecht zum Gruppenrecht? Multikulturelle Politik in den USA." In *Die multikulturelle Herausforderung*, ed. K.J. Bade. Munich, 1996.

Puhle, Hans-Jürgen, and H.-U. Wehler, eds. *Preussen im Rückblick*. Göttingen, 1980.

Quirk, Tom. "Bergson in America." *Prospects* 11 (1987).

Radcliffe-Brown, A. R. *Method in Social Anthropology*. Chicago and London, 1976.

Radtke, Frank-Olaf. "Lob der Gleich-Gültigkeit: Zur Konstruktion des Fremden im Diskurs des Multikulturalismus."In *Das Eigene und das Fremde*, ed. Uli Bielefeld. Hamburg, 1991.

———. "Multikulturell—Das Gesellschaftsdesign der 90er Jahre." *Informationsdienst zur Ausländerarbeit* no. 4 (1990).

———. "Multikulturalismus: Ein Postmoderner Nachfahre des Nationalismus." In *Multikulturelle Gesellschaft. Modell Amerika?*, ed. Berndt Ostendorf. Munich, 1994.

Raeithel, Gert. "Die zweite Zeit der Büffel." *Spiegel* 17 (1993).

Ravitch, D."Multiculturalism: E Pluribus Plures." *The American Scholar* 59 (1990).

Ray, William B. *The Ups and Downs of Radio-TV Regulations*. Ames, 1990.

Reich, Robert B. *The Work of Nations*. New York, 1991.

Remmler, Karen. "Sheltering Battered Bodies in Language: Imprisonment Once More?" In *Displacements: Cultural Identities in Question*, ed. Angelika Bammler. Bloomington and Indianapolis, 1994.

Riedel, Manfred, "Gesellschaft, Gemeinschaft." *Geschichtliche Grundbegriffe* vol. 2 Stuttgart, 1979.

Riley, Denise. *Am I That Name? Feminism and the Category of "Women" in History.* New York, 1988.

Safran, William. "Diasporas in Modern Societies: Myths of Homeland and Return." *Diaspora* 1 (Spring 1991).

Said, Edward W. *Culture and Imperialism.* New York, 1993.

Saldívar, José David. *The Dialectics of America: Genealogy, Cultural Critique, and Literary History.* Durham, 1991.

———. "The Limits of Cultural Studies." *American Literary History* 2 (1990).

Saldívar, Ramón. *Chicano Narrative: The Dialectics of Difference.* Madison, 1990.

Sassen, Saskia. *The Global City: New York, London, Tokyo.* Princeton, 1991.

———. *Cities in a World Economy.* Thousand Oaks, 1994.

———. "Whose City Is It? Globalization and the Formation of New Claims." *Public Culture* 8 (1996).

Scheller, Bernard. "Stichwörter statt eines Nachworts." In *Giovannis Zimmer,* J. Baldwin. Leipzig, 1981.

Schlesinger, Arthur M. Jr. *The Disuniting of America: Reflections on a Multicultural Society.* New York, 1992.

Schmidt, Michael. *Heute gehört uns die Strasse.* Düsseldorf, 1993.

Schmidt, Sarah. *Horace M. Kallen: Prophet of American Zionism.* Brooklyn, 1995.

———. "Horace M. Kallen and the Americanization of Zionism." Ph.D. Thesis, University of Maryland, 1973.

Schmitter, P.C. "Corporative Democracy: Oxymoronic? Just Plain Moronic? Or a Promising Way Out of the Present Impasse?" Stanford, 1988.

Schröder, Karsten and Hermann Horstkotte. "Foreigners in Germany." *Sozial-Report* 2 (1993).

Schuck, Peter H. and Rogers M. Smith. *Citizenship without Consent.* New Haven, 1985.

Schulte, Axel. "Multikulturelle Gesellschaft: Chance, Ideologie oder Bedrohung?" *Aus Politik und Zeitgeschichte* 23/24 (1990).

Schumm, Petra. "'Mestizaje' und 'culturas híbridas'—kulturtheoretische Konzepte im Vergleich." In *Lateinamerika denken: Kulturtheoretische Grenzgänge zwischen Moderne und Postmoderne,* ed. Birgit Scharlau. Tübingen, 1994.

Schwarz, Benjamin. "The Diversity Myth: America's Leading Export." *Atlantic Monthly,* May 1995.

Scott, Joan. *Gender and the Politics of History.* New York, 1988

———. "Multiculturalism and the Politics of Identity." *October* 61 (1992).

Schlaeger, Jürgen. "Cultural Poetics or Literary Anthropology?" *Real* 10 (1994).

Schmidt, Ricarda. "Theoretische Orientierungen in feministischer Literaturwissenschaft und Sozialphilosophie." In *Women in German Yearbook 7.* Lincoln, 1991.

Seeba, Hinrich C. "'Zeitgeist' und 'deutscher Geist': Zur Nationalisierung der Epochentendenz um 1800." In *Deutsche Vierteljahrsschrift für Literaturwissenschaft und Geistesgeschichte: Von der gelehrten zur disziplinären Gemeinschaft* (Sonderheft, 1987), ed. Jürgen Fohrmann and Wilhelm Vosskamp. Stuttgart, 1987.

———. "Nationalbücher: Zur Kanonisierung nationaler Bildungsmuster in der frühen Germanistik." In *Wissenschaft und Nation. Studien zur Entstehungsgeschichte der deutschen Literaturwissenschaft,* vol.1, ed. Jürgen Fohrmann and Wilhelm Vosskamp. Munich, 1991.

———. "Schwerterhebung. Zur Konstruktion des heroischen Subjekts / Raising the Sword: On the Construction of the Heroic Subject." *Daidalos. Architektur-Kunst-Kultur* 49 (15 September 1993).

Shain, Zossi. "Ethnic Diasporas and U.S. Foreign Policy." *Political Science Quarterly* 109, no. 5 (1994–1995).

Sheehan, James J. *German Liberalism in the Nineteenth Century.* Chicago, 1978.
————. "Vorbildliche Ausnahme: Liberalismus in Amerika und Europa." In *Von der Arbeiterbewegung zum modernen Sozialstaat,* ed. J. Kocka et al. Munich, 1994.
Shohat, Ella and Robert Stam. *Unthinking Eurocentrism: Multiculturalism and the Media.* London and New York, 1994.
Siddique, Sharon, "Anthropologie, Soziologie und Cultural Analysis." In *Zwischen den Kulturen. Die Sozialwissenschaften vor dem Problem des Kulturvergleichs,* ed. Joachim Matthes, Sonder band Soziale Welt 8. Göttingen, 1992.
The Slaughter House Cases, 16 Wall. 36 (1873).
Snow, Charles Percy. *The Two Cultures and a Second Look: An Expanded Version of The Two Cultures and the Scientific Revolution.* New York, 1963.
Sollors, Werner, *Beyond Ethnicity: Consent and Descent in American Culture.* New York, 1986.
————. "A Critique of Pure Pluralism." In *Reconstructing American Literary History,* ed. Sacvan Bercovitch. Cambridge, 1986.
————. "DE PLURIBUS UNA/E PLURIBUS UNUS: Mathew Arnold, George Orwell, Holocaust und Assimilation. Bemerkungen zur amerikanischen Multikulturalismusdebatte." In *Multikulturelle Gesellschaft. Modell Amerika?,* ed. Berndt Ostendorf. Munich, 1994.
Sontheimer, Kurt. *Die verunsicherte Republik.* Munich, 1979.
Spiegel. "Die Schale wird zum Kern." 48 (1993)
Spivak, Gayatri. "French Feminism Revisited: Ethics and Politics." In *Feminists Theorize the Political,* ed. Judith Butler and Joan Scott. New York, 1992.
Stark, Andrew. "Vive le Québec anglophone!" *TLS,* 22 September 1995.
Steinberg, S. *The Ethnic Myth: Race, 'Ethnicity,' and Class in America.* New York, 1981.
Strathern, Marilyn. "Parts and Wholes: Refiguring Relationships in a Post-Plural World." In *Conceptualizing Society,* ed. Adam Kuper. London, 1992.
Super, Robert Henry, ed. *Philistinism in England and America: The Complete Prose Works of Matthew Arnold.* Ann Arbor, 1974.
Swidler, Ann. "Inequality and American Culture: The Persistence of Voluntarism." *American Behavioral Scientist* 35, no. 4/5 (March/June 1992).
Taylor, Charles. *Multiculturalism and "The Politics of Recognition".* Princeton, 1992.
Thomä, Dieter. "Multikulturalismus, Demokratie, Nation: Zur Philosophie der deutschen Einheit." *Deutsche Zeitschrift für Philosophie* 43 (1995).
Tölölyan, Khachig. "The Nation-state and Its Others: In Lieu of a Preface." *Diaspora* 1, no.1 (1991).
Tomlinson, John. *Cultural Imperialism: A Critical Introduction.* Baltimore, 1991.
Trilling, Lionel. "The Leavis-Snow Controversy." *Beyond Culture: Essays on Literature and Learning.* New York, 1968.
Ungar, Sanford J., ed. *Estrangement: America and the World.* New York, 1985.
U.S. Constitution, amend. 14, sec.1
United States v Wong Kim Ark, 169 U.S. 649 (1898).
Vasey, Ruth. "Foreign Parts: Hollywood's Global Distribution and the Representation of Ethnicity." *American Quarterly* 44 (1992).
Vorländer, Hans, "Ein vorläufiges Nachwort zur deutschen Kommunitarismusdebatte." *Forschungsjournal NSB* 8, no. 3 (1955).
Wachler, Ludwig. *Vorlesungen über die Geschichte der teutschen Nationallitteratur.* 2nd ed. vol. 1, 3. Frankfurt/Main, 1834.
Walker, Alice. *Meridian.* New York, 1976.
————. *The Color Purple.* New York, 1982.
————. *The Temple of My Familiar.* New York, 1989.
Walker, Margaret. *Jubilee,* New York, 1966.

Walzer, Michael. *Multiculturalism: Examining the Politics of Recognition.* Princeton, 1994.

———. "Pluralism: A Political Perspective." In *Harvard Encyclopedia of American Ethnic Groups,* ed. Stephan Thernstrom et al. Cambridge, 1980.

———. "Multiculturalism and Individualism," *Dissent* (Spring 1994).

Waters, Mary. *Ethnic Options. Choosing Identities in America.* Berkeley, 1990.

Weber, M. "Parliament und Regierung im neugeordneten Deutschland." *Gesammelte Politische Schriften* 3rd ed. Tübingen, 1971.

Wehler, Hans Ulrich. *Deutsche Gesellschaftsgeschichte.* vols. 1–3. Munich, 1987 and 1995.

Weimann, Robert. *Literaturgeschichte und Mythologie: Methodologische und historische Studien.* Frankfurt/Main, 1977.

———. "Literaturwissenschaft und historisch-materialistische Theorie: Aktuelle Fragen der Entwicklung der Literaturtheorie und Methodologie in der Anglistik-Amerikanistik." *Zeitschrift für Anglistik und Amerikanistik* 1 (1980).

Weiner, Marc. "Letter from the New Editor of The German Quarterly." *AATG Newsletter* 30, no. 1 (Fall 1994).

Weir, M. et al. *The Politics of Social Policy in the United States.* Princeton, 1988.

Welz, Gisela, *Inszenierungen kultureller Vielfalt: Frankfurt am Main und New York City.* Berlin, 1996.

———. "Anthropology, Minority Discourse, and the 'Creolization' of Cultures." In *Mediating Cultures: Probleme des Kulturtransfers,* ed. Norbert H. Platz. (Essen, 1991).

———. "Multikulturelle Diskurse: Differenzerfahrung als ethnologischer and gesellschaftlicher Topos in Deutschland und den USA." In *Amerikastudien/American Studies* 38, no. 2 (1993).

———. "Die soziale Organisation kultureller Differenz: Zur Kritik des Ethnosbegriffs in der anglo-amerikanischen Kulturanthropologie." In *Nationales Bewußtsein und kollektive Identität,* ed. Helmut Berding. Frankfurt/Main, 1994.

Werz, Nikolaus. "'Multikulturelle Gesellschaft'—ein umstrittener Begriff: Zur Diskussion in Frankreich und Deutschland." *Dokumente* 47 (1991).

West, Cornel. *Prophetic Reflections: Notes on Race and Power in America.* Monroe, 1993.

———. "The New Cultural Politics of Difference." *October* 53 (Summer 1990).

———. "Beyond Eurocentrism and Multiculturalism." In *Beyond Eurocentrism and Multiculturalism,* vol. 2: *Prophetic Reflections.* Monroe, 1992.

West, Cornel, and Bill Brown. "Beyond Eurocentrism and Multiculturalism." *Modern Philology* 90, Suppl. (1993).

Winchester, Boyd. "Citizenship in Its International Relation." *American Law Review* (1897).

Wirzberger, Karl-Heinz. "Probleme der Bürgerrechtsbewegung in der amerikanischen Prosaliteratur der Gegenwart." In *Vom Cooper bis O'Neill. Beiträge zur USA-Literatur,* ed. idem. Berlin, 1979.

Wolf, Christa. "Parting from Phantoms: The Business of Germany." *PMLA* 111, no. 2 1996.

Whiting-Sorrell, Anna. "Life Is Belonging." *Treatment Today* 7, no. 1 (Spring 1995).

Williams, Raymond. *Culture and Society, 1780–1959.* London, 1987.

Wolfe, Alan. "Democracy versus Sociology: Boundaries and Their Political Consequences." In *Cultivating Differences: Symbolic Boundaries and the Making of Inequality,* ed. Michèle Lamong and Marcel Fournier. Chicago, 1992.

———. "Algorithmic Justice." In *Deconstruction and the Possibility of Justice,* ed. Drucilla Cornell, Michel Rosenfeld, and David Gray Carlson. New York, 1992.

Wolfen, Adrian. "Die dunklere Schwester. Alice Walker—Wege zum Verständnis." *ultimo* (February 1987).

Woodworth, Marshall B. "Citizenship of the United States under the Fourteenth Amendment." *American Law Review* 30 (1896).

————. "Who Are Citizens of the United States? Wong Kim Ark Case—Interpretation of Citizenship Clause of Fourteenth Amendment." *American Law Review* 32 (1898).

Woolf, Virginia. *A Room of One's Own.* New York, 1957.

Wunder, Bernd. *Geschichte der Bürokratie in Deutschland.* Frankfurt/Main, 1986.

Wüstenhagen, Heinz. *Krisenbewußtsein und Kunstanspruch. Roman und Essay in den USA seit 1945.* Berlin, 1981.

————. "James Baldwins Essays und Romane. Versuch einer ersten Einschätzung." *Zeitschrift für Anglistik und Amerikanistik* 13, no. 2 (1965).

————. "American Literary Naturalism and the Anti-Imperialist Movement and Thought." *Zeitschrift für Anglistik und Amerikanistik* 4 (1983).

Wuthnow, Robert. *The Restructuring of American Religion.* Princeton, 1988.

————. "The Voluntary Sector: Legacy of the Past, Hope for the Future?" In *Between States and Markets: The Voluntary Sector in Comparative Perspective,* ed. Robert Wuthnow. Princeton, 1991.

Yankelovich, Daniel. "Three Destructive Trends: Can They Be Reversed." Lecture presented at the National Civic League's one hundredth National Conference on Governance, 11 November 1994.

Young, Robert. *White Mythologies: Writing History and the West.* New York, 1990.

Zimmermann, Johann Georg. *Vom Nationalstolz. Über die Herkunft der Vorurteile gegenüber anderen Menschen und Völkern.* (1758) Reprint of 4th ed. of 1768. Zürich, 1980.

Index